T0205763

Lecture Notes in Computer Science 13008

More information about this subseries at http://www.springer.com/series/7408

Hakjoo Oh (Ed.)

Programming Languages and Systems

19th Asian Symposium, APLAS 2021
Chicago, IL, USA, October 17–18, 2021
Proceedings

 Springer

Editor
Hakjoo Oh
Korea University
Seoul, Korea (Republic of)

ISSN 0302-9743 ISSN 1611-3349 (electronic)
Lecture Notes in Computer Science
ISBN 978-3-030-89050-6 ISBN 978-3-030-89051-3 (eBook)
https://doi.org/10.1007/978-3-030-89051-3

LNCS Sublibrary: SL2 – Programming and Software Engineering

This Springer imprint is published by the registered company Springer Nature Switzerland AG
The registered company address is: Gewerbestrasse 11, 6330 Cham, Switzerland

Preface

This volume contains the papers presented at the 19th Asian Symposium on Programming Languages and Systems (APLAS 2021). APLAS 2021 was co-located with SPLASH 2021 and held during October 17–18, 2021, as a hybrid physical/virtual meeting. The physical meeting was held in Chicago, Illinois, USA.

APLAS aims to stimulate programming language research by providing a forum for the presentation of the latest results and the exchange of ideas in programming languages and systems. APLAS is based in Asia but is an international forum that serves the worldwide programming languages community.

Following the tradition from previous years, APLAS 2021 solicited contributions in the form of regular research papers and tool papers. Among others, solicited topics included the following: semantics, logics, and foundational theory; design of languages, type systems, and foundational calculi; domain-specific languages; compilers, interpreters, and abstract machines; program derivation, synthesis, and transformation; program analysis, verification, and model-checking; logic, constraint, probabilistic, and quantum programming; software security; concurrency and parallelism; tools and environments for programming and implementation; and applications of SAT/SMT to programming and implementation.

This year we employed a lightweight double-blind reviewing process with an author response period. Each paper received at least three reviews before the author response period, which was followed by a 10-day period of Program Committee (PC) discussion. We received 43 submissions, out of which 17 papers (14 regular papers and 3 tool papers) were accepted after the thorough review process by the PC. We were also honored to include two invited talks by distinguished researchers:

- Zhendong Su (ETH Zurich) on "Solidifying and Advancing the Software Foundations"
- Justin Hsu (Cornell University) on "A Separation Logic for Probabilistic Independence"

I would like to thank everyone who helped make APLAS 2021 successful. First of all, I would like to express my sincere thanks to the Program Committee who spent a lot of time and effort on the review process. I am also grateful for the external reviewers for their thorough and constructive reviews. I thank the General Chair, Wei-Ngan Chin (National University of Singapore), and Atsushi Igarashi (Kyoto University) who handled all the details of the conference from the very beginning. Finally, I would like to sincerely thank the PC chair of APLAS 2020, Bruno C. d. S. Oliveira (The University of Hong Kong), for his very helpful advice and resources.

October 2021   Hakjoo Oh

Organization

General Chair

Wei-Ngan Chin   National University of Singapore, Singapore

Program Chair

Hakjoo Oh   Korea University, South Korea

Program Committee

Andreas Abel	Gothenburg University, Sweden
Kyungmin Bae	POSTECH, South Korea
Edwin Brady	University of St Andrews, UK
Yu-Fang Chen	Academia Sinica, Taiwan
Andreea Costea	National University of Singapore, Singapore
Rayna Dimitrova	CISPA, Germany
Yu Feng	University of California, Santa Barbara, USA
Giulio Guerrieri	University of Bath, UK
Kihong Heo	KAIST, South Korea
Uday Khedker	IIT Bombay, India
Yue Li	Nanjing University, China
Sam Lindley	The University of Edinburgh, UK
Sergio Mover	École Polytechnique, France
Alex Potanin	Victoria University of Wellington, New Zealand
Xiaokang Qiu	Purdue University, USA
Jiasi Shen	MIT, USA
Xujie Si	McGill University, Canada
Gagandeep Singh	UIUC, USA
Youngju Song	Seoul National University, South Korea
Kohei Suenaga	Kyoto University, Japan
Yulei Sui	University of Technology Sydney, Australia
Tachio Terauchi	Waseda University, Japan
Xinyu Wang	University of Michigan, USA
Qirun Zhang	Georgia Institute of Technology, USA
Xin Zhang	Peking University, China

Additional Reviewers

Simon Fowler
Daniel Hillerström
Dylan McDermott
Orestis Melkonian
Garrett Morris
Wei-Lun Tsai
Di-De Yen

Abstracts of Invited Talks

Solidifying and Advancing the Software Foundations

Zhendong Su

ETH Zurich
zhendong.su@inf.ethz.ch

Abstract. Software applications and technologies are built on top of foundational systems such as compilers, databases, and theorem provers. Such foundations form the trusted computing base, and fundamentally impact software quality and security. Thus, it is a critical challenge to solidify and advance them. This talk highlights general, effective techniques, and extensive, impactful efforts on finding hundreds of critical issues in widely-used compilers, database management systems, and SMT solvers. It focuses on the high-level principles and core techniques, their significant practical successes, and future opportunities and challenges.

A Separation Logic for Probabilistic Independence

Justin Hsu

Cornell University
email@justinh.su

Abstract. Probabilistic independence is a useful concept for describing the result of random sampling—a basic operation in all probabilistic languages—and for reasoning about groups of random variables. Nevertheless, existing verification methods handle independence poorly, if at all. We propose a probabilistic separation logic PSL, where separation models probabilistic independence, based on a new, probabilistic model of the logic of bunched implications (BI). The program logic PSL is capable of verifying information-theoretic security of cryptographic constructions for several well-known tasks, including private information retrieval, oblivious transfer, secure multi-party addition, and simple oblivious RAM, while reasoning purely in terms of independence and uniformity. If time permits, we will also discuss ongoing work for reasoning about conditional independence.

Contents

Analysis and Synthesis

Scalable and Modular Robustness Analysis of Deep Neural Networks   3
Yuyi Zhong, Quang-Trung Ta, Tianzuo Luo, Fanlong Zhang,
and Siau-Cheng Khoo

Function Pointer Eliminator for C Programs   23
Daisuke Kimura, Mahmudul Faisal Al Ameen, Makoto Tatsuta,
and Koji Nakazawa

PyCT: A Python Concolic Tester   38
Yu-Fang Chen, Wei-Lun Tsai, Wei-Cheng Wu, Di-De Yen, and Fang Yu

Program Synthesis for Musicians: A Usability Testbed for Temporal Logic
Specifications   47
Wonhyuk Choi, Michel Vazirani, and Mark Santolucito

Server-Side Computation of Package Dependencies
in Package-Management Systems   62
Nobuhiro Kasai and Isao Sasano

Compilation and Transformation

Fully Abstract and Robust Compilation: And How to Reconcile the Two,
Abstractly   83
Carmine Abate, Matteo Busi, and Stelios Tsampas

A Dictionary-Passing Translation of Featherweight Go 102
Martin Sulzmann and Stefan Wehr

Hybrid Quantum-Classical Circuit Simplification with the ZX-Calculus 121
Agustín Borgna, Simon Perdrix, and Benoît Valiron

A Compilation Method for Dynamic Typing in ML 140
Atsushi Ohori and Katsuhiro Ueno

Language Design

The Choice Construct in the Soufflé Language 163
    Xiaowen Hu, Joshua Karp, David Zhao, Abdul Zreika, Xi Wu,
    and Bernhard Scholz

Latent Effects for Reusable Language Components 182
    Birthe van den Berg, Tom Schrijvers, Casper Bach Poulsen, and Nicolas Wu

Adaptable Traces for Program Explanations 202
    Divya Bajaj, Martin Erwig, Danila Fedorin, and Kai Gay

A Typed Programmatic Interface to Contracts on the Blockchain 222
    Thi Thu Ha Doan and Peter Thiemann

Verification

Simplifying Alternating Automata for Emptiness Testing 243
    Pavol Vargovčík and Lukáš Holík

Termination Analysis for the π-Calculus by Reduction to Sequential
Program Termination 265
    Tsubasa Shoshi, Takuma Ishikawa, Naoki Kobayashi, Ken Sakayori,
    Ryosuke Sato, and Takeshi Tsukada

Proving LTL Properties of Bitvector Programs and Decompiled Binaries 285
    Yuandong Cyrus Liu, Chengbin Pang, Daniel Dietsch, Eric Koskinen,
    Ton-Chanh Le, Georgios Portokalidis, and Jun Xu

Solving Not-Substring Constraint with Flat Abstraction 305
    Parosh Aziz Abdulla, Mohamed Faouzi Atig, Yu-Fang Chen,
    Bui Phi Diep, Lukáš Holík, Denghang Hu, Wei-Lun Tsai, Zhillin Wu,
    and Di-De Yen

Author Index 321

Analysis and Synthesis

Scalable and Modular Robustness Analysis of Deep Neural Networks

Yuyi Zhong[1(✉)], Quang-Trung Ta[1], Tianzuo Luo[1], Fanlong Zhang[2], and Siau-Cheng Khoo[1]

[1] School of Computing, National University of Singapore, Singapore, Singapore
{yuyizhong,taqt,tianzuoluo,khoosc}@comp.nus.edu.sg
[2] School of Computer, Guangdong University of Technology, Guangzhou, China

Abstract. As neural networks are trained to be deeper and larger, the scalability of neural network analyzer is urgently required. The main technical insight of our method is modularly analyzing neural networks by segmenting a network into blocks and conduct the analysis for each block. In particular, we propose the *network block summarization* technique to capture the behaviors within a network block using a block summary and leverage the summary to speed up the analysis process. We instantiate our method in the context of a CPU-version of the state-of-the-art analyzer DeepPoly and name our system as *Bounded-Block Poly (BBPoly)*. We evaluate BBPoly extensively on various experiment settings. The experimental result indicates that our method yields comparable precision as DeepPoly but runs faster and requires less computational resources. Especially, BBPoly can analyze *really* large neural networks like SkipNet or ResNet that contain up to one million neurons in less than around 1 hour per input image, while DeepPoly needs to spend even 40 hours to analyze one image.

Keywords: Abstract interpretation · Formal verification · Neural nets

1 Introduction

Deep neural networks are one of the most well-established techniques and have been applied in a wide range of research and engineering domains such as image classification, autonomous driving etc. However, researchers have found out that neural nets can sometimes be brittle and show unsafe behaviors. For instance, a well-trained network may have high accuracy in classifying the testing image dataset. But, if the testing image is perturbed subtly without changing the context of the image, it could fool the network into classifying the perturbed image as something else; this perturbation is known as adversarial attack [1, 2]. To tackle the issue, robustness verification is used to guarantee that unsafe states will not be reached within a certain perturbation size. Several verification techniques have been proposed to verify the robustness of neural networks.

© Springer Nature Switzerland AG 2021
H. Oh (Ed.): APLAS 2021, LNCS 13008, pp. 3–22, 2021.
https://doi.org/10.1007/978-3-030-89051-3_1

In general, these techniques can be categorized into incomplete methods (e.g. abstract interpretation [3–5]) and complete methods (e.g. constraint solving [6, 7]). Complete methods reason over exact result, but also require long execution time and heavy computational power. On the contrary, incomplete methods run much faster but will lose precision along the way.

One of the most state-of-the-art neural network verification methods proposed in recent years is DeepPoly [5]. It is an incomplete but efficient method that uses abstract interpretation technique to over-approximate operations in neural network. In particular, DeepPoly designs the abstract domain to contain symbolic lower and upper constraints, together with concrete lower and upper bounds of a neuron's value. The symbolic constraints of a neuron are defined over neurons in the previous layer; during analysis, they will be revised repeatedly into constraints defined over neurons of even earlier layers. This computation is named as *back-substitution* and is aimed to obtain more precise analysis results [5].

Considering a network with n affine layers and each layer has at most N neurons, the time complexity of this back-substitution operation is $O(n^2 \cdot N^3)$ [8]. When the neural network has many layers (n is large), this computation is heavy and it also demands extensive memory space. This is the main bottleneck of the abstract-interpretation-based analysis used by DeepPoly.

Motivation. As deep neural networks are trained to be larger and deeper to achieve higher accuracy or handle more complicated tasks, the verification tools will inevitably need to scale up so as to analyze more advanced neural networks.

To mitigate the requirement for high computational power of DeepPoly, we propose a *network block summarization* technique to enhance the scalability of the verification tool. Our key insight is to define a method that enables trade-off between precision requirement, time-efficiency requirement and computing-resource limitation. Our method, specially tailored to handle very deep networks, leads to faster analysis and requires less computational resources with reasonable sacrifice of analysis precision. We instantiate our method in the context of a CPU-version of DeepPoly, but it can also be implemented for the GPU version of DeepPoly (named as GPUPoly [8]) which can lead to even more gain in speed.

Contribution. We summarize our contributions below:

- We propose *block summarization technique* supplemented with bounded back-substitution heuristic to scale up the verification process to handle large networks like ResNet34 [9] with around one million neurons.
- We design two types of block summaries that allow us to take "shortcuts" in the back-substitution process for the purpose of reducing the time complexity and memory requirement during the analysis process.
- We implement our proposal into a prototype analyzer called BBPoly, which is built on top of the CPU-version of DeepPoly, and conduct extensive experiments on fully-connected, convolutional and residual networks. The experimental results show that BBPoly is faster and requires less memory allocation compared to the original DeepPoly, while achieves comparable precision.

2   Overview

We present an overview of the whole analysis process with an illustrative example. Our analyzer is built on top of DeepPoly system, leveraging their design of abstract domains and abstract transformers. But we will analyze the network *in blocks* and generate block summarization to speed up the analysis process. Formal details of our proposed method will be provided in Sect. 3.

The illustrative example is a fully-connected network with ReLU activation function as shown in Fig. 1. The network has 4 layers with 2 neurons in each layer and the two input neurons i_1, i_2 can independently take any real number between $[-1, 1]$. The weights of the connections between any two neurons from two adjacent layers are displayed at their corresponding edges, the bias of each neuron is indicated either above or below the neuron. Computation for a neuron in a hidden layer undergoes two steps: (i) an *affine transformation* based on the inputs, weights and biases related to this neuron, which generates a value v, followed by (ii) a *ReLU activation* which outputs v if $v > 0$, or 0 if $v \leq 0$. For the output layer, only affine transformation is applied to generate the final output of the entire network.

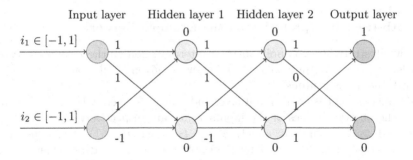

Fig. 1. Example fully-connected network with ReLU activation (cf. [5])

To analyze a neural network, we follow the approach taken by DeepPoly where each hidden layer is perceived as a combination of an affine layer and a ReLU layer. Therefore, network in Fig. 1 will be represented by the network depicted in Fig. 2 for analysis purpose, where a neuron in a hidden layer is expanded into two nodes: (i) one affine node for the related affine transformation (such as x_3, x_4, x_7, x_8), and (ii) one ReLU node which is the output of ReLU function (such as $x_5.x_6, x_9, x_{10}$).

2.1   Preliminary Description on Abstract Domain

We use the abstract domain designed from DeepPoly system [5] to verify neural networks. For each neuron x_i, its abstract value is comprised of four elements: a symbolic upper constraint u_i^s, a symbolic lower constraint l_i^s, a concrete lower bound l_i and a concrete upper bound u_i. And we have $l_i^s \leq x_i \leq u_i^s$, $x_i \in$

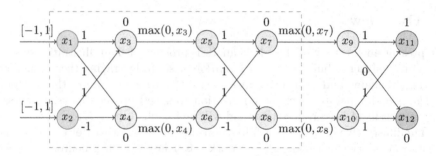

Fig. 2. The transformed network from Fig. 1 to perform analysis (cf. [5])

$[l_i, u_i]$. All the symbolic constraints associated with x_i can be formulated as $b_i + \sum_j w_j \cdot x_j$, where $w_j \in \mathbb{R}, b_i \in \mathbb{R}, j < i$. Here, the constraint $j < i$ asserts that the constraints for x_i only refer to variables "before" x_i, since the value of one neuron (at a layer) only depends on the values of the neurons at preceding layers. For the concrete bounds of x_i, we have $l_i \in \mathbb{R}, u_i \in \mathbb{R}, l_i \le u_i$ and the interval $[l_i, u_i]$ over-approximates all the values that x_i can possibly take.

2.2 Abstract Interpretation on the Example Network

We now illustrate how to apply abstract interpretation on the example network in order to get the output range of the network, given an abstract input $[-1, 1]$ for both the input neurons.

The analysis starts at the input layer and processes layer by layer until output layer. The abstract values of the inputs x_1, x_2 are respectively $\langle l_1^s = -1, u_1^s = 1, l_1 = -1, u_1 = 1 \rangle$ and $\langle l_2^s = -1, u_2^s = 1, l_2 = -1, u_2 = 1 \rangle$. Next, the affine abstract transformer (designed by DeepPoly [5]) for x_3 and x_4 generates the following symbolic constraints, where the coefficients (and the constant terms, if any) in constraints are the weights (and bias) in the fully connected layer:

$$x_1 + x_2 \le x_3 \le x_1 + x_2; \quad x_1 - x_2 \le x_4 \le x_1 - x_2 \tag{1}$$

The concrete bounds are computed using concrete intervals of x_1, x_2 and symbolic constraints in Eq. (1), thus $l_3 = l_4 = -2$ and $u_3 = u_4 = 2$ (the process of computing concrete bound is formally described in Appendix A in our technical report).

The activation transformer (designed by DeepPoly [5]) is then applied to get the abstract elements for x_5, x_6 from x_3, x_4 respectively. In general, given that $x_i = \text{ReLU}(x_j)$, if $u_j \le 0$, x_i is always 0, therefore we have $0 \le x_i \le 0, l_i = 0, u_i = 0$. If $l_j \ge 0$, then $x_i = x_j$ and we get $x_j \le x_i \le x_j, l_i = l_j, u_i = u_j$. For the case where $l_j < 0$ and $u_j > 0$, an over-approximation error will be introduced and we set the abstract element as followed for x_i:

$$x_i \ge c_i \cdot x_j, \quad x_i \le \frac{u_j(x_j - l_j)}{u_j - l_j}, \quad l_i = 0, \quad u_i = u_j, \tag{2}$$

where $c_i = 0$ if $|l_j| > |u_j|$ and $c_i = 1$ otherwise. For example, $x_5 = \mathrm{ReLU}(x_3)$ and since $l_3 < 0, u_3 > 0$, it belongs to the last case described in Eq. (2). $|l_3| = |u_3| = 2$ therefore $c_5 = 1$. Finally, we get the abstract value for x_5: $l_5 = 0, u_5 = 2, l_5^s = x_3, u_5^s = 0.5 \cdot x_3 + 1$. Similar computation can be done for x_6 to yield $l_6 = 0, u_6 = 2, l_6^s = x_4, u_6^s = 0.5 \cdot x_4 + 1$.

Next, we work on the symbolic bounds for x_7, x_8, beginning with:

$$x_5 + x_6 \leq x_7 \leq x_5 + x_6; \quad x_5 - x_6 \leq x_8 \leq x_5 - x_6 \tag{3}$$

From the symbolic constraints in Eq. (3), we recursively substitute the symbolic constraints *backward* layer by layer until the constraints are expressed in terms of the input variables. Upon reaching back to an earlier layer, constraints defined over neurons in that layer are constructed and concrete bound values are evaluated and recorded. Finally the most precise bound among all these layers will be selected as the actual concrete bound for x_7 and x_8 respectively. This process is called *back-substitution* and is the key technique proposed in Deep-Poly to achieve tighter bounds. We follow the back-substitution procedure in DeepPoly and construct constraints for x_7, x_8 defined over x_3, x_4:

$$
\begin{aligned}
x_3 + x_4 &\leq x_7 \leq 0.5 \cdot x_3 + 0.5 \cdot x_4 + 2 \\
x_3 - (0.5 \cdot x_4 + 1) &\leq x_8 \leq 0.5 \cdot x_3 + 1 - x_4,
\end{aligned} \tag{4}
$$

And we further back-substitute to have them defined over x_1, x_2:

$$
\begin{aligned}
2x_1 &\leq x_7 \leq x_1 + 2 \\
0.5 \cdot x_1 + 1.5 \cdot x_2 - 1 &\leq x_8 \leq -0.5 \cdot x_1 + 1.5 \cdot x_2 + 1
\end{aligned} \tag{5}
$$

Finally, we determine the best bound for x_7 to be $l_7 = 0, u_7 = 3$ and that for x_8 to be $l_8 = -2, u_8 = 2$. Note that we have additionally drawn a dashed orange box in Fig. 2 to represent a network *block*. Here, we propose a *block summarization* method which captures the relations between the input (leftmost) layer and output (rightmost) layer of the block. Thus Eq. (5) can function as the block summarization for the dashed block in Fig. 2; we leverage on this block summarization to make "jumps" during back-substitution process so as to save both running time and memory (details in Sect. 3).

To continue with our analysis process, we obtain next:

$$
\begin{aligned}
l_9 = 0, \quad & u_9 = 3, \quad l_9^s = x_7, \quad u_9^s = x_7 \\
l_{10} = 0, \quad & u_{10} = 2, \quad l_{10}^s = x_8, \quad u_{10}^s = 0.5 \cdot x_8 + 1 \\
l_{11} = 1, \quad & u_{11} = 6, \quad l_{11}^s = x_9 + x_{10} + 1, \quad u_{11}^s = x_9 + x_{10} + 1 \\
l_{12} = 0, \quad & u_{12} = 2, \quad l_{12}^s = x_{10}, \quad u_{12}^s = x_{10},
\end{aligned} \tag{6}
$$

Here, we can quickly construct the constraints of x_{11} defined over x_1, x_2 by using the block summarization derived in Eq. (5); yielding $2.5 \cdot x_1 + 1.5 \cdot x_2 \leq x_{11} \leq 0.75 \cdot x_1 + 0.75 \cdot x_2 + 4.5$. By doing so, our analysis will return $x_{11} \in [1, 6]$ and $x_{12} \in [0, 2]$. Note that we lose some precision when making "jumps" through block summarization; the interval for x_{11} would be $[1, 5.5]$ if we were to stick to layer-by-layer back-substitution as originally designed in DeepPoly.

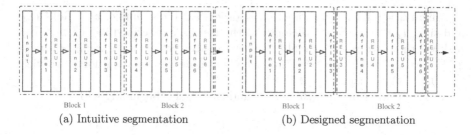

      Block 1   Block 2   Block 1   Block 2

(a) Intuitive segmentation   (b) Designed segmentation

Fig. 3. Example on segmenting network into blocks

2.3   Scaling up with Block Summarization

As illustrated in Eq. (4) and Eq. (5), we conduct back-substitution to construct symbolic constraints defined over neurons at earlier layer in order to obtain a tighter concrete bound. In DeepPoly, every affine layer initiates layer-by-layer back-substitution until the input layer. Specifically, we assume a network with n affine layers, maximum N neurons per layer and consider the kth affine layer (where the input layer is indexed as 0). Every step of back-substitution for layer k through a preceding affine layer requires $O(N^3)$ time complexity and every back-substitution through a preceding ReLU layer requires $O(N^2)$, it takes $O(k \cdot N^3)$ for the kth affine layer to complete the back-substitution process. Overall, DeepPoly analysis requires $O(n^2 \cdot N^3)$ time complexity. This can take a toll on DeepPoly when handling large networks. For example, in our evaluation platform, Deep-Poly takes around 40 hours to analyze one image on ResNet18 [9] with 18 layers. Therefore, we propose to divide the neural networks into blocks, and compute the summarization for each block. This summarization enables us to charge up the back-substitution operation by speeding across blocks, as demonstrated in Eq. (5) where constraints of neuron x_7 are directly defined over input neurons.

3   Network Block Summarization

3.1   Network Analysis with Modularization

For better scalability, we propose a modularization methodology to decrease the computational cost as well as the memory usage, where we segment the network into blocks and analyze each block in sequence. Specifically, we propose the following two techniques to reduce computation steps:

1. Generate summarization between the input and output neurons for each block, and leverage block summarization to make "jumps" during back-substitution instead of doing it layer by layer.
2. Leverage block summarization by bounding back-substitution operation to terminate early.

As illustrated by the simplified network representation in Fig. 3, we segment a network into two blocks. We then show (1) how to generate summarization given

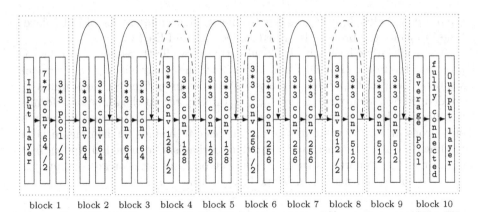

block 1   block 2   block 3   block 4   block 5   block 6   block 7   block 8   block 9   block 10

Fig. 4. ResNet18 [9] and the corresponding block segmentation

the network fragment and (2) how to leverage the summarization to perform back-substitution. The details are as follows.

Network Segmentation. We parameterize network segmentation with a parameter σ, which is the number of affine layers required to form a block. For example, σ is set to 3 in Fig. 3. Since each layer in the neural network ends with the ReLU function, an intuitive segmentation solution is to divide the network so that each block always *ends at a ReLU layer*, as depicted in Fig. 3a. However, doing so requires more computation during the back-substitution but does not gain more accuracy as compared to the segmentation method in which *each block ends by an affine layer*.[1] Therefore, we choose the later segmentation option, as shown in Fig. 3b.

Moreover, special care is required to segment a residual network. As illustrated in Fig. 4, the most important feature of residual network is the *skip connection* that enables a layer to take "shortcut connections" with a much earlier layer [9] (displayed by the curved line). Thus, a set of layers residing in between a layer and its skip-connected layer forms an "intrinsic" residual block, to be used to segment the network (e.g., blocks #2 to #9 in Fig. 4). A more dynamic choice of block size or block number could potentially lead to better trade-off between speed and precision; we leave it as future work.

Back-Substitution with Block Summarization. We present the analysis procedure which implements our block summarization method (Sect. 3.2) and bounded back-substitution heuristic in Algorithm 1. Given an input neural network, it will be first segmented (line 1) using the method described in previous subsection. For a block consisting of layers $\gamma_a, \ldots, \gamma_k$, the start layer and the end layer of the block will be remembered by the markers GetStartLayer and IsEndLayer respectively. The analysis of ReLU layers (line 3) only depends on

---

[1] An explanation of our choice to end blocks at an affine layer instead of a ReLU layer can be found in Appendix B of our technical report.

the preceding affine layer it connects to (line 4). The computation of ReLU layer (line 5) follows the process described in Sect. 2.2 and Eq. (2).

To handle affine layer with back-substitution, we firstly assign γ_{pre} to be the preceding layer of γ_k (line 7). Then, we initialize the constraint set of γ_k to be the symbolic lower and upper constraints for neurons in γ_k (line 8). Constraints Υ_k are defined over neurons in layer γ_{pre} and directly record the affine transformation between layer γ_k and γ_{pre}. Thus, we could use Υ_k and the concrete bounds of neurons in γ_{pre} to compute the initial concrete bounds for neurons in layer γ_k (line 9), using the constraint evaluation mechanism described in Appendix A of our technical report. As such, we conduct back-substitution to compute the concrete bounds for neurons in affine layer γ_k (lines 11–27).

Algorithm 1: Overall analysis procedure in BBPoly

Input: M is the network (eg. Figure 2); τ is the back-substitution threshold; σ is the network segmentation parameter

Annotatation: input layer of M as γ_{in}; constraint set of affine layer γ_k as Υ_k; the set of concrete bounds for neurons in layer $\gamma_k \in M$ as C_k; the *segmented network model* as $\mathcal{M}$

Assumption: the analysis is conducted in ascending order of the layer index

Output: tightest concrete bounds C_k computed for all layer $\gamma_k \in M$

  1: $\mathcal{M} \leftarrow$ SegmentNetwork(M, σ)
  2: **for all** layer $\gamma_k \in \mathcal{M}$ **do**
  3:     **if** IsReluLayer(γ_k) **then**
  4:         $\gamma_{pre} \leftarrow$ PredecessorLayer(γ_k)
  5:         $C_k \leftarrow$ ComputeReluLayer(γ_{pre})
  6:     **else**
  7:         $\gamma_{pre} \leftarrow$ PredecessorLayer(γ_k)
  8:         $\Upsilon_k \leftarrow$ GetSymbolicConstraints(γ_k)
  9:         $C_k \leftarrow$ EvaluateConcreteBounds$(\Upsilon_k, \gamma_{pre})$
10:         $counter_k = 0$
11:         **while** $\gamma_{pre} \neq \gamma_{in}$ **do**
12:             **if** IsEndLayer(γ_{pre}) **then**
13:                 $sum \leftarrow$ ReadSummary(γ_{pre})
14:                 $\Upsilon_k \leftarrow$ BacksubWithBlockSummary(Υ_k, sum)
15:                 $counter_k \leftarrow counter_k + 1$
16:                 $\gamma_{pre} \leftarrow$ GetStartLayer(γ_{pre})
17:             **else**
18:                 $sym\_cons \leftarrow$ GetSymbolicConstraints(γ_{pre})
19:                 $\Upsilon_k \leftarrow$ BacksubWithSymbolicConstraints(Υ_k, sym_cons)
20:                 $counter_k \leftarrow counter_k + 1$
21:                 $\gamma_{pre} \leftarrow$ PredecessorLayer(γ_{pre})
22:         **if** IsEndLayer(γ_k) **and** $\gamma_{pre} =$ GetStartLayer(γ_k) **then**
23:             StoreSummary(γ_k, Υ_k)
24:         $temp\_ck \leftarrow$ EvaluateConcreteBounds$(\Upsilon_k, \gamma_{pre})$
25:         $C_k \leftarrow$ UpdateBounds$(C_k, temp\_ck)$
26:         **if** $counter_k \geq \tau$ **and** $\neg($IsEndLayer(γ_k) **and** LackSummary$(\gamma_k))$ **then**
27:             **break**
28: **return** all C_k for all layer $\gamma_k \in \mathcal{M}$

We have two types of back-substitution and executing either one of the two will be considered as one step of back-substitution which leads to an increment of the counter for layer γ_k (lines 15, 20):

- If γ_{pre} is the end layer of a block, we first read the block summary of γ_{pre} (lines 12–13), and then call BacksubWithBlockSummary(Υ_k, sum) to perform back-substituion over a block (line 14). After execution, Υ_k will be updated to be defined over the start layer of the block. Lastly, in preparation for next iteration of execution, γ_{pre} is set to the start layer of the block (line 16).
- Otherwise, we conduct *layer-by-layer* back-substitution (lines 18–21) similarly to DeepPoly. We obtain *sym_cons*, the symbolic constraints built for γ_{pre}, and call BacksubWithSymbolicConstraints(Υ_k, sym_cons) (line 19). Then, Υ_k will be updated to be defined over the predecessor layer of γ_{pre}. Pertaining to block summarization construction, if γ_{pre} and γ_k are the start and the end layer of the same block, Υ_k will be recorded as the block summary (lines 22–23).

After generating a new set of constraints (lines 14, 19), we can compute a set of potential concrete bounds *temp_ck* using the new constraints Υ_k defined over the new γ_{pre} (line 24). Then we update C_k by the most precise bounds between *temp_ck* and the previous C_k (line 25) as proposed in DeepPoly, where *the most precise* means the smallest upper bound and biggest lower bound.

Bounded Back-Substitution. Normally, we continue new constraint construction, constraint evaluation and concrete bound update for γ_k until the input layer (line 11). The goal here is to explore the opportunity for cancellation of variables in the constraints defined over a particular layer. Such opportunity may lead to attaining tighter bounds for abstract values of neurons at layer k. Nevertheless, it is possible to terminate such back-substitution operation earlier to save computational cost, at the risk of yielding less precise results.[2] This idea is similar in spirit to our introduction of block summarization. We term such earlier termination as *bounded back-substitution*. It may appear similar to the "limiting back-substitution" suggested in DeepPoly [5] or GPUPoly [8]. However, we note that one step in back-substitution in our approach can either be a back-substitution over one layer or *over a block summary*. Therefore, even though we bound the same number of steps of back-substitution, our method allows us to obtain constraints defined over more preceding layers compared to limiting back-substitution in DeepPoly or GPUPoly.

Bounded back-substitution is incorporated in Algorithm 1, by accepting an input τ, which is a threshold for the maximum number of steps to be taken during back-substitution. More specifically, we initialize a counter when processing layer γ_k (line 10), and increment the counter accordingly during the analysis (lines 15, 20). Finally, we end the back-substitution iteration for layer γ_k once the threshold is reached (line 26).

---

[2] As a matter of fact, our empirical evaluation (detailed in Appendix C in our technical report) shows that the degree of improvement in accuracy degrades as we explore further back into earlier layers during back-substitution.

During the construction of block summarization, *we suspend this threshold checking when* γ_k *is the end layer of a block* (second test in line 26). This ensures that the algorithm can generate its block summarization without being forced to terminate early. In summary, suppose each block has at most ℓ layers, under bounded back-substitution, the layer γ_k will back-substitute either ℓ layers (if γ_k is the end layer of a block) or τ steps (if γ_k is not the end layer of a block).

3.2   Summarization Within Block

Block Summarization. The summarization captures the relationship between the output neurons and input neurons within a block. Given a block with k affine layers inside, we formally define it as $\Gamma = \{\gamma_{\text{in}}, \gamma_1, \gamma_1', \ldots, \gamma_k\}$ (e.g. block1 in Fig. 3b) or $\Gamma = \{\gamma_0', \gamma_1, \gamma_1', \ldots, \gamma_k\}$ (like block2 in Fig. 3b), where γ_i refers to an affine layer, γ_{in} refers to the input layer and γ_i' refers to the ReLU layer with ReLU function applied on γ_i, for $i \in \{0, 1, 2, \cdots, k\}$.

Suppose the last layer $\gamma_k = \{x_{k1}, \cdots, x_{kN}\}$ contains N neurons in total. The block summarization $\Phi_\Gamma = \{\langle \phi^L_{x_{k1}}, \phi^U_{x_{k1}} \rangle, \cdots, \langle \phi^L_{x_{kN}}, \phi^U_{x_{kN}} \rangle\}$ is defined as a set of constraint-pairs. For $j \in \{1, 2, \cdots, N\}$, each pair $\langle \phi^L_{x_{kj}}, \phi^U_{x_{kj}} \rangle$ corresponds to the lower and upper constraints of neuron x_{kj} defined over the neurons in the first layer of the block (be it an affine layer γ_{in} or a ReLU layer γ_0'). As these lower and upper constraints encode the relationship between output neurons and input neurons with respect to the block Γ, they function as the block summarization.

Back-Substitution with Block Summarization. To explain our idea, we present the overall back-substitution process as the matrix multiplication (cf. [8]) depicted in Fig. 5. Matrix M^k encodes the current constraints for neurons in layer l defined over neurons in previous layer k, where $1 \le k < l$. The cell indexed by the pair (x^l_{hm}, x^k_{ic}) in the matrix records the coefficient between neuron x^l_{hm} in layer l and neuron x^k_{ic} in layer k. The same notation also applies for matrix F^k and M^{k-1}, where F^k denotes next-step back-substitution and M^{k-1} represents a newly generated constraint for neurons in layer l defined over neurons in the preceding layer $k-1$. As we always over-approximate ReLU function to a linear function, without loss of generality, we therefore discuss further by considering a network as a composition of affine layers.

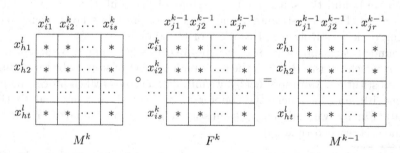

Fig. 5. Back-substitution process can be represented as matrix multiplication with constant terms (e.g. biases) being omitted, cf. [8]

Next, we describe how to perform back-substitution with the generated block summarization. After completing the layer-by-layer back-substitution process within a given block (take block 2 in Fig. 3b as example), we obtain constraints of neurons in the affine layer 6 (γ_6) defined over neurons in the ReLU layer 3 (γ_3'), which corresponds to M^k. This matrix is then multiplied with matrix F^{k1} which captures the affine relationship between neurons in layer γ_3' and γ_3 (this affine relationship is actually an over-approximation since $\gamma_3' = \mathrm{ReLU}(\gamma_3)$), followed by another multiplication with matrix F^{k2} constructed from block summarization for block 1 (in Fig. 3b), denoted here by Φ_{Γ_1}. Φ_{Γ_1} is a set of constraints for neurons in the affine layer 3 (γ_3) defined over neurons in the input layer (γ_{in}) and is computed already during the analysis of block 1. Hence, the resulting matrix $M^k \circ F^{k1} \circ F^{k2}$ encodes the coefficients of neurons in layer γ_6 defined over neurons in layer γ_{in}. Through this process, we achieve back-substitution of the constraints of layer γ_6 to the input layer.

Memory Usage and Time Complexity. In the original method, the memory usage of DeepPoly is high since it associates all neurons with symbolic constraints and maintains all symbolic constraints throughout the analysis process for the sake of layer-by-layer back-substitution. In work of [10] and [11], they all faced with out-of-memory problem when running DeepPoly on their evaluation platform. In our block summarization approach, a block captures only the relationship between its end and start layers. Consequently, all the symbolic constraints for intermediate layers within the block can be released early once we complete the block summarization computation. Thus our method requires less memory consumption when analyzing the same network, and the memory usage can also be controlled using the network segmentation parameter σ.

For time complexity, consider a network with n affine layers and each layer has at most N neurons, DeepPoly's complexity is $O(n^2 \cdot N^3)$. In our method, with bounded back-substitution (detail in Sect. 3.1), we can bound the number of steps for back-substitution to a constant for each layer. Thus the time complexity can be reduced to $O(n \cdot N^3)$. Without bounded back-substitution, we have constant-factor reduction in time complexity, yielding the same $O(n^2 \cdot N^3)$.

3.3 Summarization Defined over Input Layer

Previously, Sect. 3.2 describes a back-substitution mechanism on "block-by-block" basis. To further simplify the back-substitution process and save even more on the execution time and memory, we also design a variation of block summarization that is *defined over the input layer*. As the overall procedure of back-substitution with summarization defined over input layer is similar to the block summarization described in Algorithm 1, we provide the algorithm for this new summary in Appendix G of our technical report.

Summary over Input. Just as in Sect. 3.2, the summary-over-input is still formulated as Φ_Γ. However, $\langle \phi^L_{x_{jk}}, \phi^U_{x_{jk}} \rangle$ corresponds to constraints of neuron x_{jk} which are now *defined over the input neurons*. To generate summary for block Γ_i, we firstly do layer-by-layer analysis within the block, then we back-substitute further with the summary for block Γ_{i-1} which is defined over input neurons, thus we get Φ_{Γ_i} defined over the input neurons.

Back-Substitution with Summary over Input. The back-substitution process also follows the formulation described in Sect. 3.2. The resulting matrix $M^k \circ F^{k1} \circ F^{k2}$ will directly be defined over input neurons since F^{k2} is the summary of preceding block directly defined over input neurons.

Memory Requirement and Time Complexity. Once the summary generation for block Γ_i has completed, all symbolic constraints and summaries from previous $i-1$ blocks could be released, only the input layer needs to be kept. For time complexity, each layer back-substitutes at most $l + 1$ steps (if each block has maximum l layers), the time complexity will be $O(n \cdot N^3)$.

4   Experiment

We implemented our proposed method in a prototype analyzer called BBPoly, which is built on top of the state-of-the-art verifier DeepPoly. We conducted extensive experiments to evaluate the performance of both our tool and Deep-Poly, in terms of precision, memory usage and runtime. In the following subsections, we will describe the details of our experiment.

4.1   Experiment Setup

We propose two types of block summary in our BBPoly system:

- Block summarization as described in Sect. 3.2. It can be supplemented with bounded back-substitution heuristic in Sect. 3.1 to facilitate the analysis of extremely large network;
- Block summary defined over input layer that is introduced in Sect. 3.3

We compare our methods with the state-of-the-art system DeepPoly [5]. DeepPoly is publicly available at the GitHub repository of the ERAN system [12]. On the other hand, we do not compare with existing work that uses MILP solving [13] since the latter can only handle small networks, such as MNIST/CIFAR10 networks with 2 or 3 hidden layers while our BBPoly can analyze large networks of up to 34 hidden layers.

Evaluation Datasets. We chose the popular MNIST [14] and CIFAR10 [15] image datasets that are commonly used for robustness verification. MNIST contains gray-scale images with 28×28 pixels and CIFAR10 consists of RGB 3-channel images of size 32×32. Our test images were obtained from DeepPoly paper where they selected the first 100 images of the test set of each dataset. The test images are also publicly available at [12].

Evaluation Platform and Networks. The evaluation machine is equipped with a 2600 MHz 24 core GenuineIntel CPU with 64 GB of RAM. The implementation is 64-bit based, while soundness under floating-point arithmetic is also preserved as in DeepPoly [5]. We conducted experiments on networks of various sizes as itemized in Table 1; these include fully-connected, convolutional and (large sized) residual networks where the number of hidden neurons is up to 967K. All networks use ReLU activation, and we list the layer number and number of hidden neurons in the table. Specifically, the networks whose names suffixed by "DiffAI" were trained with adversarial training DiffAI [16]. These benchmarks are also collected from [12].

Verified Robustness Property. We verified the robustness property against the L_∞ norm attack [17] which is paramterized by a constant ϵ of perturbation. Originally, each pixel in an input image has a value p_i indicating its color intensity. After applying the L_∞ norm attack with a certain value of ϵ, each pixel now corresponds to an intensity interval $[p_i - \epsilon, p_i + \epsilon]$, forming an adversarial region defined by $\times_{i=1}^{n} [p_i - \epsilon, p_i + \epsilon]$. Our job was to verify whether a given neural network can classify all perturbed images within the given adversarial region by the same label as the original input image. If so, we conclude that robustness is verified for this input image, the given perturbation ϵ and the tested network. For images that fail the verification, due to the over-approximation error, we fail to know if the robustness actually holds and deem the results as inconclusive. We set a 3-h timeout for the analysis of each image, if the verifier fails to return a result within 3 hours, we also deem it as inconclusive.

Table 1. Experimental networks

Neural network	Dataset	#Layer	#Neurons	Type	Candidates
MNIST_9_200	MNIST	9	1,610	Fully connected	97
ffcnRELU_Point_6_500	MNIST	6	3,000	Fully connected	100
convBigRELU	MNIST	6	48,064	Convolutional	95
convSuperRELU	MNIST	6	88,544	Convolutional	99
ffcnRELU_Point_6_500	CIFAR10	6	3,000	Fully connected	56
convBigRELU	CIFAR10	6	62,464	Convolutional	60
SkipNet18_DiffAI	CIFAR10	18	558K	Residual	41
ResNet18_DiffAI	CIFAR10	18	558K	Residual	46
ResNet34_DiffAI	CIFAR10	34	967K	Residual	39

4.2 Experiments on Fully-Connected and Convolutional Networks

We firstly present the experiment results on fully-connected and convolutional networks for both the MNIST and CIFAR10 datasets. We set the block segmentation parameter to be 3;[3] this means there will be 3 affine layers contained in a block. We conduct experiments on both block-summarization and summary-over-input methods. And the bounded back-substitution heuristic is disabled for

---

[3] We have conducted preliminary experiments on the effectiveness of having different block sizes; the results are available in Appendix F of our technical report.

this part of experiments. We set six different values of perturbation ϵ for different networks according to the settings in DeepPoly (details in Appendix D of our technical report). The verified precision is computed as follows:

$$\frac{\text{Number of verified images}}{\text{Number of candidate images}} \tag{7}$$

where candidate images are those which have been correctly classified by a network. The numbers of candidate images for each network are presented in Table 1. Figure 6 shows the precision comparison among different methods on MNIST networks, and Fig. 7 shows the precision on CIFAR10 networks.[4] As expected, DeepPoly $\geq$ BBPoly (block summary) $\geq$ BBPoly (input summary) with respect to precision and execution time. Apart from MNIST_9_200 network, our methods actually achieve comparable precision with DeepPoly.

With regard to the execution time, for larger networks such as the three convolutional networks experimented, our block-summarization method can

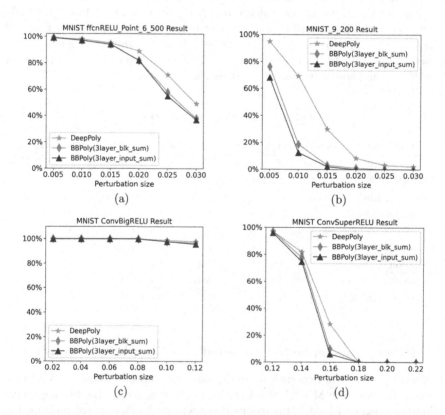

Fig. 6. Verified robustness precision comparison between our BBPoly system and Deep-Poly for MNIST fully-connected and convolutional networks

---

[4] Due to page constraint, full details of the precision and average execution time per image for the experiments are recorded in Table 5 in our technical report.

save around half of the execution time in comparison with that by Deep-Poly. Interested readers may find the details in Table 5 in Appendix E of our technical report. The execution time can be significantly reduced for even larger network, such as the deep residual networks, as demonstrated in Sect. 4.3.

4.3 Experiments on Residual Networks

Network Description. We selected three residual networks that have 18 or 34 layers and contain up to almost one million neurons as displayed in Table 1. The SkipNet18, ResNet18 and ResNet34 were all trained with DiffAI defence.

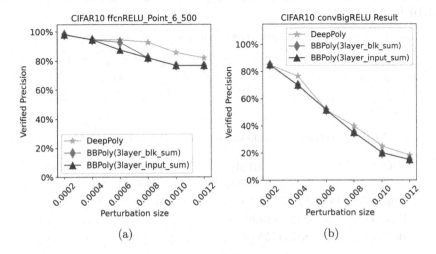

Fig. 7. Verified robustness precision comparison between our BBPoly system and Deep-Poly for CIFAR10 fully-connected and convolutional networks.

Perturbation Size. DeepPoly is not originally designed to handle such large networks and is inconclusive within our timeout. However, an efficient GPU implementation of DeepPoly (called GPUPoly) [8] was proposed for much larger networks. GPUPoly achieves the same precision as DeepPoly and it selects $\epsilon = 8/255$ for our experimental residual networks. Thus we follow the same setting as in GPUPoly. Unfortunately, GPUPoly does not run in one-CPU environment, and thus not comparable with our experimental setting.

Precision Comparison with DeepPoly. We only conducted robustness verification on candidate images as in Sect. 4.2. We set our baselines to be block-summarization method with bounded back-substitution in four steps (abbreviated by "BlkSum_4bound"), and summary-over-input method (abbreviated by "Input_Sum"). The number of candidate images, verified images and the average execution time per image for our experiment are listed in Table 2. As illustrated in Table 2, the "Input_Sum" method verifies more or at least the same number of images as compared to the "BlkSum_4bound" method but requires less execution time, which demonstrates the competitive advantage of our summary-over-input method.

Verified precision is computed using formula 7 with data from Table 2; the results are displayed in Table 3 for residual networks. DeepPoly fails to verify any image within the timeout of 3 hours in our evaluation platform (indicated by '-') whereas our methods yield reasonable verified precision within this time limit, supporting our hypothesis that BBPoly can scale up to analyze large networks with fair execution time and competitive precision.

Table 2. The number of verified images and average execution time per image for CIFAR10 residual networks

Neural net	ϵ	Candidates	BBPoly (BlkSum_4bound)		BBPoly (Input_Sum)		DeepPoly	
			Verified	Time (s)	Verified	Time (s)	Verified	Time (s)
SkipNet18_DiffAI	8/255	41	35	4027.08	36	1742.93	–	–
ResNet18_DiffAI	8/255	46	29	3212.26	29	984.43	–	–
ResNet34_DiffAI	8/255	39	21	2504.89	22	1296.78	–	–

Table 3. Verified precision comparison computed from Table 2

Neural net	ϵ	BBPoly (BlkSum_4bound)	BBPoly (Input_Sum)	DeepPoly
SkipNet18_DiffAI	8/255	85.3%	87.8%	–
ResNet18_DiffAI	8/255	63.0%	63.0%	–
ResNet34_DiffAI	8/255	53.8%	56.4%	–

Memory Comparison with DeepPoly. We mention earlier that our methods utilize less memory. To empirically testify this, we compared the peak memory usage between DeepPoly and summary-over-input method with respect to ResNet18_DiffAI, on the first input image in our dataset and $\epsilon = 8/255$. We used the following command to check the peak memory usage of our analysis process:

```
grep VmPeak /proc/$PID/status
```

According to the results, DeepPoly took up to 20.6 GB of memory while our summary-over-input method needed much less memory. It took only 11.4 GB of memory, which is 55% of the memory usage of DeepPoly.

Time Comparison with DeepPoly. To the best of our knowledge, there is no public experimental result of using DeepPoly to analyze ResNets. We initially used DeepPoly to analyze input images in our dataset with a smaller $\epsilon = 0.002$ for ResNet18_DiffAI. Since DeepPoly took around 29 hours to complete the verification of an image, we could not afford to run DeepPoly for all 100 test images. In contrast, our summary-over-input method took only 1319.66 s (≈ 22 min) for the same image. We also tried to analyze ResNet18_DiffAI with $\epsilon = 8/255$ according to the original perturbation setting, and DeepPoly took around 41 hours to complete the verification of one image. On the other hand, our block-summarization with bounded back-substitution in 4 steps used average 3212.26 s ($\approx$54 min) for one image.

5 Discussion

We now discuss the limitation of our work. There are two limitations as follows. Firstly, although the experimental results in Sect. 4.2 demonstrate that our tool yields comparable precision with DeepPoly for majority of the tested networks, it still significantly less precise than DeepPoly in certain benchmarks, such as the MNIST_9_200 network. We have explained earlier that this loss of precision is due to our current block summarization technique which cannot capture a precise enough relationship between neurons in the start and the end layer of a block. In the future, we aim to generate a more tightened summarization to reduce the over-approximation error and increase the precision of our analyzer. Secondly, our current construction of a block is simple and straightforward. We currently fix the block size to be a constant (e.g. 3), and have not considered the intricate information related to the connectivity between layers when choosing the block size. For future work, we will investigate how to utilize such information to assign the block size dynamically. This could potentially help the analysis to find a better trade-off between speed and precision.

Our proposed method on block summarization could potentially be applied to other neural network verification techniques to enhance their scalability. For instance, in constraint-based verification, the network is formulated by the conjunction of the encoding of all neurons and all connections between neurons [18]. This heavy encoding is exact but lays a huge burden on the constraint solver. Following our block summary method, we could generate over-approximate encoding of the network block to summarize the relationship between the start layer and end layer of the block. This could potentially lead to a significant decrease in the number of constraints and make such analyzer more amenable to handle larger networks.

6 Related Work

Existing works on analyzing and verifying the robustness of neural networks can be broadly categorized as *complete* or *incomplete* methods: given sufficient time and computational resource, a complete verifier can always provide a definite answer (*yes* or *no*) indicating whether a neural network model is robust or not, while an incomplete verifier might return an *unknown* answer.

Typical complete methods include the works in [6,7,19,20], which encode the verification problems into arithmetic constraints, and utilize the corresponding sound and complete solvers to solve them. In particular, the techniques in [6,19] are based on MILP (mixed integer liner program) solvers, while the verifiers in [7,20] use SMT (satisfiability modulo theory) solvers in the theory of linear real arithmetic with ReLU constraints. Although these solvers can give precise answers, they are also costly when handling a large set of constraints with many variables. Hence, it is difficult for complete verifiers to scale up.

In a different approach, the works [3–5] introduce incomplete methods which over-approximate the behavior of neural networks using techniques like abstraction interpretation, reachability analysis etc. Even though they might lose precision in certain situations, they are more scalable than those complete methods. The abstract domain devised for abstract interpretation is the essential part of the analysis. There has been progress in the design of abstract domains, from interval domains in [3] to zonotope domains in [4] and finally to polyhedral domains in [5]. These domains allow the verifiers to prove more expressive specifications, such as the robustness of neural networks, and handle more complex networks, like the deep convolutional networks. Especially, the polyhedral domain in [5] can scale up the performance of the verifier DeepPoly to handle large networks. Recently, there have been also efforts on combining both incomplete method (such as abstraction) and complete method (MILP encoding and solving), such as the works [19] and [21].

All above-mentioned verification methods are actually doing qualitative verification by considering only two cases: whether the network satisfies the property, or not. In most recent years, researchers have been looking into quantitative verification to check how often a property is satisfied by a given network under a given input distribution. For instance, the work [10] examines if majority portion of the input space still satisfies the property with a high probability.

7   Conclusion

We have proposed the block summarization and bounded back-substitution to reduce the computational steps during back-substitution process, making it more amenable for analyzer to handle larger network with limited computational resources, such as having only CPU setup. We instantiated our idea on top of DeepPoly and implement a system called BBPoly. Experiment shows that BBPoly can achieve the verified precision comparable to DeepPoly but save both running time and memory allocation. Furthermore, our system is capable of analyzing large networks with up to one million neurons while DeepPoly cannot conclude within a decent timeout. We believe that our proposal can assist with efficient analysis and be applied to other methods for better scalability.

Acknowledgement. We are grateful to Gagandeep Singh and Mark Niklas Müller for their prompt and patient answer to our queries on DeepPoly/GPUPoly. This research is supported by a Singapore Ministry of Education Academic Research Fund Tier 1 T1-251RES2103. The second author is supported by both a Singapore Ministry of Education Academic Research Fund Tier 3 MOE2017-T3-1-007 and a Singapore National Research Foundation Grant R-252-000-B90-279 for the project Singapore Blockchain Innovation Programme.

References

1. Ren, K., Zheng, T., Qin, Z., Liu, X.: Adversarial attacks and defenses in deep learning. Engineering **6**(3), 346–360 (2020)
2. Yuan, X., He, P., Zhu, Q., Li, X.: Adversarial examples: attacks and defenses for deep learning. IEEE Trans. Neural Netw. Learn. Syst. **30**(9), 2805–2824 (2019)
3. Pulina, L., Tacchella, A.: An abstraction-refinement approach to verification of artificial neural networks. In: Touili, T., Cook, B., Jackson, P. (eds.) CAV 2010. LNCS, vol. 6174, pp. 243–257. Springer, Heidelberg (2010). https://doi.org/10.1007/978-3-642-14295-6_24
4. Gehr, T., Mirman, M., Drachsler-Cohen, D., Tsankov, P., Chaudhuri, S., Vechev, M.T.: AI2: safety and robustness certification of neural networks with abstract interpretation. In: IEEE Symposium on Security and Privacy (SP), pp. 3–18. IEEE Computer Society (2018)
5. Singh, G., Gehr, T., Püschel, M., Vechev, M.T.: An abstract domain for certifying neural networks. Proc. ACM Program. Lang. **3**(POPL), 41:1–41:30 (2019)
6. Tjeng, V., Xiao, K.Y., Tedrake, R.: Evaluating robustness of neural networks with mixed integer programming. In: International Conference on Learning Representations (ICLR). OpenReview.net (2019)
7. Katz, G., Barrett, C., Dill, D.L., Julian, K., Kochenderfer, M.J.: Reluplex: an efficient SMT solver for verifying deep neural networks. In: Majumdar, R., Kunčak, V. (eds.) CAV 2017. LNCS, vol. 10426, pp. 97–117. Springer, Cham (2017). https://doi.org/10.1007/978-3-319-63387-9_5
8. Müller, C., Singh, G., Püschel, M., Vechev, M.T.: Neural network robustness verification on GPUs. CoRR, abs/2007.10868 (2020)
9. He, K., Zhang, X., Ren, S., Sun, J.: Deep residual learning for image recognition. In: IEEE Conference on Computer Vision and Pattern Recognition (CVPR), pp. 770–778 (2016)
10. Baluta, T., Chua, Z.L., Meel, K.S., Saxena, P.: Scalable quantitative verification for deep neural networks, pp. 312–323. IEEE (2021)
11. Tran, H.-D., Bak, S., Xiang, W., Johnson, T.T.: Verification of deep convolutional neural networks using ImageStars. In: Lahiri, S.K., Wang, C. (eds.) CAV 2020. LNCS, vol. 12224, pp. 18–42. Springer, Cham (2020). https://doi.org/10.1007/978-3-030-53288-8_2
12. ETH: ETH Robustness Analyzer for Neural Networks (ERAN) (2021). https://github.com/eth-sri/eran. Accessed 18 June 2021
13. Botoeva, E., Kouvaros, P., Kronqvist, J., Lomuscio, A., Misener, R.: Efficient verification of ReLU-based neural networks via dependency analysis. In: The Thirty-Fourth AAAI Conference on Artificial Intelligence, AAAI 2020, The Thirty-Second Innovative Applications of Artificial Intelligence Conference, IAAI 2020, The Tenth AAAI Symposium on Educational Advances in Artificial Intelligence, EAAI 2020, New York, NY, USA, 7–12 February 2020, pp. 3291–3299. AAAI Press (2020)
14. LeCun, Y., Cortes, C.: MNIST handwritten digit database (2010)
15. Krizhevsky, A., Nair, V., Hinton, G.: CIFAR-10 (Canadian Institute for Advanced Research)
16. Mirman, M., Gehr, T., Vechev, M.T.: Differentiable abstract interpretation for provably robust neural networks. In: International Conference on Machine Learning (ICML), pp. 3575–3583 (2018)
17. Carlini, N., Wagner, D.A.: Towards evaluating the robustness of neural networks. In: IEEE Symposium on Security and Privacy (SP), pp. 39–57 (2017)

18. Albarghouthi, A.: Introduction to Neural Network Verification. verifieddeeplearning.com (2021). http://verifieddeeplearning.com
19. Botoeva, E., Kouvaros, P., Kronqvist, J., Lomuscio, A., Misener, R.: Efficient verification of ReLU-based neural networks via dependency analysis, pp. 3291–3299. AAAI Press (2020)
20. Katz, G., et al.: The Marabou framework for verification and analysis of deep neural networks. In: Dillig, I., Tasiran, S. (eds.) CAV 2019. LNCS, vol. 11561, pp. 443–452. Springer, Cham (2019). https://doi.org/10.1007/978-3-030-25540-4_26
21. Singh, G., Gehr, T., Püschel, M., Vechev, M.T.: Boosting robustness certification of neural networks. In: International Conference on Learning Representations (ICLR). OpenReview.net (2019)

Function Pointer Eliminator for C Programs

Daisuke Kimura[1]([✉]), Mahmudul Faisal Al Ameen[2], Makoto Tatsuta[3],
and Koji Nakazawa[4]

[1] Toho University, Chiba, Japan
kmr@is.sci.toho-u.ac.jp
[2] University of Tokyo, Tokyo, Japan
faisal@kb.is.s.u-tokyo.ac.jp
[3] National Institute of Informatics/Sokendai, Tokyo, Japan
tatsuta@nii.ac.jp
[4] Nagoya University, Nagoya, Japan
knak@is.nagoya-u.ac.jp

Abstract. Verification of memory safety such as absence of null pointer
dereferences and memory leaks in system software is important in practice. O'Hearn's group proposed a new method of memory safety analy-
sis/verification by modular abstract interpretation with separation logic
and biabduction. To realize this method, one has to construct a call
graph before the modular abstract interpretation. This paper aims to ana-
lyze/verify memory safety of system software written in C programming
language by this method, and as the first step this paper provides a function pointer eliminator tool to eliminate function pointer calls in order
to construct a call graph. The tool uses SVF for pointer analysis. First
C programs are translated into LLVM programs by Clang and then SVF
analyses the LLVM programs. The tool given in this paper finds correspondence between function pointer calls in C programs and those in LLVM
programs, and transforms the C programs into C programs with the same
functionality and without any function pointer calls. The experimental
results for gzip, git, and OpenSSL using this function pointer eliminator
are presented and they show that this tool is sufficiently efficient and precise for the purpose.

1 Introduction

Large and complicated software is being increasingly used in mission critical
settings making software verification more and more important. In particular,
memory safety of software is important, since unsafe software may cause runtime
errors. It is necessary for controlling software such as airplane controllers and
car controllers. It is also necessary for communication software, since memory
unsafe program may lose robustness against attackers.

There is theoretically and practically successful work for automatic analyzer
of memory safety by O'Hearn's group [2,4,9]. They use abstract interpretation for

© Springer Nature Switzerland AG 2021
H. Oh (Ed.): APLAS 2021, LNCS 13008, pp. 23–37, 2021.
https://doi.org/10.1007/978-3-030-89051-3_2

the abstract domain of separation logic formulas with lists [3]. They use footprint analysis for precondition generation [1] and biabduction for modular analysis [2].

Their approach is modular and they first make a dependency list of functions, based on function call relation, and then they analyze all functions from the bottom functions, namely, functions that do not call other functions, to the top level function such as main. However, if programs contain a function pointer call such as (*fp)(); where fp is a function pointer variable, we cannot make a dependency list and we cannot analyze programs in a modular way.

In this paper, we will present a tool for function pointer elimination for this purpose. More specifically, in order to analyze/verify memory safety of system software written in C programming language by their method, as the first step this paper provides a tool that eliminates function pointer calls by keeping the program semantics. Moreover one can also use our tool as a frontend for any C program analyzers and transformers, since our tool is so general by inputting a C program and outputting another C program without function pointer calls.

Our tool FPE (Function Pointer Eliminator) uses Clang and SVF. SVF is a tool that enables scalable and precise interprocedural Static Value-Flow analysis for C programs by leveraging recent advances in sparse analysis [10]. It uses Andersen's algorithm for pointer analysis. Our tool works as a client program in [10]. SVF computes function names for each function pointer call in LLVM code translated from C source code by Clang. Our tool analyzes the correspondence between function pointer calls in C source code and those in LLVM code. With this information, we find function names for function calls in C source code. After that, when function names for a function pointer call (*fp)() is { F1, F2, F3 }, then we transform this call into (fp == F1 ? F1() : fp == F2 ? F2() : F3()). By this transformation, eventually all function pointer calls will be eliminated while keeping the semantics from C source code.

Our main challenge is to find a value for a C expression from an LLVM expression even for complicated expressions, so that our tool can work for OpenSSL and git. In particular, our tool can handle nested structures with arrays. Moreover, for solving struct field name renaming, we added an index number for each field.

We evaluated our function pointer eliminator on software like gzip, git, and OpenSSL. Our eliminator processes gzip quickly and processes git and OpenSSL in 16 min. Results show that our eliminator is sufficiently efficient and precise for our purpose, where precision meant the number of candidates of function names for an indirect function call.

As related work, there are papers [5–8,11] for function pointer analysis for C language and assembly languages such as LLVM language, for example, for malware detection. However, we have not found any other function pointer eliminator tools for C programming language in the literature, even though those function pointer analysis papers could give sufficient theory for a function eliminator tool. Optimizers in compilers can replace some indirect function calls by direct function calls, but some indirect function calls sometimes may be left unchanged. On the other hand, our tool replaces every indirect function call by a direct function call.

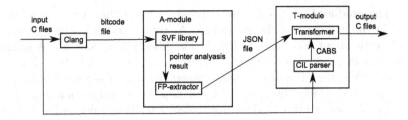

Fig. 1. The design of FPE

Section 2 explains our function pointer eliminator FPE. Section 3 discusses our tool. Section 4 discusses experimental results. We conclude in Sect. 5.

2 The Function Pointer Eliminator FPE

2.1 Usage of FPE

This section explains the usage of the function pointer eliminator FPE.

FPE is invoked through the command

```
fpe <dir>
```

where the directory `<dir>` has input C files. Then the output C files, which have the same functionality as the input C files and do not have any function pointer calls, are created in the directory `<dir>-fpe` with the same file names and subdirectory names and tree structure as the original ones. The input condition is that the input C files are preprocessed and compilable. For simplicity of implementation, FPE does not cover some complicated function pointer call expressions. This point will be discussed in the next section. However FPE covers the entirety of gzip, git, and OpenSSL. FPE is open source and is publically available for download at https://github.com/d-kmr/fpe.git.

2.2 Implementation of FPE

This section explains implementation of the function pointer eliminator FPE. The whole design of FPE is illustrated in Fig. 1. The input to FPE is a list of C files, and the output is transformed C files that have the same functionality as the original ones but do not have any function pointer calls.

The FPE system works as follows. (1) An input C file (say `input.c`) is translated into LLVM-IR by Clang. A bitcode file (`input.bc`), which is a binary file of LLVM-IR, is produced by the command:

```
clang -c -fno-discard-value-names -emit-llvm input.c
```

where the option `-emit-llvm` is to produce LLVM-IR code, and `-fno-discard-value-names` is to keep value names in the source code. A bitcode file is produced for each input C file. The produced bitcode files are combined into a single bitcode file by the `llvm-dis` command when the input is several C files.

(2) The produced bitcode file is analyzed by using the SVF library [10]. It is done in the first part of the A-module (Analyzer module), which is written in C++ with about 800 lines, in Fig. 1. The library functions use Andersen's algorithm, and produce a result of pointer analysis for LLVM files. From the result from SVF, the FP-extractor part extracts information related to function-pointers for input C files, by finding relationships between function pointer calls in the input C files and those in the LLVM files. Then it produces a JSON-format file, which contains the extracted data, namely, over-approximations of values for function pointer variables in the input C files.

(3) The T-module (Transformer module) transforms the input C files into output C files without function pointer calls, by using the JSON file produced by the A-module. This module is written in OCaml with 14k lines using the CIL library to parse C files. It first parses the input C files and creates C abstract syntax (CABS) data and also reads the JSON file, and replaces each function pointer call in the input C files with an expression of the same semantics without function pointers. Finally it outputs the resulting C files.

2.3 Analyzer Module (A-module)

This subsection shows how the analyzer module works with an example given in Fig. 2. The example defines a function pointer type FP from void to int, struct A that contains a field fp of type FP, struct B that contains a field toA of the pointer type to struct A, and the functions one, two, and three of type from void to int. The global function pointer f is called twice in the main function.

The first function pointer call f() at the line 10 is actually two() because of the preceding assignment f = two. The second one at the line 12 is actually three() because f is updated by f = three. Hence an over-approximation of f computed by SVF is {two, three}. A two-dimensional array a of type FP is declared and initialized at the line 13 and is called as a[1][0]() at the next line. SVF calculates an over-approximation {two, three} for the values of a.

A struct sA of type struct A initialized at the line 15, and a pointer pA for it is given in the next line. Then two function pointer calls pA->fp() appear twice at the lines 17 and 19. The first call and the second one are actually one() and two(), respectively. So SVF obtains {one, two} as an over-approximation for the possible values of pA->fp. Another struct sB of type struct B and a pointer pB for sB are given. The function pointer call pB->toA->fp() at the line 22 is actually two(), since pB->toA has the same value as pA by the initialization of sB. Hence SVF returns an over-approximation for pB->toA->fp that is the same as that for pA->fp.

The A-module outputs a JSON format text file as in Fig. 3. The output JSON format is a list of the following three kinds of objects:

(1) ["FPVAR",{"name":<FP>,"in_fun":<FN>,"to_funs":<FNS>}],

```
1  typedef int (*FP)();
2  struct A { int x; FP fp; };
3  struct B { struct A* toA; };

4  FP f;

5  int one(){ return 1; }
6  int two(){ return 2; }
7  int three(){ return 3; }

8  int main(){
9    f = two;
10   int n = f();

11   f = three;
12   n = f();

13   FP a[2][1] = { {two}, {three} };
14   n = a[1][0]();

15   struct A sA = { 0, one };
16   struct A* pA = &sA;
17   n = pA->fp();
18   pA->fp = two;
19   n = pA->fp();

20   struct B sB = { pA };
21   struct B* pB = &sB;
22   n = pB->toA->fp();
23   return 0;
24 }
```

Fig. 2. Example input file

(2) ["FPARR",{"ptr":<ARR>,"in_fun":<FN>,"to_funs":<FNS>}], and
(3) ["FPFLD",{"ptr":<SP>,"fld":<FLD>,"in_fun":<FN>,"to_funs":<FNS>}].

Each object corresponds to a function pointer call that appears in a source code.

The first form starting from the key "FPVAR" is used for a function pointer call of a function pointer, like f() in the example. The pair "name":<FP> means that the function pointer name of the current call is <FP>. The pair "in_fun":<FN> means that the current function pointer call appears in the body of the function <FN>. The pair "to_funs":<FNS> means that the possible values of <FP> are <FNS>, where <FNS> is a list of function names.

The second form starting from the key "FPARR" is used for a function pointer call with a function pointer array, like a[1][0]() in the example. The pair "ptr":<ARR> means that the array name of the current call is <ARR>. The meanings of the pairs "in_fun":<FN> and "to_funs":<FNS> of FPARR are the same as those of "FPVAR".

The third form starting from the key "FPFLD" is used for a function pointer call with a function pointer struct field, like pA->fp() and pB->toA->fp() in the example. This form is handled with a similar idea to the first and second forms and we omit it for space limitation.

```
[
  ["FPARR",  {"ptr":"a",  "in_fun":"main",  "to_funs":["two",  "three"] }],
  ["FPVAR",  {"name":"f",  "in_fun":"main",  "to_funs":["two",  "three"] }],
  ["FPVAR",  {"name":"f",  "in_fun":"main",  "to_funs":["two",  "three"] }],
  ["FPFLD",  {"ptr":"pA",  "fld":[{"tp":"struct.A","fld_name":"fp","fld_index":1}],
            "in_fun":"main",  "to_funs":["one",  "two"] }],
  ["FPFLD",  {"ptr":"pA",  "fld":[{"tp":"struct.A","fld_name":"fp6","fld_index":1}],
            "in_fun":"main",  "to_funs":["one",  "two"] }],
  ["FPFLD",  {"ptr":"pB",  "fld":[{"tp":"struct.B","fld_name":"toA8","fld_index":0},
            {"tp":"struct.A","fld_name":"fp9","fld_index":1}],
            "in_fun":"main",  "to_funs":["one",  "two"] }]
]
```

Fig. 3. JSON output for the example file

2.4 Transformer Module (T-module)

The T-module transforms the input C files into C files without function pointer calls by using the JSON output generated by the A-module.

- For a JSON object of the first form
  ["FPVAR",{"name":"f","in_fun":"G","to_funs":["F1","F2"]}], the corresponding function pointer call f(x1,x2) is replaced by f==F1 ? F1(x1,x2) : F2(x1,x2). Note that SVF is sound so either f==F1 or f==F2 holds.
- For a JSON object of the second form
  ["FPARR",{"ptr":"a","in_fun":"G","to_funs":["F1","F2"]}], the corresponding function pointer call a[2](x1,x2) is replaced by a[2]==F1 ? F1(x1,x2) : F2(x1,x2).
- For a JSON object of the third form
  ["FPFLD"
  {"ptr":"s","fld":<FLD>,"in_fun":"G","to_funs":["F"]}], where <FLD> is [{"fld_name":"fp1","fld_index":0}], the corresponding function pointer call s->fp(x) is replaced by F(x).

A function pointer call may appear in an expression e[fp(x)], which is obtained by filling a function pointer call fp(x) into the hole of an expression e[-] with a hole -. This form is replaced by e[fp==F1 ? F1(x) : F2(x)] using the JSON output with "to_funs":["F1","F2"].

The output of the T-module, namely the output of FPE, for the example is shown in Fig. 4. For readability, the spacings of it are slightly modified from the output of FPE. A function pointer call at the line n is transformed into the line $n + 4$ in Fig. 4.

3 Discussion

The advantages of FPE are efficiency and scalability. It works efficiently even for practical software such as gzip, git, and OpenSSL (see the next section for more detailed results). The current FPE supports the forms of function pointer calls that appear in the example and the following forms of function pointer calls:

```
1  typedef int  (*FP)() ;
2  struct A { int x; FP fp; } ;
3  struct B { struct A* toA ; } ;
4  int one () ;
5  int two () ;
6  int three () ;
7  int main () ;
8  FP f ;
9  int one () { return 1; }
10 int two () { return 2; }
11 int three () { return 3; }
12 int main (){
13   f = two;
14   int n  = f == two ? two() : three();
15   f = three;
16   n = f == two ? two() : three();
17   FP  a[2][1]  = {{two}, {three}};
18   n = a[1][0] == two ? two() : three();
19   struct A sA  = {0, one};
20   struct A *  pA  = & sA;
21   n = pA-> fp == one ? one() : two();
22   pA-> fp = two;
23   n = pA-> fp == one ? one() : two();
24   struct B sB  = {pA};
25   struct B *  pB  = & sB;
26   n = pB-> toA-> fp == one ? one() : two();
27   return 0;
28 }
```

Fig. 4. Output for the example file

$d(e, \ldots, e) \mid \, * d(e, \ldots, e) \mid (d)(e, \ldots, e) \mid (*d)(e, \ldots, e)$
where
$a ::= fp \mid a[e]$
$d ::= a \mid d\text{->}f \mid d.f$
and fp, f are names and e is an expression.
For example, FPE covers

```
open_istream_tbl[src](st, &oi, real, type)
```

that appears in OpenSSL. We believe that these forms would cover a enough large class of (normally written) C code. On the other hand, some forms, such as (b?f:G)() where f is a function pointer, are not supported yet. FPE also assumes that in input C files a global struct declaration has a struct name (a local struct declaration does not have this limitation). These restrictions are just to simplify implementation of the FP-extractor part in the A-module. If necessary, we can relax these restrictions in future. Since currently we are using CIL together with Clang according to our whole project of automatic program verification, we need to manually handle some keywords that CIL does not support by removing _Noreturn and putting typedef for _Float128x, _Float64x, _Float32x, _Float128, _Float64, _Float32 for the input C files.

Target system	Files	Lines	Time (A-mod.) SVF	FP-extractor	Time (T-mod.)	Time (Total)
gzip-1.10	132	26073	0.325s	0.089s	1.301s	1.715s
git-2.9.5	378	177594	744.398s	7.414s	74.951s	13m46.763s
OpenSSL-1.1.1b	940	498879	878.105s	8.945s	86.085s	16m13.134s

Target system	# of FP-calls	Max # of func.names	Ave. # of func. names
gzip-1.10	4	7	4
git-2.9.5	105	16	2.6
OpenSSL-1.1.1b	64	64	4.3

Fig. 5. Experimental results

4   Experimental Results

This section shows some experimental results of FPE. The tests were done on a laptop PC with 1.80 GHz Intel(R) Core(TM) i7-10510U CPU, 16 GB memory, and Linux Mint 20. The results are given in the tables of Fig. 5.

The first table shows execution times of FPE for each target systems. The column named "Files" shows the numbers of C source files (before preprocessing), and the column named "Lines" shows the total numbers of lines in these files. The column named "Time (A-mod.)" presents the execution times for SVF and FP-extractor invoked in the A-module. The columns "Time (T-mod.)" and "Time (total)" show the execution times for T-module and whole FPE (namely, A-module + T-module), respectively.

The second table shows a summary of outputs from FPE. The column named "# of FP-calls" shows the numbers of function pointer calls in the input C files. The column named "Max # of func.names" shows the maximum number of candidates of function names for a function pointer call. The right-most column "Ave. # of func.names" presents the average number of candidates of function names for a function pointer call.

These results show that FPE is sufficiently efficient. Note that it is sufficiently precise for modular program analysis, which is originally guaranteed by SVF.

5   Conclusion

We have implemented a function pointer elimination tool FPE, and by experimental results we have also shown that the tool FPE is sufficiently efficient and precise for modular program analysis.

Appendix

A   Screenshot

We give a screenshot of the command FPE.

```
% fpe.sh example_aplas
Enter /home/share/fpe/example_aplas
DELETE old .bc files
START: Making .bc files
/home/share/fpe/example_aplas/input.pp.c
llvm-dis: /lib64/libtinfo.so.5: no version information available (required by l\
lvm-dis)
FINISH: making .bc files
START: linking .bc files
llvm-link: /lib64/libtinfo.so.5: no version information available (required by \
llvm-link)
Writing 'pag_initial.dot'...
Writing 'pag_final.dot'...
Writing 'callgraph_initial.dot'...
Writing 'callgraph_final.dot'...
FINISH: linking .bc files
[
["FPARR", {"ptr":"a", "in_fun":"main", "to_funs":["two", "three"] }],
["FPVAR", {"name":"f", "in_fun":"main", "to_funs":["two", "three"] }],
["FPVAR", {"name":"f", "in_fun":"main", "to_funs":["two", "three"] }],
["FPFLD", {"ptr":"pA", "fld":[{"tp":"struct.A","fld_name":"fp","fld_index":1}],\
 "in_fun":"main", "to_funs":["one", "two"] }],
["FPFLD", {"ptr":"pA", "fld":[{"tp":"struct.A","fld_name":"fp6","fld_index":1}]\
, "in_fun":"main", "to_funs":["one", "two"] }],
["FPFLD", {"ptr":"pB", "fld":[{"tp":"struct.B","fld_name":"toA8","fld_index":0}\
, {"tp":"struct.A","fld_name":"fp9","fld_index":1}], "in_fun":"main", "to_funs"\
:["one", "two"] }]
]

real    0m0.002s
user    0m0.002s
sys     0m0.000s
Transformation begins
Transformation is finished

real    0m0.027s
user    0m0.015s
sys     0m0.013s
```

B Examples

We give some examples of how the command FPE transforms an input C file
into an output C file.

B.1 Example

The input file:

```
int func(void);

int main() {
        int (*po)() = func;
        po();
        return 0;
}

int func() {
        return 1;
}
```

The output file:

```
int  func (void   ) ;
int  main ()
{    int  ( * po ) ()  = func;
func();
return 0;
}
int  func ()
{    return 1;
}
```

B.2   Example

The input file:

```
int func(int, int);

int main() {
        int (*po)(int, int), i;
        po = func;
        i = (*po)(10, 3);
        return 0;
}

int func(int i, int j) {
        return i << j;
}
```

The output file:

```
int  func (int    , int   ) ;
int  main ()
{    int ( * po ) (int    , int   ) , i ;
po = func;
i = func(10, 3);
return 0;
}
int  func (int  i , int  j )
{    return i << j;
}
```

B.3   Example

The input file:

```
int one(void);
int two(void);
int three(void);

int main() {
        int (*po[])() = {one , two , three};
        int i = 0;

        if ((i < 0) || (i > 2)) return 0;
        (*po[i])();
        return 0;
}

int one() {
        return 1;
}
```

```
int two() {
        return 2;
}

int three() {
        return 3;
}
```

The output file:

```
int   one (void    )  ;
int   two (void    )  ;
int   three (void    )  ;
int   main ()
{     int   ( *  po[] )  ()   = {one, two, three};
int   i   = 0;
if ((i < 0) || (i > 2))
      return 0;

else
      ;

po[i] == one ? one() : po[i] == two ? two() : three();
return 0;
}
int   one ()
{     return 1;
}
int   two ()
{     return 2;
}
int   three ()
{     return 3;
}
```

B.4   Example

The input file:

```
typedef struct PString {
        char *chars;
        int (*length)(struct PString *self);
} PString;

int slen(char *c) {
        int i;
        for(i = 0; *(c + i) != 0; i++);
        return i;
}

int length(struct PString *self) {
        return slen(self -> chars);
}

struct PString str;

struct PString *initializeString(int n) {
        char *buf = "            ";
        str.chars = buf;
        str.length = length;

        str.chars[0] = '\0';

        return &str;
}
```

```
int main() {
        struct PString *p = initializeString(30);
        char *hello = "Hello";
        p -> chars = hello;
        int l =  p -> length(p);
        return 0;
}
```

The output file:

```
typedef struct PString {    char  *  chars ;
int  ( *  length ) (struct PString *  self ) ;
} PString ;
struct PString {    char  *  chars ;
int  ( *  length ) (struct PString *  self ) ;
} ;
typedef struct PString PString ;
struct PString str ;
int  slen (char  *  c )
{    int  i ;
for (i = 0; * (c + i) != 0; i++)
    ;

return i;
}
int  length (struct PString *  self )
{    return slen(self-> chars);
}
struct PString *  initializeString (int  n )
{    char  *  buf  = "           ";
str. chars = buf;
str. length = length;
str. chars[0] = '\000';
return & str;
}
int  main ()
{    struct PString *  p  = initializeString(30);
char  *  hello  = "Hello";
p-> chars = hello;
int  l  = length(p);
return 0;
}
```

B.5   Example

The input file:

```
typedef int FUNC(int, int);

FUNC sum, subtract, mul, div;
FUNC *p[4] = {sum, subtract, mul, div};

int main(void)
{
    int result;
    int i = 2, j = 3, op = 2;

    result = p[op](i, j);
}

int sum(int a, int b) { return a+b; }

int subtract(int a, int b) { return a-b; }

int mul(int a, int b) { return a*b; }

int div(int a, int b) { return a/b; }
```

The output file:

```
typedef int  FUNC (int    , int   ) ;
FUNC  sum , subtract , mul , div ;
FUNC  *  p[4]  = {sum, subtract, mul, div};
int  main (void   )
{   int  result ;
int  i  = 2, j  = 3, op  = 2;
result = p[op] == sum ? sum(i, j) : p[op] == subtract ? subtract(i, j) : p[op] \
== mul ? mul(i, j) : div(i, j);
}
int  sum (int  a , int  b )
{   return a + b;
}
int  subtract (int  a , int  b )
{   return a - b;
}
int  mul (int  a , int  b )
{   return a * b;
}
int  div (int  a , int  b )
{   return a / b;
}
```

B.6   Example

The input file:

```
typedef int (*funcptr)();     /* generic function pointer */
typedef funcptr (*ptrfuncptr)();  /* ptr to fcn returning g.f.p. */

int main()
{
        funcptr start_function();
        ptrfuncptr state = start_function;

        while (state != (void *)0)
                state = (ptrfuncptr)(*state)();

        return 0;
}

funcptr start_function()
{
        static int i=0;
        ++i;

        if(i == 5)
                return (void *)0;
        else
                return start_function;
}
```

The output file:

```
typedef int  ( *  funcptr ) () ;
typedef funcptr  ( *  ptrfuncptr ) () ;
int  main ()
{   funcptr  start_function () ;
ptrfuncptr  state  = start_function;
while (state != (void *  )0)
    state = (ptrfuncptr )start_function();

return 0;
}
```

```
funcptr start_function ()
{    static int  i  = 0;
++ i;
if (i == 5)
    return (void  *  )0;

else
    return start_function;

}
```

B.7   Example

The input file:

```
double callback(double x)
{
        return x + 1.0;
}

double g(double x, double (*f)(double))
{
        return f(x);
}

int main(void)
{
        double ans = g(5.0, callback);
        ans = g(5.0, sqrt);
        return 0;
}
```

The output file:

```
double  callback (double  x )
{    return x + 1.0;
}
double  g (double  x , double  ( *  f ) (double   ) )
{    return f == callback ? callback(x) : sqrt(x);
}
int  main (void   )
{    double  ans  = g(5.0, callback);
ans = g(5.0, sqrt);
return 0;
}
```

References

1. Calcagno, C., Distefano, D., O'Hearn, P.W., Yang, H.: Footprint analysis: a shape analysis that discovers preconditions. In: Nielson, H.R., Filé, G. (eds.) SAS 2007. LNCS, vol. 4634, pp. 402–418. Springer, Heidelberg (2007). https://doi.org/10.1007/978-3-540-74061-2_25
2. Calcagno, C., Distefano, D., O'Hearn, P.W., Yang, H.: Compositional shape analysis by means of bi-abduction. J. ACM 58(6), 26:1–26:66 (2011)
3. Distefano, D., O'Hearn, P.W., Yang, H.: A local shape analysis based on separation logic. In: Hermanns, H., Palsberg, J. (eds.) TACAS 2006. LNCS, vol. 3920, pp. 287–302. Springer, Heidelberg (2006). https://doi.org/10.1007/11691372_19
4. Distefano, D., Fähndrich, M., Logozzo, F., O'Hearn, P.W.: Scaling static analyses at Facebook. Commun. ACM 62(8), 62–70 (2019)

5. Faruki, P., Laxmi, V., Gaur, M.S., Vinod, P.: Mining control flow graph as API call-grams to detect portable executable malware. In: Proceedings of the Fifth International Conference on Security of Information and Networks (SIN 2012), pp. 130–137 (2012)
6. Gascon, H., Yamaguchi, F., Arp, D., Rieck, K.: Structural detection of android malware using embedded call graphs. In: Proceedings of the 2013 ACM Workshop on Artificial Intelligence and Security (AISec 2013), pp. 45–54 (2013)
7. Hu, X., Chiueh, T.-C., Shin, K.G.: Large-scale malware indexing using function-call graphs. In: Proceedings of the 16th ACM Conference on Computer and Communications Security (CCS 2009), pp. 611–620 (2009)
8. Jang, J.-W., Woo, J., Yun, J., Kim, H.K.: Mal-Netminer: malware classification based on social network analysis of call graph, In: Proceedings of the 23rd International Conference on World Wide Web Companion (WWW 2014 Companion), pp. 731–734 (2014)
9. O'Hearn, P.W.: Separation logic. Commun. ACM **62**(2), 86–95 (2019)
10. Sui, Y., Xue, J.: SVF: interprocedural static value-flow analysis in LLVM. In: Proceedings of the 25th International Conference on Compiler Construction (CC 2016), pp. 265–266 (2016)
11. Zhang, W., Zhang, Yu.: Lightweight function pointer analysis. In: Lopez, J., Wu, Y. (eds.) ISPEC 2015. LNCS, vol. 9065, pp. 439–453. Springer, Cham (2015). https://doi.org/10.1007/978-3-319-17533-1_30

PyCT: A Python Concolic Tester

Yu-Fang Chen[1]([⊠]), Wei-Lun Tsai[1], Wei-Cheng Wu[2], Di-De Yen[1],
and Fang Yu[3]

[1] Academia Sinica, Taipei, Taiwan
{yfc,alan23273850,bottle}@iis.sinica.edu.tw
[2] Information Sciences Institute, University of Southern California, Los Angeles, USA
wwu@isi.edu
[3] National Chengchi University, Taipei, Taiwan
yuf@nccu.edu.tw

Abstract. Concolic testing is a software testing technique for generating concrete inputs of programs to increase code coverage and has been developed for years. For programming languages such as C, JAVA, x86 binary code, and JavaScript, there are already plenty of available concolic testers. However, the concolic testers for Python are relatively less. Since Python is a popular programming language, we believe there is a strong need to develop a good one.

Among the existing testers for Python, PyExZ3 is the most well-known and advanced. However, we found some issues of PyExZ3: (1) it implements only a limited number of base types' (e.g., integer, string) member functions and (2) it automatically downcasts concolic objects and discards related symbolic information as it encounters built-in types' constructors.

Based on the concept of PyExZ3, we develop a new tool called PyCT to alleviate these two issues. PyCT supports a more complete set of member functions of data types including integer, string, and range. We also propose a new method to upcast constants to concolic ones to prevent unnecessary downcasting. Our evaluation shows that with more member functions being supported, the coverage rate is raised to (80.20%) from (71.55%). It continues to go up to (85.68%) as constant upcasting is also implemented.

1 Introduction

Python language has been widely adopted to develop modern applications such as web applications, data analytics, machine learning, and robotics due to its high-level interactive nature and its maturing ecosystem of scientific libraries. As a general-purpose language, it is increasingly used not only in academic settings but also in industry. While it is an appealing choice for algorithmic development and exploratory data analysis, a systematic approach to analyze behaviors of Python programs is of the essence for software security. Systematic input generation that can cover all (or most critical) program behaviors is critical for software testing and debugging. While a concrete execution can only explore a specific path, randomly generating inputs is hard to hit honeypot and in most

© Springer Nature Switzerland AG 2021
H. Oh (Ed.): APLAS 2021, LNCS 13008, pp. 38–46, 2021.
https://doi.org/10.1007/978-3-030-89051-3_3

cases under-approximates program behaviors. It is desired having program properties hold under any usage scenarios.

Static analysis on formally modeling programs with symbolic and abstraction models provides a sound approach to analyze all potential behaviors of programs, but it may raise false alarms and requires runtime analysis for validation. Dynamic analysis on running and analyzing real executions helps to witness violations, but it requires effective input generation to trigger critical executions and cover sufficient program behaviors. Symbolic execution [5] poses an elegant solution for systematic input generation by executing programs on symbolic inputs (instead of concrete ones). During the execution, symbolic constraints are generated to represent program behaviors and path conditions. Solving these constraints yields inputs to trigger program execution. The main issue with symbolic execution is that its capability is limited by the power of the underlying constraint solvers. If the solver cannot solve a path constraint, it cannot find an input to cover that path and thus may lower its coverage rate.

Concolic testing combines symbolic execution and concrete testing to improve code coverage. When encountered constraints that cannot be handled by the solvers, a concolic tester can substitute some parts of the constraints with their corresponding concrete values to simplify them. Still, if the solver finds a solution of the simplified constraint, it is a valid solution of the original constraint. There have been quite a few useful concolic testing tools, targeting different languages and platforms, e.g., CUTE [8] and DART [3] for C, SAGE [4] for x86 binaries, jDART [6] for Java, Jalangi [7] for JavaScript, and PyExZ3 [1] for Python scripts.

Although Python is a popular language, concolic testers supporting Python are lacking. To the best of our knowledge, PyExZ3 is the most well-known and advanced Python concolic tester. It uses an object-oriented approach to implement concolic testing. It substitutes each basic data type (e.g., integer and string) with a concolic version that maintains both a concrete and a symbolic value. The concolic objects' member functions are also lifted to support both symbolic and concrete values. We believe this concept would lead to a very clean implementation of concolic testing.

However, the implementation of PyExZ3 suffers from two major issues. First, it implements only a limited number of basic types' member functions. For example, common functions such as "abs" and "round" of the integer type are not supported. This is fine for a proof-of-concept implementation, but would result in a low code coverage when used to analyze large projects.

Second and more importantly, PyExZ3 automatically downcasts concolic objects to primitive objects, which consists of only concrete values, and discards related symbolic information when it encounters built-in types' member functions. For instance, assume the symbolic and concrete values of the concolic value c_x of the variable x are e and 7, respectively, where e is an expression over variables occurred in the code. When we execute the statement "if int$(x) > 5$", it triggers the constructor int(x), which discards the symbolic value e and leave only the concrete value 7.

Based on the concept of PyExZ3, we develop a new tool called PyCT to alleviate these two issues. PyCT supports a more complete set of member functions of data types including integer, string, and range (Sect. 3). We also propose a new method to upcast constant values for the prevention of unnecessary downcasting (Sect. 4). We evaluate PyCT on a well-known GitHub project[1] related to algorithm implementations, and the experiment shows that these two optimizations lead to a significant improvements in terms of code coverage. With more member functions being supported, the coverage rate is raised to (80.20%) from (71.55%). It goes up to (85.68%) as constant upcasting is also implemented (Note that there are different means to define code coverage, in the paper, we consider the line coverage of programs).

2   Object-Oriented Concolic Testing Algorithm

We first recap the object oriented concolic testing algorithm and its implementation introduced in [1] for being self-contained. Here we consider two types of objects, integer type and string type. We implement the classes *concolic integer* and *concolic string* that inherit the classes integer and string, respectively. Taking concolic integer as an example, it has two member values, the concrete and the symbolic values, and overrides all integer classes' member functions. The concrete value is with the integer type and the symbolic value is a *symbolic expression* that is expressible in SMT theory of strings and linear arithmetic, i.e., T_{SLIA} [2]. For a member function $f(\bar{x})$ of concolic integer type, it updates the concrete value in the same way that $f(\bar{x})$ of integer type does. For a symbolic value, the basic version just update its value to a special symbol $\perp$ to denote that it does not have symbolic value. We say that a member function is not supported if its implementation is the basic version. If this member function is *supported*, we need to replace the symbol $\perp$ in the basic version with a symbolic expression that captures the semantics of f.

Such object-oriented implementation has the advantage that, any time when the tester feeds a concolic object c to a non-supported function, c is automatically downcast to the basic type and the tester can still run without encounter a runtime exception. One can then step-wisely improve the amount of supported member functions by replacing the basic version with the one capturing the function's semantic. For a *concolic object* c, we use $c.val$ to denote its the *concrete value* and $c.exp$ to denote its *symbolic expression*. If c is of concolic integer type (resp., concolic string type), then $c.val$ is a constant integer in $\mathbb{Z}$ (resp., a constant string in Σ^*) and $c.exp$ is an integer expression (resp., a string expression). We write $c = (x, s)$ for $c.val = x$ and $c.exp = s$.

To increase the line coverage, a concolic tester simulates the behaviors of a program in an iterative manner and collects the constraints relating to the program's input variables during one execution for generating input values for the subsequent iterations.

---

[1] We use The Algorithms/Python project (https://github.com/TheAlgorithms/Python), the 4th top-starred Python project on GitHub, introducing plenty of common algorithm implementations learning purposes.

More specifically, each variable x of the program corresponds to a concolic object c_x. Value $c_x.val$ is updated along with x and $c_x.exp$ describes the relation between the current value of x and the initial variable values. For instance, if $c_x = (2, x + 1)$ and $c_y = (3, 2z)$ are two integer concolic objects, then, after executing "$x := x + 2y + 1$", c_x is updated to $(9, x + 4z + 2)$ since $2 + 2 * 3 + 1 = 9$ and $(x + 1) + 2(2z) + 1 = x + 4z + 2$. Besides, a concolic tester maintains a tree T to remember the path constraints corresponding to all executed program traces. It also maintains a queue Q of formulae whose models correspond to input values that is guaranteed to cover some unexplored program lines. In what follows, we use the program P given in Fig. 1 as an example to illustrate how the algorithm works, including how T and Q are maintained. Integer variables x, y, z correspond to integer concolic objects c_x, c_y, c_z, respectively.

1st Iteration: The integer variable x is the input argument of function isPalindrome. Initially, we randomly pick an integer value for x, say 0, and create the concolic integer $c_x = (0, x)$ as the input. Now T is an empty tree, and Q is an empty queue. After executing line 2 and 3, we have $c_y = (0, 0)$ and $c_z = (0, x)$. In line 4, the Boolean statement $z > 0$ is encountered. Since $c_z.exp = x$ and the tree T is empty, the node n_1 with label $\psi_1 := (x > 0)$ is inserted into T as a root. See Fig. 2. Because that $c_z.val = 0$ does not satisfy the statement, the current execution will take the false branch. We push the formula ψ_1, whose model corresponds to input values going to the true branch, into the queue Q (the result is Q_1 in the figure) Then, line 8 is executed. From the condition $x == y$, we create the constraint $\psi_2 := (c_x.exp == c_y.exp) = (0 == x)$. Since we are coming from the left (false) branch of n_1, we add the node n_2 with label ψ_2 into T as a left-child of n_1. Then we push the formula $\neg\psi_1 \wedge \neg\psi_2$, which corresponds to taking n_1's left branch and followed by taking n_2's left branch, is pushed into Q (to obtain Q_2 in the figure). Notice that the models of both formullae in Q_2 will lead to some unexplored program lines, as they take different branch direction then we did in the current execution. At the end, line 9 is executed and the first iteration finished.

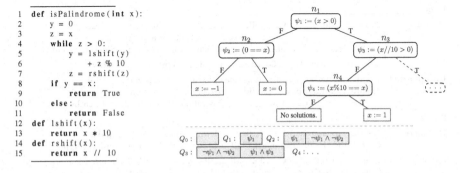

```
1   def isPalindrome(int x):
2       y = 0
3       z = x
4       while z > 0:
5           y = lshift(y)
6               + z % 10
7           z = rshift(z)
8       if y == x:
9           return True
10      else:
11          return False
12  def lshift(x):
13      return x * 10
14  def rshift(x):
15      return x // 10
```

Fig. 1. Program P checks if x is a palindrome.

Fig. 2. The tree of the concolic testing process on program P.

2nd Iteration: The *halting conditions* for the process are either the queue Q is empty or all lines of P are covered after an iteration. Neither of the halting conditions is satisfied, then the process continues (until a given timeout period is reached). At the beginning of the 2nd iteration, the formula ψ_1 is removed from the front of Q and the new initial value c_x can be set as $(1, x)$ since $x = 1$ is a solution of ψ_1. (Note that, in implementation, the formula is sent to an SMT solver for a solution.) We then repeat the procedure in a similar way as we did before. In this example, entire procedure will stop in three iterations when all programs lines are covered. We refer the readers to our appendix for further details.

3   Function Support and Implementation

The tool PyExZ3 only implements a very limited amount of member functions, so it is expected that the code coverage would increase as more functions are supported. In PyCT, we support almost all member functions of concolic integer and string whose semantic are expressible in T_{SLIA} (SMT theory of strings and linear arithmetic). In Table 1 we lists the member functions of integer and string in Python that we support and do not support. Member functions are divided into three groups in the tables, (i) complete; (ii) partial; and (iii) unsupported. Functions in group (i) can be well expressed in T_{SLIA} and implemented in PyCT thoroughly. In group (ii), functions are basically supported, excepts certain special input arguments because of implementation difficulty. For example, lexicographic orderings in Python and Z3's T_{SLIA} implementation are different, so member functions of string type related to lexicographic order are not completely supported. Group (iii) includes member functions we do not provide support the update of symbolic expressions. Some functions are in this group

Table 1. Member functions of integer and string types and their PyCT implementation.

Integer	
Complete	__abs__, __add__, __bool__, __ceil__, __eq__, __floor__, __ge__, __gt__, __le__, __lt__, __mul__, __ne__, __neg__, __pos__, __radd__, __rmul__, __round__, __rsub__, __sub__, __trunc__, conjugate, denominator, imag, numerator, real
Partial	__floordiv__, __mod__, __rfloordiv__, __rmod__, __rtruediv__, __truediv__
Unsupported	__and__, __divmod__, __format__, __hash__, __index__, __invert__, __lshift__, __rshift__, __or__, __pow__, __rand__, __rdivmod__, __rlshift__, __ror__, __rpow__, __rrshift__, __rxor__, __xor__, as_integer_ratio, bit_length, to_bytes
String	
Complete	__add__, __contains__, __eq__, __iter__, __len__, __mul__, __ne__, __rmul__, count, find, index, isalpha, isdigit, islower, isupper, lower, replace, upper
Partial	__ge__, __getitem__, __gt__, __le__, __lt__, __mod__, endswith, isalnum, isnumeric, lstrip, rstrip, split, splitlines, startswith, strip
Unsupported	__format__, __hash__, __rmod__, capitalize, casefold, center, encode, expandtabs, format, format_map, isascii, isdecimal, isidentifier, isprintable, isspace, istitle, join, ljust, partition, rfind, rindex, rjust, rpartition, rsplit, swapcase, title, translate, zfill

because they are not expressible in T_{SLIA}. One major class of this type is the bitwise operations, which usually requires the use of SMT bit-vector theory to model them precisely and efficiently. Another class of examples are those whose return types are not expressible in T_{SLIA}. For example, "as_integer_ratio" returns a tuple and "to_bytes" returns a list. Our preliminary study over the top 5 starred GitHub projects suggests that in totally 421,214 lines of code, the unsupported functions (not counting the magic functions which cannot be found by simple pattern matching) only occur 381 times (less than 0.1%).

The Range Class. In Python, "range()" is often used in the "for" statement and is one of the most frequently used functions. However, different from many other programming languages, in Python, "range" is a class like string and integer and therefore, refers to a set of member functions, listed in Table 2. To increase the coverage, some member functions of range type are supported in PyCT.

Table 2. Member functions of range type.

Complete	__init__, __contains__, __iter__, __len__, count, index
Partial	__getitem__
Unsupported	__bool__, __eq__, __ge__, __gt__, __hash__, __le__, __lt__, __ne__, __reversed__

Consider the statement "for i in range (a, b, c): S", where S is a Python statement. Expression range (a, b, c) corresponds to the sequence $\pi : a, a + c, \ldots, a + c*n$ when $c \geq 0$, where n is the greatest non-negative integer s.t. $a + c*n < b$. So the statement S is covered when π is a non-empty sequence. The case of $c \leq 0$ is symmetric.

To support member functions of range type, we introduce *concolic range*. For the concolic object of range (a, b, c), the concrete value is the sequence π and the symbolic expression is a quadruple (start, stop, step, current), where start, stop, and step refer to $c_a.exp$, $c_b.exp$, and $c_c.exp$, respectively, and "current" is the element in π of the current loop, i.e., $i.val$. Each $i.val \in \pi$ refers to a branch $c_a.exp + c_c.exp * j < c_b.exp$, where $j = (i.val - c_a.val)/c_c.val$, i.e., the index of loop corresponding to $i.val$. The constraint $c_a.exp + c_c.exp * n < c_b.exp$ is then pushed into the queue as S is not covered. We use the example given in Fig. 3 to explain why this setting can help increase coverage.

```
1  def range_example(b):
2      for e in range(0, b, 4):
3          if e == 8:
4              return
```

Fig. 3. "range" in the "for" statement.

At the beginning, c_b is set as $(0, b)$. Obviously, lines 3 and 4 are not covered, then after the 1st iteration is completed, constraint $0 + 4 * 0 < b$ is pushed into the queue and $b = 1$ is a solution to the constraint. Similarly, constraints $0 + 4 * 1 < b$ and $0 + 4 * 2 < b$ are pushed into the queue at the ends of the 2nd and 3rd iterations and $b = 5$, $b = 9$ are solutions, respectively. Accordingly, program P is fully covered as the input value $b = 9$. In this example in range (a, b, c), a and c are set as two constants, the other cases where a, c are variables can be derived similarly.

Exception Handling. The execution of a program may halt when an exception is triggered, e.g., divided-by-zero, str-to-int conversion exceptions, etc. Essentially, exceptions can be viewed as branch conditions. If the current input value triggers an exception, the tester would like to find another input without trigger that exception, and vice versa, to increase code coverage. We realize it by pre-inserting some branch statements into the source code without modifying the semantics of the program. Consider the statement "x = y / z". A divided-by-zero exception is thrown as the value of z = 0. In PyCT, the statement is automatically rewritten as "if z == 0: S; else: x = y / z", where S is a statement throwing a divided-by-zero exception. The other exceptional cases are handled in a similar manner.

Function Decomposition. It happens that some Python expressions are not immediately expressible in T_{SLIA}. So for supporting those functions, we decompose them into T_{SLIA} expressible fragments. For instance, in Python, "abc" $* 2$ represents the string "abcabc". However, in T_{SLIA}, a multiplication of a string and an integer is not valid. We handle the string-integer multiplication by transforming them to a recursive statement. Observe that $s * n = s * (n - 1) + s$ for all string s and positive integer n. So we translate "t = s * n" into the recursive statement S(s, n): "if $(n - 1) == 0$: then t = s; else: t = S(s, n − 1) + s", and it becomes expressible in T_{SLIA}.

Another example is the "str.count(sub)" function that counts the number of occurrences of sub in str. We need to handle the special case when sub is an empty string. In such a case, "count" simply returns the length of str plus one. Otherwise, we create a temporary string $temp$ whose value is obtained by replacing all occurrences of sub in str with empty strings, and then we can obtain str.count(sub) = $\frac{\text{len}(str) - \text{len}(temp)}{\text{len}(sub)}$.

The "str.replace(old, new, max)" function replaces at most "max" occurrences of "old" with "new". This is also handled by translating to recursive statement and invoking the single entry replace function in SMT2 in the recursive function body. Other functions we support using a similar approach include "lower" and "upper".

4   Constant Upcasting

In PyExZ3, besides non-supported member function calls, constant values being callers may also downcast concolic objects to primitive ones, i.e., integers or strings. For instance, for constant string 'abcd', the function call 'abcd'.__contains__(x) with input argument x causes the concolic object c_x corresponding to x to be downcasted. This would reduce the total coverage rate because in the subsequent program execution, we lost the symbolic information of x, and hence cannot switch to some unexplored path when encountered branch statements involving x. Our experiments (Sect. 5) shows that such downcast has significant negative impact to code coverage.

A naive solution is to make Python constant/primitive strings' member functions (such as "__contains__") also accept concolic objects as input arguments.

To achieve this, one has to modify, for example, Python's source codes, which is cumbersome and needs a great effort. Besides, they also have to update the modification frequently for maintaining the compatibility as Python's official version advances.

In PyCT, a more feasible and reliable solution is implemented instead. The idea is to upcast constant values to their corresponding concolic objects. More specifically, each constant value s is upcasted to the concolic object (s, s). So the primitive string "abcd" is upcasted to the concolic string ("abcd", "abcd") and the appearance of the function call "abcd". __contains__(x) is replaced with the concolic string member function call introduced in the last section, i.e., the function __contains__ in Table 1. Accordingly, c_x is not downcasted and so we can use its symbolic value afterward. By replacing each occurrence of constants in the AST of the source code under testing with its corresponding concolic object, then the idea, upcasting constant values to concolic objects, is instantly realized. This constant upcasting technique is also used to conquer a similar problem that PyExZ3 only outputs concrete values from Python's common built-in constructors such as int(x), str(x), and range(x, y, z) in PyCT.

5   Experiment Results

To evaluate PyCT, we compare it with PyExZ3 on the following five benchmarks: (1) UnitTest(PyExZ3) provided by PyExZ3; (2) UnitTest(PyCT) which we compose for testing; (3) LeetCode collected from the LeetCode platform; (4) PythonLib, the Python core libraries, where both LeetCode and Python-Lib involve diverse usages of string-number conversion in Python such as parsing date-time, verifying and restoring IP addresses from strings, etc.; (5) The Algorithms/Python[2], the 4th top-starred Python project on GitHub, introducing plenty of common algorithm implementations in Python language for learning purposes, and therefore including many integer and string type-hinting functions. The experiments are run in a Docker container on a PC with an Intel Core i7-10700 (2.90 GHz) processor with 8 cores and 16 threads, a 48 GB of RAM, and a 1.8 TB, 7200 rpm hard disk drive running the Ubuntu 20.04.1 LTS operating system. The versions of Python and the SMT solver CVC4 are 3.8.5 and 1.7[3], respectively.

For the evaluation of the constant upcasting technique, in the experiments, PyCT are run in two modes, the mode without and with constant upcasting, denoted PyCT (Sect. 3 only) and PyCT+Up (Sect. 3 and 4), respectively. For each concolic tester, each function in the benchmarks is tested at most 15 min. The timeout of one concolic testing iteration is set to 15 s. The timeout of an SMT constraint solving is set to 10 s. We use the package "coverage"[4] to compute line coverage (the number of executed lines ÷ the number of lines in the source code).

---

[2] https://github.com/TheAlgorithms/Python.

[3] https://github.com/cvc5/cvc5/tree/d1f3225e26b9d64f065048885053392b10994e71.

[4] https://pypi.org/project/coverage/4.5.4/.

Table 3 shows the results. Both PyCT and PyCT+Up outperform PyExZ3 on all benchmarks in terms of coverage. The results show that constant upcasting technique significantly improves PyCT's line coverage. One can tell that comparing with PyExZ3, on average, PyCT and PyCT+Up take more time on testing a function. Whereas that the median times of the three testers on all benchmarks are almost equivalent, which suggests that PyCT and PyCT+Up spend more time on solving difficult cases to increase coverage rate.

Table 3. Results on the benchmarks.

No. of functions		UnitTest (PyExZ3)	UnitTest (PyCT)	Leetcode	PythonLib	The Algorithms/ Python	TOTAL
		73	23	15	9	376	496
Line coverage	PyExZ3	493/536	183/219	180/290	177/312	2258/3156	3291/4513
		(91.98%)	(83.56%)	(62.07%)	(56.73%)	(71.55%)	(72.92%)
	PyCT	499/536	210/219	242/290	183/312	2531/3156	3665/4513
		(93.10%)	(95.89%)	(83.45%)	(58.65%)	(80.20%)	(81.21%)
	PyCT+Up	499/536	214/219	287/290	251/312	2704/3156	3955/4513
		(93.10%)	(97.72%)	(98.97%)	(80.45%)	(85.68%)	(87.64%)
Average time	PyExZ3	26.26	39.35	85.63	201.77	16.47	24.43
	PyCT	25.04	84.64	61.11	207.62	23.38	30.95
	PyCT+Up	25.05	39.97	102.99	209.32	52.23	52.04
Median time	PyExZ3	0.03	0.02	0.03	0.12	1.29	1.28
	PyCT	0.11	0.11	0.15	0.76	2.5	1.27
	PyCT+Up	0.13	0.11	1.02	13.83	2.54	1.29

References

1. Ball, T., Daniel, J.: Deconstructing dynamic symbolic execution. In: Dependable Software Systems Engineering, pp. 26–41 (2015)
2. Barrett, C., Stump, A., Tinelli, C.: The SMT-LIB Standard: Version 2.0. Technical report (2010). www.SMT-LIB.org
3. Godefroid, P., Klarlund, N., Sen, K.: DART: directed automated random testing. In: ACM SIGPLAN Notices, vol. 40, pp. 213–223. ACM (2005)
4. Godefroid, P., Levin, M.Y., Molnar, D.A.: SAGE: whitebox fuzzing for security testing. ACM Queue 10(1) (2012)
5. King, J.C.: Symbolic execution and program testing. Commun. ACM 19(7), 385–394 (1976)
6. Luckow, K., et al.: JDART: a dynamic symbolic analysis framework. In: Chechik, M., Raskin, J.-F. (eds.) TACAS 2016. LNCS, vol. 9636, pp. 442–459. Springer, Heidelberg (2016). https://doi.org/10.1007/978-3-662-49674-9_26
7. Sen, K., Kalasapur, S., Brutch, T.G., Gibbs, S.: Jalangi: a tool framework for concolic testing, selective record-replay, and dynamic analysis of Javascript. In: ESEC/FSE 2013, pp. 615–618 (2013)
8. Sen, K., Marinov, D., Agha, G.: CUTE: a concolic unit testing engine for C. In: ACM SIGSOFT Software Engineering Notes, vol. 30, pp. 263–272. ACM (2005)

Program Synthesis for Musicians: A Usability Testbed for Temporal Logic Specifications

Wonhyuk Choi[1]([✉]), Michel Vazirani[1], and Mark Santolucito[2]

[1] Columbia University, New York, NY 10027, USA
{wonhyuk.choi,mvv2114}@columbia.edu
[2] Barnard College, Columbia University, New York, NY 10027, USA
msantolu@barnard.edu

Abstract. In recent years, program synthesis research has made significant progress in creating user-friendly tools for Programming by example (PBE) and Programming by demonstration (PBD) environments. However, program synthesis from logical specifications, such as reactive synthesis, still faces large challenges in widespread adoption. In order to bring reactive synthesis to a wider audience, more research is necessary to explore different interface options. We present The SynthSynthesizer, a music-based tool for designing and testing specification interfaces. The tool enables researchers to prototype different interfaces for reactive synthesis and run user studies on them. The tool is accessible to both researchers and users by running on a browser on top of a **docker**-containerized synthesis toolchain. We show sample implementations with the tool by creating dropdown interfaces, and by running a user study with 21 users.

Keywords: Reactive synthesis · Program synthesis · Computer music

1 Introduction

Over the last two decades, program synthesis has seen much progress [15] and researchers have made significant headway into making program synthesis accessible to a wider audience [13]. Specifically, research in Programming by example (PBE) and Programming by demonstration (PBD) has led to a wide array of user-friendly tools [8,22,23,31], including Wrangler [21], StriSynth [14], Sketch-n-Sketch [16].

However, building user-friendly tools for program synthesis from logical specifications remains a challenge. In particular, for reactive synthesis [4], despite development in both theory [3,33] and tooling [19], the complexity of writing specifications has limited the adoption of reactive synthesis to a highly technical audience. In order to bring synthesis to non-technical users, more research is necessary to understand effective means of creating logical specifications.

In this paper, we present The SynthSynthesizer, a tool that enables researchers to try out different interfaces and logic fragments for reactive synthesis.

© Springer Nature Switzerland AG 2021
H. Oh (Ed.): APLAS 2021, LNCS 13008, pp. 47–61, 2021.
https://doi.org/10.1007/978-3-030-89051-3_4

Fig. 1. Autumn Leaves Lead Sheet indicating the changes in signal topology

Researchers can define interfaces by simply implementing a single `JavaScript` function, after which a non-technical audience can interact with the tool. In order to appeal to a larger base of users, The SynthSynthesizer uses computer music as an reactive environment that is also interactive and creative.

The SynthSynthesizer runs on a browser, making it easily to deploy user studies. The tool is also easy to install and modify for researchers; the synthesis toolchain is provided in `docker` container so that even researchers without a deep knowledge of reactive synthesis can explore the specification interface space.

Using our tool, we explored dropdowns as a way of specifying reactive control by implementing three different interfaces. We ran a user study on these interfaces by presenting them to 21 participants with a mix of music and programming backgrounds. From the study, we found that users experienced a tradeoff between ease of use and expressivity, and enjoyed the no-code nature of synthesis. These experiences motivate further exploration of specification interface design, which our tool aims to facilitate.

In summary, our contributions are as follows:

1. We present The SynthSynthesizer, a music-based tool that enables rapid prototyping and user studies for studying different reactive synthesis interfaces.
2. We explored dropdowns as an interface for specifying reactive control, and implemented the example interfaces using our tool.
3. We ran a user study with 21 users, and found a tradeoff between expressivity and ease-of-use as well as a possible appeal of synthesis to a wider user-base.

2   Motivating Example

As an illustrative example, consider a user that would like a reactive system to manipulate audio signals as phrases of a music piece are played. Specifically, AM synthesis should be toggled whenever the note G4 is played, and LFO vibrato should be toggled whenever the note E4 is played, as shown in Fig. 1.

To build such a reactive system, a user could write a program that specifies when and how the signals should change. However, writing this program is generally not an easy task. It not only requires the user to be a competent programmer, but also requires them to be comfortable using specific API's such as `Web Audio`. Moreover, even if a user can write such a program, the solution is verbose, requiring nearly 100 lines of code to satisfy two logical conditions.

In order to concisely encapsulate the time-varying nature of the signal topology, the user might turn to reactive synthesis. In this case, the user would need to choose a temporal logic and write a specification that determines when AM synthesis and LFO vibrato are toggled. Such a specification, using Temporal Stream Logic (TSL) [11], can be written as follow:

$$\texttt{play G4} \leftrightarrow [\texttt{AM} \leftarrowtail \texttt{toggle AM}]$$
$$\texttt{play E4} \leftrightarrow [\texttt{LFO} \leftarrowtail \texttt{toggle LFO}]$$

Though reactive synthesis brings the user closer to building their instrument, this solution generally involves too much prerequisite knowledge. Users must understand the notion of formal guarantees, time steps, and other particularities of temporal logic, making the approach unrealistic for a broad population.

To overcome the above challenges, we need a framework where non-technical users can easily specify temporal properties. Here, we present The SynthSynthesizer as a tool for exploring the space of such frameworks, where researchers can prototype different interfaces and run user studies.

3   Preliminaries

Temporal Stream Logic (TSL) is a logic designed around the synthesis of reactive programs [11]. TSL is built upon the same temporal logic operators (i.e. next $\bigcirc$, until $\mathcal{U}$) found in logics such as Linear Temporal Logic. In addition, TSL introduces *predicate terms* τ_P, *function terms* τ_F, and *update terms* to describe reactive systems that manipulate data. In TSL, the conceptualization of a reactive system revolves around signals s which carry data values of arbitrary complexity; A TSL specification describes how functions should be applied to these signals over time. Signals may be pure outputs, or *cells*, as a one-timestep delayed input. These terms are defined as shown in the grammar of TSL below:

$$\varphi := \tau \in \mathcal{T}_P \cup \mathcal{T}_U \mid \neg\varphi \mid \varphi \wedge \varphi \mid \bigcirc\varphi \mid \varphi\,\mathcal{U}\,\varphi$$

$$\tau_F := \texttt{s} \mid \texttt{f}(\tau_F^0, \tau_F^1, \ldots, \tau_F^{n-1})$$
$$\tau_P := \texttt{p}(\tau_F^0, \tau_F^1, \ldots, \tau_F^{n-1})$$
$$\tau_U := [s \leftarrowtail \tau_F]$$

4   The SynthSynthesizer

In this section, we introduce The SynthSynthesizer, a testbed tool for running user studies on different logical fragments and interfaces for program synthesis.

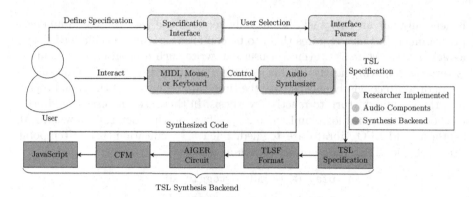

Fig. 2. Overview of The SynthSynthesizer

The framework allows researchers to create interfaces by defining them through HTML and implementing a single function in JavaScript to parse the interface. The tool also allows researchers to experiment with different fragments of logics, and explore the tradeoffs between expressivity and usability.

The overview of the process is shown in Fig. 2. First, a user submits their specification through an interface. This gets parsed into a logic formula, which is then synthesized into JavaScript code. The resulting code is embedded back into the tool, controlling the audio synthesizer that the user plays with either their mouse, QWERTY keyboard, or USB MIDI controller. The researcher is free to use any temporal logic that can synthesize to JavaScript (such as LTL), but we include our TSL synthesis backend for completeness and usability.

We implemented the audio components of The SynthSynthesizer using Web Audio [28] and Web MIDI [36], both standard Web APIs maintained by the W3C. The frontend uses framework-less JavaScript, and the backend runs on Node.js. The server backend is responsible for synthesizing TSL specifications to JavaScript, with Strix [26] as its synthesis backend and tsltools [10] to convert between formats such as TLSF [20] and AIGER [18].

We designed The SynthSynthesizer so that researchers can easily access the tool. Most notably, installation is hassle-free: we provide a docker container with all the dependencies pre-installed. In particular, this makes the tool accessible to researchers outside the formal methods community; researchers do not a deep understanding of the synthesis procedure to use our tool. Additionally, since the tool runs on a web browser, running user studies is as simple as just sharing a link. A live demo of the tool is available at https://tslsynthesissynthesizer.com.

5   Evaluation

As an example of how The SynthSynthesizer can be used to explore interfaces for synthesis, we implemented three separate interfaces and presented them to users for a user study. Each interface utilizes a different fragment of TSL.

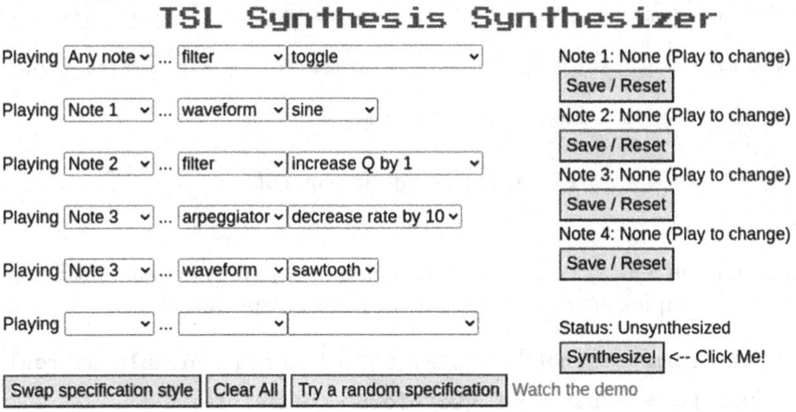

TSL Synthesis Synthesizer

Playing [Any note ▾] ... [filter ▾] [toggle ▾]   Note 1: None (Play to change)
                                                         [Save / Reset]
Playing [Note 1 ▾] ... [waveform ▾] [sine ▾]   Note 2: None (Play to change)
                                                         [Save / Reset]
Playing [Note 2 ▾] ... [filter ▾] [increase Q by 1 ▾]   Note 3: None (Play to change)
                                                         [Save / Reset]
Playing [Note 3 ▾] ... [arpeggiator ▾] [decrease rate by 10 ▾]   Note 4: None (Play to change)
                                                         [Save / Reset]
Playing [Note 3 ▾] ... [waveform ▾] [sawtooth ▾]

Playing [▾] ... [▾] [▾]   Status: Unsynthesized
                                                         [Synthesize!] <-- Click Me!
[Swap specification style] [Clear All] [Try a random specification] Watch the demo

Fig. 3. Interface of TSL$_\alpha$

5.1   Interface Implementations

We explored dropdowns as an interface for specifying reactive control, as drop-downs are a ubiquitous design element. We created two dropdown interfaces with different frontends, and included a third written interface as a control case. All three interfaces use TSL to synthesize user specifications, but with varying parts of the grammar and subsequently varying levels of expressivity.

We now present each implementation separately.

TSL$_\alpha$. In our first implementation, we use a fragment of TSL that we call TSL$_\alpha$. Let $\tau_U \in \mathcal{T}_U$ update terms, $\tau_p \in \mathcal{T}_P$ predicate terms. Then, every formula φ in TSL$_\alpha$ is built according to the following grammar:

$$\varphi := \Box \tau_u \mid \Box \tau_p \leftrightarrow \tau_u \mid \varphi \wedge \varphi$$

The syntax of TSL$_\alpha$ allows users to specify predicates that reconfigure the signal flow topology of the underlying synthesizer. In particular, the TSL specification in the motivating example can be captured by TSL$_\alpha$.

The grammar is concise, allowing us to build a compact interface as in Fig. 3. With this interface, users can define specifications by selecting from a set of predefined options. TSL$_\alpha$ specifications also synthesize quickly; 1,000 random synthesis queries took, on average, only 1.76 s (cf. Appendix A.2).

TSL$_\beta$. Our second implementation still features a dropdown interface, but with a more expressive grammar. Its syntax is constructed as follows:

$$\psi = \tau_u \mid \tau_p \leftrightarrow \tau_u \mid \tau_u \rightarrow \tau_u$$
$$\varphi = \Box \psi \mid \Box \tau_u \rightarrow \psi \ \mathcal{W} \ \neg \tau_u \mid \varphi \wedge \varphi$$

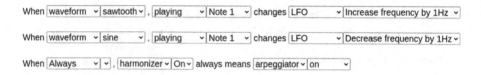

Fig. 4. Partial interface of TSL$_\beta$

Expanding upon TSL$_\alpha$, TSL$_\beta$ adds terms of $\tau_u \rightarrow \tau_u$ and the weak until operator $\mathcal{W}$ for more complex specifications. For instance, a specification

$$\square[\texttt{waveform} \leftarrowtail \texttt{sine()}] \leftrightarrow (\texttt{play C4} \leftrightarrow [\texttt{amFreq} \leftarrow \texttt{double amFreq}])$$
$$\mathcal{W} \neg[\texttt{waveform} \leftarrowtail \texttt{sine()}] \wedge \neg[\texttt{waveform} \leftarrowtail \texttt{waveform}]$$

states that playing C4 doubles AM frequency only when the waveform is sine.

To suit the additional complexity in TSL$_\beta$, we arranged the dropdowns as natural language sentences for user readability. The interface is shown in Fig. 4. This fragment of TSL also synthesizes quickly, with a mean of 10.09 s for 1,000 random specification synthesis queries (cf. Appendix A.2).

TSL$_\mu$. TSL$_\mu$ subsumes TSL$_\alpha$ and TSL$_\beta$ by offering the full syntax of TSL, but with the restriction that predicates cannot be applied to cells (cf. Appendix A.1). We can easily implement the tool using a written interface. Here, users type TSL$_\mu$ formulas directly into a textbox, accessing the syntax TSL$_\mu$ without any restrictions. In a user study, this interface would serve as the control case. Since the UI is a simple textbox, we omit a figure of TSL$_\mu$.

5.2 User Study

We presented the TSL$_\alpha$, TSL$_\beta$, and TSL$_\mu$ instantiations of The SynthSynthesizer to 21 users for a usability study. The participants were recruited through online forums focused on programming and computer music, such as reddit or discord. Users first watched a video tutorial[1] and answered preliminary questions on a scale of 1 (not at all experienced) - 7 (very experienced), to rate their own experience in music ($mean = 4.0, SD = 2.2$), audio signal processing ($mean = 2.6, SD = 2.1$), and programming ($mean = 4.5, SD = 2.0$). The users then manipulated the tool to define specifications, synthesize them, and interact with the resulting reactive system. Afterwards, users responded to a variety of questions, such as rating each interface on its 'Ease of Use' and 'Flexibility', or answering if they had a favorite interface and why. The full list of questions is included in Appendix A.3. Note that we did not time users for any of their activities, since our user study was focused on creativity and music production instead of concrete task completion.

From the user study, we found that participants found TSL$_\alpha$ and TSL$_\beta$ equally understandable (Q2) and intuitive (Q3), while also being expressive and

---

[1]   https://tslsynthesissynthesizer.com/tutorial.html.

flexible (Q4). However, while users rated TSL_μ to be expressive and flexible, participants rated its usability to be lower than TSL_α and TSL_μ across all questions. Since we organized our study by showing TSL_α, TSL_β, and TSL_μ in the same sequential order, we intentionally created a bias for users to have a more solid understanding of TSL and temporal logic by the time they reached the TSL_μ interface. However, as users still expressed difficulty in using TSL_μ, this strengthens our claim that we need a more user-friendly interface than text-based interfaces to expose reactive synthesis to a wider audience. From this, we do not conclude that dropdowns are necessarily the right choice of interface - instead we remark that this is complex design space that requires further investigation.

A total of 18 participants responded to an optional qualitative question asking which interface was their favorite. Three chose TSL_α, nine chose TSL_β, and six chose TSL_μ. The preference for the more complex interfaces shows how users are intrigued by the expressivity and possibilities of TSL. Although larger fragments of TSL make interfaces harder to use, users are willing to accept a more complex logic if the interface for the specifications is sufficiently constrained. The balance struck by TSL_β was also reflected in the user explanations. One user responded *"TSL_β: offers the most flexibility while still being incredibly intuitive."* and another user responded *"TSL_β had the best tradeoff in intuitiveness/ease of use and freedom/flexibility".* Two other users mentioned they preferred to avoid writing code, responding *"TSL_β! It felt like it had a lot more layers that you could add on, without the complexity of writing your own code to make it work."* and *"TSL_β. It has lots of flexibility and no need to write code.".*

A video of users interacting with the tool is available at tslsynthesissynthesizer.com/demo.html. Visualizations of the user study results are available in Appendix A.4.

6   Related Work

The SynthSynthesizer is a tool for exploring logic and interface design for program synthesis with temporal logics. In recent years, there has been an increased interest in usability design of language tools [5], including program synthesis tools [7,32]. Frameworks to bring program synthesis to broader audiences have also been explored in the context of games [25], graphics [16], and data science [35], but synthesis tools for non-technical users have not yet included reactive synthesis specifically. The tool Flax [34,35] specifically looks at nontraditional interfaces to synthesis by using visualization as a mode of specification.

Some existing tools have explored the usability design space of temporal logics for more technical users. TERMITE [29,30] was designed to bring reactive synthesis to software developers. Another critical design problem in the usability of reactive synthesis is the task of providing explanations for reactive synthesis results [1]. Additionally, the UPPAAL tool provides an application-specific engineered interface for TCTL (timed computation tree logic) specifications; however, UPPAAL is more focused on verification than synthesis [2].

While interfaces for interactive music generation with reactive synthesis is a new research problem, computer-assisted composition has a long history [6]. In terms of usability, recent results have found that users preferred to have more control over automated music generation rather than having a monolithic end-to-end model [17]. Similarly, user studies on a music generation tool for video editing [12] found participants objecting to too much automation, as it made them feel as if they had not created music. These insights can directly contribute to interface research of reactive synthesis, since synthesized automata may be counter-intuitive to users.

We have built our tool around TSL [11], but our interface could be used to explore specification interface for other temporal logic. Of particular interest would be adding support for TSL-Modulo Theories [9,24], which would allow for more fine-grained manipulations of music parameters.

7   Conclusions

We have introduced The SynthSynthesizer, a music-based user study tool that allows rapid prototyping of different fragments of logic and interfaces. We hope our tool can be used to start research into designing interfaces for different logics, and make synthesis more accessible to a broader audience.

A   Appendix

A.1   TSL$_\mu$ and its Decidability

For our tool, we use the TSL fragment TSL$_\mu$ that has no predicate term application on cell values. While our tool has many internal cell values – such as modulation frequencies or waveforms – predicate terms are only applied to fresh user inputs (i.e. which notes they pressed, the velocity of key press, etc.). This allows us to use the fragment TSL$_\mu$, which is decidable, unlike the full syntax of TSL.

Here, we formalize the definition of TSL$_\mu$ and prove the decidability of its synthesis problem.

Definition 1 (TSL$_\mu$). *Let function terms τ_F and update terms τ_U be defined as in Sect. 3. Let predicate terms τ_P be defined as follows:*

$$\tau_P := p(s_{i_0}, s_{i_1}, \cdots s_{i_j})$$

where s_{i_j} refers to input signals, and p any predicate. Then, a TSL$_\mu$ formula is defined by the following syntax:

$$\varphi := \tau \in T_P \cup T_U \mid \neg\varphi \mid \varphi \wedge \varphi \mid \bigcirc\varphi \mid \varphi \, \mathcal{U} \, \psi$$

Intuitively, this is a fragment of TSL where predicate terms are evaluated only on input signals, and not cells. In particular, synthesizing this fragment of TSL is decidable.

We now show that synthesis of this fragment of TSL is decidable by showing that every TSL_μ formula can be reduced to an LTL formula.

Theorem 1 (TSL$_\mu$-LTL Equivalence). *Every TSL_μ formula can be transformed to an equivalent LTL formula in polynomial time.*

Proof. In TSL synthesis, the environment player chooses the predicate terms τ_P and the system player chooses the update terms τ_U. In TSL_μ, the environment inputs τ_P's are always fresh at each timestep, and their values do not depend on previous outputs τ_U of the system player.

Now, we can use the translation procedure from TSL to LTL presented in [11]:

$$\varphi_{LTL} = \square \Big(\bigwedge_{s_o \in \mathbb{O} \cup \mathbb{C}} \bigvee_{\tau \in \mathcal{T}_{U/\mathtt{id}}^{s_o}} \big(\tau \wedge \bigwedge_{\tau' \in \mathcal{T}_{U/\mathtt{id}}^{s_o} \backslash \{\tau\}} \neg \tau' \big) \Big)$$
$$\wedge \; \textsc{SyntacticConversion}\big(\varphi_{TSL}\big)$$

Finkbeiner et al. show the soundness of this procedure, that the realizability of φ_{LTL} implies the realizability of φ_{TSL}. In the full syntax of TSL, this procedure may still produce φ_{LTL} that returns unrealizable even though φ_{TSL} is realizable since the procedure removes the semantic meanings of update terms. However, in TSL_μ, the environment inputs do not depend on the previous system outputs, and no semantic interpretation of update terms is necessary; it follows that an unrealizable φ_{LTL} always implies an unrealizable φ_{TSL} formula.

Table 1. Synthesis times for different grammars

Interface type	Realizable	Unrealizable	Timeout	Median (s)	Average (s)
TSL_α	446	554	0	1.72	1.76
TSL_β	911	1	71	51.50	10.09

Furthermore, this procedure is bounded in polynomial time with respect to the formula size. The first part of the equation partially reconstructs the semantic meaning of updates by ensuring that a signal is not update with multiple values at a time. This is bounded in the size of update terms, $\binom{n}{2} \in \mathcal{O}(n^2)$. The second part of the equation simply transforms predicate terms to environment inputs and update terms to system outputs, and is in done in linear time, so the entire procedure is bounded in polynomial time.

Finally, we state the decidability as a corollary.

Corollary 1 (Decidability of TSL$_\mu$ Synthesis). *The synthesis problem of TSL_μ is decidable.*

Proof. The syntheis problem of LTL is 2EXP-COMPLETE [27]. Therefore, it follows from Theorem 1 that the synthesis problem of TSL_μ is also 2EXP-COMPLETE, and decidable.

A.2 Experimental Results

In order for users to interact with an interface, it is necessary that it synthesizes in a reasonable amount of time. Therefore, we decided to measure synthesis times of our TSL fragments by randomly generating 1,000 specifications using The SynthSynthesizer's random specification generator. The runtimes of random specifications is particularly relevant to our tool, as the interfaces for TSL_α and TSL_β included a "generate random specification" button, allowing users to explore the specification design space without needing to have a goal in mind. The random specification generator chooses an option randomly from each dropdown menu in the UI, effectively doing a random search through the combinatorial space of all possible specifications in TSL_α and TSL_β. We did not run a experimental result on the TSL_μ syntax as we did not include random generation of specifications for TSL_μ.

Synthesis was executed on a quad-core Intel Xeon processor (2.30 Ghz, 16 Gb RAM) running Ubuntu 64bit LTS 18.04. Timeout was defined as any synthesis request that took over 10 s. Average and median time exclude these timed out synthesis requests. The results are shown in Table 1.

Overall, we found that TSL_α specifications synthesized much faster than TSL_β specifications, without any timeouts. This was an expected result, given the relative simplicity of TSL_α's grammar compared to that of TSL_β. However, we were surprised to find that only one TSL_β specification was unrealizable. After a careful investigation, we discovered that the additional complexity in the grammar more tightly constrained each specification. Since each specification made weaker requirements, the grammar had less probability to create mutually exclusive specifications.

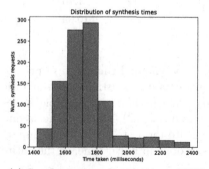

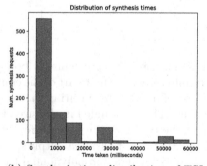

(a) Synthesis time distribution of TSL_α (b) Synthesis time distribution of TSL_β

Fig. 5. Synthesis times of 1000 random specifications

We visualize the distribution of the synthesis times in Fig. 5. TSL_α synthesis times follow a quasi-Gaussian distribution, but even the longest-taking query completes in under 2.4 s. On the other hand, the distribution of TSL_β specifications skew right; the number of specifications decreases with increasing synthesis time. The majority of specifications synthesize quickly, with 68.5% specifications taking less than 10 s to synthesize. From our experimental results, we see a clear tradeoff between expressivity and synthesis times. TSL_α has a limited grammar, but on average synthesis takes less than two seconds to complete. On the other hand, TSL_β uses a larger fragment of TSL and provides more expressivity to the user, but at the cost of timeout; 7.1% of specifications timed out, and on average took almost 10 times as longer to synthesize than TSL_α.

A.3   User Study Questions

In this section, we present the full set of questions for the comprehensive user study in Tables 2, 3, and 4. Note that Q5 is repeated in the table because the question is phrased slightly different for TSL_μ. The question is meant to ask about the intuitiveness of the structure of the specification interface. For TSL_α and TSL_β, the specification interface is structured around dropdown menus. For TSL_μ, the specification interface is structured around a text box.

A.4   User Study Results Visualizations

In this section, we present visualizations of the user study results. Figure 6a shows the user responses for each question for each separate interface. Figures 6b and 6c demonstrate the tradeoff between flexibility and ease-of-use of TSL_α, TSL_β, and TSL_μ.

Table 2. Please rate the TSL-[x] interface for creating and synthesizing specifications from 1 to 7 (7 is highest) on the following

Question number	Question
Q1	Intuitiveness
Q2	Understandability
Q3	Ease of use
Q4	Flexibility and expressivity

Table 3. On a scale from 1 to 7, how much do you agree with the following statements about TSL_[x]

Question number	Question
Q5(α, β)	The dropdown menus in TSL_[x] are an intuitive interface for specifying control flow
Q5(μ)	The text box in TSL_μ is an intuitive interface for specifying control flow
Q6	TSL_[x] can help me create music that I previously wanted to create
Q7	TSL_[x] can give me new ideas for music that I hadn't thought of
Q8	I can teach others how to use TSL_[x]
Q9	I would use TSL_[x] again to make music
Q10	I understand what specifications in TSL_[x] mean
Q11	After clicking "Synthesize!", the program did what I expected it to
QD.α	I understood sequential structure of the dropdown menus
QD.β	I understood the natural language descriptions between the dropdown menus
QS.μ	I understood the syntax of TSL_[x]

Table 4. Paragraph responses

Question number	Question
QG.1	What are your general thoughts on TSL_[x]?
QG.2	Which of the three specification interfaces was your favorite? Why?
QG.3	Would you like to share anything else?

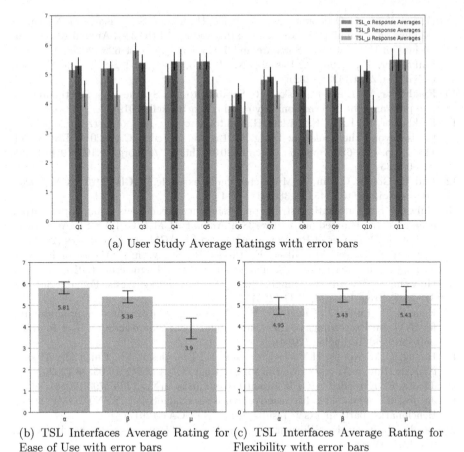

(a) User Study Average Ratings with error bars

(b) TSL Interfaces Average Rating for (c) TSL Interfaces Average Rating for Ease of Use with error bars   Flexibility with error bars

Fig. 6. User study average ratings

References

1. Baumeister, T., Finkbeiner, B., Torfah, H.: Explainable reactive synthesis. In: Automated Technology for Verification and Analysis (2020)
2. Behrmann, G., et al.: Uppaal 4.0 (2006)
3. Bloem, R., Jobstmann, B., Piterman, N., Pnueli, A., Saar, Y.: Synthesis of reactive (1) designs. J. Comput. Syst. Sci. **78**, 911–938 (2012)
4. Church, A.: Application of recursive arithmetic to the problem of circuit synthesis. J. Symbol. Logic **28**, 289–290 (1963)
5. Coblenz, M., et al.: User-centered programming language design: a course-based case study (2020)
6. Cope, D.: An expert system for computer-assisted composition. Comput. Music J. **11**(4), 30–46 (1987)
7. Crichton, W.: Human-centric program synthesis. CoRR abs/1909.12281 (2019)

8. Ferdowsifard, K., Ordookhanians, A., Peleg, H., Lerner, S., Polikarpova, N.: Small-step live programming by example. In: Proceedings of the 33rd Annual ACM Symposium on User Interface Software and Technology, pp. 614–626 (2020)
9. Finkbeiner, B., Heim, P., Passing, N.: Temporal stream logic modulo theories. CoRR abs/2104.14988 (2021)
10. Finkbeiner, B., Klein, F., Piskac, R., Santolucito, M.: Synthesizing functional reactive programs. In: International Symposium on Haskell (2019)
11. Finkbeiner, B., Klein, F., Piskac, R., Santolucito, M.: Temporal stream logic: synthesis beyond the bools. In: Dillig, I., Tasiran, S. (eds.) CAV 2019. LNCS, vol. 11561, pp. 609–629. Springer, Cham (2019). https://doi.org/10.1007/978-3-030-25540-4_35
12. Frid, E., Gomes, C., Jin, Z.: Music creation by example. In: CHI 2020. ACM (2020). https://doi.org/10.1145/3313831.3376514
13. Gulwani, S.: Automating string processing in spreadsheets using input-output examples. In: Proceedings of the 38th Annual ACM SIGPLAN-SIGACT Symposium on Principles of Programming languages. ACM Sigplan Notices (2011)
14. Gulwani, S., Mayer, M., Niksic, F., Piskac, R.: Strisynth: synthesis for live programming. In: International Conference on Software Engineering (2015)
15. Gulwani, S., Polozov, O., Singh, R., et al.: Program synthesis. Foundations and Trends®.Prog. Lang. **4**, 1–119 (2017)
16. Hempel, B., Lubin, J., Chugh, R.: Sketch-n-sketch: Output-directed programming for SVG. In: Proceedings of the 32nd Annual ACM Symposium on User Interface Software and Technolog (2019)
17. Huang, C.A., Koops, H.V., Newton-Rex, E., Dinculescu, M., Cai, C.J.: AI song contest: Human-AI co-creation in songwriting. CoRR abs/2010.05388 (2020)
18. Jacobs, S.: Extended AIGER format for synthesis. arXiv:1405.5793 (2014)
19. Jacobs, S., et al.: The 4th reactive synthesis competition (SYNTCOMP 2017): Benchmarks, participants & results. In: SYNT@CAV (2017)
20. Jacobs, S., Klein, F., Schirmer, S.: A high-level ITI synthesis format: Tlsf v1. 1. Synthesis Workshop at CAV (2016)
21. Kandel, S., Paepcke, A., Hellerstein, J., Heer, J.: Wrangler: Interactive visual specification of data transformation scripts. In: CHI (2011)
22. Lerner, S.: Projection boxes: On-the-fly reconfigurable visualization for live programming. In: CHI (2020)
23. Lubin, J., Collins, N., Omar, C., Chugh, R.: Program sketching with live bidirectional evaluation. In: ICFP (2020)
24. Maderbacher, B., Bloem, R.: Reactive synthesis modulo theories using abstraction refinement. arXiv preprint arXiv:2108.00090 (2021)
25. Mayer, M., Kuncak, V.: Game programming by demonstration. In: Proceedings of the 2013 ACM International Symposium on New Ideas, New Paradigms, and Reflections on Programming & Software (2013)
26. Meyer, P.J., Sickert, S., Luttenberger, M.: Strix: explicit reactive synthesis strikes back! In: Chockler, H., Weissenbacher, G. (eds.) CAV 2018. LNCS, vol. 10981, pp. 578–586. Springer, Cham (2018). https://doi.org/10.1007/978-3-319-96145-3_31
27. Pnueli, A., Rosner, R.: On the synthesis of an asynchronous reactive module. In: International Colloquium on Automata, Languages, and Programming (1989)
28. Rogers, C.: Web audio API specification. World Wide Web Consortium (2021)
29. Ryzhyk, L., Walker, A.: Developing a practical reactive synthesis tool: experience and lessons learned. In: Workshop on Synthesis at CAV (2016)
30. Ryzhyk, L., et al.: User-guided device driver synthesis. In: OSDI (2014)

31. Santolucito, M.: Human-in-the-loop program synthesis for live coding. In: Proceedings of the 9th ACM SIGPLAN International Workshop on Functional Art, Music, Modelling, and Design (2021)
32. Santolucito, M., Goldman, D., Weseley, A., Piskac, R.: Programming by example: Efficient, but not "helpful". In: PLATEAU@SPLASH (2018)
33. Schewe, S., Finkbeiner, B.: Bounded synthesis. In: International Symposium on Automated Technology for Verification and Analysis (2007)
34. Wang, C., Feng, Y., Bodik, R., Cheung, A., Dillig, I.: Visualization by example. In: Proceedings of the ACM on Programming Languages (POPL) (2019)
35. Wang, C., Feng, Y., Bodik, R., Dillig, I., Cheung, A., Ko, A.J.: Falx: synthesis-powered visualization authoring. In: CHI Conference on Human Factors in Computing Systems (2021)
36. Wilson, C., Kalliokoski, J.: Web midi API W3C, Working Draft (2021)

Server-Side Computation of Package Dependencies in Package-Management Systems

Nobuhiro Kasai$^{(\boxtimes)}$ ⓘ and Isao Sasano ⓘ

Shibaura Institute of Technology, Tokyo, Japan
ma20024@shibaura-it.ac.jp, sasano@sic.shibaura-it.ac.jp

Abstract. Package managers are often used in recent software development to obtain directly-dependent packages recursively. Typically, package managers make requests to the package registry more than once when computing indirect dependencies. Moreover, much amount of computations are duplicated by clients of package managers. This duplication can be avoided by computing indirect dependencies in advance on the server-side of package-management systems. Therefore, we propose two algorithms functioning in parallel on the server-side: one to compute the indirect dependencies when copying all packages in existing package managers to the server and one to add packages to the server. Based on these parallelized algorithms, we implement a server `fpms-server` and a client `fpms` for npm packages. By our experiments, our client obtains dependencies of some package more than two times faster than clients in existing npm and yarn systems.

Keywords: Package manager · Parallelization · Server-side computation

1 Introduction

Package-management systems (or package managers) are often used in recent software development. For example, npm is used for Node.js, cargo is used for Rust, and RubyGems is used for Ruby. Package-management systems consist of clients and servers. A server (or package registry) has a set of packages and information on each package that includes a set of directly-dependent packages. Servers usually just send back packages and their information when receiving requests from clients.

When getting packages from a package registry, package manager clients resolve package dependencies recursively by accessing the registry one or more times. The deeper the package dependencies are, the more package registry accesses are needed. Also, more than one client may perform the same computation regarding package dependencies. We should not ignore the time for computing dependencies, since computing indirect dependencies takes as around one-fourth or half time as downloading packages, as shown in Table 1.

ⓒ Springer Nature Switzerland AG 2021
H. Oh (Ed.): APLAS 2021, LNCS 13008, pp. 62–79, 2021.
https://doi.org/10.1007/978-3-030-89051-3_5

Table 1. Time for computing and downloading package indirect dependencies in npm

Package name	Computing indirect dependencies [s]	Download [s]
react	1.6	3.4
gatsby	11.0	39.0

When computing package dependencies, we have to consider circularity of package dependencies, which frequently appears in programming language package-management systems such as npm. Figure 1 shows an example of circularity in dependencies on npm package d, where package versions are written after @. There is a circularity among packages {es5 − ext, ex6 − iterator} and another circularity among packages {d, es5 − ext, es6 − symbol}.

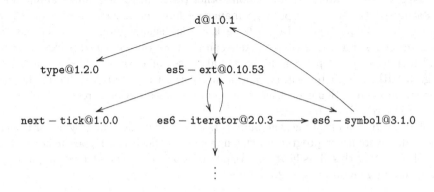

Fig. 1. An example of circularity in dependencies on npm

In this paper, we propose algorithms for computing package dependencies on the server-side that can cope with circularities, which will allow computation sharing among clients and reduce the number of accesses to the package registry by clients. Many package-management systems enable packages to specify a version range for each directly-dependent package. Our proposed algorithms support the description of version ranges. There are also various package-management systems with functionalities beyond describing version ranges. We describe the functionalities our approach supports in Sect. 2.

For simplicity, we focus on package managers for programming languages, many of which do not permit publishers to specify any conditions between packages being installed and installed packages. This allows package dependencies to be computed on the server-side.

We implement a prototype system based on the algorithms and find that a considerable amount of time is required to compute package dependencies for all packages in npm. For improved efficiency, we parallelize the algorithms.

Based on the parallelized algorithms, we implement a client and server called fpms and fpms-server, respectively, for npm packages. The server sends back package dependencies in one transaction for a request from clients. Using fpms-server, Internet transactions are reduced by our experiments.

The rest of the paper is organized as follows. Section 2 describes package managers and the functionalities supported by our approach. Section 3 shows our sequential algorithms, and Sect. 4 shows the parallelized algorithms. Section 5 describes system implementation based on the parallelized algorithms. Section 6 shows the experimental results for all npm packages using the system. Section 7 discusses the applicability of our approach to other package managers and our implementation from various viewpoints, and Sect. 8 concludes the paper.

2   Package Managers

Package managers are tools for (among other tasks) installing, uninstalling, and updating packages. Many package managers have package registries on their servers to hold package data, with package publishers publishing packages to their registries. Package manager users can then obtain published packages from said registries. Many package managers also use some form of files as packages (e.g., a URL of a git repository) and a directory or a compressed file in the file system on clients. Some package managers use an additional registry to allow users to store private packages.

The various kinds of package managers can be classified roughly as for either operating systems or programming languages [8]. Section 2.1 goes into greater detail regarding this classification. We describe package dependencies in package managers in general in Sect. 2.2.

2.1   Package Managers for Programming Languages and Operating Systems

Package managers for operating systems include apt (used in Ubuntu), nix (used in Nix OS), and Pacman (used in Arch Linux). These operating system package managers manage packages globally from a location, enabling users to manage software in their OS more easily than doing it by themselves.

Package managers for programming languages include npm (used for Node.js), cargo (used for Rust), and RubyGems (used for Ruby). In many cases, programming language package managers are used to develop programs for individual projects. Programming language package managers also support global locations for installing software developed in the programming language.

2.2   Package Dependencies

When developing a new package p, developers specify a set S of packages that are used directly by p. S may be empty. We say that p depends directly on another package p' when $p' \in S$. We consider the transitive closure of the direct-dependency relation to be an "indirect dependency." When the client of the package manager installs p, the client also installs all the packages on which p

depends indirectly. We write $D(p)$ for the set of all packages on which p depends indirectly, solving for dependencies of p when computing $D(p)$.

Package managers associate packages with names and occasionally versions. We write p_v for the package whose name is p and whose version is v. Many package managers allow developers to specify direct dependency for a developing package, requiring either a fixed version or a range of version conditions for each package in the set by writing a set of pairs (package names and version conditions). For example, in npm, when the version condition for p is ^1.0.0, a version of p that satisfies the condition is more than or equal to 1.0.0 and less than 2.0.0.

Package developers can use URLs (for git repositories, zip archives of a package, etc.) instead of packages for S, depending on the package manager in use. Some packages managers also allow developers to specify conflict packages (when p does not exist locally and a locally existing p' conflicts with p, preventing installation), optional dependencies (allowing package managers to attempt specified package installations that do not cause errors if the installation fails), and peer dependencies (where the package manager notifies users of the dependencies and does not install package specified by the dependencies).

When solving for dependencies of p, there may be packages q_x and q_y with the same name q and different versions x and y in $D(p)$, but dealing with such instances depends on the package manager in question.

Packages in npm average 7.34 dependencies with a standard deviation of 22.52 [4], probably because npm package developers often use *trivial packages* [1], with a high standard deviation. In npm, there are about 1.5 million package names and about 15 million packages.

Npm clients do not save the package data locally, so they may generally access the package registry more than once when solving package dependencies. In contrast, some package managers, such as apt, get and save all package data locally before solving package dependencies.

Many programming language package managers generate a file possessing dependencies among the packages (e.g., npm generates `package-lock.json` and cargo generates `Cargo.lock`), for installing packages with keeping versions of installed packages unchanged, for example. When such files exist, the package manager gets packages written in the file without solving package dependencies.

3   Algorithms

The algorithms we present in this section use a direct graph, which we call a *package-dependency graph*. Each node in this graph is a package that has edges to directly-dependent packages. As for indirect dependencies, one of the algorithms maintains a mapping that maps each package to a set of packages indirectly dependent on the package.

This section details two cases for computing indirect dependencies on the server-side and an algorithm corresponding to each case. One is for computing indirect dependencies for many packages at once, which is used for adding all packages existing in some other package-management system to the server. The other is for updating indirect dependencies, which is used when a developer adds new packages to the server.

For the first case, we compute the set of indirectly-dependent packages for each package in two phases: initializing the package-dependency graph (shown in Sect. 3.1) and computing the set of indirectly-dependent packages for each package using the package-dependency graph (show in Sect. 3.2).

For the second case, we give an algorithm for adding packages to the registry (shown in Sect. 3.3).

As packages may have circular dependencies, we employ an idea used in iterative algorithms for data-flow analysis for imperative languages with looping constructs [2] for computing indirectly-dependent packages. We leave a comparison between our algorithms and iterative algorithms in the data-flow analysis as a future study.

3.1 Initializing Package-Dependency Graph

We initialize a package-dependency graph before computing a set of indirectly-dependent packages for every package (see in Algorithm 1).

Algorithm 1. An algorithm for initializing a package-dependency graph

---

function DEPS($pack, package\_map$)
   $result \leftarrow \emptyset$
   for $(name, condition) \in pack.depspec$ **do**
      $targets \leftarrow package\_map[name]$
      $filtered \leftarrow ()$
      for $target \in targets$ **do**
         if $t.version$ satisfies $condition$ **then**
            $filtered \leftarrow filtered \cup t$
      $result \leftarrow result \cup \{\text{LATEST}(filtered)\}$
   return $result$
function INITIALIZE_GRAPH($package\_map$)
   for $packs\_set \in package\_map$ **do**
      for $pack \in packs\_set$ **do**
         $dset \leftarrow \text{DEPS}(pack, package\_map)$
         SAVE_DSET($pack, dset$)

As preparation for initializing the graph by function INITIALIZE_GRAPH, we get all package data from the registry of the package-management system and save the data persistently somewhere, such as a database, by using the function SAVE_PACK, which is also used in Algorithm 3.

Each package p has a property $p.depspec$, a set of pairs of names and conditions on version ranges, as its specification of direct dependencies. The obtained package data is then stored as an associative array $package\_map$, with each entry possessing a package name n as its key and a set of packages having n as the value, before *package_map* is passed to the INITIALIZE_GRAPH function as its argument in Algorithm 1.

For each value of *packs_set* in *package_map*, we compute a set of directly-dependent packages for each package *pack* in *packs_set* by using the function DEPS.

DEPS takes as its arguments a package p and an associative array a, computing a set of directly-dependent packages for each package. Here, we let $P(n, c)$ be the set of all packages of name n satisfying the version condition c. Following the specification of npm, we have to determine the latest package in $P(n, c)$ for each pair of n and c in *p.depspec*, which is the specification of dependency in p. DEPS does this by using the function LATEST, which takes as its argument a set of packages and returns the package that is the latest in the set.

The result of DEPS is assigned to *deps* and is also saved persistently somewhere, such as a database, by the function SAVE_DSET.

When initializing the server, we call the INITIALIZE_GRAPH function and then call the COMPUTE_INDEP function in Algorithm 2.

3.2   Computing the Set of Indirectly-Dependent Packages for Every Package

Algorithm 2 computes the set of indirectly-dependent packages for every package.

In the function COMPUTE_INDEP, the variable *all_packs* is the set of all packages, obtained by the function GET_ALL_PACKS, which obtains package data saved by the function SAVE_PACK (see in Sect. 3.1).

The variable *all_deps* is initialized as an empty associative array that has packages as keys and sets of packages as values, which is used for updating the indirect dependencies in each iteration.

Before entering the while loop in the function COMPUTE_INDEP, we assign false to *complete*, which is used as the condition for the while loop, and assign an empty set to upd_{pre}, which holds the indirect dependencies computed in the previous iteration, except for the first iteration. We then call UPDATE_DEPS(*all_packs*, *all_deps*, upd_{pre}) to update the indirect dependencies. The return value of UPDATE_DEPS is a set of packages assigned to *upd* and is used as a flag to indicate whether the indirectly-dependent packages of each package are updated. When a package p is an element in *upd*, it means that *all_deps*[p] was updated.

In the loop of UPDATE_DEPS, *iset* is initially set as *all_deps*[p], which is the set of packages on which the package p indirectly depends that were obtained in the previous iteration. In the first iteration, *all_deps*[p] is an empty set for every p. The variable *iset* is then augmented by the set *dset* of packages that p directly depends on, which is obtained by GET_DSET(p) at its first iteration, represented by $upd_{pre} = \emptyset$. Note that GET_DSET(p) returns a set of packages that was saved by SAVE_DSET, which is called in Algorithms 1 and 3. From the second iteration, *iset* is augmented by *all_deps*[d], which is the set of packages that the package d indirectly depends on, as computed in the previous iteration. This augmentation

Algorithm 2. An algorithm for computing the set of indirectly-dependent packages for every package

---

function UPDATE_DEPS($packs, all\_deps, upd_{pre}$)
    $upd \leftarrow \emptyset$
    for $p \in packs$ **do**
        $iset \leftarrow all\_d[p]$
        $size \leftarrow iset.size$
        $dset \leftarrow$ GET_DSET(p)
        if $upd_{pre} = \emptyset$ **then**
            $iset \leftarrow iset \cup dset$
        else
            for $d \in dset$ **do**
                if $d \in upd_{pre}$ **then**
                    $iset \leftarrow iset \cup all\_deps[d]$
        if $iset.size > size$ **then**
            $all\_deps[p] \leftarrow iset$
            $upd \leftarrow upd \cup \{p\}$
    return upd
function COMPUTE_INDEP()
    $all\_packs \leftarrow$ GET_ALL_PACKS()
    $all\_deps \leftarrow emptyMap()$
    for $p \in all\_packs$ **do**
        $all\_deps[p] \leftarrow \emptyset$
    $upd_{pre} \leftarrow \emptyset$
    $complete \leftarrow false$
    while !$complete$ **do**
        $complete \leftarrow true$
        $upd \leftarrow$ UPDATE_DEPS($all\_packs, all\_deps, upd_{pre}$)
        if $upd! = \emptyset$ **then**
            $complete \leftarrow false$
            $upd_{pre} \leftarrow upd$
    SAVE_ALL_DEPS(all_deps)

---

is done only when $all\_deps[d]$ has been updated in the previous iteration, which is represented by the condition $d \in upd_{pre}$. Thanks to this optimization, our experiments have found Algorithm 2 is at least twice as fast as it was prior to optimization.

In Algorithm 2, $all\_deps[p]$ monotonically increases with respect to the ordering of the set inclusion. In addition, the value of $iset$ increases for each iteration; therefore, we only need to check if the size of $iset$ is larger than the size of the initial value of $iset$ in the current iteration, when determining whether all_deps and the flags upd should be updated. We omit the formal argument about properties of Algorithm 2.

3.3   Adding Packages to the Server

Algorithm 3 indicates how packages are added to the server, which has packages
with indirect dependencies already computed.

Algorithm 3. An algorithm for adding packages to the server

---

function ADD_PACKAGES(*packs*)
    for *pack* ∈ *packs* **do**
        SAVE_PACK(*pack*)
        dset ← ∅
        for (*name*, *condition*) ∈ *pack.depspec* **do**
            filtered ← ∅
            for *p* ∈ GET_PACKAGES(*name*) **do**
                if *p.version* satisfies *condition* **then**
                    filtered ← *filtered* ∪ {*p*}
            dset ← *dset* ∪ {LATEST(*filtered*)}
        SAVE_DSET(*pack*, *dset*)
        for *p* ∈ PACKS_DEPENDS_ON(*pack.name*) **do**
            for (*name*, *cond*) ∈ *p.depspec* **do**
                if *name* = *pack.name* **then**
                    condition ← *cond*
                    break
            if *pack.version* satisfies *condition* **then**
                p_dset ← GET_DSET(*p*)
                for *d* ∈ *p_dset* **do**
                    if *d.name* = *pack.name* **then**
                        pack_old ← *d*
                        break
                if *pack.version* > *pack_old.version* **then**
                    p_dset ← (*p_dset* \ {*pack_old*}) ∪ {*pack*}
                    SAVE_DSET(*p*, *p_dset*)
    COMPUTE_INDEP()

The function ADD_PACKAGES takes a set of packages *packs* as its argument,
which are added to the server. For each *pack* in *packs*, *pack* is initially saved by
SAVE_PACK as in the preparation for calling INITIALIZE_GRAPH in Sect. 3.1.

In the first **for** loop of the outermost **for** loop, we compute the set of directly-
dependent packages *dset* of *pack* similarly to the DEPS function in Algorithm 1.
The GET_PACKAGES function takes a name *name* and returns the set of packages with that *name* before saving it in the function SAVE_PACK. The result of
collecting directly-dependent packages is saved by the function SAVE_DSET.

To compute the set of indirectly-dependent packages for all packages including *pack*, we reuse COMPUTE_INDEP in Algorithm 2.

In the second **for** loop of the outermost **for** loop, we check whether an
update is required for directly-dependent packages of packages that depend

on a package with the name *pack.name*. Those packages are obtained by the PACK_DEPENDS_ON function. The detailed explanation of the second **for** loop is left for readers.

Finally, we compute the set of indirectly-dependent packages using the COMPUTE_INDEP function in Algorithm 2.

4   Parallelization

We implemented a prototype system based on the algorithms in the previous sections, finding that initialization took around 30 min for about 15 million packages in npm.

To improve efficiency, we have parallelized Algorithms 1, 2, and 3, illustrating how to parallelize these algorithms in this section. After parallelization, initialization completed in around 15 min.

4.1   Initializing Package-Dependency Graph

In the DEPS function of Algorithm 1, the newest directly-dependent packages of each package are computed independently. Therefore, we divide PACKAGE_MAP into several groups and run the INITIALIZE_GRAPH function for each group in parallel.

Algorithm 4 shows a parallel algorithm for initializing a package-dependency graph.

Algorithm 4. A parallel algorithm for initializing a package-dependency graph

function INITIALIZE_GRAPH_IN_PARALLEL(*package_map*)
    thread_num ← GET_THREAD_NUM()
    pack_groups ← GROUP(*package_map*, *thread_num*)
    threads ← ∅
    for *map* ← *pack_groups* **do**
        thread ← MAKE_THREAD(λ().(
            INITIALIZE_GRAPH(*map*)
        ))
        thread.run()
        threads ← *threads* ∪ {*thread*}
    WAITALL(*threads*)

We begin by dividing the mapping *package_map* by the number of threads. The GET_THREAD_NUM function then returns the number of threads, and the GROUP function takes *package_map* and a number *thread_num*, which is the number of threads, and divides *package_map* by *thread_num*.

For each map, we create threads that each call the INITIALIZE_GRAPH function in Algorithm 1. We let *threads* be all the threads created and wait for all threads to finish using the WAITALL function.

4.2 Computing the Set of Indirectly-Dependent Packages for Every Package in Parallel

Algorithm 5 shows a parallel algorithm for computing the set of indirectly-dependent packages for every package.

Algorithm 5. A parallel algorithm for computing the set of indirectly-dependent packages for every package

---

function COMPUTE_INDEP_IN_PARALLEL()
    $all\_packs \leftarrow$ GET_ALL_PACKS()
    $all\_deps \leftarrow emptyMap()$
    for $p \in all\_packs$ **do**
        $all\_deps[p] \leftarrow \emptyset$
    $thread\_num \leftarrow$ GET_THREAD_NUM()
    $pack\_groups \leftarrow$ GROUP($all\_packs, thread\_num$)
    $upd_{pre} \leftarrow \emptyset$
    $complete \leftarrow false$
    while $!complete$ **do**
        $updarr \leftarrow \emptyset$
        $threads \leftarrow \emptyset$
        for $(packs, i) \in$ ENUMERATE($pack\_groups$) **do**
            $thread \leftarrow$ MAKE_THREAD($\lambda().($
                $updarr[i]$
                    $\leftarrow$ UPDATE_DEPS($packs, all\_deps, upd_{pre}$)
)
            $thread.run()$
            $threads \leftarrow threads \cup \{thread\}$
        WAITALL($threads$)
        $upd_{pre} \leftarrow$ UNIONALL($updarr$)
        if $upd_{pre} = \emptyset$ **then**
            $complete \leftarrow true$
    SAVE_ALL_DEPS(all_deps)

In the COMPUTE_INDEP_IN_PARALLEL function, we start by dividing the packages into groups PACK_GROUPS by the number of threads.

For each group in PACK_GROUPS, we create a thread that calls the UPDATE_DEPS function in Algorithm 2. The ENUMERATE function enumerates groups in $pack\_groups$ with their indices.

To collect packages whose indirect dependencies are updated, we use an array $updarr$ of length $thread\_num$, each element of which holds the set of updated packages computed by the function UPDATE_DEPS. After waiting for all threads computing each indirect dependencies, we assign the union of all sets in $updarr$ to upd_{pre}, which was computed by the UNIONALL function.

In each iteration of the while loop, the indirect dependencies held in all_deps depend on the order of the computation done in the threads. However, the final result of the indirect-dependencies held in *all_deps* was the same as the one computed in Algorithm 2. We omit the formal argument about this fact.

4.3   Adding Packages to the Server

To parallelize Algorithm 3, we call the COMPUTE_INDEP_IN_PARALLEL function in Algorithm 5 instead of the COMPUTE_INDEP function.

Algorithm 3 updates the package-dependency graph before calling COMPUTE_INDEP. The package-dependency graph can be updated just by adding directly-dependent packages of each new package, which does not take much time. Therefore, we do not parallelize Algorithm 3 except when replacing COMPUTE_INDEP with the COMPUTE_INDEP_IN_PARALLEL function.

5   Implementation

We implemented a server **fpms-server** (fast package manager server) in Scala, making the source code public at https://github.com/sh4869/fpms-server. We also made the server public temporarily at http://202.18.65.18/.

The **fpms-server** provides a web API that we named **indep**. The **indep** API takes package name *name* and optionally a version condition *condition*, which we write as **indep**(*name*, *condition*). The syntax and semantics of *condition* are the same as those used in npm. The server then returns the set of indirectly-dependent packages of the latest package whose name is *name* and whose version satisfies *condition*. When a *condition* is not given, the server returns the set of indirectly-dependent packages of the latest package of name *name*.

If we wanted to obtain the indirectly-dependent packages of the package **react** whose version is **17.0.2**, then we would just need to access http://202. 18.65.18/calculated/react?range=17.0.2.

When the server **fpms-server** receives a request, the request path (given as the argument of GET method) is matched against the pattern: GET/calculated/*name*(?range=*condition*)?. As a result, the package name given in the request is assigned to the pattern variable *name*, allowing the version condition to be assigned to the pattern variable *condition*. Our implementation supports version conditions following the grammar given in https://github.com/npm/node-semver#range-grammar. For example, when the GET method is

GET /calculated/react?range=17.0.2,

name becomes **react**, *condition* becomes **17.0.2**, and the response is obtained in JSON format. The response is shown Fig. 2 using the Firefox browser.

We used two databases in the server (PostgreSQL and Redis) to save package data as well as the direct and indirect dependencies, respectively, for all packages.

We saved package data as the **package** table on PostgreSQL, showing its definition in Table 2. We used a JSON type [9] for the column **deps**. PostgreSQL provided the **json_extract_path** function [10] that received a column name and

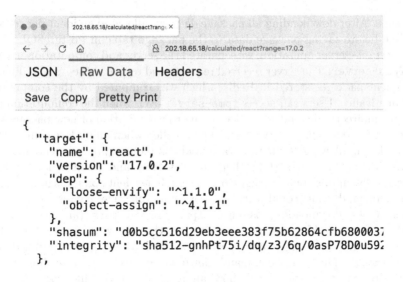

```
{
  "target": {
    "name": "react",
    "version": "17.0.2",
    "dep": {
      "loose-envify": "^1.1.0",
      "object-assign": "^4.1.1"
    },
    "shasum": "d0b5cc516d29eb3eee383f75b62864cfb6800037
    "integrity": "sha512-gnhPt75i/dq/z3/6q/0asP78D0u59z
  },
```

Fig. 2. Part of the result of calling indep(react, 17.0.2)

Table 2. The definition of the package table

Column name	Column type	Description
id	Integer	Identifier of package
name	String	Package name
version	String	Package version
deps	JSON	Specification of dependencies

key name as its arguments to return the value mapped from the key in the column as JSON data, and that is used in function PACK_DEPENDS_ON in Algorithm 3.

The direct-dependencies and the set of indirectly-dependent packages for every package were saved into Redis.

We implemented functions SAVE_DSET, GET_DSET, and SAVE_ALL_DEPS in Algorithms 1, 2, and 3, to save data to and get data from Redis. We also implemented the SAVE_PACK and GET_ALL_PACKS functions in Algorithm 2 and 3, so that they would save data and get data from PostgreSQL.

In implementing Algorithm 2, we represented a package using an identifier to reduce memory usage.

When sending back the set of indirectly-dependent packages for an API call indep($name, condition$), the server obtained packages of $name$ from PostgreSQL, found the identifier of the latest version of $P(name, condition)$, got the identifiers of indirectly-dependent packages, and then obtained the package data from PostgreSQL using the identifiers. Direct and indirect dependencies for every package were saved into Redis as the set of identifiers.

To use our system with npm packages, it was necessary to download all package data from the npm package registry prior to starting the server for the first time. After downloading all package data, we allocated an identifier to every package before saving package data to the `package` table in PostgreSQL.

For stable server operation, we separated the server and computation parts on the `fpms-server`. The server received requests and returned the set of indirectly-dependent packages stored in Redis, which was computed by the computation part in advance. Users can access `fpms-server` even when the computation part updates indirectly-dependent packages due to the addition of new packages. As presented in Algorithm 5, SAVE_ALL_DEPS is called when an update computation is completed, allowing Redis to always hold complete indirect dependencies.

We implemented a system client named `fpms` and published to npm at https://www.npmjs.com/package/fpms-client. The client `fpms` was implemented as a command that could take one or more package names as its arguments. When downloading packages, `fpms` invoked `yarn` (an alternative of npm). Before invoking `yarn`, `fpms` created the file `yarn.lock` [12], where the dependency of some packages was described by using data fetched from `fpms-server`. The `yarn` command downloaded packages according to the description in `yarn.lock`. We show an example of the file `yarn.lock` for the package `log4js` at https://raw.githubusercontent.com/sh4869/fpms-server/master/docs/yarn_lock_example.txt. We also made the source code of the client `fpms` public at https://github.com/sh4869/fpms.

6   Experiments

To show the effectiveness of our approach, we measured the response and execution times in our system's server, then compared them with those in `yarn`. We experimented in a machine with an AMD Ryzen 9 3950X CPU with a 16-Core Processor, 32 threads at 3.5 GHz, 128 GB of memory, and an Ubuntu 20.04 64-bit OS. The experiments used all 32 available threads.

6.1   Comparison Between `fpms` and `yarn`

We measured the time to execute each client command for downloading packages with solving dependencies and the number of requests to the server while solving dependencies via `fpms` and `yarn`. The results of this experimentation are available in Tables 3 and 4. When solving dependencies for a package p, the `yarn` client accesses the server at most as many times as the number of indirectly-dependent packages of the package p. By contrast, the `fpms` client always accesses the server just once for solving dependencies for a package, since dependency was computed on the server in advance.

In this experiment, each client installed eight packages to the corresponding server. Following the default behavior of npm, each client obtained the latest version for each package name and requested each package three times. The clients accessed the servers through the Internet in the same environment. The average times are shown in Table 3.

The fpms client ran faster than the yarn client when installing packages except for underscore and react. When installing the gatsby package (which contained multiple indirectly-dependent packages), fpms ran much faster than yarn. When installing the react, underscore, tslib, and typescript packages, yarn solved dependencies using a small number of requests to the registry. The fpms client was slightly slower than yarn, since the fpms client invokes yarn command as a child process while yarn client does not create any child process. The difference is around a little less than 0.1 s, which corresponds to the time spent on invoking yarn as a child process by our experiments. We believe this is solved by implementing the function of downloading packages by ourselves, instead of using yarn.

Table 3. Comparison of times to install packages using fpms and yarn commands

Package name	fpms [s]	yarn [s]
underscore	0.73	0.65
tslib	0.39	0.33
typescript	1.00	0.98
react	0.44	0.40
log4js	0.60	1.28
express	1.00	1.50
typeorm	2.40	2.70
gulp	3.10	3.70
firebase-tools	6.40	10.00
gatsby	23.41	32.45

Table 4. Comparison of the number of server requests used by commands fpms and yarn while solving dependencies

Package name	fpms	yarn
underscore	1	1
tslib	1	1
typescript	1	1
react	1	4
log4js	1	11
express	1	52
typeorm	1	72
gulp	1	297
firebase-tools	1	633
gatsby	1	1435

6.2   Initialization

Prior to server initialization, we downloaded all packages information (about 15 million packages) from the npm package registry, which took a few hours.

The time spent initializing the server is shown in Table 5. During initialization, most of the time was spent initializing the package table in PostgreSQL. It bears mention that initialization is not necessary even if the server machine is restarted, since the package data, direct dependencies, and indirect dependencies are saved on PostgreSQL and Redis.

6.3   Adding Packages

When adding packages to the server, each package developer sent an HTTP POST request to the server. The URL for the request was http://202.18.65.18/add and the request body was in a JSON format, which was posted on https://github.com/sh4869/fpms-server#post-add.

Table 5. Server initialization times

Initializing database [s]	Creating the package-dependency graph [s]	Computing the sets of indirectly-dependent packages [s]	Saving data to Redis [s]
1020	70	300	180

Although the server accepted requests for adding packages at all times, the server could only start adding packages after previous additions were finished. The server started adding packages if any requests remained, with all remaining requests being processed together. The server also started adding packages when one minute had passed after the previous addition to allow multiple requests to be processed at once. Table 6 shows the time required to add new package versions to the server. We also show the number of packages with updated directly-dependent packages and the number of packages that each of added packages directly-depends on in Table 7. When adding a package, the number of packages with their directly-dependent packages updated by adding the package had a significant negative effect on the execution time, yet the number of packages that the added package directly depends on did not matter as much. Table 6 shows that the number of packages to be added does not have an appreciable effect on the time for adding packages, and that adding multiple packages at once was much more efficient than adding packages individually.

Table 6. Execution time for adding packages

Package to be added	Execution time [s]
gatsby	480
react	420
firebase-tools	420
debug	780
underscore	747
underscore, gatsby	750

Table 7. The number of packages with their directly-dependent packages updated when adding a package (a) and the number of packages that the added package directly depends on (b)

Package name	(a)	(b)
gatsby	41	153
react	1	2
firebase-tools	11	57
debug	172506	2
underscore	138223	0

7 Discussions

Here we discuss the applicability of our approach to other package managers with unique functionalities, examine the Nix package manager (which allows the sharing of build binaries), and discuss our implementation from various viewpoints.

7.1   Applicability to Other Package Managers

Our algorithm can be used with package managers that support version ranges in the dependency condition descriptions. For example, Ruby Gems supports only version ranges in the dependency condition descriptions, so we expect our approach can be applied to Ruby Gems. We also expect our approach can be applied to many package managers for programming languages, such as Ruby Gems and Pip, save those that support features other than the description of version ranges.

7.2   Complex Specification of Dependencies and Local Environments

Some package managers, especially OS package managers, can impose more complex conditions than ours on packages to be installed. For example, apt can specify conflict packages and can use disjunction in dependency conditions. When a package to be installed has conflict packages, package managers have to check whether the conflict packages are installed globally. Opium [11] was developed to cope with these situations using the SAT solver. Disjunctions in the description of version conditions have been argued about in terms of the semantics of concurrency in functional languages [3].

   To support the complex dependencies described above in our system, we may have to compute indirect dependencies for all possible disjunction selections in the conditions. In this case, clients will have to get a set of indirect dependencies and select one by checking the installed packages.

7.3   Multiple Package Registries

Some package-management systems allow clients to get packages from multiple package registries. In such systems, developers can specify any package on some of the registries as a directly-dependent package of the package being developed.

   In our algorithm, direct and indirect dependencies are saved in the server. As package registries are not connected to each other generally, when we extend our approach to support multiple registries, we may support communication between package registries for computing indirectly-dependent packages among multiple registries.

7.4   Nix Package Manager

The Nix package manager is mainly used with the Nix OS [5]. It allows build packages to be shared with other machines that have Nix installed as binary caches, which are mainly used for distributing binaries provided by software developers because of security reasons. By contrast, indirect dependencies are shared in our system.

7.5 Dependencies in Build Systems

Build systems, such as `make` and `bazel`, compute dependencies of build tasks.
`Bazel` [6] is a build system that shares obtained results among cloud users. In
cloud builds, build systems compute build task dependencies, then check whether
there are shared results for cloud dependencies. Our approach may be applied
to build systems with build tasks that are performed in the cloud, preventing
identical build tasks from being performed on many local machines.

Build systems are classified in the study [7] according to the way they solve
the dependencies for understanding the build system features. Similar to that
study, we may classify package managers to clarify what kind of package managers our approach can be applied to.

7.6 Security

In our system, we establish a third-party server between the client and the
package registry. The client may provide an option for checking that indirect
dependencies have not been tampered with on the server. In the option, the
client checks that each installed package is required by the user or any of the
installed packages. It is faster than computing indirectly-dependent packages
from scratch in the client. Note that direct dependencies are assumed to be
correct, since our client obtains package data, including direct dependencies,
from the npm package registry.

8   Conclusions and Future Work

We proposed computing package dependencies on the server-side of package-
management systems. Based on this idea, we proposed two parallel algorithms
for computing indirect dependencies on the server and for adding packages to
the server.

Based on our algorithms, we implemented a server `fpms-server` and a client
`fpms` for 15 million npm packages. The server provided a web API for users
to get indirectly-dependent packages of a package by sending a package name
and a version condition. It took roughly 15 min to initialize package dependencies on the server and another 12 min to update package dependencies on the
server. Such an update can be performed without interrupting the service. We
experimented installing some packages with their indirectly-dependent packages
by using two clients: `fpms` and `yarn`. Our results indicated that the `fpms` client
worked faster than `yarn` in cases where there were many indirectly-dependent
packages.

Npm supports some features that specify special dependencies, such as
optional and peer dependencies, which will be a future study.

References

1. Abdalkareem, R., Nourry, O., Wehaibi, S., Mujahid, S., Shihab, E.: Why do developers use trivial packages? An empirical case study on NPM. In: Proceedings of the 2017 11th Joint Meeting on Foundations of Software Engineering, pp. 385–395 (2017)
2. Aho, A.V., Lam, M.S., Sethi, R., Ullman, J.D.: Compilers: Principles, Techniques, and Tools, 2nd edn. Addison-Wesley Longman Publishing Co. Inc., Boston (2006)
3. Bazerman, G., Puzio, R.: The topological and logical structure of concurrency and dependency via distributive lattices (2020). https://arxiv.org/abs/2004.05688
4. Dietrich, J., Pearce, D., Stringer, J., Tahir, A., Blincoe, K.: Dependency versioning in the wild. In: 2019 IEEE/ACM 16th International Conference on Mining Software Repositories, pp. 349–359. IEEE (2019)
5. Dolstra, E., Löh, A.: NixOS: a purely functional Linux distribution. In: Proceedings of the 13th ACM SIGPLAN International Conference on Functional Programming, pp. 367–378 (2008)
6. Google: Bazel - a fast, scalable, multi-language and extensible build system - Bazel. https://bazel.build/
7. Mokhov, A., Mitchell, N., Jones, S.P.: Build systems à la carte: theory and practice. J. Funct. Program. **30**, e11 (2020)
8. Muhammad, H., Real, L.C.V., Homer, M.: Taxonomy of package management in programming languages and operating systems. In: Proceedings of the 10th Workshop on Programming Languages and Operating Systems, pp. 60–66 (2019)
9. The PostgreSQL Global Development Group: PostgreSQL: Documentation: 13: 8.14. JSON types. https://www.postgresql.org/docs/13/datatype-json.html
10. The PostgreSQL Global Development Group: PostgreSQL: Documentation: 9.3: JSON functions and operators. https://www.postgresql.org/docs/9.3/functions-json.html
11. Tucker, C., Shuffelton, D., Jhala, R., Lerner, S.: OPIUM: optimal package install/uninstall manager. In: Proceedings of the 29th International Conference on Software Engineering, pp. 178–188 (2007)
12. Yarn: yarn.lock. Yarn. https://classic.yarnpkg.com/en/docs/yarn-lock/

Compilation and Transformation

Fully Abstract and Robust Compilation
And How to Reconcile the Two, Abstractly

Carmine Abate[1], Matteo Busi[2], and Stelios Tsampas[3(✉)]

[1] MPI-SP Bochum, Bochum, Germany
carmine.abate@mpi-sp.org
[2] Università di Pisa, Pisa, Italy
matteo.busi@di.unipi.it
[3] KU Leuven, Leuven, Belgium
stelios.tsampas@cs.kuleuven.be

Abstract. The most prominent formal criterion for secure compilation is *full abstraction*, the preservation and reflection of contextual equivalence. Recent work introduced *robust compilation*, defined as the preservation of *robust satisfaction* of hyperproperties, i.e., their satisfaction against arbitrary attackers. In this paper, we initially set out to compare these two approaches to secure compilation. To that end, we provide an exact description of the hyperproperties that are robustly satisfied by programs compiled with a fully abstract compiler, and show that they can be meaningless or trivial. We then propose a novel criterion for secure compilation formulated in the framework of Mathematical Operational Semantics (MOS), guaranteeing both full abstraction and the preservation of robust satisfaction of hyperproperties in a more sensible manner.

Keywords: Secure compilation · Fully abstract compilation · Robust hyperproperty preservation · Language-based security · Mathematical Operational Semantics

Remark. To ease reading, we highlight the elements of source languages in blue, sans-serif, the target elements in red, bold and the common ones in black [33].

1 Introduction

Due to the complexity of modern computing systems, engineers make substantial use of *layered design*. Higher layers hide details of the lower ones and come with abstractions that ease reasoning about the system itself [39]. A layered design of programming languages allows to benefit from modules, interfaces or dependent types of a *source, high-level* language to write well-structured programs, and execute them efficiently in a *target, low-level* language, after *compilation*. Unfortunately, an attacker may exploit the lack of abstractions at the low-level to mount a so-called *layer-below attack* [39], which is otherwise impossible at the high-level [17,18].

H. Oh (Ed.): APLAS 2021, LNCS 13008, pp. 83–101, 2021.
https://doi.org/10.1007/978-3-030-89051-3_6

Secure compilation [35] devises both principles and proof techniques to preserve the (security-relevant) abstractions of the source and prevent layer-below attacks. Abadi [1] hinted that secure compilers must respect *equivalences*, as some security properties can be expressed in terms of indistinguishability w.r.t. arbitrary attackers, or *contextual equivalence*. Fully abstract compilers preserve and reflect (to avoid trivial translations) contextual equivalence.

Two decades of successes [1,8,9,13,14,19,34,36,43,45] made full abstraction the gold-standard for secure compilation. However, some ad-hoc examples from recent literature [4,37] showed that fully abstract compilers may still introduce bugs that were not present in source programs, e.g.,

Example 1 (See also Appendix E.5 of [4]). Consider source programs to be functions $\mathbb{B} \to \mathbb{N}$ (from booleans to natural numbers) and target ones to be functions $\mathbb{N} \to \mathbb{N}$. Define contextual equivalence to be equality of outputs on equal inputs. Next, identify $\mathbb{B}$ with $\{0,1\} \subseteq \mathbb{N}$, and compile a program P to $[\![\mathsf{P}]\!] : \mathbb{N} \to \mathbb{N}$ that coincides with $\mathsf{P} : \mathbb{B} \to \mathbb{N}$ on $\{0,1\}$ and returns a default value – denoting a bug – otherwise,

$$[\![\mathsf{P}]\!](n) = \begin{cases} \mathsf{P}(n) & \text{for } n = 0,1 \\ 42 & \text{otherwise} \end{cases}$$

$[\![\cdot]\!]$ is fully abstract, yet a source program that "never outputs 42", will no longer enjoy this property. ∎

This simple example underlines the fact that if a security property like "never output 42" is not captured by contextual equivalence, there is no guarantee it will be preserved by a fully abstract compiler. Abadi [1] tellingly wrote

> [...] we still have only a limited understanding of how to specify and prove that a translation preserves particular security properties. [...]

Abate et al. [4] proposed to specify security in terms of *hyperproperties*, sets of sets of traces of observable events [15]. In this setting, they consider a compiler *secure* only if it *robustly preserves* a class of hyperproperties, i.e., if it preserves their satisfaction against arbitrary attackers. For Example 1, "never output 42" can be specified as a *safety* hyperproperty, where function inputs and outputs are the observable events. The above compiler $[\![\cdot]\!]$ is *not* secure according to Abate et al. [4], as it does not robustly preserve the class of safety hyperproperties. More generally, each particular class of hyperproperties, e.g., the one for data integrity or the one for data confidentiality [15], determines a precise formal secure compilation criterion.

Despite the introduction of the robust criteria, full abstraction is still widely adopted [14,19,43,45], for at least two reasons. First, contextual equivalence can model security properties such as noninterference [13], isolation [14], well-bracketed control flow or local state encapsulation [43] for programs that don't expose events externally. Second, even though fully abstract compilers do not *in general* preserve data integrity or confidentiality, they often do so in practice.

Fully abstract and robust compilation both embody valuable notions of secure compilation and neither is stronger than the other nor are they orthogonal, which makes us believe their relation deserves further investigation. Our goal is to have criteria with well understood security guarantees for compiled programs, so that both users and developers of compilers may decide which criterion better fits their needs. For that, we assume an abstract trace semantics, collecting observables events and internal steps, is given for both source and target languages, and start our quest not by asking *if* a given fully abstract compiler preserves *all* hyperproperties, but *which ones do* and *which ones do not* preserve.

Contributions. First, we make explicit the guarantees given by full abstraction w.r.t. arbitrary source hyperproperties. We achieve this by showing that for every fully abstract compiler $[\![\cdot]\!]$, there exists a translation or interpretation of source hyperproperties into target ones, $\tilde{\tau}$, such that if P robustly satisfies a source hyperproperty H, $[\![P]\!]$ robustly satisfies $\tilde{\tau}(H)$ (Theorem 1). However, we observe that a fully abstract compiler may fail to preserve the robust satisfaction of some hyperproperty, as $\tilde{\tau}$ may map interesting hyperproperties to trivial ones (Example 2). We then provide a sufficient and necessary condition to preserve the robust satisfaction of hyperproperties (Corollary 1), but argue that it is unfeasible to be proven true for an arbitrary fully abstract compiler. To overcome the above issues, we introduce a novel criterion, that we formulate in the abstract framework of Mathematical Operational Semantics (MOS). We show that our novel criterion implies full abstraction and the preservation of robust satisfaction of arbitrary hyperproperties (Sect. 5). We illustrate effectiveness and realizability of our criterion in Example 3.

2 Fully Abstract and Robust Compilation

Let us briefly recall the intuition of fully abstract and robust compilation, and provide their rigorous definitions. We refer the interested reader to [3,4,35] for more details.

2.1 Fully Abstract Compilation

Abadi [1] proposed fully abstract compilation to preserve security properties such as confidentiality and integrity when these are expressed in terms of indistinguishability w.r.t. the observations of arbitrary attackers, the latter modeled as execution contexts. For a concrete example, if no source context C_S can distinguish a program P_1 that uses some confidential data k from a program P_2 that does not, we can deduce that k is kept confidential by P_1. Thus, a compiler $[\![\cdot]\!]$ from a source language to a target one, that aims to preserve confidentiality, must ensure that also $[\![P_1]\!]$ and $[\![P_2]\!]$ are equivalent w.r.t. the observations of any target context C_T. To avoid trivial translations, one typically asks for the reflection of the equivalence as well.

Definition 1 (Fully abstract compilation [1]). *A compiler $[\![\cdot]\!]$ is fully abstract iff for any P_1 and P_2,*

$$(\forall \mathsf{C_S}.\mathsf{C_S}\,[\mathsf{P_1}] \approx \mathsf{C_S}\,[\mathsf{P_2}]) \Leftrightarrow (\forall \mathsf{C_T}.\mathsf{C_T}\,[\![\mathsf{P_1}]\!] \approx \mathsf{C_T}\,[\![\mathsf{P_2}]\!])$$

where $\mathsf{C_S}$, $\mathrm{C_T}$ denote source and target contexts resp., $\approx$, $\approx$ denote the two contextual equivalences, i.e., equivalence relations on programs.

Notice that the security notions one can preserve and reflect with a fully abstract compiler are those captured by the contextual equivalence relation $\approx$, that determines both the meaningfulness and the effectiveness of full abstraction. Indeed, if $\approx$ is too coarse-grained, some interesting security properties may be ignored. Dually, if $\approx$ is too fine-grained, equivalent source programs may not have counterparts that are equivalent in the target. In Sect. 3, we pick $\approx$ to be equality of execution traces which, under mild assumptions [20,28], coincides with other common choices of $\approx$ (see also Sect. 6).

2.2   Robust Compilation

Abate et al. [4] suggest a family of secure compilation criteria that depend on the security notion one is interested in preserving. The key idea in their criteria is the preservation of *robust satisfaction*, i.e., satisfaction of (classes of) security properties against arbitrary attackers, modeled as contexts. More concretely, Abate et al. [3,4] assume that every execution of a program exposes a trace of observable events $t \in Trace$ for a fixed set $Trace$ and model interesting security notions like data integrity, confidentiality or observational determinism as sets of sets of traces, i.e., *hyperproperties* denoted by $H \in \wp(\wp(Trace))$ [15].

Definition 2 (Robust satisfaction [3,4]). *A program P robustly satisfies a hyperproperty H iff $\forall C.\ C\,[P] \models H$, where $C\,[P] \models H \triangleq beh(C\,[P]) \in H$ and $beh(C\,[P])$ is the set of all traces that can be observed when executing $C\,[P]$.*

Secure compilation criteria can then be defined as the preservation of robust satisfaction of classes of hyperproperties such as safety or liveness [4], in this paper we consider the class of *all* hyperproperties and *robust hyperproperty preservation* (RHP$^\tau$ from [3]). For that, consider a function τ that takes a source-level hyperproperty and returns its interpretation (or translation) at the target level. Intuitively, a compiler $[\![\cdot]\!]$ is RHP$^\tau$ if, for any source hyperproperty H robustly satisfied by P, its interpretation $\tau(H)$ is robustly satisfied by $[\![P]\!]$, formally:

Definition 3 (Robust hyperproperty preservation). *A compiler $[\![\cdot]\!]$ preserves the robust satisfaction of hyperproperties according to a translation $\tau : \wp(\wp(\mathsf{Trace_S})) \to \wp(\wp(\mathrm{Trace_T}))$ iff the following RHP$^\tau$ holds*

$$\mathsf{RHP}^\tau \equiv \forall \mathsf{P}\ \forall \mathsf{H} \in \wp(\wp(Trace)).\ (\forall \mathsf{C_S}.\ \mathsf{C_S}\,[\mathsf{P}] \models \mathsf{H}) \Rightarrow$$
$$(\forall \mathsf{C_T}.\ \mathsf{C_T}\,[\![\mathsf{P}]\!] \models \tau(\mathsf{H}))$$

when τ is clear from the context we simply say that $[\![\cdot]\!]$ is robust.

RHP$^\tau$ can be formulated without quantification on hyperproperties [3,4].

Lemma 1 (Property-free RHP$^\tau$). *For a compiler* $[\![\cdot]\!]$*, RHP$^\tau$ is equivalent to*[1]

$$\forall P \; \forall C_T \; \exists C_S. \; \mathrm{beh}_T(C_T \, [\![P]\!]) = \tau(\mathrm{beh}_S(C_S \, [P]))$$

Notice that, while Definition 3 describes—through τ—the target *guarantees* for $[\![P]\!]$ against arbitrary target contexts, Lemma 1 enables proofs by *back-translation*. In fact, similarly to fully abstract compilation [35], one can prove that a compiler is RHP$^\tau$ by exhibiting a so-called *back-translation* map producing a source context C_S whose interaction with P exposes "the same" observables as C_T does with $[\![P]\!]$:

Remark 1 (RHP$^\tau$ by back-translation). RHP$^\tau$ holds if there exists a back-translation function *bk* such that for any C_T and any P, $bk(C_T \, [\![P]\!]) = C_S$ is such that $\mathrm{beh}_T(C_T \, [\![P]\!]) = \tau(\mathrm{beh}_S(C_S \, [P]))$.

3 Comparing **FAC** and **RHP$^\tau$**

In the previous section we defined fully abstract compilation as the preservation and reflection of contextual equivalence, i.e., what the contexts can observe about programs. Instead, RHP$^\tau$ was defined as the preservation of (robust satisfaction of) hyperproperties of externally observable traces of events. To enable any comparison, we first provide an intuition on how to accommodate the mismatch in *observations* between full abstraction and RHP$^\tau$ (see the online appendix [5] for all the details). We assume the operational semantics of our languages exhaustively specify the execution of programs in contexts, including both internal steps and steps that expose externally observable *events* like inputs and outputs. Also, we say that a trace is *abstract* if it collects both internal steps and externally observable events. In a slight abuse of notation, we still denote with $beh(C \, [P])$ the set of all the possible *abstract* traces allowed by the semantics when executing P in C. Moreover, since hyperproperties just express predicates over events , we now write $beh(C \, [P]) \in H$ to mean that the traces of events for $C \, [P]$ satisfy the hyperproperty H. Finally, we elect to express contextual equivalence as the equality of the (sets of) abstract traces in an arbitrary context.

Definition 4 (Equality of $beh(\cdot)$). *For programs P_1, P_2 and a context C,*

$$C \, [P_1] \approx C \, [P_2] \iff beh(C \, [P_1]) = beh(C \, [P_2])$$

In Sect. 6 we discuss other common choices for $\approx$ such as *equi-termination*, and the hypotheses under which they are equivalent to ours. We now instantiate Definition 1 on the contextual equivalence from Definition 4 and make explicit the notion of fully abstract compilation we are going to use from now on. Note how we are only interested in the *preservation* of contextual equivalence, as reflection is often subsumed by compiler correctness (e.g., in absence of internal non-determinism) [1,35].

---

[1] $\tau(\mathrm{beh}_S(C_S \, [P]))$ is a shorthand for $\tau(\{\mathrm{beh}_S(C_S \, [P])\})$.

Definition 5 (FAC). *For a compiler* $[\![\cdot]\!]$, FAC *is the following predicate*

$$\mathsf{FAC} \equiv \forall \mathsf{P}_1 \mathsf{P}_2.(\forall \mathsf{C}_\mathsf{S}.\ \mathrm{beh}_\mathsf{S}(\mathsf{C}_\mathsf{S}\,[\mathsf{P}_1]) = \mathrm{beh}_\mathsf{S}(\mathsf{C}_\mathsf{S}\,[\mathsf{P}_2])) \Rightarrow$$
$$(\forall \mathsf{C}_\mathsf{T}.\ \mathrm{beh}_\mathsf{T}(\mathsf{C}_\mathsf{T}\,[\![\mathsf{P}_1]\!]]) = \mathrm{beh}_\mathsf{T}(\mathsf{C}_\mathsf{T}\,[\![\mathsf{P}_2]\!]]))$$

Abate et al. [4], Patrignani and Garg [37] have previously investigated the relation between FAC as in Definition 5 and RHP$^\tau$. In particular, Abate et al. [4] showed that FAC does not imply any of the robust criteria, with an example similar to the one we sketched in Sect. 1. In this section, we provide further evidence of this fact: a fully abstract compiler that does not preserve the robust satisfaction of a security-relevant hyperproperty, namely noninterference. More details on the example can be found in the online appendix [5].

Example 2. Let Source and Target to be two WHILE-like languages [31] with a mutable state. A state $s \in S \triangleq (\mathit{Var} \rightarrow \mathbb{N})$ assigns every variable $\mathsf{v} \in \mathit{Var}$ a natural number. We assume Var to be partitioned into a "high" (private) and a "low" (public) part. We write $\mathsf{v} \in \mathit{Var}_H$ ($\mathsf{v} \in \mathit{Var}_L$, resp.) to denote that the variable v is private (public, resp.). Partial programs are defined in the same way in both Source and Target, whereas whole programs, or terms, are obtained by filling the hole(s) of a context with a partial program (Fig. 1). The only context in Source is $[\cdot]$, called the *identity* context and such that for any P, $[\mathsf{P}] = \mathsf{P}$. Instead, contexts in Target additionally include $\lceil \cdot \rceil$ that is able to observe the *internal* event $\mathcal{H}$ (intuitively, a form of *information leakage* that is not observed by source contexts) and report it by emitting !.

$$\langle P \rangle ::= \text{skip} \mid \mathsf{v} := \langle \mathit{expr} \rangle \mid \langle P \rangle; \langle P \rangle \mid \text{while } \langle \mathit{expr} \rangle \ \langle P \rangle$$
$$\langle \mathsf{C}_\mathsf{S} \rangle ::= [\cdot] \qquad\qquad \langle \mathbf{C_T} \rangle ::= [\cdot] \mid \lceil \cdot \rceil$$

Fig. 1. $\langle P \rangle$ defines the syntax of both Source and Target partial programs, where $\langle \mathit{expr} \rangle$ denotes the usual arithmetic expressions over $\mathbb{N}$. $\langle \mathsf{C}_\mathsf{S} \rangle$ and $\langle \mathsf{C_T} \rangle$ define instead the contexts of Source and Target, respectively.

The semantics of Source and Target are partially given in Fig. 2. Rule asnL is for assignments that do not involve high variables. asnH is for assignments of high variables, and – upon a change in their value – the internal trace $\mathcal{H}$ is emitted. The Target counterparts, asnL and asnH, work similarly. Finally, the most interesting rule is bang2, where we see how context $\lceil \cdot \rceil$ reports a ! upon encountering an $\mathcal{H}$.

$$\text{asnL} \ \frac{\mathsf{v} \in \mathit{Var}_L \qquad e \cap \mathit{Var}_H = \emptyset}{s, \mathsf{v} := e \rightarrow s_{[\mathsf{v} \leftarrow [e]_s]}, \checkmark} \qquad \text{asnH} \ \frac{\mathsf{v} \in \mathit{Var}_H \qquad s(\mathsf{v}) \neq [e]_s}{s, \mathsf{v} := e \xrightarrow{\mathcal{H}} s_{[\mathsf{v} \leftarrow [e]_s]}, \checkmark}$$

$$\text{bang2} \ \frac{s, \mathbf{p} \xrightarrow{\mathcal{H}} s', \mathbf{p}'}{s, \lceil \mathbf{p} \rceil \xrightarrow{!} s', \mathbf{p}'}$$

Fig. 2. Selected rules of Source and Target.

For example, consider a high variable $v \in Var_H$ and the Source program $P \triangleq v := 42$. When P is plugged in the identity context $[\cdot]$, the resulting behavior is $beh_S([P]) = \{ s \cdot \mathcal{H} \cdot s' \cdot \checkmark \mid s \in S \wedge s' = s_{[v \leftarrow 42]} \}$. Intuitively, the traces in $beh_S([P])$ express that the execution starts in a state s, then a high variable is updated ($\mathcal{H}$) leading to state s' and then the program terminates ($\checkmark$). For the same $v \in Var_H$, target program $P \triangleq v := 42$ in $\lceil \cdot \rceil$, we have that $beh_T(\lceil P \rceil) = \{ s \cdot ! \cdot s' \cdot \checkmark \mid s \in S \wedge s' = s_{[v \leftarrow 42]} \}$. Notice the additional ! w.r.t. the source, due to the fact that the context observed a change in a high variable. Informally, we say that a program satisfies noninterference if, executing it in two low-equivalent initial states, it transitions to two low-equivalent states. More rigorously, noninterference can be defined for both Source and Target as the following hyperproperty $NI \in \wp(\wp(Trace))$,

$$NI = \{ \pi \in \wp(Trace) \mid \forall t_1, t_2 \in \pi. \ t_1^0 =_L t_2^0 \Rightarrow t_1 =_L t_2 \}$$

where t_i^0 stands for the first observable of the trace t_i and $=_L$ denotes the fact that two states are low-equivalent (i.e., they coincide on all $x \in Var_L$). Also, we lift the notation to traces and write $t_1 =_L t_2$ to denote that t_1 and t_2 are pointwise low-equivalent. More precisely, $=_L$ ignores all occurrences of $\mathcal{H}$ (as it is internal) and compares traces observable-by-observable, relating $\checkmark$ and ! to themselves and comparing states with the above notion of low-equivalence.

The identity compiler preserves trace equality (see the online appendix [5] for the proof), but does not preserve the robust satisfaction of noninterference as the Target context $\lceil \cdot \rceil$ can detect changes in high variables and report a !. ∎

On the one hand, RHP^τ provides an explicit description of the target hyperproperty $\tau(H)$ that is guaranteed to be robustly satisfied after compilation under the hypothesis that H is robustly satisfied in the source. However, RHP^τ does not imply the preservation of contextual equivalence (or trace equality) because hyperproperties cannot specify which traces are allowed for every single context. On the other hand, it is possible that FAC does not preserve (the robust satisfaction of) hyperproperties, because contextual equivalence may not capture some hyperproperty such as noninterference, as shown in Example 2. So, what kind of hyperproperties a FAC compiler is guaranteed to preserve? If P robustly satisfies H (possibly not captured by $\approx$), what is the hyperproperty that is robustly satisfied by $[\![P]\!]$ for $[\![\cdot]\!]$ being FAC?

We answer this question by defining a map $\tilde{\tau} : \wp(\wp(Traces)) \rightarrow \wp(\wp(Trace_T))$ so that FAC implies $RHP^{\tilde{\tau}}$. The map $\tilde{\tau}$ enjoys an optimality condition making it the *best possible* description of the target guarantee for programs compiled by a FAC compiler.

Theorem 1. *If $[\![\cdot]\!]$ is FAC, then there exists a map $\tilde{\tau}$ such that $[\![\cdot]\!]$ is $RHP^{\tilde{\tau}}$. Moreover, $\tilde{\tau}$ is the smallest (pointwise) with this property.*

To avoid any misunderstanding, we stress the fact that, akin to [32, Theorem 1], neither the existence, nor the optimality of $\tilde{\tau}$ can be used to argue that a FAC compiler $[\![\cdot]\!]$ is reasonably robust. The robustness of $[\![\cdot]\!]$ depends on the image of $\tilde{\tau}$ on the hyperproperties of interest: it should not be trivial, e.g., $\tilde{\tau}(\mathsf{NI_S}) = \top$ like in Example 2 nor distort the intuitive meaning of the hyperproperty itself, e.g., $\tilde{\tau}(\mathsf{NI_S}) =$ "never output 42". In a setting in which observables are coarse enough to be common to source and target traces, i.e., $\mathsf{Trace_S} = \mathrm{Trace_T}$, it is possible to establish whether $\tilde{\tau}(H)$ has "the same meaning" as H:

Corollary 1. *If $[\![\cdot]\!]$ is FAC, then for every hyperproperty H, $[\![\cdot]\!]$ preserves the robust satisfaction of H iff $\tilde{\tau}(H) \subseteq H$, where $\tilde{\tau}$ is the map from Theorem 1.*

The rigorous definition of $\tilde{\tau}$ and the proof of Theorem 1 and Corollary 1 can be found in the online appendix [5]. Here, we only mention that the definition of $\tilde{\tau}$ requires information on the compiler itself, thus it can be unfeasible to compute and assess the meaningfulness of $\tilde{\tau}(H)$. Corollary 1 partially mitigates this problem by allowing to approximate $\tilde{\tau}(H)$ rather than computing it, e.g., by showing an intermediate K such that $\tilde{\tau}(H) \subseteq K \subseteq H$. We leave as future work any approximation techniques for $\tilde{\tau}$ that would make substantial use of Corollary 1.

To overcome the issues highlighted above, we extend the categorical approach to secure compilation of Tsampas et al. [48] and propose an abstract criterion that implies both FAC and RHP$^{\tau}$ for a τ defined via co-induction and therefore independent of the compiler. In Sect. 4 we shall summarize the underlying theory before introducing our criterion in Sect. 5.

4   Secure Compilation, Categorically

The basis of our approach and that of Tsampas et al. [48] is the framework of *Mathematical Operational Semantics* (MOS) [50]. Here, we briefly explain how MOS gives a mathematical description of programming languages as well as (secure) compilers and show how our earlier Example 2 fits such a framework. We refer the interested reader to the seminal paper of Turi and Plotkin [50] and the excellent introductory material of Klin [24] for more details. Further examples and applications can be found in the literature [48,49,51].

4.1   Distributive Laws and Operational Semantics

The main idea of MOS is that the semantics of programming languages, or systems in general, can be formally described through distributive laws (i.e., natural transformations of varying complexity) of a *syntax functor* Σ over a *behavior functor* B in a suitable category (in our case the category **Set** of sets and total functions [24]). The functor $\Sigma : \textbf{Set} \rightarrow \textbf{Set}$ represents the algebraic signature of the language and thus acts as an abstract description of its syntax. Instead, the functor $B : \textbf{Set} \rightarrow \textbf{Set}$ describes the behavior of the language in terms of its observable events (e.g., the behavior of a non-deterministic labeled transition system can be modeled by the functor $BX = \wp(X)^{\Delta}$, where Δ is a set of trace labels [52]);

Recall now the languages Source and Target of Example 2. The syntax functor for Source for a set of terms X builds terms $\Sigma\, X$ according to (the sum of all) the constructors of the language:

$$\Sigma\, X \triangleq \top \uplus (\mathbb{N} \times E) \uplus (X \times X) \uplus (E \times X),$$

where E is the set of arithmetic expressions. The behavior functor for Source is a map that for an arbitrary set X, updates a store $s \in S$, and either terminates ($\checkmark$) or returns another term in X, possibly recording that some high-variable has been modified ($\mathcal{H}$):

$$\mathsf{B}\, X \triangleq (S \times (\text{Maybe } \mathcal{H}) \times (X \uplus \checkmark))^S.$$

In Target, the syntax functor is $\Sigma\, X = \Sigma\, X \uplus X$, where the extra occurrence of X corresponds to the target context $\lceil \cdot \rceil$, and $\mathsf{B}\, X \triangleq (S \times (\text{Maybe } (\mathcal{H} \uplus !)) \times (X \uplus \checkmark))^S$. We explicitly notice that syntactic "holes" are represented by the identity functor $\text{Id}\, X = X$ and, to make this connection clearer, the syntax functor for Source can be equivalently written as $\Sigma \triangleq \top \uplus (\mathbb{N} \times E) \uplus (\text{Id} \times \text{Id}) \uplus (E \times \text{Id})$.

Next, we can define the operational semantics, a *distributive law* of Σ over B, in the format of a *GSOS law* ([24, Section 6.3]). A GSOS law of Σ over B is a natural transformation $\rho : \Sigma(\text{Id} \times B) \Longrightarrow B\Sigma^*$, where Σ^* is the free monad over Σ. For instance, the rules of sequential composition in Source (see seq1 and seq2 in the online appendix [5, Fig. 4]) correspond to the following component of the GSOS law $\rho : \Sigma(\text{Id} \times B) \Longrightarrow B\Sigma^*$:

$$(\mathsf{p},\mathsf{f}) \; ; (\mathsf{q},\mathsf{g}) \mapsto \lambda\, s. \begin{cases} (s', \delta, \mathsf{p}' \; ; \; \mathsf{q}) & \text{if } \mathsf{f}(s) = (s', \delta, \mathsf{p}') \\ (s', \delta, \mathsf{q}) & \text{if } \mathsf{f}(s) = (s', \delta, \checkmark) \end{cases}$$

Here, $\mathsf{p}, \mathsf{q} \in X$ with X a generic set of terms, i.e., p and q can be programs, contexts or programs within a context, and $\mathsf{f}, \mathsf{g} \in \mathsf{B}X$. The image of ρ is an element of $\mathsf{B}\Sigma^* X = (S \times (\text{Maybe } \mathcal{H}) \times (\Sigma^* X \uplus \checkmark)))^S$, depending on whether p transitions to a term p' (thus involving seq2), or terminates with $\checkmark$ (seq1).

Lastly, we informally recall that when the formal semantics of a language is given through a GSOS law $\rho : \Sigma(\text{Id} \times B) \Longrightarrow B\Sigma^*$, for $\Sigma, B : \mathbf{Set} \to \mathbf{Set}$, the set of programs is (isomorphic to) the initial algebra $A = \Sigma^*\emptyset$, while the final coalgebra $Z = B^\infty \top^2$ describes the set of all possible behaviors.

Remark 2. A distributive law ρ induces a map $f : A \to Z$ that assigns to every closed term or program its behaviors as specified by the law ρ itself.

For Source and Target from Example 2 f and f are just another, equivalent representation of $\mathsf{beh}_S(\cdot)$ and $\mathsf{beh}_T(\cdot)$, e.g., for v private variable,

$$\mathsf{f}([\mathsf{v}:=\mathsf{42}]) = \lambda s.\ \langle s_{[x \leftarrow 42]}, \langle \mathcal{H}, \checkmark \rangle \rangle$$
$$\mathsf{f}(\lceil \mathsf{v}:=\mathsf{42} \rceil) = \lambda s.\ \langle s_{[x \leftarrow 42]}, \langle !, \checkmark \rangle \rangle$$

In other words, map $f : A \to Z$ is the abstract counterpart of map $beh(\cdot)$ that assigns to every program the set of all its possible execution traces.

---

[2] Σ^* is the *free monad* over Σ and B^∞ is the *co-free comonad* over B [22, Ch. 5].

4.2 Maps of Distributive Laws as Fully Abstract Compilers

Watanabe [51] first introduced maps of distributive laws (MoDL) as *well-behaved translations* between two GSOS languages. Tsampas et al. [48] showed how MoDL can also be used as a formal, abstract criterion for secure compilation. Let us recall the definition of MoDL for two GSOS laws in the same category.

Definition 6 (MoDL). *A map of distributive law between* $\rho : \Sigma(\mathrm{Id} \times \mathsf{B}) \Longrightarrow \mathsf{B}\Sigma^*$ *and* $\rho : \Sigma(\mathrm{Id} \times \mathsf{B}) \Longrightarrow \mathsf{B}\Sigma^*$ *is a pair of natural transformations* $s : \Sigma \Longrightarrow \Sigma^*$ *and* $b : \mathsf{B} \Longrightarrow \mathsf{B}$ *such that the following diagram commutes,*

$$
\begin{array}{ccc}
\Sigma(\mathrm{Id} \times \mathsf{B}) & \xrightarrow{\ \rho\ } & \mathsf{B}\Sigma^* \\
{\scriptstyle s^* \circ \Sigma(id \times b)}\Big\downarrow & & \Big\downarrow{\scriptstyle b \circ \mathsf{B}s^*} \\
\Sigma(\mathrm{Id} \times \mathsf{B}) & \xrightarrow{\ \rho\ } & \mathsf{B}\Sigma^*
\end{array}
$$

where $s^* : \Sigma^* \Longrightarrow \Sigma^*$ *extends* $s : \Sigma \Longrightarrow \Sigma^*$ *to a morphism of free monads, i.e., to terms of arbitrary depth via structural induction.*

The diagram in Definition 6 expresses a form of *compatibility* of the source and the target semantics. Considering any source term, executing it w.r.t. the source semantics ρ and then translating the behavior (together with the resulting source term) is equivalent to first compiling the source term (and translating the behavior of its subterms) and then executing it w.r.t. the target semantics ρ.

We recall that the set of source (resp. target) programs is $\mathsf{A} \triangleq \Sigma^* \emptyset$ ($\mathsf{A} \triangleq \Sigma^* \emptyset$ resp.), and that $[\![\cdot]\!] \triangleq s_\emptyset^* : \mathsf{A} \to \mathsf{A}$ is the *compiler* induced by s. On the behaviors side, the natural transformation $b : \mathsf{B} \Longrightarrow \mathsf{B}$ induces a translation of behaviors $d := b_\top^\infty : \mathsf{Z} \to \mathsf{Z}$ where $\mathsf{Z} \triangleq \mathsf{B}^\infty \top$. The compiler $[\![\cdot]\!] = s_\emptyset^*$ preserves (and also reflects when all the components of b are injective) *bisimilarity* (see [48], Section 4.3). Whenever bisimilarity coincides with trace equality (see Definition 4), for example under the assumption of *determinacy*[3], the following holds ([48]).

Corollary 2. *In absence of internal non-determinism, MoDL implies* FAC.

Similarly to FAC, the definition of MoDL does not ensure that $[\![\cdot]\!] = s_\emptyset^*$ is robust. Indeed, the obvious embedding compiler from Example 2 is a MoDL (let $s = i_1$ and $b = (S \times (\text{Maybe } i_1) \times (1 \uplus \checkmark))^S$). Intuitively, MoDL adequately captures the fact that compilation preserves the behavior of terms, but fails to capture the observations target contexts can make on compiled terms.

5 Reconciling Fully Abstract and Robust Compilation

To account for the shortcoming of MoDL, we introduce a new, complementary definition that allows reasoning explicitly on the semantic power of contexts in

---

[3] It is possible to eliminate the hypothesis of determinacy when B is an endofunctor over categories richer that **Set**, e.g., **Rel** the category of sets and relations.

some target language relative to contexts in a source language. This definition acts (in conjunction with MoDL) as an abstract criterion of robust compilers.

For the new definition, we elect to qualify some constructors in Σ as *contexts* constructors so that $\Sigma \triangleq \mathfrak{C} \uplus \mathfrak{P}$ where $\mathfrak{C}$ defines the constructors for contexts and $\mathfrak{P}$ for all the rest. We also assume that the GSOS law $\rho : \Sigma(\mathrm{Id} \times B) \Longrightarrow \Sigma^* B$ respects this "logical partition" of Σ in that $\rho = [B \; i_1 \circ \rho_1, \; \rho_2]$ where $\rho_1 : \mathfrak{C}(\mathrm{Id} \times B) \Longrightarrow B\mathfrak{C}^*$ and $\rho_2 : \mathfrak{P}(\mathrm{Id} \times B) \Longrightarrow B\Sigma^*$.

Definition 7 (MMoDL). *A many layers map of distributive laws (MMoDL) between* $\rho : \Sigma(\mathrm{Id} \times B) \Longrightarrow B\Sigma^*$ *and* $\rho : \Sigma(\mathrm{Id} \times B) \Longrightarrow B\Sigma^*$ *is given by natural transformations* $b : B \Longrightarrow B$ *and* $t : \mathfrak{C} \Longrightarrow \mathfrak{C}^*$ *making the following commute:*

$$
\begin{array}{ccccccc}
\mathfrak{C}\Sigma(\mathrm{Id} \times B) & \xrightarrow{\;\mathfrak{C}^*(\Sigma\pi_1,\rho)\;} & \mathfrak{C}(\mathrm{Id} \times B)\Sigma^* & \xrightarrow{\;t\;} & \mathfrak{C}^*(\mathrm{Id} \times B)\Sigma^* & \xrightarrow{\;\rho_1\;} & B\mathfrak{C}^*\Sigma^* \\
\Big\downarrow{\scriptstyle \mathfrak{C}^*(\Sigma\pi_1,\rho)} & & & & & & \Big\downarrow{\scriptstyle b} \\
\mathfrak{C}(\mathrm{Id} \times B)\Sigma^* & \xrightarrow{\;\mathfrak{C}(\mathrm{Id}\times b)\;} & \mathfrak{C}(\mathrm{Id} \times B)\Sigma^* & \xrightarrow{\;\rho_1\;} & B\mathfrak{C}^*\Sigma^* & \xrightarrow{\;Bt^*\;} & B\mathfrak{C}^*\Sigma^*
\end{array}
$$

The top-left object, $\mathfrak{C}\Sigma(\mathrm{Id} \times B)$, represents a target context which is filled with some source term, whose subterms exhibit some source behavior. In both paths, the plugged source terms are initially evaluated w.r.t. the source semantics. On the upper path, we first *back-translate* [16] the target context using t, then we run the resulting program w.r.t. the source semantics (ρ_1), and finally we translate the resulting behavior back to the target via b. Instead, in the lower path we first translate the resulting behavior through $\mathfrak{C}(\mathrm{Id} \times b)$, then we let the target context observe (ρ_1), and finally we back-translate *the behavior* via Bt^*.

To relate MMoDL with RHP$^\tau$, we formulate the latter in the framework of MOS. Recall (see Remark 1) that RHP$^\tau$ holds if there exists a *back-translation* map bk that for every target context $\mathrm{C_T}$ and program P, produces a source context $bk(\mathrm{C_T}, \mathrm{P}) = \mathrm{C_s}$ such that $\mathrm{beh_T}(\mathrm{C_T}[\![\mathrm{P}]\!]) = \tau(\mathrm{beh_S}(\mathrm{C_s}[\mathrm{P}]))$.

Remark 3 ((Abstract) RHP$^\tau$). For $\tau : Z \to Z$, a compiler $[\![\cdot]\!]$ is RHP$^\tau$ iff there exists bk such that

$$
\tau \circ \mathsf{f} \circ \mathsf{plug} \circ bk = \mathsf{f} \circ \mathsf{plug} \circ id \times [\![\cdot]\!],
$$

where $f : A \to Z$ associates to every program its behaviors as specified by ρ (see Remark 2) and *plug* is the operation of plugging a term into a context.

We are now ready to state our second contribution, namely that the pairing of a MoDL (s, b) and a MMoDL (t, b) gives an (abstract) RHP$^\tau$ compiler.

Theorem 2 (MMoDL imply RHP$^\tau$). *Let* $s : \Sigma \Longrightarrow \Sigma^*$, $b : B \Longrightarrow B$ *and* $t : \mathfrak{C} \Longrightarrow \mathfrak{C}$ *such that* (s, b) *and* (t, b) *are (respectively) a MoDL and a MMoDL from* $\rho : \Sigma(\mathrm{Id} \times B) \Longrightarrow B\Sigma^*$ *to* $\rho : \Sigma(\mathrm{Id} \times B) \Longrightarrow B\Sigma^*$. *The compiler* $[\![\cdot]\!] = s^*_\emptyset$ *is (abstract) RHP$^\tau$ for* $\tau = b^\infty_\top$ *coinductively induced by* b.

Proof (Sketch). The back-translation $bk := t^*_\emptyset \times id$ satisfies the equation in Remark 3 (details in the online appendix [5]). □

Before fixing the compiler from Example 2 to make it satisfy both MoDL (Definition 6) and MMoDL (Definition 7), let us see why the back-translation mapping both target contexts to the identity source context $[\cdot]$ is not a MMoDL. Let $v \in Var_H$ be a private variable, on the upper path of Definition 7 we have

$$\lceil v := 42 \rceil \xrightarrow{\mathfrak{C}^*(\Sigma\pi_1, \rho)} \lceil \checkmark \rceil, \lambda s.\langle s_{[v \leftarrow 42]}, \mathcal{H} \rangle \xrightarrow{\quad t \quad} [, \checkmark], \ldots \mathcal{H} \xrightarrow{\rho_1} \checkmark, \ldots \mathcal{H} \xrightarrow{\quad b \quad} \checkmark, \ldots \mathcal{H}$$

Note how the identity context fails to report !. On the lower path, we have instead

$$\lceil v := 42 \rceil \xrightarrow{\mathfrak{C}^*(\Sigma\pi_1, \rho)} \lceil \checkmark \rceil, \lambda s.\langle s_{[v \leftarrow 42]}, \mathcal{H} \rangle \xrightarrow{\mathfrak{C}(\mathrm{Id} \times b)} \lceil \checkmark \rceil, \ldots \mathcal{H} \xrightarrow{\rho_1} \checkmark, \ldots ! \xrightarrow{Bt^*} \checkmark, \ldots !$$

Here, it is evident that the context $\lceil \cdot \rceil$ "picks up" $\mathcal{H}$ and reports !, unlike $[\cdot]$.

Example 3 (Example 2, revisited). We now show how to fix the compiler from Example 2 by making it RHP$^\tau$ for a suitable τ. For that, we first need to slightly modify the language Target. The idea is that variable assignments in Target should now be *sandboxed*, so that the interactions with the context $\lceil \cdot \rceil$ do not expose sensitive information. Formally, we extend the algebraic signature of Target with a constructor for sandboxing assignments, i.e., $\Sigma \uplus (E \times \mathrm{Id})$, so that Target terms are generated by grammar

$$<P> ::= \mathrm{skip} \,|\, v := <expr> \,|\, \langle P \rangle; \langle P \rangle \,|\, \mathrm{while}\ <expr>\ \langle P \rangle \,|\, \lfloor v := <expr> \rfloor$$

where the semantics of $\lfloor \cdot \rfloor$ is described in Fig. 3. We can now define the new (i.e., fixed) compiler $[\![\cdot]\!]$ and the appropriate map τ, so that $[\![\cdot]\!]$ is RHP$^\tau$. Both $[\![\cdot]\!]$ and τ are determined by the natural transformations s, t, and b, such that (s, b) is a MoDL and (t, b) is a MMoDL. The natural transformation $s : \Sigma \Longrightarrow (\Sigma \uplus (E \times \mathrm{Id}))^*$, and therefore the inductively defined compiler $[\![\cdot]\!] \triangleq s_\emptyset^*$, wraps assignments in the sandbox $\lfloor \cdot \rfloor$, i.e., $[\![v := e]\!] = \lfloor v := e \rfloor$ and acts as the identity on other terms. The natural transformation $t : \mathfrak{C} \Longrightarrow \mathfrak{C}^*$ maps every Target context to the identity context $[\cdot]$. Finally, the translation of behaviors $b : B \Longrightarrow B$ erases the occurrences of $\mathcal{H}$, implying that the compiled terms are not expected to report changes in high variables.

$$\mathrm{sb1} \frac{s, \mathbf{p} \xrightarrow{\mathcal{H}} s', \checkmark}{s, \lfloor \mathbf{p} \rfloor \to s', \checkmark} \qquad \mathrm{sb2} \frac{s, \mathbf{p} \xrightarrow{\mathcal{H}} s', \mathbf{p}'}{s, \lfloor \mathbf{p} \rfloor \to s', \mathbf{p}'}$$

Fig. 3. Rules extending the semantics of Target.

Recall that the diagram from Definition 7 failed to commute for Example 2, because (s, b) being a MoDL imposed b to not erase any occurrences of $\mathcal{H}$. The same diagram for the new Target language and natural transformations s, b, and t now commutes. More specifically, in the upper path we have

$$\lceil v := 42 \rceil \xrightarrow{\mathfrak{C}^*(\Sigma\pi_1, \rho)} \lceil \checkmark \rceil, \lambda s.\langle s_{[v \leftarrow 42]}, \mathcal{H} \rangle \xrightarrow{\quad t \quad} [, \checkmark], \ldots \mathcal{H} \xrightarrow{\rho_1} \checkmark, \ldots \mathcal{H} \xrightarrow{\quad b \quad} \checkmark, \ldots$$

while in the lower path we get

$$\lceil v := 42 \rceil \xrightarrow{\mathfrak{C}^*(\Sigma\pi_1, \rho)} \lceil \checkmark \rceil, \lambda s.\langle s_{[v \leftarrow 42]}, \mathcal{H} \rangle \xrightarrow{\mathfrak{C}(\mathrm{Id} \times b)} \lceil \checkmark \rceil, \ldots \xrightarrow{\rho_1} \checkmark, \ldots \xrightarrow{Bt^*} \checkmark, \ldots$$

We point the reader interested to the online appendix [5] for more details in showing that the above (s, b) is a MoDL and that (t, b) is a MMoDL.

Hereafter, we discuss one of the benefits of the abstract definitions presented so far, namely that we can easily compute τ, and immediately establish if programs that robustly satisfy NI_S (noninterference in Source) are compiled to programs that robustly satisfy NI_T. In order to do so, we need to connect Z and Z to traces and hyperproperties of Source and Target. Elements of Z are functions that assign to every $s \in S$ a new state s' and *maybe* an extra symbol like ! or $\mathcal{H}$, and a continuation, i.e., another function of the same type. Traces are instead sequences of stores possibly exhibiting the extra symbols $\mathcal{H}$ and !. It is easy to show (see the online appendix [5]) that every trace corresponds to an element of Z – the function that returns the head of the trace and continues as the tail of the same trace – and that every function in Z corresponds to a set of traces – one trace for every fixed $s \in S$. Thus, we can prove that τ maps (the set of functions in Z corresponding to) NI_S to a subset of (the set of functions corresponding to) NI_T, i.e., the compiler $\llbracket \cdot \rrbracket$ preserves robust satisfaction.   ∎

6   Related Work

In this section, we discuss related work regarding origins and applications of full abstraction, trace based criteria, MoDL and relevant proof techniques.

Full abstraction was introduced to relate the operational and the denotational semantics of programming languages [40]. A denotational semantics of a language is said to be fully abstract w.r.t. an operational one for the same language *iff* the same denotation is given to contextually equivalent terms, i.e., those terms that result the *same* when evaluated according to the operational semantics. Common choices to establish when the result of the evaluation is *the same*, and hence to define contextual equivalence, are *equi-convergence* and *equi-divergence* (e.g., in [13,14,23,28,38]). Notice that there is no loss of generality with these choices, if (and only if!) contexts are powerful enough [28], e.g., when all inputs can be thought as part of the context, and the context itself may select one final value as the result of the execution or diverge.

Fully abstract translations as in Definition 1 have been adopted for comparing expressiveness of languages (see, e.g., the works by Mitchell [28] and Patrignani et al. [38]), but Gorla and Nestmann [21] showed that they may lead to false positive results. The interested reader can find out more in the online appendix [5], where we also sketch how to use RHP^τ for expressiveness comparisons.

Full Abstraction and Secure Compilation. Abadi [1] originally proposed to use full abstraction to preserve security properties in translations from a source language L_1 to a target one L_2. A fully abstract translation or compiler preserves and reflects equivalences, and can therefore be a way to preserve security properties when these are expressed as equivalences. Remarkable examples from the literature are given by Bowman and Ahmed [13], Busi et al. [14] and Skorstengaard et al. [43]. In the first two works the authors model contexts so that contextual equivalence captures (forms of) noninterference and preserve it through a fully abstract translation. Skorstengaard et al. [43] consider a source language with well-bracketed control flow (WBCF) and local state encapsulation (LSE), then model target contexts so that these two properties are captured by contextual equivalence and, they exhibit a fully abstract translation so that both WBCF and LSE are guaranteed also in the target. We stress the fact that, all security properties that are not captured by contextual equivalence are not necessarily preserved by a fully abstract compiler, thus allowing for counterexamples similar to Example 1. Finally, it is worth noting that fully abstract compilation does not prevent source programs to be insecure, nor suggests how to fix them, quoting Abadi [1]:

> An expression of the source language L_1 may be written in a silly, incompetent, or even malicious way. For example, the expression may be a program that broadcasts some sensitive information—so this expression is insecure on its own, even before any translation to L_2. Thus, full abstraction is clearly not sufficient for security [...]

Beyond Full Abstraction. Several definitions of "well-behaved translations" exist, depending both on the scenario and on the properties one aims to preserve during the translation. For example, if the goal is to preserve functional correctness, then it is natural to require the compiled program to *simulate* the source one [29]. This can be expressed both as a relation between the operational semantics of the source and the target (see for example [27,42,51]), or extrinsically as a relation between the execution traces of programs before and after compilation [3,12,46]. *Trace based criteria for compiler correctness* The CompCert [12,26] and CakeML [46] projects are milestones in the formal verification of compilers. Preservation of functional correctness can be expressed in both cases in terms of execution traces [3]. For the CompCert compiler, executing ⟦P⟧ w.r.t. the target semantics yields the same observable events as executing P w.r.t. the source semantics, as long as P does not encounter an undefined behavior. Similarly, CakeML ensures that executing ⟦P⟧ w.r.t. the target semantics yields the same observable events as executing P w.r.t. the source semantics, as long as there is enough space in target memory. In both cases, correctness is proven by exhibiting a simulation between ⟦P⟧ and P.

Trace Based Criteria for Secure Compilation. Similarly to what happens for functional correctness, relations between the execution traces of a program and of its compiled version, can be used to express preservation of noninterference through compilation [10,11,30]. The simulation-based techniques introduced in CompCert sometimes suffice also to show the preservation of noninterference, e.g., when the source and the target semantics are equipped with a notion of leakage [10, Sections 5.2–5.4]. However, in more general cases a stronger, *cube-shaped simulation* is needed (see [10, Section 5.5], and [11,30]). Stewart et al. [44] propose a variant of CompCert that also gives some guarantees w.r.t. source contexts, and their compilation in the target. Still, this does not guarantee security against *arbitrary* target contexts, that can be strictly stronger than source ones. Abate et al. [3,4] propose a family of criteria with the goal of preserving satisfaction of (classes of) security properties against arbitrary contexts. Also, they show that their criteria can be formulated in at least two equivalent ways. The first one explicitly describes the target guarantees ensured for compiled programs, for example which safety properties are guaranteed for programs written in unsafe languages and compiled according to the criterion proposed by Abate et al. [2] (see their Appendix A). The second way is instead more amenable to proofs, e.g., by enabling proofs by back-translation Abate et al. [2, Fig. 4].

Maps of Distributive Laws (MoDL). Mathematical Operational Semantics (MOS) and distributive laws ensure *well-behavedness* of the operational semantics of a language while also providing a formal description for it. Such semantics have been given for languages with algebraic effects [6] and for stochastic calculi [25]. In their biggest generality distributive laws are defined between monads and comonads [24], but it is often convenient to consider the slightly less general GSOS laws that correspond bijectively to GSOS rules [7,24,41].

Proof Techniques for fully abstract compilation include both cross-language logical relations between source and compiled programs [13,35,43] and back-translation of target contexts into source ones [14,16,35]. The latter technique sometimes exploits information from execution traces [16], and can be adapted also to some of the robust criteria of Abate et al. [4]. Ongoing work is aiming to formalize the back-translation technique needed to prove some of the robust preservation of safety (hyper)properties in the Coq proof assistant [2,47]. The best results in mechanization of secure compilation criteria have been achieved for the criteria that can be proven via simulations, especially when extending the CompCert proof scripts, e.g., [10]. The complexity of many proofs is relatively contained as they show a *forward* simulation—the source program simulates the one in the target—and "flip" it into a *backward* one—the compiled program simulates the source one—with a general argument. We are not aware of mechanized proofs for MoDL, but we believe it would be convenient to first express maps between GSOS laws as relations between GSOS rules (see also Sect. 7).

7   Conclusions and Future Work

The scope of this work has been to clarify the guarantees provided by criteria for secure compilation, make them explicit and immediately accessible to users and developers of (provably) secure compilers. We investigated the relation between fully abstract and robust compilation, provided an explicit description of the hyperproperties robustly preserved by a fully abstract compiler, and noticed that these are not always meaningful, nor of practical utility. We have therefore introduced a novel criterion that ensures both fully abstract and robust compilation, and such that the meaningfulness of the hyperproperty guaranteed to hold after compilation can be easily established. The proposed example shows that our criterion is achievable.

   Future work will focus on proof techniques for MoDL and MMoDL that are amenable to formalization in a proof assistant. For that we can either build on existing formalizations of polynomial functors as containers, or exploit the correspondence between GSOS laws and GSOS rules, and characterize MoDL and MMoDL as relations between source and target rules. Another interesting line of work consists in devising over (under) approximation for the map $\tilde{\tau}$ from Theorem 1, and use our Corollary 1 to establish whether existing fully abstract compilers preserve (violate) a given hyperproperty.

Acknowledgements. We are grateful to Pierpaolo Degano, Letterio Galletta, Catalin Hritcu, Marco Patrignani, Frank Piessens, and Jeremy Thibault for their feedback on early versions of this paper. We would also like to thank the anonymous reviewers for their insightful comments and suggestions that helped to improve our presentation.

Carmine Abate is supported by the European Research Council https://erc.europa.eu/ under ERC Starting Grant SECOMP (715753). Matteo Busi is partially supported by the research grant on *Formal Methods and Techniques for Secure Compilation* from the Department of Computer Science of the University of Pisa.

References

1. Abadi, M.: Protection in programming-language translations. In: Secure Internet Programming, Security Issues for Mobile and Distributed Objects, pp. 19–34 (1999)
2. Abate, C., et al.: When good components go bad: formally secure compilation despite dynamic compromise. In: Proceedings of the 2018 ACM SIGSAC Conference on Computer and Communications Security, pp. 1351–1368 (2018)
3. Abate, C., et al.: Trace-relating compiler correctness and secure compilation. In: ESOP 2020. LNCS, vol. 12075, pp. 1–28. Springer, Cham (2020). https://doi.org/10.1007/978-3-030-44914-8_1
4. Abate, C., Blanco, R., Garg, D., Hritcu, C., Patrignani, M., Thibault, J.: Journey beyond full abstraction: exploring robust property preservation for secure compilation. In: 2019 IEEE 32nd Computer Security Foundations Symposium (CSF), pp. 256–25615. IEEE (2019)
5. Abate, C., Busi, M., Tsampas, S.: Fully abstract and robust compilation and how to reconcile the two, abstractly (2021)
6. Abou-Saleh, F., Pattinson, D.: Towards effects in mathematical operational semantics. Electr. Notes Theor. Comput. Sci. **276**, 81–104 (2011)
7. Aceto, L., Fokkink, W., Verhoef, C.: Structural operational semantics. In: Handbook of Process Algebra, pp. 197–292. Elsevier (2001)
8. Ahmed, A., Blume, M.: Typed closure conversion preserves observational equivalence. In: Hook, J., Thiemann, P. (eds.) Proceeding of the 13th ACM SIGPLAN International Conference on Functional Programming, ICFP 2008, Victoria, BC, Canada, 20–28 September 2008, pp. 157–168. ACM (2008)
9. Ahmed, A., Blume, M.: An equivalence-preserving CPS translation via multi-language semantics. In: Chakravarty, M.M.T., Hu, Z., Danvy, O. (eds.) Proceeding of the 16th ACM SIGPLAN International Conference on Functional Programming, ICFP 2011, Tokyo, Japan, 19–21 September 2011, pp. 431–444. ACM (2011). https://doi.org/10.1145/2034773.2034830
10. Barthe, G., et al.: Formal verification of a constant-time preserving C compiler. Proc. ACM Program. Lang. 4(Popl), 1–30 (2019)

11. Barthe, G., Grégoire, B., Laporte, V.: Secure compilation of side-channel counter-measures: the case of cryptographic "constant-time". In: 2018 IEEE 31st Computer Security Foundations Symposium (CSF), pp. 328–343. IEEE (2018)

12. Besson, F., Blazy, S., Wilke, P.: A verified compcert front-end for a memory model supporting pointer arithmetic and uninitialised data. J. Autom. Reason. **62**(4), 433–480 (2019)

13. Bowman, W.J., Ahmed, A.: Noninterference for free. ACM SIGPLAN Not. **50**(9), 101–113 (2015)

14. Busi, M., et al.: Provably secure isolation for interruptible enclaved execution on small microprocessors. In: 33rd IEEE Computer Security Foundations Symposium (CSF 2020) (2020)

15. Clarkson, M.R., Schneider, F.B.: Hyperproperties. J. Comput. Secur. **18**(6), 1157–1210 (2010)

16. Devriese, D., Patrignani, M., Piessens, F.: Fully-abstract compilation by approximate back-translation. In: Proceedings of the 43rd Annual ACM SIGPLAN-SIGACT Symposium on Principles of Programming Languages, pp. 164–177 (2016)

17. D'Silva, V., Payer, M., Song, D.X.: The correctness-security gap in compiler optimization. In: 2015 IEEE Symposium on Security and Privacy Workshops, SPW 2015, San Jose, CA, USA, 21–22 May 2015, pp. 73–87 (2015)

18. Durumeric, Z., et al.: The matter of heartbleed. In: Proceedings of the 2014 Conference on Internet Measurement Conference, pp. 475–488 (2014)

19. El-Korashy, A., Tsampas, S., Patrignani, M., Devriese, D., Garg, D., Piessens, F.: CapablePtrs: securely compiling partial programs using the pointers-as-capabilities principle. CoRR abs/2005.05944 (2020)

20. Engelfriet, J.: Determinacy - (observation equivalence = trace equivalence). Theor. Comput. Sci. **36**(1), 21–25 (1985)

21. Gorla, D., Nestmann, U.: Full abstraction for expressiveness: history, myths and facts. Math. Struct. Comput. Sci. **26**(4), 639–654 (2016)

22. Jacobs, B.: Introduction to Coalgebra: Towards Mathematics of States and Observation, Cambridge Tracts in Theoretical Computer Science, vol. 59. Cambridge University Press (2016). ISBN 9781316823187

23. Jacobs, K., Timany, A., Devriese, D.: Fully abstract from static to gradual. Proc. ACM Program. Lang. **5**(Popl), 1–30 (2021)

24. Klin, B.: Bialgebras for structural operational semantics: an introduction. Theoret. Comput. Sci. **412**(38), 5043–5069 (2011)

25. Klin, B., Sassone, V.: Structural operational semantics for stochastic process calculi. In: Amadio, R. (ed.) FoSSaCS 2008. LNCS, vol. 4962, pp. 428–442. Springer, Heidelberg (2008). https://doi.org/10.1007/978-3-540-78499-9_30

26. Leroy, X.: Formal certification of a compiler back-end or: programming a compiler with a proof assistant. In: Morrisett, J.G., Jones, S.L.P. (eds.) Proceedings of the 33rd ACM SIGPLAN-SIGACT Symposium on Principles of Programming Languages, POPL 2006, Charleston, South Carolina, USA, 11–13 January 2006, pp. 42–54. ACM (2006)

27. Melton, A., Schmidt, D.A., Strecker, G.E.: Galois connections and computer science applications. In: Pitt, D., Abramsky, S., Poigné, A., Rydeheard, D. (eds.) Category Theory and Computer Programming. LNCS, vol. 240, pp. 299–312. Springer, Heidelberg (1986). https://doi.org/10.1007/3-540-17162-2_130

28. Mitchell, J.C.: On abstraction and the expressive power of programming languages. Sci. Comput. Program. **21**(2), 141–163 (1993)

29. Morris, F.L.: Advice on structuring compilers and proving them correct. In: Proceedings of the 1st Annual ACM SIGACT-SIGPLAN Symposium on Principles of Programming Languages, pp. 144–152 (1973)

30. Murray, T., Sison, R., Pierzchalski, E., Rizkallah, C.: Compositional verification and refinement of concurrent value-dependent noninterference. In: 2016 IEEE 29th Computer Security Foundations Symposium (CSF), pp. 417–431. IEEE (2016)

31. Nielson, H.R., Nielson, F.: Semantics with Applications: An Appetizer. Undergraduate Topics in Computer Science. Springer. London (2007). https://doi.org/10.1007/978-1-84628-692-6. ISBN 978-1-84628-691-9

32. Parrow, J.: General conditions for full abstraction. Math. Struct. Comput. Sci. **26**(4), 655–657 (2016)

33. Patrignani, M.: Why should anyone use colours? Or, syntax highlighting beyond code snippets. CoRR abs/2001.11334 (2020)

34. Patrignani, M., Agten, P., Strackx, R., Jacobs, B., Clarke, D., Piessens, F.: Secure compilation to protected module architectures. ACM Trans. Program. Lang. Syst. **37**(2), 6:1–6:50 (2015)

35. Patrignani, M., Ahmed, A., Clarke, D.: Formal approaches to secure compilation: a survey of fully abstract compilation and related work. ACM Comput. Surv. (CSUR) **51**(6), 1–36 (2019)

36. Patrignani, M., Clarke, D.: Fully abstract trace semantics for protected module architectures. Comput. Lang. Syst. Struct. **42**, 22–45 (2015)

37. Patrignani, M., Garg, D.: Secure compilation and hyperproperty preservation. In: 2017 IEEE 30th Computer Security Foundations Symposium (CSF), pp. 392–404. IEEE (2017)

38. Patrignani, M., Martin, E.M., Devriese, D.: On the semantic expressiveness of recursive types. Proc. ACM Program. Lang. **5**(Popl), 1–29 (2021)

39. Piessens, F.: Security across abstraction layers: old and new examples. In: 2020 IEEE European Symposium on Security and Privacy Workshops (EuroS&PW), pp. 271–279. IEEE (2020)

40. Plotkin, G.D.: LCF considered as a programming language. Theoret. Comput. Sci. **5**(3), 223–255 (1977)

41. Plotkin, G.D.: A structural approach to operational semantics. Aarhus university (1981)

42. Sabry, A., Wadler, P.: A reflection on call-by-value. ACM Trans. Program. Lang. Syst. (TOPLAS) **19**(6), 916–941 (1997)

43. Skorstengaard, L., Devriese, D., Birkedal, L.: StkTokens: enforcing well-bracketed control flow and stack encapsulation using linear capabilities. Proc. ACM Program. Lang. **3**(Popl), 19:1–19:28 (2019)

44. Stewart, G., Beringer, L., Cuellar, S., Appel, A.W.: Compositional compcert. In: Proceedings of the 42nd Annual ACM SIGPLAN-SIGACT Symposium on Principles of Programming Languages, pp. 275–287 (2015)

45. Strydonck, T.V., Piessens, F., Devriese, D.: Linear capabilities for fully abstract compilation of separation-logic-verified code. Proc. ACM Program. Lang. **3**(ICFP), 84:1–84:29 (2019)

46. Tan, Y.K., Myreen, M.O., Kumar, R., Fox, A., Owens, S., Norrish, M.: The verified cakeML compiler backend. J. Func. Program. **29** (2019)

47. Thibault, J., Hritcu, C.: Nanopass back-translation of multiple traces for secure compilation proofs. In: 5th Workshop on Principles of Secure Compilation, PriSC 2021, Virtual Event, 17 January 2021 (2021). http://perso.eleves.ens-rennes.fr/people/Jeremy.Thibault/prisc2021.pdf

48. Tsampas, S., Nuyts, A., Devriese, D., Piessens, F.: A categorical approach to secure compilation. In: Petrişan, D., Rot, J. (eds.) CMCS 2020. LNCS, vol. 12094, pp. 155–179. Springer, Cham (2020). https://doi.org/10.1007/978-3-030-57201-3_9

49. Turi, D.: Categorical modelling of structural operational rules: case studies. In: Category Theory and Computer Science, 7th International Conference, CTCS 1997, Santa Margherita Ligure, Italy, 4–6 September 1997, Proceedings, pp. 127–146 (1997)

50. Turi, D., Plotkin, G.: Towards a mathematical operational semantics. In: Proceedings of Twelfth Annual IEEE Symposium on Logic in Computer Science, pp. 280–291. IEEE (1997)

51. Watanabe, H.: Well-behaved translations between structural operational semantics. Electr. Notes Theoret. Comput. Sci. **65**(1), 337–357 (2002)

52. Winskel, G., Nielsen, M.: Models for concurrency. DAIMI Rep. Ser. **22**(463) (1993)

A Dictionary-Passing Translation of Featherweight Go

Martin Sulzmann[1][(✉)] and Stefan Wehr[2]

[1] Karlsruhe University of Applied Sciences, Karlsruhe, Germany
martin.sulzmann@h-ka.de
[2] Offenburg University of Applied Sciences, Offenburg, Germany
stefan.wehr@hs-offenburg.de

Abstract. The Go programming language is an increasingly popular language but some of its features lack a formal investigation. This article explains Go's resolution mechanism for overloaded methods and its support for structural subtyping by means of translation from Featherweight Go to a simple target language. The translation employs a form of dictionary passing known from type classes in Haskell and preserves the dynamic behavior of Featherweight Go programs.

1 Introduction

The Go programming language [22], introduced by Google in 2009, is syntactically close to C and incorporates features that are well-established in other programming languages. For example, a garbage collector as found in Java [6], built-in support for concurrency and channels in the style of Concurrent ML [17], higher-order and anonymous functions known from functional languages such as Haskell [12]. Go also supports method overloading for structures where related methods can be grouped together using interfaces. Unlike Java, where subtyping is nominal, Go supports structural subtyping among interfaces.

Earlier work by Griesmer and co-authors [7] introduces Featherweight Go (FG), a minimal core calculus that includes the essential features of Go. Their work specifies static typing rules and a run-time method lookup semantics for FG. However, the actual Go implementation appears to employ a different dynamic semantics. Quoting Griesmer and co-workers:

> Go is designed to enable efficient implementation. Structures are laid out in memory as a sequence of fields, while an interface is a pair of a pointer to an underlying structure and a pointer to a dictionary of methods.

To our knowledge, nobody has so far formalized such a dictionary-passing translation for FG and established its semantic equivalence with the FG run-time method lookup dynamic semantics. Hence, we make the following contributions:

- Section 5 specifies the translation of source FG programs to an untyped lambda calculus with pattern matching. We employ a dictionary-passing

© Springer Nature Switzerland AG 2021
H. Oh (Ed.): APLAS 2021, LNCS 13008, pp. 102–120, 2021.
https://doi.org/10.1007/978-3-030-89051-3_7

translation scheme à la type classes [8] to statically resolve overloaded FG method calls. The translation is guided by the typing of the FG program.
- Section 6 establishes the semantic correctness of the dictionary-passing translation. The proof for this result is far from trivial. We require step-indexed logical relations [1] as there can be cyclic dependencies between interfaces and method declarations.

Section 3 specifies Featherweight Go (FG) and Sect. 4 specifies our target language. Section 7 covers related works and concludes. The upcoming section gives an overview.

2   Overview

We introduce Featherweight Go [7] (FG) by an example and then present the ideas of our dictionary-passing translation for FG.

2.1   FG by Example

FG is a syntactic subset of the full Go language, supporting structures, methods and interfaces. The upper part in Fig. 1, lines 1–22, shows an example slightly adopted from [7]. The original example covers equality in FG. We extend the example and include an ordering relation (less or equal than) as well.

FG programs consist of a sequence of declarations defining structures, methods, interfaces and a main function. Method bodies in FG only consist of a return statement. For clarity, we sometimes identify subexpressions via variable bindings introduced with var. In such a declaration, the name of a variable precedes its type, the notation var _ (line 21) indicates that we do not care about the variable name given to the main expression. The example uses primitive types int and bool and several operations on values of these types (==, &&, ...). These are not part of FG.

Structures in FG are similar to structures known from C/C++. A syntactic difference is the FG convention that field names precede the types. In FG, structures and methods are always declared separately, whereas C++ groups methods together in a class declaration. Methods in FG can be overloaded on the *receiver*. The receiver is the value on which the method operates on.

Interfaces in FG consist of a set of method declarations that share the same receiver. For example, interface Eq introduces method eq and interface Ord introduces methods eq and lt (line 3 and 4). The (leading) receiver argument is left implicit and method names in interfaces must always be distinct. Interfaces are types and can be used in type declarations for structures and methods. For example, structure Pair defines two fields left and right, each of type Eq. Declarations of structures must be non-recursive whereas an interface may appear in the method declaration of the interface itself. For example, see interface Eq.

FG uses the keyword func to introduce methods and functions. Methods can be distinguished from ordinary functions as the receiver argument always precedes the method name. In FG, the only function is the main function, all other declarations introduced by func are methods.

```
1   type Int    struct { val int }
2   type Pair   struct { left  Eq; right Eq }
3   type Eq     interface { eq(that Eq) bool }
4   type Ord    interface { eq(that Eq) bool; lt(that Ord) bool }
5
6   func (this Int) eq(that Eq) bool {
7           return this.val == (that.(Int)).val
8   }
9   func (this Pair) eq(that Eq) bool {
10          return this.left.eq(that.(Pair).left) &&
11                 this.right.eq(that.(Pair).right)
12  }
13  func (this Int) lt(that Ord) bool {
14          return this.eq(that) ||
15                 (this.val < (that.(Int)).val)
16  }
17  func main() {
18    var i Int = Int{1}
19    var j Int = Int{2}
20    var p Pair = Pair{i, j}
21    var _ bool = p.eq(p)
22  }
23  -- Field access assuming constructors K_Int and K_Pair.
24  val (K_Int y) = y
25  left (K_Pair (x,_)) = x
26  right (K_Pair (_,x)) = x
27
28  -- Interface-value construction assuming constructors K_Eq, K_Ord.
29  toEq_Int y = K_Eq (y, eq_Int)
30  toEq_Pair y = K_Eq (y, eq_Pair)
31  toEq_Ord (K_Ord (x,eq,_)) = K_Eq (x,eq)
32
33  -- Interface-value destruction.
34  fromEq_Int (K_Eq (K_Int y, _)) = K_Int y
35  fromEq_Pair (K_Eq (K_Pair (x,y) , _)) = K_Pair (x,y)
36  fromOrd_Int (K_Ord (K_Int y, _, _)) = K_Int y
37
38  -- Method definitions.
39  eq_Eq (K_Eq (x, eq)) = eq x
40  eq_Int this that = val this == val (fromEq_Int that)
41  eq_Pair this that = eq_Eq (left this) (left (fromEq_Pair that))
42                  && eq_Eq (right this) (right (fromEq_Pair that))
43  lt_Int this that = eq_Int this (toEq_Ord that)
44                  || (val this < val (fromOrd_Int that))
45  main =
46    let i = K_Int 1
47        j = K_Int 2
48        p = K_Pair (toEq_Int i, toEq_Int j)
49    in eq_Pair p (toEq_Pair p)
```

Fig. 1. Equality and ordering in FG and its translation

Consider the method implementation of eq for receiver this of type Int starting at line 6. This definition takes care of equality among Int values by making use of primitive equality == among int. We would expect argument that to be of type Int. However, to be able to use an Int value everywhere an Eq value is expected (to be discussed shortly), the signature of eq for Int must match exactly the signature declared by interface Eq. Hence, that has declared type Eq, and we resort to a type assertion, written that.(Int), to convert it to Int. Type assertions involve a run-time check that may fail. The same observation applies to the implementation of Eq for receiver Pair (line 9).

FG supports structural subtyping among structures and interfaces. A structure is a subtype of an interface if the structure implements the methods as declared by the interface. For example, Int and Pair both implement interface Eq. This implies the structural subtype relations (1) Int <: Eq and (2) Pair <: Eq. Relation (1) ensures that the construction of the pair at line 20 type checks: variables i and j have type Int but can also be viewed as type Eq thanks to structural subtyping. Relation (2) resolves the method call p.eq(p) at line 21 as the Pair variable p also has the type Eq. The method definition starting at line 9 will be chosen.

An interface I is a structural subtype of another interface J if I contains all of J's method declarations. For example, the set of methods of interface Ord is a superset of the method set of Eq. This implies (3) Ord <: Eq, which is used in the method implementation of lt for receiver type Int. See line 14 where (3) yields that variable that with declared type Ord also has type Eq. Thus, the method call this.eq(that) is resolved via the method definition from line 6.

2.2   Dictionary-Passing Translation

We translate FG programs by applying a form of dictionary-passing translation known from type classes [8]. As our target language we consider an untyped functional language with pattern matching where we use Haskell style syntax for expressions and patterns. Each FG interface translates to a pair consisting of a structure value and a dictionary. The dictionary holds the set of methods available as specified by the interface whereas the structure implements these methods. We refer to such pairs as *interface-values*. The translation is type-directed as we need type information to resolve method calls and construct the appropriate dictionaries and interface values.

Lines 23–49 show the result of applying our dictionary-passing[1] translation scheme to the FG program (lines 1–22). We use a tagged representation to encode FG structures in the target language. Hence, for each structure S, we assume a data constructor K_S, where we use pattern matching to represent field access (lines 23–26). For example, structure Pair implies the data constructor K_{Pair}. For convenience, we assume tuples and make use of don't care patterns _ .

A method call on an interface type translates to a lookup of the method in the dictionary of the corresponding interface-value. Like structures, interface-values

---

[1] Technically, we are passing around interface-values wrapping dictionaries of methods.

are tagged in the target language. For example, line 39 introduces the helper function eq_{Eq} to perform method lookup for method eq of interface Eq. The constructor for an Eq interface-value is K_{Eq}. Hence, we pattern match on K_{Eq} and extract the underlying structure value and method definition. A method call such as this.left.eq(...) in the source program (line 10) with receiver this.left of type Eq then translates to eq_{Eq} (left this)... (line 41).

A method call on a structure translates to the method definition for this receiver type. For example, we write eq_{Int} to refer to the translation of the method definition of eq for receiver type Int. A method call such as this.eq(...) in the source program (line 14) with receiver this of type Int then translates to eq_{Int} this... (line 43).

The construction of interface-values is based on structural subtype relations. Recall the three structural subtype relations we have seen earlier: (1) Int <: Eq and (2) Pair <: Eq and (3) Ord <: Eq. Relation (1) implies the interface-value constructor $toEq_{Int}$ (line 29), which builds an Eq interface-value via the given structure value y and a dictionary consisting only of the method eq_{Int}. Relation (2) implies a similar interface-value constructor $toEq_{Pair}$ (line 30). Relation (3) gives raise to the interface-value constructor $toEq_{Ord}$ (line 31), which transforms some Ord into an Eq interface-value. We assume that in case a dictionary consists of several methods, methods are kept in fixed order.

Type assertions imply interface-value destructors. For example, the source expression that.(Int) (line 7) performs a run-time check, asserting that that has type Int. In terms of the dictionary-passing translation, function $fromEq_{Int}$ (line 34) performs this check. Via the pattern K_{Eq} (K_{Int} y,) _) , we assert that the underlying target structure must result from Int. If the interface-value contains a value not tagged with K_{Int}, the pattern matching fails at run-time, just as the type assertion in FG. Interface-value destructors $fromEq_{Pair}$ and $fromOrd_{Int}$ (lines 35, 36) result from similar uses of type assertions.

To summarize, each use of structural subtyping implies a interface-value constructor being inserted in the target program. For example, typing the source expression p.eq(p) in line 21 relies on structural subtyping Pair <: Eq because argument p has type Pair but method eq requires a parameter of type Eq. Thus, the translation of this expression is eq_{Pair} p ($toEq_{Pair}$ p) in line 49.

Similarly, type assertions imply interface-value destructors. For example, the source expression that.(Pair).left in line 10 use a type assertion on that, which has type Eq. Thus, it translates to the target expression left ($fromEq_{Pair}$ that) in line 41.

We continue by introducing FG and our target language followed by the full details of the dictionary-passing translation.

3   Featherweight Go

Featherweight Go (FG) [7] is a tiny fragment of Go containing only structures, methods and interfaces. Figure 2 gives the syntax of FG. With the exception of variable bindings in function bodies, the primitive type int with operations ==

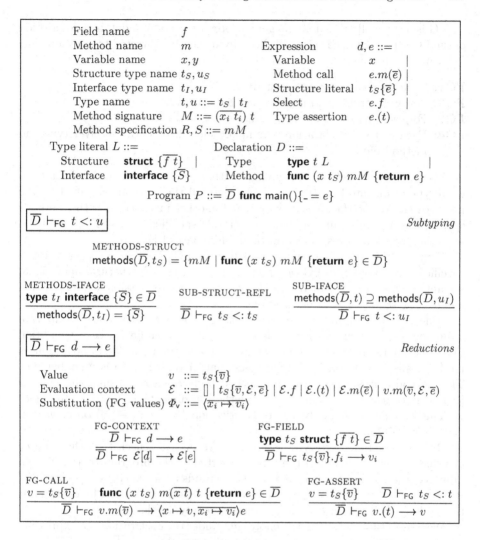

Fig. 2. Featherweight Go (FG)

and $<$, and the primitive type **bool** with operations **&&** and **||**, we can represent the example from Fig. 2 in FG. Compared to the original presentation of FG [7] we use symbol L instead of T (for type literals), and omit the **package** keyword at the start of a FG program. Overbar notation $\overline{\xi}^n$ denotes the sequence $\xi_1 \ldots \xi_n$ for some syntactic construct ξ, where in some places commas separate the sequence items. If irrelevant, we omit the n and simply write $\overline{\xi}$. Using the index variable i under an overbar marks the parts that vary from sequence item to sequence item; for example, $\overline{\xi' \xi_i}^n$ abbreviates $\xi' \xi_1 \ldots \xi' \xi_n$ and $\overline{\xi_j}^q$ abbreviates $\xi_{j1} \ldots \xi_{jq}$.

FG is a statically typed language. For brevity, we omit a detailed description of the FG typing rules as they will show up in the type-directed translation. The following conditions must be satisfied.

FG1: Structures must be non-recursive.

FG2: For each struct, field names must be distinct.

FG3: For each interface, method names must be distinct.

FG4: Each method declaration is uniquely identified by the receiver type and method name.

FG supports structural subtyping, written $\overline{D} \vdash_{\mathsf{FG}} t <: u$. A struct t_S is a subtype of an interface t_I if t_S implements all the methods specified by the interface t_I. An interface t_I is a subtype of another interface u_I if the methods specified by t_I are a superset of the methods specified by u_I. The structural subtyping relations are specified in the middle part of Fig. 2.

Next, we consider the dynamic semantics of FG. The bottom part of Fig. 2 specifies the reduction of FG programs by making use of structural operational semantics rules of the form $\overline{D} \vdash_{\mathsf{FG}} d \longrightarrow e$ to reduce expression d to expression e under the sequence $\overline{D}$ of declarations.

Rule FG-CONTEXT makes use of evaluation contexts with holes to apply a reduction inside an expression. Rule FG-FIELD deals with field access. Condition FG2 guarantees that field name lookup is unambiguous. Rule FG-CALL reduces method calls. Condition FG4 guarantees that method lookup is unambiguous. The method call is reduced to the method body e where we map the receiver argument to a concrete value v and method arguments x_i to concrete values v_i. This is achieved by applying the substitution $\langle x \mapsto v, \overline{x_i \mapsto v_i} \rangle$ on e, written $\langle x \mapsto v, \overline{x_i \mapsto v_i} \rangle e$.

Rule FG-ASSERT covers type assertions. We need to check that the type t_S of value v is consistent with the type t asserted in the program text. If t is an interface, then t_S must implement all the methods as specified by this interface. If t is a struct type, then t must be equal to t_S. Both checks can be carried out by checking that t_S and t are in a structural subtype relation.

We write $\overline{D} \vdash_{\mathsf{FG}} e \longrightarrow^* v$ to denote that under the declarations $\overline{D}$, expression e reduces to the value v in a finite number of steps. We write $\overline{D} \vdash_{\mathsf{FG}} e \longrightarrow^k v$ to denote that under the declarations $\overline{D}$, expression e reduces to the value v within at most k steps. This means we might need fewer than k steps but k are clearly sufficient to reduce the expression to some value. If there is no such v for any number of steps, we say that e is *irreducible* w.r.t. $\overline{D}$, written $\mathsf{irred}(\overline{D}, e)$.

4 Target Language

$$
\begin{array}{llll}
\text{Expression} & E ::= \\
\quad\text{Variable} & X \mid Y & | & \text{Pattern clause} \quad Cls ::= Pat \to E \\
\quad\text{Constructor} & K & | & \text{Pattern} \qquad\quad Pat ::= K\,\overline{X} \\
\quad\text{Application} & E\ E & | & \text{Program} \qquad\ \ Prog ::= \textbf{let}\ \overline{Y_i = \lambda X_i.E_i} \\
\quad\text{Abstraction} & \lambda X.E & | & \qquad\qquad\qquad\qquad \textbf{in}\ E \\
\quad\text{Pattern case} & \textbf{case}\ E\ \textbf{of}\ [\overline{Cls}] &
\end{array}
$$

$$
\begin{array}{lll}
\text{TL values} & V & ::= X \mid K\,\overline{V} \\
\text{TL evaluation context} & \mathcal{R} & ::= [\,] \mid K\,\overline{V}\mathcal{R}\overline{E} \mid \textbf{case}\ \mathcal{R}\ \textbf{of}\ [\overline{Pat \to E}] \mid \mathcal{R}\ E \mid V\ \mathcal{R} \\
\text{Substitution (TL values)} & \varPhi_{\mathsf{V}} & ::= \langle \overline{X \mapsto V} \rangle \\
\text{Substitution (TL methods)} & \varPhi_{\mathsf{m}} & ::= \langle \overline{Y \mapsto \lambda X.E} \rangle
\end{array}
$$

$\boxed{\varPhi_{\mathsf{m}} \vdash_{\mathsf{TL}} E \longrightarrow E'}$ $\hfill$ *TL expression reductions*

TL-CONTEXT
$$\dfrac{\varPhi_{\mathsf{m}} \vdash_{\mathsf{TL}} E \longrightarrow E'}{\varPhi_{\mathsf{m}} \vdash_{\mathsf{TL}} \mathcal{R}[E] \longrightarrow \mathcal{R}[E']}$$

TL-LAMBDA
$$\varPhi_{\mathsf{m}} \vdash_{\mathsf{TL}} (\lambda X.E)\ V \longrightarrow \langle X \mapsto V \rangle E$$

TL-CASE
$$\dfrac{K\ \overline{X_i}^n \to E' \in [\overline{Pat \to E}]}{\varPhi_{\mathsf{m}} \vdash_{\mathsf{TL}} \textbf{case}\ K\ \overline{V_i}^n\ \textbf{of}\ [\overline{Pat \to E}] \longrightarrow \langle \overline{X_i \mapsto V_i}^n \rangle E'}$$

TL-METHOD
$$\varPhi_{\mathsf{m}} \vdash_{\mathsf{TL}} Y\ E \longrightarrow \varPhi_{\mathsf{m}}(Y)\ E$$

$\boxed{\vdash_{\mathsf{TL}} Prog \longrightarrow Prog'}$ $\hfill$ *TL reductions*

TL-PROG
$$\dfrac{\langle \overline{Y_i \mapsto \lambda X_i.E_i} \rangle \vdash_{\mathsf{TL}} E \longrightarrow E'}{\vdash_{\mathsf{TL}} \textbf{let}\ \overline{Y_i = \lambda X_i.E_i}\ \textbf{in}\ E \longrightarrow \textbf{let}\ \overline{Y_i = \lambda X_i.E_i}\ \textbf{in}\ E'}$$

Fig. 3. Target Language (TL)

Figure 3 specifies the syntax and dynamic semantics of our target language (TL). We use capital letters for constructs of the target language. Target expressions E include variables X, Y, data constructors K, function application, lambda abstraction and case expressions to pattern match against constructors. In a case expression with only one pattern clause, we often omit the brackets and just write **case** E **of** $Pat \to E$. A program consists of a sequence of function definitions and a (main) expression. The function definitions are the result of translating FG method definitions.

We assume data constructors for tuples up to some fixed but arbitrary size. The syntax $(\overline{E}^n)$ constructs an n-tuple when used as an expression, and deconstructs it when used in a pattern context. At some places, we use nested patterns as an abbreviation for nested case expressions. The notation $\lambda Pat.E$ stands for $\lambda X.\textbf{case}\ X\ \textbf{of}\ [Pat \to E]$, where X is fresh.

Representing the example from Fig. 2 in the target language requires some more straightforward extensions: integers with operations == and <, booleans with operations && and | |, let-bindings inside expressions, and top-level bindings. The target language can encode the last two features via lambda-abstractions and top-level let-bindings.

The structural operational semantics employs two types of substitutions. Substitution Φ_V records the bindings resulting from pattern matching and function applications. Substitution Φ_m records the bindings for translated method definitions (i.e. for top-level let-bindings). Target values consist of constructors and variables. A variable may be a value if it refers to a yet to be evaluated method binding.

Reduction of programs is mapped to reduction of expressions under a method substitution. See rule TL-PROG. The remaining reduction rules are standard.

We write $\Phi_m \vdash_{TL} E \longrightarrow^* V$ to denote that under substitution Φ_m, expression E reduces to the value V in a finite number of steps. We write $\Phi_m \vdash_{TL} E \longrightarrow^k V$ to denote that under substitution Φ_m, expression E reduces to V within at most k steps. This means we might need fewer than k steps but k are clearly sufficient. If there is no such V for any number of steps, we say that E is *irreducible* w.r.t. Φ_m, written $\mathsf{irred}(\Phi_m, E)$.

5   Dictionary-Passing Translation

We formalize the dictionary-passing translation of FG to TL. The translation rules are split over two figures. Figure 4 covers methods, programs and some expressions. Figure 5 covers structural subtyping and type assertions. The translation rules are guided by type checking the FG program. The gray shaded parts highlight target terms that are generated. If these parts are ignored, the translation rules are effectively equivalent to the FG type checking rules [7]. We assume that conditions FG1-4 hold as well.

We use the following conventions. We assume that each FG variable x translates to the TL variable X. For each structure t_S we introduce a TL constructor K_{t_S}. For each interface t_I we introduce a TL constructor K_{t_I}. In the translation, a source value of an interface type t_I translates to an interface-value tagged by K_{t_I}. The interface-value contains the underlying structure value and a dictionary consisting of the set of methods as specified by the interface. For each method declaration **func** $(x\ t_S)\ mM\ \{\textbf{return}\ e\}$ we introduce a TL variable X_{m,t_S}, thereby relying on FG4 which guarantees that m and t_S uniquely identify this declaration. We write Δ to denote typing environments where we record the types of FG variables. The notation $[n]$ is a short-hand for the set $\{1, \ldots, n\}$.

5.1   Translating Programs, Methods and Expressions

The translation of programs and methods boils down to the translation of expressions involved. Rule TD-METHOD translates a specific method declaration, rule TD-PROG collects all method declarations and also translates the main expression. See Fig. 4.

Convention for mapping source to target terms

$$x \rightsquigarrow X \quad t_S \rightsquigarrow K_{t_S} \quad t_I \rightsquigarrow K_{t_I} \quad \textbf{func } (x\ t_S)\ mM\ \{\textbf{return } e\} \rightsquigarrow X_{m,t_S}$$

$$\text{FG Environment } \Delta ::= \{\} \mid \{x:t\} \mid \Delta \cup \Delta$$

$$\boxed{\overline{D} \vdash_{\textsf{meth}} \textbf{func } (x\ t_S)\ m(\overline{x\ t})\ t \rightsquigarrow E} \qquad\qquad \textit{Translating method declarations}$$

TD-METHOD
$$\frac{\text{distinct}(x,\overline{x}^n) \qquad \langle \overline{D}, \{x:t_S, \overline{x_i:t_i}^n\}\rangle \vdash_{\textsf{exp}} e:t \rightsquigarrow E}{\overline{D} \vdash_{\textsf{meth}} \textbf{func } (x\ t_S)\ m(\overline{x\ t}^n)\ t\ \{\textbf{return } e\} \rightsquigarrow \lambda X.\lambda(\overline{X}^n).E}$$

$$\boxed{\vdash_{\textsf{prog}} P \rightsquigarrow Prog} \qquad\qquad \textit{Translating programs}$$

TD-PROG
$$\frac{\begin{array}{c}\langle \overline{D}, \{\}\rangle \vdash_{\textsf{exp}} e:t \rightsquigarrow E \\ \overline{D} \vdash_{\textsf{meth}} D'_i \rightsquigarrow E_i \qquad D'_i = \textbf{func } (x_i\ t_{Si})\ m_iM_i\ \{\textbf{return } e_i\} \\ (\text{for all } i \in [n], \text{where } \overline{D'}^n \text{ are the } \textbf{func} \text{ declarations in } \overline{D})\end{array}}{\vdash_{\textsf{prog}} \overline{D}\ \textbf{func } \text{main}()\{\_=e\} \rightsquigarrow \textbf{let } \overline{X_{m_i,t_{Si}} = E_i}^n \textbf{ in } E}$$

$$\boxed{\langle \overline{D}, \Delta\rangle \vdash_{\textsf{exp}} e:t \rightsquigarrow E} \qquad\qquad \textit{Translating expressions}$$

TD-VAR
$$\frac{(x:t) \in \Delta}{\langle \overline{D}, \Delta\rangle \vdash_{\textsf{exp}} x:t \rightsquigarrow X}$$

TD-STRUCT
$$\frac{\textbf{type } t_S \textbf{ struct } \{\overline{f\ t}^n\} \in \overline{D} \qquad \langle \overline{D}, \Delta\rangle \vdash_{\textsf{exp}} e_i:t_i \rightsquigarrow E_i \quad (\text{for all } i \in [n])}{\langle \overline{D}, \Delta\rangle \vdash_{\textsf{exp}} t_S\{\overline{e}^n\}:t_S \rightsquigarrow K_{t_S}\ (\overline{E}^n)}$$

TD-ACCESS
$$\frac{\langle \overline{D}, \Delta\rangle \vdash_{\textsf{exp}} e:t_S \rightsquigarrow E \qquad \textbf{type } t_S \textbf{ struct } \{\overline{f\ t}^n\} \in \overline{D}}{\langle \overline{D}, \Delta\rangle \vdash_{\textsf{exp}} e.f_i:t_i \rightsquigarrow \textbf{case } E \textbf{ of } K_{t_S}\ (\overline{X}^n) \to X_i}$$

TD-CALL-STRUCT
$$\frac{m(\overline{x\ t}^n)\ t \in \textsf{methods}(\overline{D}, t_S) \\ \langle \overline{D}, \Delta\rangle \vdash_{\textsf{exp}} e:t_S \rightsquigarrow E \qquad \langle \overline{D}, \Delta\rangle \vdash_{\textsf{exp}} e_i:t_i \rightsquigarrow E_i \quad (\text{for all } i \in [n])}{\langle \overline{D}, \Delta\rangle \vdash_{\textsf{exp}} e.m(\overline{e}^n):t \rightsquigarrow X_{m,t_S}\ E\ (\overline{E}^n)}$$

TD-CALL-IFACE
$$\frac{\langle \overline{D}, \Delta\rangle \vdash_{\textsf{exp}} e:t_I \rightsquigarrow E \qquad \textbf{type } t_I \textbf{ interface } \{\overline{S}\} \in \overline{D} \\ S_j = m(\overline{x\ t}^n)t \qquad \langle \overline{D}, \Delta\rangle \vdash_{\textsf{exp}} e_i:t_i \rightsquigarrow E_i \quad (\text{for all } i \in [n]) \qquad X, \overline{X}^q \text{ fresh}}{\langle \overline{D}, \Delta\rangle \vdash_{\textsf{exp}} e.m(\overline{e}^n):t \rightsquigarrow \textbf{case } E \textbf{ of } K_{t_I}\ (X, \overline{X}^q) \to X_j\ X\ (\overline{E}^n)}$$

Fig. 4. Translation of methods, programs and expressions

$$\boxed{\langle \overline{D}, \Delta \rangle \vdash_{\mathsf{exp}} e : t \rightsquigarrow E} \qquad\qquad \textit{Translating structural subtyping and type assertions}$$

TD-SUB
$$\frac{\langle \overline{D}, \Delta \rangle \vdash_{\mathsf{exp}} e : t \rightsquigarrow E_2 \qquad \overline{D} \vdash_{\mathsf{iCons}} t <: u \rightsquigarrow E_1}{\langle \overline{D}, \Delta \rangle \vdash_{\mathsf{exp}} e : u \rightsquigarrow E_1\ E_2}$$

TD-ASSERT
$$\frac{\langle \overline{D}, \Delta \rangle \vdash_{\mathsf{exp}} e : t_I \rightsquigarrow E_2 \qquad \overline{D} \vdash_{\mathsf{iDestr}} t_I \searrow u \rightsquigarrow E_1}{\langle \overline{D}, \Delta \rangle \vdash_{\mathsf{exp}} e.(u) : u \rightsquigarrow E_1\ E_2}$$

$$\boxed{\overline{D} \vdash_{\mathsf{iCons}} t <: u_I \rightsquigarrow E} \qquad\qquad \textit{Interface-value construction}$$

TD-CONS-STRUCT-IFACE
$$\frac{\textbf{type } t_I \textbf{ interface } \{\overline{S}\} \in \overline{D} \qquad \mathsf{methods}(\overline{D}, t_S) \supseteq \overline{S} \qquad \overline{S} = \overline{mM}^n}{\overline{D} \vdash_{\mathsf{iCons}} t_S <: t_I \rightsquigarrow \lambda X.K_{t_I}\ (X, \overline{X_{m_i, t_S}}^n)}$$

TD-CONS-IFACE-IFACE
$$\frac{\begin{array}{c}\textbf{type } t_I \textbf{ interface } \{\overline{R}^n\} \in \overline{D} \\ \textbf{type } u_I \textbf{ interface } \{\overline{S}^q\} \in \overline{D} \qquad S_i = R_{\pi(i)} \quad (\text{for all } i \in [q])\end{array}}{\overline{D} \vdash_{\mathsf{iCons}} t_I <: u_I \rightsquigarrow \lambda X.\textbf{case } X \textbf{ of } K_{t_I}\ (X, \overline{X}^n) \rightarrow K_{u_I}\ (X, X_{\pi(1)}, \ldots, X_{\pi(q)})}$$

$$\boxed{\overline{D} \vdash_{\mathsf{iDestr}} t_I \searrow u \rightsquigarrow E} \qquad\qquad \textit{Interface-value destruction}$$

TD-DESTR-IFACE-STRUCT
$$\frac{\textbf{type } t_I \textbf{ interface } \{\overline{R}^n\} \in \overline{D} \qquad \overline{D} \vdash_{\mathsf{FG}} t_S <: t_I}{\overline{D} \vdash_{\mathsf{iDestr}} t_I \searrow t_S \rightsquigarrow \lambda X.\textbf{case } X \textbf{ of } K_{t_I}\ (K_{t_S}\ Y, \overline{X}^n) \rightarrow K_{t_S}\ Y}$$

TD-DESTR-IFACE-IFACE
$$\frac{\begin{array}{c}X, Y, Y', \overline{X}^n \text{ fresh} \qquad \textbf{type } t_I \textbf{ interface } \{\overline{R}^n\} \in \overline{D} \\ \text{for all } \textbf{type } t_{Sj} \textbf{ struct } \{\overline{f\ u}\} \in \overline{D} \text{ with } \overline{D} \vdash_{\mathsf{iCons}} t_{Sj} <: u_I \rightsquigarrow E_j : \\ Cls_j = K_{t_{Sj}}\ Y' \rightarrow (E_j\ (K_{t_{Sj}}\ Y'))\end{array}}{\overline{D} \vdash_{\mathsf{iDestr}} t_I \searrow u_I \rightsquigarrow \lambda X.\textbf{case } X \textbf{ of } K_{t_I}\ (Y, \overline{X}^n) \rightarrow \textbf{case } Y \textbf{ of } [\overline{Cls}]}$$

Fig. 5. Translation of structural subtyping and type assertions

The translation rules for expressions are of the form $\langle \overline{D}, \Delta \rangle \vdash_{\mathsf{exp}} e : t \rightsquigarrow E$ where $\overline{D}$ refers to the sequence of FG declarations, Δ refers to type binding of local variables, e is the to be translated FG expression, t its type and E the resulting target term. Departing from FG's original typing rules [7], the translation rules are non-syntax directed due the structural subtyping rule TD-SUB defined in Fig. 5. We could integrate this rule via the other rules but this would make all the rules harder to read. Hence, we prefer to have a separate rule TD-SUB.

We now discuss the translations rules for the expression forms in Fig. 4. (The remaining expression forms are covered in Fig. 5, to be explained in the next section.) Rule TD-VAR translates variables and follows our convention that x translates to X. Rule TD-STRUCT translates a structure creation. The translated field elements E_i are collected in a tuple and tagged via the constructor K_{t_S}. Rule TD-ACCESS uses pattern matching to capture field access in the translation.

Method calls are dealt with by rules TD-CALL-STRUCT and TD-CALL-IFACE. Rule TD-CALL-STRUCT covers the case that the receiver e is of the structure type t_S. The first precondition guarantees that an implementation for this specific method call exists. (See Fig. 2 for the auxiliary methods.) Hence, we can assume that we have available a corresponding definition for X_{m,t_S} in our translation. The method call then translates to applying X_{m,t_S} first on the translated receiver E, followed by the translated arguments collected in a tuple $(\overline{E}^n)$.

Rule TD-CALL-IFACE assumes that receiver e is of interface type t_I, so e translates to interface-value E. Hence, we pattern match on E to access the underlying value and the desired method in the dictionary. We assume that the order of methods in the dictionary corresponds to the order of method declarations in the interface. The preconditions guarantee that t_I provides a method m as demanded by the method call, where j denotes the index of m in interface t_I.

5.2   Translating Structural Subtyping and Type Assertions

Rule TD-SUB deals with structural subtyping and yields an interface-value constructor derived via rules TD-CONS-STRUCT-IFACE and TD-CONS-IFACE-IFACE in Fig. 5. These rules correspond to the structural subtyping rules in Fig. 2 but additionally yield an interface-value constructor.

The preconditions in rule TD-CONS-STRUCT-IFACE check that structure t_S implements the interface t_I. This guarantees the existence of method definitions X_{m_i,t_S}. Hence, we can construct the desired interface-value.

The preconditions in rule TD-CONS-IFACE-IFACE check that t_I's methods are a superset of u_I's methods. This is done via the total function $\pi : \{1,\ldots,q\} \to \{1,\ldots,n\}$ that matches each (wanted) method in u_I against a (given) method in t_I. We use pattern matching over the t_I's interface-value to extract the wanted methods. Recall that dictionaries maintain the order of method as specified by the interface.

Type assertions $e.(u)$ are dealt with in rule TD-ASSERT and translate to an interface-value destructor. In the static semantics of FG there are two cases to consider. Both cases assume that the expression e is of some interface type t_I. The first case asserts the type of a structure and the second case asserts the type of an interface. Asserting that a structure is of the type of another structure is not allowed in FG, because such a type assertion would never succeed.

Rule TD-DESTR-IFACE-STRUCT deals with the case that we assert the type of a structure t_S. If t_S does not implement the interface t_I, the assertion can never be successful. Hence, we find the precondition $\overline{D} \vdash_{\mathsf{FG}} t_S <: t_I$. We pattern match over the interface-value that represents t_I to check the underlying value matches t_S and extract the value. It is possible that some other value has been used to implement the interface-value that represents t_I. In such a case, the pattern match fails and we experience run-time failure.

Rule TD-DESTR-IFACE-IFACE deals with the case that we assert the type of an interface u_I on a value of type t_I. The outer case expression extracts the value Y underlying interface-value t_I (this case never fails). We then check if we can construct an interface-value for u_I via Y. This is done via an inner case expression. For each structure t_{Sj} implementing u_I, we have a pattern clause Cls_j that matches against the constructor $K_{t_{Sj}}$ of the structure and then constructs an interface-value for u_I. There are two reasons for run-time failure here. First, Y (used to implement t_I) might not implement u_I; that is, none of the pattern clauses Cls_j match. Second, $\overline{Cls}$ might be empty because no receiver at all implements u_I. This case is rather unlikely and could be caught statically.

6 Properties

We wish to show that the dictionary-passing translation preserves the dynamic behavior of FG programs. To establish this property we make use of (binary) logical relations [16,20]. Logical relations express that related terms behave the same. We say that source and target terms are *equivalent* if they are related under the logical relation. The goal is to show that FG expressions and target expressions resulting from the dictionary-passing translation are equivalent.

For example, in FG the run-time value associated with an interface type is a structure that implements the interface whereas in our translation each interface translates to an interface-value. To establish that a structure $t_S\{\overline{v}\}$ and an interface-value $K_{t_I}(V, \overline{V})$ are equivalent w.r.t. some interface t_I we need to require that

- (Struct-I-Val-1) $t_S\{\overline{v}\}$ and V are equivalent w.r.t. t_S, and
- (Struct-I-Val-2) method definitions for receiver type t_S are equivalent to $\overline{V}$.

Because signatures in method specifications of an interface may refer to the interface itself, there may be cyclic dependencies that then result in well-foundness issues of the definition of logical relations. To solve this issue we include a step index [1]. We explain this technical point via the example in Fig. 1. We will write $e \approx E \in [\![t]\!]_k$ to denote that FG expression e and TL expression E are in a logical relation w.r.t. the FG type t, where k is the step index. Similarly, **func** $(x\ t_S)\ R\ \{\mathbf{return}\ e\} \approx V \in [\![R]\!]_k$ expresses that a FG method declaration and a TL value V are in a logical relation w.r.t. the FG method specification R.

$$\boxed{e \approx E \in [\![t]\!]_k^{\langle \overline{D}, \Phi_m \rangle}} \qquad\qquad \text{\textit{FG expressions versus TL expressions}}$$

RED-REL-EXP
$$\frac{\forall k_1 < k, k_2 < k, v, V.(k - k_1 - k_2 > 0 \wedge \overline{D} \vdash_{\mathsf{FG}} e \longrightarrow^{k_1} v \wedge \Phi_m \vdash_{\mathsf{TL}} E \longrightarrow^{k_2} V)}{\implies v \approx V \in [\![t]\!]_{k-k_1-k_2}^{\langle \overline{D}, \Phi_m \rangle}}{e \approx E \in [\![t]\!]_k^{\langle \overline{D}, \Phi_m \rangle}}$$

$$\boxed{v \approx V \in [\![t]\!]_k^{\langle \overline{D}, \Phi_m \rangle}} \qquad\qquad \text{\textit{FG values versus TL values}}$$

RED-REL-STRUCT
$$\frac{\textbf{type } t_S \textbf{ struct } \{\overline{f\ t}^n\} \in \overline{D} \qquad \forall i \in [n].v_i \approx V_i \in [\![t_i]\!]_k^{\langle \overline{D}, \Phi_m \rangle}}{t_S\{\overline{v}^n\} \approx K_{t_S}\ (\overline{V}^n) \in [\![t_S]\!]_k^{\langle \overline{D}, \Phi_m \rangle}}$$

RED-REL-IFACE
$$\frac{V = K_{u_S}\ \overline{V'} \qquad \forall k_1 < k.v \approx V \in [\![u_S]\!]_{k_1}^{\langle \overline{D}, \Phi_m \rangle} \qquad \mathsf{methods}(\overline{D}, t_I) = \{\overline{mM}^n\}}{\forall k_2 < k, i \in [n].\mathsf{methodLookup}(\overline{D}, (m_i, u_S)) \approx V_i \in [\![m_i M_i]\!]_{k_2}^{\langle \overline{D}, \Phi_m \rangle}}{v \approx K_{t_I}\ (V, \overline{V}^n) \in [\![t_I]\!]_k^{\langle \overline{D}, \Phi_m \rangle}}$$

$$\boxed{\textbf{func } (x\ t_S)\ mM\ \{\textbf{return } e\} \approx V \in [\![mM]\!]_k^{\langle \overline{D}, \Phi_m \rangle}} \quad \text{\textit{FG methods versus TL methods}}$$

RED-REL-METHOD
$$\frac{\forall k' \leq k, v', V', \overline{v_i}^n, \overline{V_i}^n.(v' \approx V' \in [\![t_S]\!]_{k'}^{\langle \overline{D}, \Phi_m \rangle} \wedge (\forall i \in [n].v_i \approx V_i \in [\![t_i]\!]_{k'}^{\langle \overline{D}, \Phi_m \rangle}))}{\implies \langle x \mapsto v', \overline{x_i \mapsto v_i}^n \rangle e \approx (V\ V')\ (\overline{V}^n) \in [\![t]\!]_{k'}^{\langle \overline{D}, \Phi_m \rangle}}{\textbf{func } (x\ t_S)\ m(\overline{x\ t}^n)\ t\ \{\textbf{return } e\} \approx V \in [\![m(\overline{x\ t}^n)\ t]\!]_k^{\langle \overline{D}, \Phi_m \rangle}}$$

$$\boxed{\langle \overline{D}, \Phi_m, \Delta \rangle \vdash_{\mathsf{red-rel}}^k \Phi_v \approx \Phi_V} \qquad \text{\textit{FG versus TL value bindings}}$$

RED-REL-VB
$$\frac{\forall (x : t) \in \Delta.\Phi_v(x) \approx \Phi_V(X) \in [\![t]\!]_k^{\langle \overline{D}, \Phi_m \rangle}}{\langle \overline{D}, \Phi_m, \Delta \rangle \vdash_{\mathsf{red-rel}}^k \Phi_v \approx \Phi_V}$$

$$\boxed{\vdash_{\mathsf{red-rel}}^k \overline{D} \approx \Phi_m} \qquad\qquad \text{\textit{FG declarations versus TL method bindings}}$$

RED-REL-DECLS
$$\frac{\forall \textbf{func } (x\ t_S)\ mM\ \{\textbf{return } e\} \in \overline{D} :}{\textbf{func } (x\ t_S)\ mM\ \{\textbf{return } e\} \approx X_{m,t_S} \in [\![mM]\!]_k^{\langle \overline{D}, \Phi_m \rangle}}{\vdash_{\mathsf{red-rel}}^k \overline{D} \approx \Phi_m}$$

Fig. 6. Relating FG to TL reduction

Consider the FG expression $\mathsf{Int}\{1\}$ from example in Fig. 1. When viewed at type Eq, our translation yields the interface-value K_{Eq} (K_{Int} 1, $\mathsf{eq}_{\mathsf{Int}}$). We need to establish $\mathsf{Int}\{1\} \approx K_{\mathsf{Eq}}$ (K_{Int} 1, $\mathsf{eq}_{\mathsf{Int}}$) $\in [\![\mathsf{Eq}]\!]_{k_1}$.

(1) $\text{Int}\{1\} \approx \mathsf{K_{Eq}} \ (\mathsf{K_{Int}} \ 1, \ \mathsf{eq_{Int}}) \in [\![\mathsf{Eq}]\!]_{k_1}$

   if (2) $\text{Int}\{1\} \approx \mathsf{K_{Int}} \ 1 \in [\![\mathsf{Int}]\!]_{k_2}$ and

      (3) **func** $(\mathsf{x} \ \mathsf{Int})$ **eq**$(\mathsf{y} \ \mathsf{Eq})$ **bool** $\{\mathbf{return}\, e\} \approx \mathsf{eq_{Int}} \in [\![\mathsf{eq(y\ Eq)\ bool}]\!]_{k_3}$
      where $k_2 < k_1, k_3 < k_1$

         if (4) $\forall v_1 \approx V_1 \in [\![\mathsf{Int}]\!]_{k_4}, v_2 \approx V_2 \in [\![\mathsf{Eq}]\!]_{k_4}.$
             $\langle x \mapsto v_1, y \mapsto v_2 \rangle e \approx \mathsf{eq_{Int}} \ V_1 \ V_2 \in [\![\mathbf{bool}]\!]_{k_4}$ where $k_4 \leq k_3$

Following (Struct-I-Val-1) and (Struct-I-Val-2), (1) holds if we can establish (2) and (3). (2) is easy to establish. (3) holds if we can establish (4). (4) states that for equivalent inputs the respective method definitions are equivalent as well. Without the step index, establishing $. \approx . \in [\![\mathsf{Eq}]\!]$ would reduce to establishing $. \approx . \in [\![\mathsf{Eq}]\!]$. We are in a cycle. With the step index, $. \approx . \in [\![\mathsf{Eq}]\!]_{k_1}$ reduces to $. \approx . \in [\![\mathsf{Eq}]\!]_{k_4}$ where $k_4 < k_1$. The step index represents the number of reduction steps we can take and will be reduced for each reduction step. Thus, we can give a well-founded definition of our logical relations.

Figure 6 gives the step-indexed logical relations to relate FG and TL terms. Rule RED-REL-EXP relates FG and TL expressions. The expressions are in a relation assuming that the resulting values are in a relation where we impose a step limit on the number of reduction steps that can be taken. We additionally find parameters $\overline{D}$ and $\varPhi_\mathsf{m}$ as FG and TL expressions refer to method definitions.

Rule RED-REL-STRUCT is straightforward. Rule RED-REL-IFACE has been motivated above. We make use of the following helper function to lookup up the method definition for a specific pair of method name and receiver type.

$$\frac{\mathbf{func}\ (x\ t_S)\ m M\ \{\mathbf{return}\ e\} \in \overline{D}}{\mathsf{methodLookup}(\overline{D}, (m, t_S)) = \mathbf{func}\ (x\ t_S)\ m M\ \{\mathbf{return}\ e\}}$$

Rule RED-REL-METHOD covers method definitions. Rule RED-REL-VB ensures that the substitutions from free variables to values are related. Rule RED-REL-DECLS ensures that our labeling for the translation of method definitions is consistent.

A fundamental property of step-indexed logical relations is that if two expressions are in a relation for k steps then they are also in a relation for any smaller number of steps.

Lemma 1 (Monotonicity). *Let* $e \approx E \in [\![t]\!]_k^{\langle \overline{D}, \varPhi_\mathsf{m} \rangle}$ *and* $k' \leq k$. *Then, we find that* $e \approx E \in [\![t]\!]_{k'}^{\langle \overline{D}, \varPhi_\mathsf{m} \rangle}$.

Proof. By induction over the derivation $e \approx E \in [\![t]\!]_k^{\langle \overline{D}, \varPhi_\mathsf{m} \rangle}$.
Case RED-REL-EXP:

$$\frac{\forall k_1 < k, k_2 < k, v, V.(k - k_1 - k_2 > 0 \land \overline{D} \vdash_\mathsf{FG} e \longrightarrow^{k_1} v \land \varPhi_\mathsf{m} \vdash_\mathsf{TL} E \longrightarrow^{k_2} V)}{\Longrightarrow v \approx V \in [\![t]\!]_{k-k_1-k_2}^{\langle \overline{D}, \varPhi_\mathsf{m} \rangle}}{e \approx E \in [\![t]\!]_k^{\langle \overline{D}, \varPhi_\mathsf{m} \rangle}}$$

If either e or E is irreducible, $e \approx E \in [\![t]\!]_{k'}^{\langle \overline{D}, \Phi_m \rangle}$ holds immediately because the universally quantified statement in the premise holds vacuously.

Otherwise, we find $\overline{D} \vdash_{\mathsf{FG}} e \longrightarrow^{k_1} v$ and $\Phi_m \vdash_{\mathsf{TL}} E \longrightarrow^{k_2} V$ for some k_1 and k_2. If $k' - k_1 - k_2 \leq 0$, $e \approx E \in [\![t]\!]_{k'}^{\langle \overline{D}, \Phi_m \rangle}$ holds again immediately.

Otherwise, by induction applied on the premise of rule RED-REL-EXP we find that $v \approx V \in [\![t]\!]_{k' - k_1 - k_2}^{\langle \overline{D}, \Phi_m \rangle}$ and we are done for this case.

Case RED-REL-STRUCT:

$$\frac{\mathbf{type}\ t_S\ \mathbf{struct}\ \{\overline{f\ t}^n\} \in \overline{D} \qquad \forall i \in [n]. v_i \approx V_i \in [\![t_i]\!]_k^{\langle \overline{D}, \Phi_m \rangle}}{t_S\{\overline{v}^n\} \approx K_{t_S}\ (\overline{V}^n) \in [\![t_S]\!]_k^{\langle \overline{D}, \Phi_m \rangle}}$$

Follows immediately by induction.

Case RED-REL-IFACE:

$$\frac{\begin{array}{c} V = K_{u_S}\ \overline{V'} \\ (1)\ \forall k_1 < k. v \approx V \in [\![u_S]\!]_{k_1}^{\langle \overline{D}, \Phi_m \rangle} \qquad \mathsf{methods}(\overline{D}, t_I) = \{\overline{mM}^n\} \\ (2)\ \forall k_2 < k, i \in [n]. \mathsf{methodLookup}(\overline{D}, (m_i, u_S)) \approx V_i \in [\![m_i M_i]\!]_{k_2}^{\langle \overline{D}, \Phi_m \rangle} \end{array}}{v \approx K_{t_I}\ (V, \overline{V}^n) \in [\![t_I]\!]_k^{\langle \overline{D}, \Phi_m \rangle}}$$

Consider the first premise (1). If there exists $k_1 < k'$ then $v \approx V \in [\![u_S]\!]_{k_1}^{\langle \overline{D}, \Phi_m \rangle}$. Otherwise, this premise holds vacuously. The same argument for $k_2 < k'$ applies to the second premise (2). Hence, $v \approx K_{t_I}\ (V, \overline{V_i}^n) \in [\![t_I]\!]_{k'}^{\langle \overline{D}, \Phi_m \rangle}$. □

A similar monotonicity result applies to method definitions and declarations. Monotonicity is an essential property to obtain the following results.

Interface-value constructors and destructors preserve equivalent expressions via logical relations as stated by the following results.

Lemma 2 (Structural Subtyping versus Interface-Value Constructors). *Let $\overline{D} \vdash_{\mathsf{iCons}} t <: u \rightsquigarrow E_1$ and $\vdash_{\mathsf{red-rel}}^k \overline{D} \approx \Phi_m$ and $e \approx E_2 \in [\![t]\!]_k^{\langle \overline{D}, \Phi_m \rangle}$. Then, we find that $e \approx E_1\ E_2 \in [\![u]\!]_k^{\langle \overline{D}, \Phi_m \rangle}$.*

Lemma 3 (Type Assertions versus Interface-Value Destructors). *Let $\overline{D} \vdash_{\mathsf{iDestr}} t \searrow u \rightsquigarrow E_1$ and $\vdash_{\mathsf{red-rel}}^k \overline{D} \approx \Phi_m$ and $e \approx E_2 \in [\![t]\!]_k^{\langle \overline{D}, \Phi_m \rangle}$. Then, we find that $e.(u) \approx E_1\ E_2 \in [\![u]\!]_k^{\langle \overline{D}, \Phi_m \rangle}$.*

Based on the above we can show that target expressions resulting from FG expressions and target methods resulting from FG methods are equivalent.

Lemma 4 (Expression Equivalence). *Let $\langle \overline{D}, \Delta \rangle \vdash_{\mathsf{exp}} e : t \rightsquigarrow E$ and Φ_v, Φ_V, Φ_m such that $\langle \overline{D}, \Phi_m, \Delta \rangle \vdash_{\mathsf{red-rel}}^k \Phi_v \approx \Phi_V$ and $\vdash_{\mathsf{red-rel}}^k \overline{D} \approx \Phi_m$ for some k. Then, we find that $\Phi_v(e) \approx \Phi_V(E) \in [\![t]\!]_k^{\langle \overline{D}, \Phi_m \rangle}$.*

Lemma 5 (Method Equivalence). *Let* $\overline{D} \vdash_{\mathsf{meth}} \mathbf{func}\ (x\ t_S)\ m(\overline{x\ t}^n)\ t$ {**return** e} $\leadsto \lambda X.\lambda(\overline{X}^n).E$. *Then, we find that* $\vdash_{\mathsf{red-rel}}^k \overline{D} \approx \varPhi_{\mathsf{m}}$ *where* $\varPhi_{\mathsf{m}}(X_{m,t_S}) = \lambda X.\lambda(\overline{X}^n).E$ *for any* k.

The lengthy proofs of the above results are given in the online version of this paper.[2]

From Lemmas 4 and 5 we can derive our main result that the dictionary-passing translation preserves the dynamic behavior of FG programs.

Theorem 1 (Program Equivalence). *Let* $\vdash_{\mathsf{prog}} \overline{D}\ \mathbf{func}\ \mathsf{main}()\{\_ = e\} \leadsto$ **let** $\overline{X_{m_i,t_{S_i}} = E_i}^n$ **in** E *where we assume that* e *has type* t. *Then, we find that* $e \approx E \in [\![t]\!]_k^{\langle \overline{D}, \varPhi_{\mathsf{m}} \rangle}$ *for any* k *where* $\varPhi_{\mathsf{m}} = \langle \overline{X_{m_i,t_{S_i}} \mapsto E_i}^n \rangle$.

Proof. Follows from Lemmas 4 and 5. □

Our main result also implies that our translation is coherent. Recall that the translation rules are non-syntax directed because of rule TD-SUB. Hence, we could for example insert an (albeit trivial) interface-value constructor resulting from $\overline{D} \vdash_{\mathsf{iCons}} t_I <: t_I \leadsto E$. Hence, there might be different target terms for the same source term. Our main result guarantees that all targets obtained preserve the meaning of the original program.

7   Related Work and Conclusion

The dictionary-passing translation is well-studied in the context of Haskell type classes [24]. A type class constraint translates to an extra function parameter, constraint resolution provides a dictionary with the methods of the type class for this parameter. In our translation from Featherweight Go [7], dictionaries are not supplied as separate parameters because FG does not support parametric polymorphism. Instead, a dictionary is always passed as part of an interface-value, which combines the dictionary with the concrete value implementing the interface. Thus, interface-values can be viewed as representations of existential types [10,13,23]. How to adapt our dictionary-passing translation scheme to FG extended with parametric polymorphism (generics) is something we plan to consider in future work.

In the context of type classes it is common to show that resulting target programs are well-typed. For example, see the work by Hall and coworkers [8]. Typed target terms in this setting require System F and richer variants depending on the kind of type class extensions that are considered [19]. Our target terms are untyped and we pattern match over constructors to check for "run-time types". For example, see rule TD-DESTR-IFACE-STRUCT in Fig. 5. There are various ways to support dynamic typing in a typed setting. For example, we could employ GADTs as described by Peyton Jones and coworkers [9]. A simply-typed first order functional language with GADTs appears then to be sufficient as a typed

---

[2] https://arxiv.org/abs/2106.14586.

target language for Featherweight Go. This will require certain adjustments to our dictionary-passing translation. We plan to study the details in future work.

Another important property in the type class context is coherence. Bottu and coworkers [3] make use of logical relations to state equivalence among distinct target terms resulting from the same source type class program. Thanks to our main result Theorem 1, we get coherence for free. We believe it is worthwhile to establish a property similar to Theorem 1 for type classes. We could employ a simple denotational semantics for source type class programs such as [14,21] which is then related to target programs obtained via the dictionary-passing translation. This is something that has not been studied so far and another topic for future work.

Method dictionaries bear some resemblance to virtual method tables (vtables) used to implement virtual method dispatch in object-oriented languages [5]. The main difference between vtables and dictionaries is that there is a fixed connection between an object and its vtable (via the class of the object), whereas the connection between a value and a dictionary may change at runtime, depending on the type the value is used at. Dictionaries allow access to a method at a fixed offset, whereas vtables in the presence of multiple inheritance require a more sophisticated lookup algorithm [2].

Subtyping for interfaces in Go is based purely on width subtyping, there is no support for depth subtyping [15]: a subtype might provide more methods than the super-interface, but method signatures must match invariantly. Method dispatch in Go is performed only on the receiver of the method call. Multidispatch [4,18] refers to the ability to dispatch on multiple arguments, but this approach turns out to be difficult in combination with structural subtyping [11].

To summarize the results of the paper at hand: we defined a dictionary-passing translation from Featherweight Go to a untyped lambda calculus with pattern matching. The compiler for the full Go language [22] employs a similar dictionary-passing approach. We proved that the translation preserves the dynamic semantics of Featherweight Go, using step-indexed logical relations.

Acknowledgments. We thank the APLAS'21 reviewers for their helpful and constructive feedback.

References

1. Ahmed, A.: Step-indexed syntactic logical relations for recursive and quantified types. In: Sestoft, P. (ed.) ESOP 2006. LNCS, vol. 3924, pp. 69–83. Springer, Heidelberg (2006). https://doi.org/10.1007/11693024_6
2. Alpern, B., Cocchi, A., Fink, S.J., Grove, D., Lieber, D.: Efficient implementation of java interfaces: invokeinterface considered harmless. In: Proceedings of OOPSLA 2001, ACM (2001)
3. Bottu, G.J., Xie, N., Marntirosian, K., Schrijvers, T.: Coherence of type class resolution. Proc. ACM Program. Lang. 3(ICFP), 1–28 (2019)
4. Chambers, C.: Object-oriented multi-methods in Cecil. In: Madsen, O.L. (ed.) ECOOP 1992. LNCS, vol. 615, pp. 33–56. Springer, Heidelberg (1992). https://doi.org/10.1007/BFb0053029

5. Driesen, K., Hölzle, U.: The direct cost of virtual function calls in C++. In: Proceedings of OOPSLA 1996, ACM (1996)
6. Gosling, J., et al.: The Java Language Specification, Java SE 16 edn (2021). https://docs.oracle.com/javase/specs/jls/se16/html/index.html
7. Griesemer, R., et al.: Featherweight go. Proc. ACM Program. Lang. **4**(OOPSLA), 1–29 (2020)
8. Hall, C.V., Hammond, K., Peyton Jones, S.L., Wadler, P.L.: Type classes in Haskell. ACM Trans. Program. Lang. Syst. **18**(2), 109–132 (1996)
9. Peyton Jones, S., Weirich, S., Eisenberg, R.A., Vytiniotis, D.: A reflection on types. In: Lindley, S., McBride, C., Trinder, P., Sannella, D. (eds.) A List of Successes That Can Change the World. LNCS, vol. 9600, pp. 292–317. Springer, Cham (2016). https://doi.org/10.1007/978-3-319-30936-1_16
10. Läufer, K.: Type classes with existential types. J. Funct. Prog. **6**(3), 485–518 (1996)
11. Malayeri, D., Aldrich, J.: Integrating nominal and structural subtyping. In: Vitek, J. (ed.) ECOOP 2008. LNCS, vol. 5142, pp. 260–284. Springer, Heidelberg (2008). https://doi.org/10.1007/978-3-540-70592-5_12
12. Marlow, S.: Haskell 2010 language report (2010). https://www.haskell.org/onlinereport/haskell2010/
13. Mitchell, J.C., Plotkin, G.D.: Abstract types have existential type. ACM Trans. Program. Lang. Syst. **10**(3), 470–502 (1988)
14. Morris, J.G.: A simple semantics for Haskell overloading. In: Proceedings of Haskell 2014, New York, ACM (2014)
15. Pierce, B.: Types and Programming Languages, 1st edn. MIT Press, Cambridge (2002)
16. Plotkin, G.: Lambda-definability and logical relations. Unpublished manuscript (1973)
17. Reppy, J.H.: Concurrent ML: design, application and semantics. In: Functional Programming, Concurrency, Simulation and Automated Reasoning, pp. 165–198. Springer, Heidelberg (1993)
18. Steele, G.L.: Common LISP: The Language, 2nd edn. Digital Press, Amsterdam (1990)
19. Sulzmann, M., Chakravarty, M.M.T., Jones, S.P., Donnelly, K.: System F with type equality coercions. In: Proceedings of TLDI 2007, New York, ACM (2007)
20. Tait, W.W.: Intensional interpretations of functionals of finite type I. J. Symb. Log. **32**(2), 198–212 (1967)
21. Thatte, S.R.: Semantics of type classes revisited. In: Proceedings of LISP 1994, pp. 208–219. ACM (1994)
22. The Go programming language (2021). https://golang.org
23. Thiemann, P., Wehr, S.: Interface types for Haskell. In: Ramalingam, G. (ed.) APLAS 2008. LNCS, vol. 5356, pp. 256–272. Springer, Heidelberg (2008). https://doi.org/10.1007/978-3-540-89330-1_19
24. Wadler, P., Blott, S.: How to make ad-hoc polymorphism less ad hoc. In: Proceedings of POPL 1989, New York, ACM (1989)

Hybrid Quantum-Classical Circuit Simplification with the ZX-Calculus

Agustín Borgna[1,2]([⊠]) [iD], Simon Perdrix[1] [iD], and Benoît Valiron[3] [iD]

[1] CNRS LORIA, Inria-MOCQUA, Université de Lorraine, 54000 Nancy, France
`agustin.borgna@loria.fr`
[2] Université Paris-Saclay, CNRS, Laboratoire Méthodes Formelles,
91405 Orsay, France
[3] École CentraleSupélec, Laboratoire Méthodes Formelles, 91405 Orsay, France

Abstract. We present a complete optimization procedure for hybrid quantum-classical circuits with classical parity logic. While common optimization techniques for quantum algorithms focus on rewriting solely the pure quantum segments, there is interest in applying a global optimization process for applications such as quantum error correction and quantum assertions. This work, based on the pure-quantum circuit optimization procedure by Duncan et al., uses an extension of the formal graphical ZX-calculus called $ZX_{\frac{\pi}{4}}$ as an intermediary representation of the hybrid circuits to allow for granular optimizations below the quantum-gate level. We define a translation from hybrid circuits into diagrams that admit the graph-theoretical focused-gFlow property, needed for the final extraction back into a circuit. We then derive a number of gFlow-preserving optimization rules for $ZX_{\frac{\pi}{4}}$ diagrams that reduce the size of the graph, and devise a strategy to find optimization opportunities by rewriting the diagram guided by a Gauss elimination process. Then, after extracting the circuit, we present a general procedure for detecting segments of circuit-like $ZX_{\frac{\pi}{4}}$ diagrams which can be implemented with classical gates in the extracted circuit. We have implemented our optimization procedure as an extension to the open-source python library PyZX.

Keywords: ZX-calculus · Optimization · Gflow · Hybrid circuits · PyZX

1 Introduction

The description of quantum algorithms commonly involves quantum operations interacting with classical data in its inputs, outputs, or intermediary steps via measurements or state preparations. Some applications such as quantum error correction [2,9] and quantum assertions [18,24] explicitly introduce classical measurements and logic between quantum computations. In general, quantum programming languages usually allow for measurements and classically controlled quantum operators mixed-in with unitary gates [7,11,15,22]. Furthermore, Jozsa [14] conjectured that any polynomial-time quantum algorithm can

© Springer Nature Switzerland AG 2021
H. Oh (Ed.): APLAS 2021, LNCS 13008, pp. 121–139, 2021.
https://doi.org/10.1007/978-3-030-89051-3_8

be simulated by polylogarithmic-depth quantum computation interleaved with polynomial-depth classical computation. As such, there is interest in contemplating this kind of structures in circuits.

A popular alternative representation of quantum circuit is based on the *ZX-calculus* [5,6], a formal diagrammatic language which presents a more granular representation of quantum circuits and has been successfully used in applications such as MBQC [10], quantum error correction [4], and quantum foundations. Carette et al. [3] introduced an extension of the calculus called ZX$_{\pm}$ which allows for the representation of operations interacting with the classical environment by adding a discarding *ground generator* to the diagrams.

It is natural to look at the problem of optimizing algorithm implementations by taking in consideration the environment in addition to the pure quantum fragments. However, most common optimization strategies focus solely on the latter without contemplating the hybrid quantum-classical structure [1,12]. One of this pure optimizations introduced by Duncan et al. [8] uses the ZX-calculus to apply granular rewriting rules that ignore the boundaries of each quantum gate. We will refer to it as the *Clifford optimization* algorithm. Their rewriting steps preserve a diagram property called *gFlow admittance* that is required for the final extraction of the ZX diagrams into circuits. The ZX optimization method was latter used by Kissinger and van de Wetering [17] in their method to reduce the number of T-gates in quantum circuits.

In this work we define the natural extension of the pure Clifford optimization algorithm by Duncan et al. to hybrid quantum-classical circuits using the ZX$_{\pm}$ calculus.

Our circuit optimization procedure forgets the difference between quantum and classical wires during the simplification process, representing connections as a single type of edge. This allows it to optimize the complete hybrid system as an homogeneous diagram, and results in similar representations for operations that can be done either quantumly or classically. Generally, in a physical quantum computer, the classical operations are simpler to implement than their quantum counterparts, and quantum simulators can exploit the knowledge of which wires carry classical data to simplify their operation. As such, it is beneficial to extract classical gates in the resulting circuit where possible.

The contribution of this paper are as follows.

- We specify a translation of hybrid circuits into ZX$_{\pm}$ diagrams in a special *graph like* form that admits a gFlow, restricting the classical segments of the input to parity circuits.
- We introduce a number of gFlow-preserving rewriting rules that interact with the discarding generator to reduce the size of the diagrams, and devise a strategy to find optimization opportunities using the biadjacency matrix of the graph cut between spiders connected to ground generators and the other nodes in the diagram.
- We define a procedure to extract ZX$_{\pm}$ diagrams with a gFlow back into hybrid quantum-classical circuits, including ancilla initialization and termination.

- We define the problem of $ZX_{\pm}$-classicalization as labelling segments of the diagrams which can be implemented classically and present an heuristic solution. Our method can be applied on the extracted circuits to maximize the number of classically implemented operations.

The paper is organized in the following manner. In Sect. 2 we define the quantum circuits, present a syntactic description of the $ZX_{\pm}$ calculus and its equation, and give an intuition behind the representation of hybrid quantum-classical circuits. Section 3 then introduces the graph-like family of $ZX_{\pm}$ diagrams and defines the focused gFlow property over the graphs. We then define the translation of quantum circuits into graph-like diagrams in Sect. 4. In Sect. 5 we introduce the optimization rules and our strategy for finding rule matches which we use to describe the complete optimization algorithm. Then in Sect. 6 we define the extraction algorithm and finally we present our classicalization procedure in Sect. 7. In Sect. 8 we discuss the results of testing our procedure on randomly generated circuits.

2   Hybrid Quantum-Classical Circuits and the Grounded ZX-Calculus

In pure quantum operations, a single qubit quantum state is represented as a unitary vector in the Hilbert space $\mathbb{C}^2$. We use Dirac notation to talk about such vectors and denote an arbitrary state as $|\phi\rangle$. States can be described as a linear combination of vectors in a basis such as the computational basis $\{|0\rangle, |1\rangle\}$ or the diagonal basis $\{|+\rangle, |-\rangle\}$, where $|\pm\rangle = \frac{1}{\sqrt{2}}(|0\rangle \pm |1\rangle)$. A third, less commonly used basis called Y is formed by the vectors $|\circlearrowleft\rangle = \frac{1}{\sqrt{2}}(|0\rangle + i|1\rangle)$ and $|\circlearrowright\rangle = \frac{1}{\sqrt{2}}(|0\rangle - i|1\rangle)$. Qubit spaces can be composed using a tensor product, and we denote $|\phi\psi\rangle = |\phi\rangle \otimes |\psi\rangle$.

Hybrid quantum-classical systems include classical data, which can be represented in a qubit space as orthonormal basis vectors (e.g. by representing a logical 0 as the state $|0\rangle$ and a logical 1 as $|1\rangle$), but additionally include a *trace* or *measurement* operation, which probabilistically projects a qubit into a vector in an orthogonal basis. The resulting probabilistic distribution of pure states is called a mixed state, and is better represented by a *density matrix*, a positive semi-definite Hermitian operator of trace one in the $(\mathbb{C}^{2\times2})^{\otimes n}$ Hilbert space, for an n-qubit system. Given a probabilistic distribution of pure states $\{(p_i, |\phi_i\rangle)\}$, their density matrix is constructed as $\sum_i p_i |\phi_i\rangle\langle\phi_i|$, where $\langle\phi| = |\phi\rangle^\dagger$.

Quantum circuit diagrams consist of horizontal lines carrying each the information of one qubit, read from right to left, with some attached gates applying unitary transformations over the qubit states. We use the universal set of operations $\{\text{CNOT}, X_\alpha, Z_\alpha, H\}$ for pure-quantum diagrams. When α is limited to multiples of $\frac{\pi}{4}$ this roughly corresponds to the approximately universal Clifford+T group. Some rotation gates have specific names, such as $Z = Z_\pi$, $X = X_\pi$, $S = Z_{\frac{\pi}{2}}$, $\text{HSH} = X_{\frac{\pi}{2}}$, and $T = Z_{\frac{\pi}{4}}$. We additionally include ancilla initialization and termination, and swaps. The representation of each mentioned gate is reproduced here.

Hybrid circuits represent bit-carrying classical wires using doubled lines and extend the set of gates with some classical operations such as {NOT, XOR, AND}, classical fan-out, bit swaps, measurement, qubit preparation, and classically controlled versions of the X_π and Z_π gates. We depict them respectively as follows.

Circuits are inductively constructed from these generators, wire identities, and parallel and serial composition, ensuring that only wires of the same type connect with each other.

In this work we restrict the input to circuits with classical parity logic, choosing not to include AND gates due to the complexity of their representation as $ZX_{\pm}$ diagrams, which might result in the introduction of additional non-Clifford gates during the extraction procedure (refer to Sect. 9 for further discussion).

The ZX-calculus is a formal graphical language which provides a fine-grained representation of quantum operations. We present a brief introduction to its definition, including the $ZX_{\pm}$ extension to represent classical operations. Refer to [23] for a complete description of both calculi.

ZX diagrams representing pure-quantum linear maps are composed by *wires*, *spiders*, and *Hadamard boxes*. We read the diagrams from right to left and represent inputs and outputs as open-ended wires. The Hadamard box ——□—— swaps the computational and diagonal basis, mapping $|0\rangle$ to $|+\rangle$, $|1\rangle$ to $|-\rangle$ and vice versa. The spiders are arbitrary-degree nodes labelled with a real phase $\alpha \in [0, 2\pi)$ that come in either green or red color, named Z- and X-spiders respectively. When α is a multiple π or $\frac{\pi}{2}$, we call them *Pauli* or *Clifford*-spiders respectively. We refer to the set of spiders connected to outputs and inputs of the diagram as O and I respectively, and call their members *output-* and *input-spiders*.

A degree-2 green (resp. red) spider corresponds to applying a Z_α (X_α) operation over a qubit. Phaseless spiders represents nodes with phase 0 and can be interpreted as copying the computational basis vectors in the case of green spiders, or the diagonal basis vectors for red spiders.

$$\alpha |00\rangle + \beta |11\rangle + \gamma |01\rangle + \theta |10\rangle \quad \longrightarrow \quad \alpha |000\rangle + \beta |111\rangle$$

Spiders of the same color can be fused together, adding their phases. It is important to note that the relative position of the nodes in ZX diagrams do not alter their interpretation, as only the topology matters.

The ZX-calculus comes equipped with a complete set of formal rewrite rules [13]. We reproduce it here ignoring scalars.

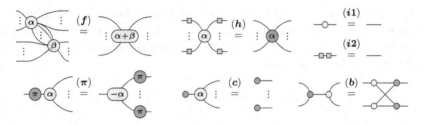

The ZX$_{\frac{1}{4}}$ calculus [3] is an extension to the ZX-calculus which is able to easily describe interactions with the environment. The diagrams have a standard interpretation as completely positive linear maps between quantum mixed states. In addition to the ZX generators and rewrite rules, the calculus introduces a *ground* generator (⊥) which represent the tracing operation, or the discarding of information. When connected to a degree-3 green spider, this can correspond to a measurement operation over the computational basis or a qubit initialization from a bit.

$$-\boxed{\nearrow}\!\!\top \quad \sim \quad -\!\!\!\!\!\bigcirc\!\!\!\!\top \quad \sim \quad =\!\!\!\top$$

We refer to the spiders attached to ⊥ generators as ⊥-spiders. Notice that we use the same kind of wire for both classical and quantum data, since as previously discussed we can encode the latter as the former. We will later introduce a method to differentiate between the two types of wire by using the ⊥-spiders in Sect. 7.

ZX$_{\frac{1}{4}}$ extends the set of rewriting rules with the following additions.

$$\Vert\!\!-\!\!\bigcirc \overset{(k)}{=} \begin{array}{c}\ulcorner\quad\urcorner\\ \lfloor\quad\rfloor\end{array} \qquad \Vert\!\!-\!\!\square\!\!- \overset{(l)}{=} \Vert\!\!- \qquad \Vert\!\!-\!\!\alpha\!\!- \overset{(m)}{=} \Vert\!\!- \qquad \begin{array}{c}\Vert\!\!-\!\!\bigcirc\!\!-\\ \Vert\!\!-\!\!\bullet\!\!-\end{array} \overset{(n)}{=} \begin{array}{c}\Vert\!\!-\\ \Vert\!\!-\end{array}$$

Intuitively, the ⊥ generator discards any operation applied over a single qubit. Multiple discards can be combined into one vio the following rule, derived from rules (m), (n), and (k).

$$\begin{array}{c}\Vert\!\!-\\ \Vert\!\!-\end{array}\!\!\!\!\!\rangle\!\!-\!\!\bigcirc\!\!- \overset{(gg)}{=} \Vert\!\!-\!\!\!-\!\!\bigcirc\!\!-$$

For simplicity in our diagrams, we replace solely as notation the Hadamard boxes with "Hadamard wires" drawn in blue, as follows.

$$-\!\!\bigcirc\!\!\cdots\!\!-\!\!\bigcirc\!\!- = -\!\!\bigcirc\!\!-\!\!\square\!\!-\!\!\bigcirc\!\!-$$

We introduce two additional derived equations. One to erase duplicated Hadamard wires, as proven by Duncan et al. [8], and another to discard them, from a combination of rules (m) and (l).

$$\vdots\!\!\rangle\!\!\bigcirc\!\!\cdots\!\!\bigcirc\!\!\langle\vdots \overset{(fh)}{=} \vdots\!\!\rangle\!\!\bigcirc \quad \bigcirc\!\!\langle\vdots \qquad \Vert\!\!-\!\!\bigcirc\!\!\cdots\!\!\bigcirc\!\!\langle\vdots \overset{(ml)}{=} \Vert\!\!-\!\!\bigcirc\!\!\langle\vdots$$

We utilise !-box notation [20] to represent infinite families of diagrams with segments that can be repeated 0 or more times. In the following sections it will be useful to use this notation for depicting more complex diagrams. Here we present an example of its usage.

$$ \multimap\!\!\fbox{α_i} \in \{\multimap , \multimap\!\!\circ\!\!\cdots\!\!\alpha_0 , \multimap\!\!\overset{\alpha_0}{\underset{\alpha_1}{<}} , \dots \} $$

3   Graph-Like Diagrams and Focused gFlow

A ZX diagram is said to be in *graph-like* form [8] when it contains only Z-spiders connected by Hadamard wires, there are no parallel edges nor self-loops, and no spider is connected to more than one input or output. We define the graph-like form for $ZX_{\pm}$ diagrams and include a weaker version allowing a node to connect to an input, a ground, and any number of outputs simultaneously. When defining a translation from quantum circuits into $ZX_{\pm}$ diagrams it will be simpler to initially generate weakly graph-like diagrams and transform the final result into the strict version afterwards.

Definition 1. *A $ZX_{\pm}$ diagram is graph-like (respectively weakly graph-like) when:*

1. *All spiders are Z-spiders.*
2. *Z-spiders are only connected via Hadamard edges.*
3. *There are no parallel Hadamard edges or self-loops.*
4. *There is no pair of connected $\pm$ -spiders.*
5. *Every input, output, or $\pm$ is connected to a Z-spider.*
6. *Every Z-spider connected to a $\pm$ has phase 0.*
7. *Every Z-spider is connected to at most one input, one output, or one $\pm$ (at most one input and at most one $\pm$).*

Proposition 1. *Every $ZX_{\pm}$ diagram is equivalent to a weakly graph-like $ZX_{\pm}$ diagram. Indeed, Duncan et al. [8] proved that any pure-ZX diagram is equivalent to a graph-like one. The proof can be extended to weakly graph-like $ZX_{\pm}$ diagrams simply by applying rule (l) to eliminate Hadamards connected to $\pm$ generators, rule (gg) to eliminate duplicated $\pm$ connected to the same spider, and rule (n) to disconnect wires between $\pm$ -spiders.*

Lemma 1. *There exists an algorithm to transform an arbitrary $ZX_{\pm}$ diagram into an equivalent strictly graph-like diagram.*

Proof. By adding identity spiders to the inputs and outputs. Cf. long version on arXiv.

Once a diagram is in a weakly graph-like form, all its spiders as well as all its internal connections are of the same kind. We can refer to its underlying structure as a simple undirected graph, marking the nodes connected to inputs and outputs. In addition, $\pm$ generators or the $\pm$ -spiders connected to them can be seen as outputs discarding information into the environment. This is known as the underlying open graph of a diagram.

Definition 2. *An open graph is a triple (G, S, T) where $G = (V, E)$ is an undirected graph, and $S \subseteq V$ is a set of sources and $T \subseteq V$ is a set of sinks. For a weakly graph-like $ZX_{\doteq}$ diagram D, the underlying open graph $G(D)$ is the open graph whose vertices are spiders D, whose edges correspond to Hadamard edges, whose set S is the subset of spiders connected to the inputs of D, and whose set T is the subset of spiders connected to the outputs of D or to ground generators.*

The underlying open graph of a ZX diagram produced from our translation of quantum circuits verify a graph-theoretic invariant called *focused gFlow* [19]. This structure—originally conceived for graph states in measurement based quantum computation—gives a notion of flow of information and time on the diagram. It will be required to guide the extraction strategy in Sect. 6.

Definition 3. *Given an open graph G, a focused gFlow $(g, \prec)$ on G consists of a function $g : \overline{T} \to 2^{\overline{S}}$ and a partial order $\prec$ on the vertices V of G such that for all $u \in \overline{T}$, $\mathsf{Odd}_G(g(u)) \cap \overline{T} = \{u\}$ and $\forall v \in g(u), u \prec v$ where $2^{\overline{S}}$ is the powerset of $\overline{S}$ and $\mathsf{Odd}_G(A) := \{v \in V(G) \mid |N(v) \cap A| \equiv 1 \bmod 2\}$ is the odd neighbourhood of A.*

4   Translation of Hybrid Quantum-Classical Circuits

We describe our translation from hybrid quantum-classical circuits into strictly graph-like $ZX_{\doteq}$ diagrams by steps. First, we translate each individual gate directly into a weakly graph-like diagram and connect them with regular wires. We define this translation $T(\cdot)$ by inductively translating the gates as described in Table 1 immediately followed by the application of the spider fusion rule (f) and rules (gg) and (fh) to remove all regular wires, duplicated $\doteq$ generators, and parallel Hadamard wires, ensuring that the final combined diagram is in a weakly graph-like form. An example of this translation is shown in Fig. 1.

Notice that the translation maps both classical and quantum wires to regular $ZX_{\doteq}$ diagram edges. We keep track of which inputs and outputs of the diagram were connected to classical wires and introduce $\doteq$ generators for the operations that interact with the environment. In Sect. 6 we present a method to detect the sections of the final circuit that can be implemented as classical operations by looking at the classical inputs/outputs and the $\doteq$ generators, independently of which wires where originally classical.

Lemma 2. *The $ZX_{\doteq}$ diagram resulting from the translation $T(\cdot)$ is weakly graph-like.*

Proof. By induction on the circuit construction. Cf. long version on arXiv.

After the translation, we can apply Lemma 1 to obtain a strictly graph-like diagram. This step essentially separates the $\doteq$ generators from the inputs and outputs, allowing the optimization procedure to move them around and let them interact with other parts of the diagram.

Table 1. Translation from hybrid quantum-classical circuits into ZX$_{\pm}$ diagrams.

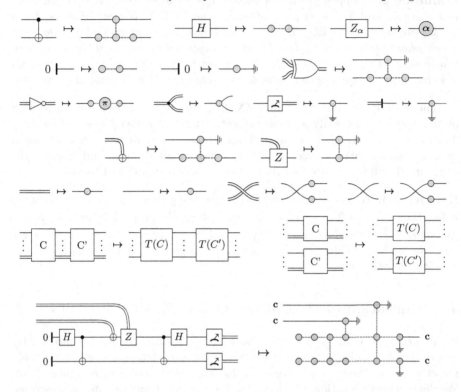

Fig. 1. Example translation of the superdense coding circuit into a ZX$_{\pm}$ diagram with labelled inputs and outputs, and subsequent application of the spider-fusion rule.

Lemma 3. *If C is a hybrid quantum-classical circuit and D is the graph-like ZX$_{\pm}$ diagram obtained from the translation $T(C)$ and Lemma 1, then $G(D)$ admits a focused gFlow.*

Proof. By induction on C. Cf. long version on arXiv.

5   Grounded ZX Optimization

Our simplification strategy for ZX$_{\pm}$ diagrams is based on eliminating nodes from the diagram by systematically applying a number of rewriting rules while preserving the existence of a focused gFlow. In this section we introduce the new rules, define a strategy to maximize their effectiveness, and finally use it together with the pure-ZX optimization to define our algorithm.

5.1   Basic Simplification Rules

Duncan et al. [8] presented the following gFlow-preserving *local complementation* and *pivoting* rules for the ZX calculus in their optimization procedure.

These rules effectively reduce the size of the diagram by at least one node on each application by eliminating internal proper-Clifford spiders and Pauli spider pairs respectively.

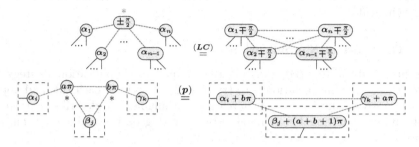

These rules can be applied directly in ZX$_\pm$ diagrams when the target spiders are not connected to a $\pm$ generator. For the cases where some of the target spiders are $\pm$-spiders, we introduce the following altered rules. Their derivation can be found in the long version on arXiv.

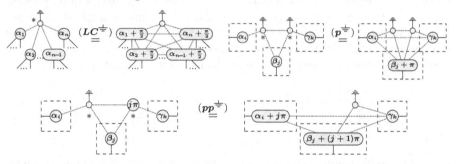

Notice that both rules $(\boldsymbol{LC^{\pm}})$ and $(\boldsymbol{p^{\pm}})$ do not decrease the number of spiders in the diagram. As such, we will focus on rule $(\boldsymbol{pp^{\pm}})$ for our optimization.

If $(\boldsymbol{pp^{\pm}})$ is applied with a non-$\pm$ spider connected to a boundary, the rule produces a $\pm$-spider connected to an input or output thus needing to add an identity operation as described in Lemma 1 to preserve the graph-like property. Since in this case we add additional nodes to the graph, we will only apply rule $(\boldsymbol{pp^{\pm}})$ on a boundary spider if it can be followed by another node-removing rule.

Additionally, we will use rules $(\boldsymbol{ml})$ and $(\boldsymbol{k})$ directly to remove nodes in the diagram when there are $\pm$-spiders with degree 1 or 0 in the graph, respectively.

Lemma 4. *If the non-$\pm$ spider in the lhs of the discarding rule $(\boldsymbol{ml})$ is not connected to an output or input, then applying the rule over a graph-like diagram D preserves the existence of a focused gFlow.*

Proof. If the non-$\pm$ spider in the lhs is not connected to an input or output of the diagram, then applying the rule does not break the graph-like property of D. The preservation of the gFlow follows from $\pm$-spiders being sinks of the underlying open graph.

Lemma 5. *Rules $(LC^{\doteq})$, $(p^{\doteq})$, and $(pp^{\doteq})$ preserve the existence of a focused gFlow.*

Proof. Notice that rules $(LC^{\doteq})$, $(p^{\doteq})$, and $(pp^{\doteq})$ are compositions of gFlow-preserving rules.

5.2   Ground-Cut Simplification

The previously introduced rewriting rules require a simplification strategy to apply them. A simple solution is to try to find a match for each rule and apply them iteratively until no more matches are available. We describe a strategy that can find additional rule matches by operating on the biadjacency matrix between the $\doteq$-spiders and the non-$\doteq$ spiders.

Definition 4. *The ground-cut of a graph-like $ZX_{\doteq}$ diagram D is the cut resulting from splitting the $\doteq$ and non-$\doteq$ spiders in $G(D)$.*

Since the diagram is graph-like, there are no internal wires in the $\doteq$ partition. Given a $ZX_{\doteq}$ diagram D, we denote M_D the biadjacency matrix of its ground-cut, where rows correspond to $\doteq$-spiders and columns correspond to non-$\doteq$ spiders. We can apply all elementary row operations on the matrix by rewriting the diagram. The addition operation between the rows corresponding to the $\doteq$-spider u and the $\doteq$-spider v can be implemented via the following rule.

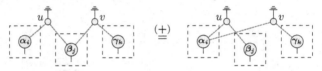

Using the elementary row operations we can apply Gaussian elimination on the ground-cut biadjacency matrix of a graph-like $ZX_{\doteq}$ diagram, generating in the process an equivalent diagram whose ground-cut biadjacency matrix is in reduced echelon form.

Any row in the ground-cut biadjacency matrix left without non-zero elements after applying Gaussian elimination corresponds to an isolated $\doteq$-spiders in the diagram that can be eliminated by rule (k). If the reduced row echelon form of the biadjacency matrix contains a row with exactly one non-zero elements, then that element corresponds to an isolated $\doteq$-spider and non-$\doteq$ spider pair in the diagram and therefore we can apply rule (ml) to remove the non-$\doteq$ spider.

5.3   The Algorithm

Based on the previous strategy, we define a terminating procedure which turns any graph-like $ZX_{\doteq}$ diagram into an equivalent *simplified* diagram that cannot be further reduced.

Definition 5. *A graph-like $ZX_{\doteq}$ diagram is in simplified-form if it does not contain any of the following, up to single-qubit unitaries on the inputs and outputs.*

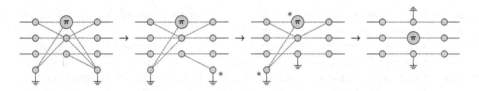

Fig. 2. Example of a diagram optimization applying a ground-cut simplification, a discard rule, and a Pauli elimination.

- *Interior proper Clifford spiders.*
- *Adjacent pairs of interior Pauli spiders.*
- *Interior Pauli spiders adjacent to boundary spiders.*
- *Interior Pauli spiders adjacent to ⩦-spiders.*
- *Degree-1 ⩦-spiders not connected to input or output spiders.*
- *Connected components not containing inputs nor outputs.*

We define an optimization algorithm that produces diagrams in simplified-form by piggybacking on the pure optimization procedure. This optimization applies the local complementations ($\boldsymbol{LC}$) and pivoting ($\boldsymbol{p}$) rules until there are no interior proper Clifford spiders or adjacent pairs of non-⩦ interior Pauli spiders. After the initial pure simplification, we continue our optimization as follows.

1. Repeat until no rule matches, removing wires between ⩦-spiders and parallel Hadamard connections after each step:
   (a) Run Gaussian elimination on the ground-cut of the diagram as described in Sect. 5.2.
   (b) Remove the grounds corresponding to null rows with rule ($\boldsymbol{k}$).
   (c) If any row of the biadjacency matrix has a single non-zero element, corresponding to a ⩦-spider connected to a spider v, then:
      i. If v is not a boundary spider, apply rule ($\boldsymbol{ml}$).
      ii. If v is a boundary spider and v is adjacent to a Pauli spider, apply rule ($\boldsymbol{ml}$) immediately followed by the procedure from Lemma 1 to make the diagram graph-like again. Then delete the Pauli neighbour using rule ($\boldsymbol{pp^{\ne}}$), to ensure that the step removes at least one node.
   (d) Apply Pauli spider elimination rule ($\boldsymbol{pp^{\ne}}$) until there are no Pauli spiders connected to ground spiders.
2. Remove any connected component of the graph without inputs or outputs.

Notice that each cycle the loop reduces the number of nodes in the graph, so this is a terminating procedure. Additionally, since each applied rule preserves the existence of a gFlow the final diagram admits a gFlow. An example run of the algorithm is shown in Fig. 2.

6   Circuit Extraction

Here we describe a general circuit extraction procedure for graph-like ZX$_{\rightleftharpoons}$ diagrams admitting a focused gFlow into hybrid quantum-classical circuits, by modifying the procedure for pure diagrams from the Clifford optimization. We present the pseudocode in Algorithm 1.

The algorithm progresses through the diagram from right-to-left, maintaining a set of spiders F, called the *frontier*, which represents the unextracted spiders connected to the extracted segment. Each frontier spider is assigned an output qubit line $Q(v)$. This set is initially populated by the nodes connected to outputs of the diagram. The strategy is to proceed backwards by steps, adding unextracted spiders into the frontier and deleting some of them to extract operations on the output circuit, in back-to-front order.

To find candidate spiders to add to the frontier we apply Gaussian elimination on the biadjacency matrix of the frontier and non-frontier spiders, similarly to the optimization method described in Sect. 5.2. The gFlow property of the graph ensures that we can always progress by extracting a node. It suffices to look at the set of non-frontier vertices maximal in the order and notice that, after the Gauss elimination, either we can choose a $\doteq$ -spider from the set, or a non-$\doteq$ spider that has a single connection to the frontier. A careful implementation of the biadjacency matrix row and column ordering can reduce the number of $\doteq$ -spider extractions when no non-$\doteq$ candidates are available. We require the following proposition to apply the row additions on the graph (Duncan et al. [8], Proposition 7.1).

Proposition 2. *For any $ZX_{\doteq}$ diagram D, the following equation holds:*

where M describes the biadjacency matrix of the relevant vertices, and M' is the matrix produced by adding row 2 to row 1 in M. Furthermore, if the diagram on the LHS has a focused gFlow, then so does the RHS.

In our pseudocode, the call to CLEANFRONTIER ensures that F only contains phaseless spiders without internal wires. Notice that it preserves the gFlow since it only modifies edges between sink nodes, and removes spiders with no other connections. After the while loop terminates, all outputs of the circuit will have been extracted. If there are inputs left unextracted, and since the diagram had a gFlow, we can discard them directly via measurement operations.

Finally, we add any necessary swap operations to map the inputs to the correct lines, and insert qubit initializations and measurements at inputs and outputs marked as classical. In Sect. 7 we detail a method to better detect the internal parts of the circuit that can be implemented classically.

In any case, each step of the while loop in Algorithm 1 line 5, preserves the gFlow of the diagram, and we can show that it terminates in at most $|V|$ steps: Indeed, if there are no non-frontier spiders, then a call to CLEANFRONTIER will

---

Algorithm 1. Circuit extraction

1: **function** EXTRACTION
2:     F : $Set\langle Node\rangle \leftarrow$ O, Q : $Map\langle Node, int\rangle \leftarrow \emptyset$
3:     **for all** $v \in$ F **do** Q$(v) \leftarrow$ Output connected to v
4:     CLEANFRONTIER(F, Q)
5:     **while** F $\neq \emptyset$ **do**
6:         Run Gauss elimination on the frontier biadjacency matrix M (Proposition 2)
7:         **if** a row of M has a single non-zero element **then**
8:             Let u and v be the corresponding non-frontier and frontier node
9:                 Q$(u) \leftarrow$ Q(v)
10:             Remove v from the diagram and add u to F
11:         **else**
12:             $v \leftarrow$ Arbitrary $\doteq$-spider in the neighbourhood of F
13:             Q$(v) \leftarrow$ New qubit line id
14:             Extract a classical bit termination on Q(v) and add u to F
15:         CLEANFRONTIER(F, Q)
16:     **for all** Unextracted $v \in I$ **do**
17:         Q$(v) \leftarrow$ Input connected to v
18:         Extract a measurement gate and a classical bit termination on Q(v)
19:         Assign the corresponding input to Q(v)
20: **function** CLEANFRONTIER(F, Q)
21:     **for all** $v \in$ F **do**
22:         **if** v is a $\doteq$-spider **then** Remove the $\doteq$, extract a measurement on Q(v)
23:         **if** v has a phase $\alpha \neq 0$ **then** Set $\alpha = 0$, extract a Z$_\alpha$ gate on Q(v)
24:         **for all** $u \in$ F, $v \sim u$ **do** Remove the wire, extract a CZ gate on Q(v), Q(u)
25:         **if** v is not connected to any other node **then**
26:             Remove v
27:             **if** $v \in$ I **then** assign the input to qubit Q
28:             **else** extract a $|+\rangle$ qubit initialization on Q(v)

---

remove all nodes from the frontier. Moreover, each step of the while loop in line 5 moves one non-frontier spider to F.

7   Circuit Classicalization

The extraction procedure described in Sect. 6 produces correct circuits that are almost completely composed by quantum gates and wires, without any classical operation. In this section we describe the general problem of detecting parts of the circuits that can be realized as classical operations, and introduce an efficient heuristic solution based on a local-search. Notice, however, that while we aim to recognize all classically realizable operations in the circuit the characteristics of each quantum computer may dictate the final choice between quantum and classical operators by taking into account the costs of exchanging data between both realms.

Given a ZX$_\pm$ diagram, we decorate its wires using the set of labels $\mathcal{L} = \{Q, X, Y, Z, \perp\}$. The label Z means that this particular wire can be replaced by a classical wire (possibly precomposed with a standard basis measurement and postcomposed by a qubit initialisation in the standard basis depending on whether the connected wires are also classical or not), and similarly for X and Y by adapting the basis of measurement/initialisation to the diagonal or Y basis. Q means that the wire is a quantum wire, and finally $\perp$ means that the wire can be removed by precomposing with a $\pm$ and postcomposing with a maximally mixed state. The set of labels form a partial order, $Q \geq X, Y, Z \geq \perp$.

A labelling L of a diagram D is a map from its edges into a pair of labels. The two labels, drawn at each end of the wire, indicate the origin of the constraint. Intuitively, $z \quad A$ means that the wire is produced in such a way that guarantees that the qubit carries classical information encoded in the computational basis, whereas $A \quad z$ means that the wire can be replaced by a classical wire because some process will force this qubit to be in that basis—for instance, it is going to be measured in the standard basis and thus one can already measure this qubit in the standard basis and use a classical wire—. We define a partial order between labellings of a diagram as the natural lift from the partial order of the labels.

Each label corresponds to a density matrix subspace of $\mathbb{C}^{2 \times 2}$, representing all possible mixed states allowed by that particular kind of wire.

$$Q = \mathbb{C}^{2 \times 2} \qquad Z = \{\alpha \,|0\rangle\langle0| + \beta \,|0\rangle\langle0| \mid \alpha, \beta \in \mathbb{R}_{\geq 0}, \alpha + \beta = 1\}$$
$$\perp = \{\tfrac{1}{2}\,|0\rangle\langle0| + \tfrac{1}{2}\,|1\rangle\langle1|\} \quad X = \{\alpha \,|+\rangle\langle+| + \beta \,|-\rangle\langle-| \mid \alpha, \beta \in \mathbb{R}_{\geq 0}, \alpha + \beta = 1\}$$
$$Y = \{\alpha \,|\circlearrowright\rangle\langle\circlearrowright| + \beta \,|\circlearrowleft\rangle\langle\circlearrowleft| \mid \alpha, \beta \in \mathbb{R}_{\geq 0}, \alpha + \beta = 1\}$$

Notice that the greatest common ancestor $A \sqcup B$ corresponds to the intersection of the sets.

Intuitively, a labelling is valid if we can cut any wire in the diagram and, after forcing a valid state in the inputs and outputs, we get a valid state in the cut terminals. That is, we rearrange the diagram to transform all outputs into inputs and connect the cut terminals as outputs, as shown on the right. Then, applying an arbitrary input $\rho \in (\bigotimes_i^n A_i) \otimes (\bigotimes_j^m D_j)$ to the diagrams produces a result in $E \otimes F$.

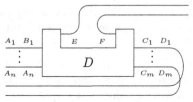

Notice that if A is a valid label for a wire then any $B \geq A$ is also valid, and in particular Q is always a valid label. We can then omit unnecessary labels in the diagrams, marking them implicitly as Q.

Given a ZX$_\pm$ diagram D with marked classical inputs and outputs, we define the classicalization problem as finding a minimal valid labeling where the inputs and outputs are labelled as Q or Z accordingly.

7.1 Local-Search Algorithm

We present a local-search labelling procedure for ZX$_\pm$ diagrams with explicit Hadamard gates—replacing the Hadamard wires—and only green spiders, that produces locally minimal labellings by propagating the labels over individual spiders. A diagram resulting from the circuit extraction in Sect. 6 can be transformed to have only green spiders by applying the color-change rule (h). This restriction is purely for simplicity in our definition, as the equivalent functions can be defined easily for red spiders.

We introduce a number of operations over the labels. First, a binary function representing the result of combining two wires via a phaseless green spider, $\star : \mathcal{L} \times \mathcal{L} \to \mathcal{L}$.

$$
\begin{array}{lllll}
Z \star A = Z & X \star A = A & Y \star Y = X & Q \star Y = Q & \bot \star Y = \bot \\
A \star Z = Z & A \star X = A & Y \star Q = Q & Q \star Q = Q & \bot \star Q = Z \\
& & Y \star \bot = \bot & Q \star \bot = Z & \bot \star \bot = \bot
\end{array}
$$

Notice that $(\mathcal{L}, \star)$ is a commutative monoid with X as neutral element. We also define a "Z rotation" operation for $\alpha \in [0, 2\pi)$, $\mathrm{rot}_\alpha : \mathcal{L} \to \mathcal{L}$.

$$
\mathrm{rot}_\alpha(Z) = Z \qquad \mathrm{rot}_\alpha(Q) = Q \qquad \mathrm{rot}_\alpha(\bot) = \bot
$$

$$
\mathrm{rot}_\alpha(X) = \begin{cases} X & \text{if } \alpha \in \{0, \pi\} \\ Y & \text{if } \alpha \in \{\frac{1}{2}\pi, \frac{3}{4}\pi\} \\ Q & \text{otherwise} \end{cases}
\mathrm{rot}_\alpha(Y) = \begin{cases} Y & \text{if } \alpha \in \{0, \pi\} \\ X & \text{if } \alpha \in \{\frac{1}{2}\pi, \frac{3}{4}\pi\} \\ Q & \text{otherwise} \end{cases}
$$

This corresponds to the identity if $\alpha \in \{0, \pi\}$, and in general $\mathrm{rot}_\alpha(A) \star b \geq \mathrm{rot}_\alpha(A \star B)$.

Finally, we define a function H representing the application of the Hadamard operation over a label, $H : \mathcal{L} \to \mathcal{L}$.

$$
H(Q) = Q \qquad H(X) = Z \qquad H(Z) = X \qquad H(Y) = Y \qquad H(\bot) = \bot
$$

Our classical detection procedure starts by labelling any classical input or output with a Z label, and any $\frac{1}{\ne}$ with a $\bot$ label, and the rest of the diagram wires with Q.

It then proceeds by propagating the labels using the following rules:

For any labels $A, B, C, D, E, F \in \mathcal{L}$.

We apply these rules until there are no more labels to change. Since each time we replace labels with lesser ones in the order, the procedure terminates. Finally, we can interpret wires with a classical label in any direction as classically realisable. We show an example of a labeled diagram in Fig. 3.

Lemma 6. *The local-search labelling algorithm produces a valid labeling according to the standard interpretation of the* $ZX_{\frac{1}{\ne}}$ *calculus.*

Proof. By proving that both rules (ch) and (cz) produce valid labellings, cf. long version on arXiv.

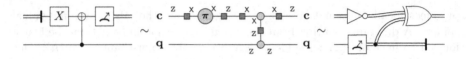

Fig. 3. Example of a local-search classicalization. Q labels are omitted.

8   Implementation

We have implemented each of the algorithms presented in this work as an extension to the open source Python library *PyZX* [16] by modifying its implementation of ZX diagrams to admit ZX$_\pm$ primitives. A repository with the code is available at http://github.com/aborgna/pyzx/tree/zxgnd. We additionally implemented a naïve ZX$_\pm$ extension of the pure Clifford optimization for comparison purposes, which doesn't use any of our $\pm$ rewriting rules. When applied to pure quantum circuits, our algorithm does not perform additional optimizations after the Clifford procedure and therefore achieves the same benchmark results recorded by Duncan et al. on the circuit set described by Amy et al. [1].

We tested the procedure over two classes of randomly generated circuits, and measured the size of the resulting diagram as the number of spiders left after the optimization. This metric correlates with the size of the final circuit, although the algorithmic noise caused by the arbitrary choices in the extraction procedure may result in some cases in bigger extracted circuit after a reduction step.

The first test generates Clifford+T circuits with measurements by applying randomly chosen gates from the set {CNOT, S, HSH, T, Meas} over a fixed number of qubits, where Meas are measurement gates on a qubit immediately followed by a qubit initialization. We fix the probability of choosing a CNOT, S, or HSH gate to 0.2 each and vary the probabilities for T and Meas in the remaining 0.4. These circuits present a general worst case, where there is no additional classical structure to exploit during the hybrid circuit optimization.

The second type of generated operations are classical parity-logic circuits. These consist on a number of classical inputs, fixed at 10, where we apply randomly chosen operations from the set {NOT, XOR, Fanout} with probabilities 0.3, 0.3, and 0.4 respectively.

In Fig. 4 we compare the results of our optimization using the Clifford optimization as baseline. Figure 4a shows the reduction of diagram size when running the algorithm on randomly generated Clifford+T circuits with measurement. We vary the probability of generating a measurement gate between 0 and 0.2 while correspondingly changing the probability of generating a T-gate between 0.4 and 0.2, and show the results for different combinations of qubit and gate quantities. We remark that the optimization produces noticeably smaller diagrams once enough $\pm$ generators start interacting with each other. There is a critical threshold of measurement gate probability, specially visible in the cases with 8 qubits and 1024 gates, where with high probability the outputs of the diagram become disconnected from the inputs due to the $\pm$ interactions. This results in

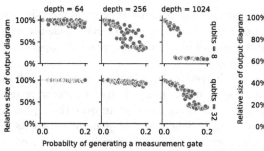

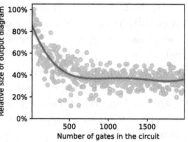

(a) Diagram size reduction on Clifford+T circuits with measurements.

(b) Diagram size reduction on parity-logic circuits.

Fig. 4. Benchmark results on randomly generated diagrams.

our algorithm optimizing the circuits to produce a constant result while discarding their input.

Figure 4b shows the comparison of diagram size between our procedure and the Clifford optimization when run over classical parity circuits. The optimization produces consistently smaller diagrams, generally achieving the theoretical minimal number of ⇌ generators, equal to the number of inputs. We further remark that in all of the tested cases the classicalization procedure was able to detect that all the extracted operations on the optimized parity-logic circuit were classically realisable.

The runtime of our algorithm implementation is polynomial in the size of the circuit. As with the Clifford optimization, the cost of our optimization and extraction processes is dominated by the Gauss elimination steps. For the ground-node rewriting rules, our unoptimized implementation is roughly $\mathcal{O}(n^2 * k^2)$ in the worst case with k being the number of measurement gates and n the number of gates, but in practice it behaves cubically on the number of gates due to the sparseness of the diagrams. The implementation was not developed with a focus on the runtime cost, and some possible optimizations may reduce this bound.

9   Discussion and Future Work

We introduced an optimization procedure for optimizing hybrid classical circuits inspired by previous work on pure circuit optimization using the ZX calculus. The process is composed by a translation step, the optimization of the diagrams, an extraction back into circuits and finally a detection of classically-realisable operations. Our translation operation produces diagrams which admit a focused gFlow, a property that we maintain during the optimization and require during the extraction. For our optimization step we defined a series of rewrite strategies to reduce the size of the diagrams, and introduced a strategy to find additional optimization opportunities by applying Gaussian elimination on the biadjacency matrix of the ground-cut of the diagram. Our extraction procedure initially generates circuits without classical operations. Hence, we introduced a classicalization heuristic for arbitrary circuits that is able to replace quantum operations by their classical equivalent, where possible.

Kissinger and van de Wetering [17] defined a procedure based on the Clifford optimization to reduce the T-gate count in quantum circuits by defining new structures in the graphs called *phase gadgets* and operating over their phases. Their work can be easily extended to $ZX_{\pm}$, where the $\pm$ generators act as an absorbing element for the gadgets phases. However, rules such as $(+)$ prove to be strictly more powerful than applying the pure phase gadget rules over $\pm$ - gadgets. In general, the phase-gadget optimization affects an independent section of the structure of the diagram compared to ours, and can be applied with it.

During our definition of the optimization process we decided to restrict the input circuits to parity classical logic, excluding AND and OR gates. This does not raise from an inherent limitation of the system but from a practical standpoint. The $ZX_{\pm}$ calculus is able to represent AND operations in what equates to the Clifford+T decomposition of the Toffoli gate, introducing multiple T-gates and CNOT gates to the circuit [21]. The multiple spiders would be dispersed around the diagram during the optimization step, potentially breaking the pattern formed by the AND gate and replacing it with multiple quantum operations. This can produce the unexpected result of introducing expensive quantum operations in an originally pure classical circuit. A possible next step for this work would be to use an alternative diagrammatic representation better adapted to represent arbitrary boolean circuit such as the ZH calculus.

Acknowledgements. The authors would like to thank Kostia Chardonnet and Renaud Vilmart for their suggestions on the classicalization problem, and John van de Wetering for his help with the pyzx library. This work was supported in part by the French National Research Agency (ANR) under the research project SoftQPRO ANR-17-CE25-0009-02, and by the DGE of the French Ministry of Industry under the research project PIA-GDN/QuantEx P163746-484124, and by the project STIC-AmSud project Qapla' 21-SITC-10.

References

1. Amy, M., Maslov, D., Mosca, M.: Polynomial-time T-depth optimization of Clifford+T circuits via matroid partitioning. IEEE Trans. Comput.-Aided Des. **33**(10), 1476–1489 (2014)
2. de Beaudrap, N., Horsman, D.: The ZX calculus is a language for surface code lattice surgery. Quantum **4**, 218 (2020)
3. Carette, T., Jeandel, E., et al.: Completeness of graphical languages for mixed states quantum mechanics. In: Proceedings of ICALP, pp. 108:1–108:15 (2019)
4. Chancellor, N., Kissinger, et al.: Graphical structures for design and verification of quantum error correction (2016)
5. Coecke, B., Duncan, R.: Interacting quantum observables. In: Aceto, L., Damgård, I., Goldberg, L.A., Halldórsson, M.M., Ingólfsdóttir, A., Walukiewicz, I. (eds.) ICALP 2008. LNCS, vol. 5126, pp. 298–310. Springer, Heidelberg (2008). https://doi.org/10.1007/978-3-540-70583-3_25

6. Coecke, B., Kissinger, A.: Picturing quantum processes. In: Chapman, P., Stapleton, G., Moktefi, A., Perez-Kriz, S., Bellucci, F. (eds.) Diagrams 2018. LNCS (LNAI), vol. 10871, pp. 28–31. Springer, Cham (2018). https://doi.org/10.1007/978-3-319-91376-6_6
7. Cross, A.W., Bishop, L.S., et al.: Open quantum assembly language (2017)
8. Duncan, R., Kissinger, A., et al.: Graph-theoretic simplification of quantum circuits with the ZX-calculus. Quantum **4**, 279 (2020)
9. Duncan, R., Lucas, M.: Verifying the steane code with quantomatic. In: Proceedings of QPL, pp. 33–49 (2013)
10. Duncan, R., Perdrix, S.: Rewriting measurement-based quantum computations with generalised flow. In: Abramsky, S., Gavoille, C., Kirchner, C., Meyer auf der Heide, F., Spirakis, P.G. (eds.) ICALP 2010. LNCS, vol. 6199, pp. 285–296. Springer, Heidelberg (2010). https://doi.org/10.1007/978-3-642-14162-1_24
11. Green, A.S., Lumsdaine, P.L.F., et al.: Quipper: a scalable quantum programming language. In: Proceedings of PLDI, pp. 333–342 (2013)
12. Heyfron, L., Campbell, E.T.: An efficient quantum compiler that reduces T count (2018)
13. Jeandel, E., Perdrix, S., Vilmart, R.: Completeness of the ZX-calculus. LMCS **16**(2), 11:1-11:72 (2020)
14. Jozsa, R.: An introduction to measurement based quantum computation. In: NATO Science Series, III, vol. 199, pp. 137–158 (2005)
15. Khammassi, N., Guerreschi, G.G., et al.: cqasm v1.0: towards a common quantum assembly language (2018)
16. Kissinger, A., van de Wetering, J.: PyZX: large scale automated diagrammatic reasoning. In: ENTCS, vol. 318, pp. 229–241 (2020)
17. Kissinger, A., van de Wetering, J.: Reducing T-count with the ZX-calculus (2020)
18. Li, G., Zhou, L., Yu, N., et al.: Projection-based runtime assertions for testing and debugging quantum programs. PAPL **4**(OOPSLA), 1–29 (2020)
19. Mhalla, M., Murao, M., Perdrix, S., Someya, M., Turner, P.S.: Which graph states are useful for quantum information processing? In: Bacon, D., Martin-Delgado, M., Roetteler, M. (eds.) TQC 2011. LNCS, vol. 6745, pp. 174–187. Springer, Heidelberg (2014). https://doi.org/10.1007/978-3-642-54429-3_12
20. Miller-Bakewell, H.: Finite verification of infinite families of diagram equations. In: Proceedings of QPL, pp. 27–52 (2019)
21. Selinger, P.: Quantum circuits of T-depth one. Phys. Rev. A **87**(4), 042302 (2013)
22. Steiger, D.S., Häner, T., Troyer, M.: ProjectQ: an open source software framework for quantum computing. Quantum **2**, 49 (2018)
23. van de Wetering, J.: ZX-calculus for the working quantum computer scientist (2020)
24. Zhou, H., Byrd, G.T.: Quantum circuits for dynamic runtime assertions in quantum computation. IEEE Comput. Arch. Lett. **18**(2), 111–114 (2019)

A Compilation Method for Dynamic Typing in ML

Atsushi Ohori[⊠] and Katsuhiro Ueno

Tohoku University, Sendai, Miyagi, 980-8577, Japan
{ohori,katsu}@riec.tohoku.ac.jp

Abstract. This paper develops a systematic method for extending a polymorphic type system of ML with dynamic typing, and implements the extension in SML#. The core of the extension consists of an adaptation of the type-directed compilation method for non-parametric polymorphism to type tag abstraction and type tag generation. To support existentially bound type variables in dynamic value elimination and user-level manipulation of dynamic values, the conventional type-directed compilation framework is extended with existential types and a mechanism to *reify* dynamic values to user-level datatypes. The resulting language achieves orthogonal integration of dynamic typing in ML: it supports all the standard features, including polymorphic type inference, user-defined datatypes and pattern matching, in programming with dynamic typing. The implementation readily provides various practical features, including polymorphic first-class pretty-printer, polymorphic deserialization, type-safe interface to database systems, and type-safe meta-programming.

1 Introduction

Dynamic typing in statically typed languages [2] is a mechanism to inject a value of static type τ to a special atomic type, called *dynamic* or *dyn* for a shorter, by pairing the value with a type tag of τ, and to inspect the type tag at run-time by typecase statement. Its usefulness has been well recognized. Using dynamic typing, one can write various type-dependent programs such as pretty-printing, type-safe evaluation, and reflection. As observed by many authors, dynamic typing is also an indispensable to communicate with external environments such as database systems [3]. Considering these benefits, we can say that dynamic typing is a basic feature that should be included in any statically typed language. Here, we focus on the problem of extending a polymorphic type system with dynamic typing and implementing it in a practical compiler.

This problem was already considered in the original proposal of dynamic typing [2], and further explored in [1]. In their studies, main focuses are on how to extend typecase patterns with type constructors (type functions) in explicitly typed second-order systems. In [11], the authors proposed a method to extend ML with dynamic typing and implemented it in the CAML compiler. Their

© Springer Nature Switzerland AG 2021
H. Oh (Ed.): APLAS 2021, LNCS 13008, pp. 140–159, 2021.
https://doi.org/10.1007/978-3-030-89051-3_9

extension is however rather restricted one: only values of closed types can be injected to type *dyn*. Due to this restriction, dynamic typing does not mix well with ML's implicit polymorphism. Another direction toward integrating dynamic typing in polymorphic languages is to investigate various encoding methods in powerful type systems such as those of Haskell. While some recent researches such as [17] showed successful result, it is difficult to see what is necessary to add dynamic typing to a polymorphic type system and to implement it in a practical compiler. As we shall demonstrate in Subsect. 6.3, dynamic typing, when properly integrated in ML, can represent type-safe meta programming without using any powerful typing mechanisms such as GADT, type classes, higher-rank polymorphism, and even without polymorphic recursion. While we do not have any formal result of relative expressive power of dynamic typing, this property suggests that dynamic typing is an independent primitive mechanism that should be investigated.

The aim of this paper is to develop a systematic method for orthogonally extending a polymorphic type system of ML with dynamic typing, and for implementing the extension in a full-scale native code compiler.

1.1 Analysis of Dynamic Typing

To clarify the technical issue in integrating dynamic typing in a polymorphic type system of ML, we briefly review dynamic typing. Its basis, as presented in [2], is to introduce primitive type *dyn*, and two language constructs:

$$\frac{\mathcal{T} \vdash e : \tau}{\mathcal{T} \vdash \texttt{dynamic}(e) : dyn}, \qquad \frac{\mathcal{T} \vdash e : dyn}{\mathcal{T} \vdash (e \textbf{ as } \tau) : \tau}.$$

$\texttt{dynamic}(e)$ injects a value of type τ into *dyn*, whose run-time object is intuitively understood as a pair $(V, tyRep(\tau))$ consisting of a run-time value V of type τ, and a type representation (or type tag) $tyRep(\tau)$ of τ. (e **as** τ) checks whether or not the stored type tag $tyRep(\tau')$ matches with static type τ, and if it matches then it returns the stored value V of type τ, otherwise it raises *RuntimeTypeError* exception. Because introduction of exception handling does not create any new technical problem, we use it implicitly.

For the purpose of our analysis, let us suppose that these two constructs are magically realized in ML. Since these two typing rules are parameterized with τ without any constraints, there should be no problem in integrating these rules in a polymorphic type system of ML. This simple observation indicates that if these constructs are (somehow magically) given, then dynamic typing are uniformly integrated in ML. We enumerate some of the features that should be readily available from this (at this moment hypothetical) integration.

- *Polymorphism*. Since τ ranges over all the monotypes of ML including type variables 'a, they are uniformly integrated in ML polymorphic type inference. For example, the ML type inference algorithm should infer principal typings for the following functions

```
val mkDyn = (fn x => dynamic(x))    : 'a -> dyn
val cast  = (fn dyn => (dyn as 'a)) : dyn -> 'a
```

Using them, one would be able to write polymorphic functions as seen below:

```
fun packFold (l:'a list, f:'a * 'a -> 'a) = myDyn (l, f)
fun doFold z dyn = (fn (l, f) => foldr f z l)
                   (cast dyn : 'a list * ('a * 'a -> 'a))
val (d1, d2) = (packFold ([1,2], op +), packFold (["a","b"], op ^))
val (r1, r2) = (doFold 0 d1, doFold "" d2)
```

– *Pattern matching.* Since ML pattern matching is orthogonal to its polymorphic type discipline, it mixes well with the two dynamic constructs. The following code pattern demonstrates this mixture:

```
fun f dyn = case (dyn as 'a T) of P₁:'a T => e₁ | ... | Pₙ => eₙ
```

A simple example is shown below.

```
fun hd dyn z =
    case (dyn as 'a list) of nil:'a list => z | h::_ => h
val (x,y) = (hd (dynamic [1,2]) 0, hd (dynamic ["a","b"]) "")
```

This mixture subsumes **typecase** constructs. To see this, consider the following type definitions and a **typecase**-like construct (generalized to patterns):

```
type cPoint = real * real
type pPoint = {r:real, theta:real}
val x = dynamiccase e of
            (d:cPoint -> real, p:cPoint) => d p
          | {distance:pPoint -> real, point:pPoint} => distance point
```

If the (hypothetical) integration of dynamic typing is achieved then the above **dynamiccase** construct could simply be regarded as a short-hand of the following term:

```
(case (e as (cPoint -> int) * cPoint) of
    (d, p) => d p)
handle RuntimeTypeError =>
  (case (e as {distance:pPoint -> int, point:pPoint}) of
     {distance, point}) => distance point)
```

– *User-defined algebraic datatypes.* Since $(e \text{ as } \tau)$ and pattern matching does not assume any special condition on the pattern P_i, ML's user-defined generative **datatype** are available in programming with dynamic typing without any additional machinery, as shown in the following (hypothetical) example:

```
datatype cPoint = C of real * real
fun cDist (x:cPoint) : real = ...
datatype pPoint = P of {r:real, theta:real}
fun pDist (x:pPoint) : real = ...
fun dist d = dynamiccase d of C c => cDist c | P p => pDist p
```

In [17], this form of uniform mixture of user-defined datatypes with dynamic typing is called the *open world* of types and is recognized as an important research goal. However, we should note that, in the ML type system, the set of all possible generative user-defined datatypes is a member of its well-defined semantic objects, and therefore there is no "openness"; the *open world* of types would already be achieved if the uniform mixture is realized.

1.2   Our Strategy and Contribution

The above simple analysis confirms that if the two primitives dynamic(e) and
(e as τ) are uniformly integrated into the polymorphic type system of ML, most
of the features of dynamic typing are automatically obtained. The important
point is the availability of the two constructs for *any type* τ. Perhaps due to the
difficulty of implementing the two constructs for all possible types, this obvious
approach had not been taken in existing works.

One first goals is to achieve this uniform integration of dynamic primitives in
a polymorphic type system of ML. The necessary type-theoretical mechanisms
are the following.

– *Type reification.* Based on the intuitive understanding of dyn as a pair (V, τ)
  consisting of a value V and its type τ, in [2], the evaluation rule is defined as

$$\frac{E \models e \Downarrow V}{E \models \mathtt{dynamic}(e : \tau) \Downarrow (V, \tau)}$$

  where τ is annotated by the type inference process. This involves cross-phase
  computation; τ is available at compile time but V is constructed at run-time.
  To realize the intended intuitive semantics, the compiler need to generate
  code that creates a type tag value $tyRep(\tau)$ at run-time.
– *Type tag abstraction and application.* Since τ may contain type variable 'a,
  we need to abstract the necessary run-time type tag information. The need
  of passing some type information has been well recognized in the history of
  dynamic typing [2,11]. The necessary mechanism is however not type-passing
  but passing the type tag of the type variables appearing in τ of dynamic($e : \tau$)
  and (e as τ). This should happen only when these constructs appear inside
  of a polymorphic function. Therefore, a proper tag-passing does not change
  the semantics of the language and also does not introduce any overhead for
  programs that do not use dynamic typing.
  This form of extra type attribute passing has been invented for various features that require non-parametric behavior, including record polymorphism
  [14], [7], tag-free garbage collection [23]. Among them we adopt the record
  compilation framework [14], which is perhaps the first proposal in this general
  approach and provides a rigorous minimal core for type tag passing.

We have developed a detailed and provably sound type-theoretical framework
to represent these mechanism and have established a type-directed compilation
method for the polymorphic construct dynamic(e) and (e as τ).

Our second goal is to extend the above dynamic typing mechanism in ML
with *existential types* and *type reification*.

– Existential types are useful in *dyn* elimination. Suppose we have a dynamic
  object consisting of a state τ and a method $\tau \rightarrow int$. This would naturally be
  regarded as a "package" (in the sense of data algebra [12]) of type $\exists t.t \times (t \rightarrow int)$. Therefore, we should be able to write a function of the form

```
fun applyMethod dyn =
    dynamiccase dyn of {'a} (s:'a, f:'a -> int) => f s
```

The newly introduced notation {'a} indicates that the type variable 'a is existentially bound in the scope of the rule, with the restriction that it must not *escape* from the scope. The ML type system assumes that any type variables are implicitly universally-bound, and therefore an explicit introduction of a different kind of type variables is inevitable. As we shall show in our development, however, the existential quantification mechanism can be simulated through ML polymorphism. Therefore, the required addition does not complicate the underlying ML typing mechanism. However, there is a subtle interaction between existential witness and type tag passing, which requires a new development in type-directed compilation.

– Type reification provides the programmer to analyze and manipulate dynamic values. This mechanism is necessary in interaction with external environment. The simplest example is pretty-printing or serialization. Writing a systematic serializer that works for all the possible ML types including arbitrary record types and user-defined datatypes, we must provide a mechanism for user program to analyze the internal structure of type *dyn*.

We carry out all the above type-theoretical development, and have implemented them in the SML# compiler [21].

1.3   Related Works

To place our contributions among a number of related works, the remainder of this section compares these results with related works.

After the proposal of dynamic typeing [2], there have been a number of researches on extensions and implementation. The work of [1] recognized the difficulty of allowing dynamic introduction for an expression that has free type variables such as fn x => dynamic(x) in ML. The work of [11] extended ML with dynamic(e) by restricting e to an expression that has a *closed type*. Due to this restriction, dynamic(e) and (e as τ) are not polymorphic so that expressions such as fn (x:'a) => fn d => (d as 'a -> int) x or fn x => dynamic(x) are prohibited. In contrast, our framework allows all the definable monotypes in both of the constructs. As we have reviewed above, this feature is the key to orthogonal extension of dynamic typing with ML's various useful features. Dynamic typing has also been implemented in Clean [18] and OCaml [10], but they do not seem to achieve the uniform integration comparable to ours.

In the context of powerful type systems such as those of Haskell, there are a number of works on encoding dynamic typing primitives using various advanced features such as type classes [4,7], GADTs [16,24], and higher-kind type constructors (type functions) [19]. Encoding inevitably introduces overhead, and it is difficult to see what is necessary to extend a polymorphic type system and implementing it in a practical optimizing compiler that does not contain various advanced typing mechanisms. Our work can be used to analyze the necessary and sufficient type-theoretical machinery for realizing dynamic typing in an ML-style polymorphic language, and to study the relationship between dynamic typing and other typing mechanisms.

In order to achieve a type-safe and flexible programming with JSON, our previous work [15] has introduced dynamic typing restricted to ground monotypes. The current work is a systematic extension to polymorphic type system.

Our development follows the type-directed compilation of record polymorphism [14]. As we have mentioned, there have been a number of related proposals [6–8,23]. All of them share a similar structure in passing some type attributes. A novel contribution toward this paradigm of type attribute passing is the integration of existential type variables, which require a new type-theoretical development.

In a more general perspective, investigation of extending statically typed language with dynamic typing is related to researches on the relationship between static and dynamic typing, including type *dyn* and explicit type coercion operation by [9], and recent investigation of gradual typing initiated by [20]. It is an interesting future research direction to investigate the relationship between compilation method of those gradually typed languages and ours.

Paper Organization. Section 2 defines the source language. Section 3 defines the target calculus and proves type soundness. It then gives a type-directed compilation algorithm. Section 4 extends the framework with pattern matching. Section 5 extends the framework with existential types. Section 6 shows some examples to demonstrate the usefulness of dynamic typing. Section 7 concludes the paper with suggestions for further investigation.

The severe page limitation prevents us to present the framework and implementation method fully; we intend to publish a full version elsewhere.

2 The Source Calculus

This section defines the source calculus as an implicitly typed polymorphic calculus of ML with data constructors, and the two constructs for dynamic typing. Let x and t range over a given countably infinite set of variables and type variables, respectively. Let c^b range over a given set of typed constants of atomic type b. To model user-defined datatypes, we let T and C respectively denote the predefined set of (first-order) type constructors and data constructors. We write $C\ e$ for a datatype term.

Following the tradition of ML [5], we let τ and σ range over the set of *monotypes* and *polytypes*, respectively. In order to identify those type variables whose type tag information is required at run-time, we introduce a simple kind system consisting of two atomic kinds, U for the set of all monotypes, and R for the set of all the monotypes whose type tag information is available.

The set of terms, monotypes, polytypes, and kinds are given below:

$$e ::= x \mid c^b \mid \lambda x.e \mid e\ e \mid C\ e \mid \texttt{case}\ e\ \texttt{of}\ \overline{C\ x\ \texttt{=>}\ e} \mid \texttt{let}\ x\ \texttt{=}\ e\ \texttt{in}\ e \mid$$
$$\texttt{dynamic}(e) \mid (e\ \texttt{as}\ \tau)$$
$$\tau ::= t \mid b \mid \tau \to \tau \mid \tau\ T \mid dyn \qquad \sigma ::= \tau \mid \forall t : k.\sigma \qquad k ::= U \mid R$$

In this definition, $\overline{C\ x\ \texttt{=>}\ e}$ indicates a finite sequence of $C\ x\ \texttt{=>}\ e$. In the sequel, we use the notation $\overline{X}$ for other syntactic category X as well.

To perform type-directed compilation for this calculus, we need to identify all the type variables used in a given typing derivation. For this purpose, we introduce a kind assignment $\mathcal{K}$, which is a mapping from a finite subset of type variables to kinds. For a given kind assignment $\mathcal{K}$, we write $\mathcal{K}\{t : k\}$ to denote $\mathcal{K} \cup \{t : k\}$ provided that $t \notin dom(\mathcal{K})$. Similar convention is used for other finite maps. Any static object containing types must be kinded by some kind assignment $\mathcal{K}$. We say that X is well-formed under $\mathcal{K}$, written $\mathcal{K} \vdash X$, if $FTV(X) \subseteq dom(\mathcal{K})$, where $FTV(X)$ denotes the set of free type variables of X.

A monotype τ has a kind k under $\mathcal{K}$, written $\mathcal{K} \vdash \tau : k$, if this is derived by the following simple kinding system:

$$\frac{\mathcal{K} \vdash \tau}{\mathcal{K} \vdash \tau : U} \qquad \frac{\mathcal{K}(t) = R \text{ for all } t \in FTV(\tau)}{\mathcal{K} \vdash \tau : R}$$

To define the set of typing rules for this calculus, we assume that each C is associated to a closed polytype σ^C, and write $\vdash C : \tau_1 \rightarrow \tau_2$ to indicate that $\tau_1 \rightarrow \tau_2$ is an instance of the polytype σ^C. A type assignment $\mathcal{T}$ is a finite mapping from variables to polytypes. The set of typing rules is given in Fig. 1.

$$\frac{\mathcal{K} \vdash \mathcal{T}\{x : \sigma\}}{\mathcal{K}, \mathcal{T}\{x : \sigma\} \vdash x : \sigma} \qquad \mathcal{K}, \mathcal{T} \vdash c^b : b \qquad \frac{\mathcal{K}, \mathcal{T}\{x : \tau_1\} \vdash e : \tau_2}{\mathcal{K}, \mathcal{T} \vdash \lambda x.e : \tau_1 \rightarrow \tau_2}$$

$$\frac{\mathcal{K}, \mathcal{T} \vdash e_1 : \tau_1 \rightarrow \tau_2 \quad \mathcal{K}, \mathcal{T} \vdash e_1 : \tau_1}{\mathcal{K}, \mathcal{T} \vdash e_1\ e_2 : \tau_2} \qquad \frac{\vdash C : \tau_1 \rightarrow \tau_2 \quad \mathcal{K}, \mathcal{T} \vdash e : \tau_1}{\mathcal{K}, \mathcal{T} \vdash C\ e : \tau_2}$$

$$\frac{\mathcal{K}, \mathcal{T} \vdash e : \tau' \quad \vdash C_i : \tau_i \rightarrow \tau' \quad \mathcal{K}, \mathcal{T}\{x : \tau_i\} \vdash e_i : \tau}{\mathcal{K}, \mathcal{T} \vdash \textbf{case}\ e\ \textbf{of}\ \overline{C_i\ x_i\ \texttt{=>}\ e_i} : \tau}$$

$$\frac{\mathcal{K}, \mathcal{T} \vdash M : \forall t{:}k.\sigma \quad \mathcal{K} \vdash \tau' : k}{\mathcal{K}, \mathcal{T} \vdash M : \sigma[\tau'/t]} \qquad \frac{\mathcal{K}\{t : k\}, \mathcal{T} \vdash e : \sigma}{\mathcal{K}, \mathcal{T} \vdash e : \forall t{:}k.\sigma}$$

$$\frac{\mathcal{K}, \mathcal{T} \vdash e : \tau \quad \mathcal{K} \vdash \tau : R}{\mathcal{K}, \mathcal{T} \vdash \texttt{dynamic}(e) : dyn} \qquad \frac{\mathcal{K}, \mathcal{T} \vdash e : dyn \quad \mathcal{K} \vdash \tau : R}{\mathcal{K}, \mathcal{T} \vdash (e\ \textbf{as}\ \tau) : \tau}$$

Fig. 1. The type system of the source calculus

A kinded substitution is a pair $(\mathcal{K}, S)$ of kind assignment $\mathcal{K}$ and a type substitution S. A kinded substitution $(\mathcal{K}, S)$ respects $\mathcal{K}'$ if $\mathcal{K} \vdash S(t) : k$ for all $t : k \in \mathcal{K}'$.

Proposition 1. *If* $\mathcal{K}, \mathcal{T} \vdash e : \sigma$ *and* $(\mathcal{K}', S)$ *respects* $\mathcal{K}$, *then* $\mathcal{K}', S(\mathcal{T}) \vdash S(e) : S(\sigma)$.

The proof is similar to the corresponding proofs in [14].

3   The Target Calculus and Compilation

The semantics for this calculus is given by the composition of type-directed compilation to the target calculus and the type-sound operational semantics of the target calculus.

3.1   The Target Calculus and Type Soundness

The main role of the target calculus is to represent typed derivation of run-time type tags and type tag passing. For this purpose, we introduce *type tags*, ranged over by L, as the set of terms given by the following syntax:

$$L ::= t \mid \mathtt{BaseTy}^b \mid \mathtt{FunTy}(L, L) \mid \mathtt{DataTy}(T, L) \mid \mathtt{DynTy}$$

This looks like a simple (user-level) datatype definition for representing type tag. The major technical novelty of the target calculus is to introduce type tag terms as a typing derivation, which are used in term typing derivation. For this purpose, we introduce a semantic object *type tag type* of the form $tyRep(\tau)$. We say that a type tag L has $tyRep(\tau)$ under $\mathcal{K}$, and write $\mathcal{K} \vdash L : tyRep(\tau)$, if it is derived by the following simple type tag derivation system:

$$\mathcal{K}\{t : R\} \vdash t : tyRep(t) \qquad \mathcal{K} \vdash \mathtt{BaseTy}^b : tyRep(b) \qquad \mathcal{K} \vdash \mathtt{DynTy} : tyRep(dyn)$$

$$\frac{\mathcal{K} \vdash L : tyRep(\tau)}{\mathcal{K} \vdash \mathtt{DataTy}(T, L) : tyRep(\tau\ T)} \qquad \frac{\mathcal{K} \vdash L_1 : tyRep(\tau_1) \quad \mathcal{K} \vdash L_2 : tyRep(\tau_2)}{\mathcal{K} \vdash \mathtt{FunTy}(L_1, L_2) : tyRep(\tau_1 \to \tau_2)}$$

This is a formulation of the intuitive understanding of $tyRep(\tau)$ to be a singleton type denoting the type tag of τ. This type tag derivation allows us to connect tag passing and tag abstraction required for a term of type of the form $\forall t : R.\sigma$.

We continue to use τ and σ for the set of monotypes and polytypes. The set of terms (ranged over by M) of the target calculus is given below:

$$M ::= x \mid c^b \mid \lambda x.M \mid M\ M \mid C\ M \mid \mathtt{case}\ M\ \mathtt{of}\ \overline{C\ x\ \texttt{=>}\ M} \mid \mathtt{let}\ x\ \texttt{=}\ M\ \mathtt{in}\ M \mid$$
$$\lambda t.M \mid M\ L \mid \mathtt{dynamic}(M : L) \mid (M\ \mathtt{as}\ L)$$

The set of typing rules is given in Fig. 2.

For this calculus, we also have the following basic property:

Proposition 2. *If $\mathcal{K}, \mathcal{T} \vdash M : \sigma$, $(\mathcal{K}', S)$ respects $\mathcal{K}$, then $\mathcal{K}', S(\mathcal{T}) \vdash S(M) : S(\sigma)$.*

$$\frac{\mathcal{K} \vdash \mathcal{T}\{x : \sigma\}}{\mathcal{K}, \mathcal{T}\{x : \sigma\} \vdash x : \sigma} \qquad \mathcal{K}, \mathcal{T} \vdash c^b : b \qquad \frac{\mathcal{K}, \mathcal{T}\{x : \tau_1\} \vdash M : \tau_2}{\mathcal{K}, \mathcal{T} \vdash \lambda x.M : \tau_1 \to \tau_2}$$

$$\frac{\mathcal{K}, \mathcal{T} \vdash M_1 : \tau_1 \to \tau_2 \quad \mathcal{K}, \mathcal{T} \vdash M_1 : \tau_1}{\mathcal{K}, \mathcal{T} \vdash M_1 \ M_2 : \tau_2} \qquad \frac{\vdash C : \tau_1 \to \tau_2 \quad \mathcal{K}, \mathcal{T} \vdash M : \tau_1}{\mathcal{K}, \mathcal{T} \vdash C \ M : \tau_2}$$

$$\frac{\mathcal{K}, \mathcal{T} \vdash M : \tau' \quad \vdash C_i : \tau_i \to \tau' \quad \mathcal{K}, \mathcal{T}\{x : \tau_i\} \vdash M_i : \tau}{\mathcal{K}, \mathcal{T} \vdash \mathtt{case} \ M \ \mathtt{of} \ C_i \ x_i \ \texttt{=>} \ M_i : \tau}$$

$$\frac{\mathcal{K}\{t : U\}, \mathcal{T} \vdash M : \sigma}{\mathcal{K}, \mathcal{T} \vdash M : \forall t : U.\sigma} \qquad \frac{\mathcal{K}\{t : R\}, \mathcal{T} \vdash M : \sigma}{\mathcal{K}, \mathcal{T} \vdash \lambda t.M : \forall t : R.\sigma}$$

$$\frac{\mathcal{K}, \mathcal{T} \vdash M : \forall t : U.\sigma \quad \mathcal{K} \vdash \tau : U}{\mathcal{K}, \mathcal{T} \vdash M : \sigma[\tau/t]} \qquad \frac{\mathcal{K}, \mathcal{T} \vdash M : \forall t : R.\sigma \quad \mathcal{K} \vdash L : tyRep(\tau)}{\mathcal{K}, \mathcal{T} \vdash M \ L : \sigma[\tau/t]}$$

$$\frac{\mathcal{K}, \mathcal{T} \vdash M_1 : \sigma \quad \mathcal{K}, \mathcal{T}\{x : \sigma\} \vdash M_2 : \tau}{\mathcal{K}, \mathcal{T} \vdash \mathtt{let} \ x \ \texttt{=} \ M_1 \ \mathtt{in} \ M_2 : \tau}$$

$$\frac{\mathcal{K}, \mathcal{T} \vdash M : \tau \quad \mathcal{K} \vdash L : tyRep(\tau)}{\mathcal{K}, \mathcal{T} \vdash \mathtt{dynamic}(M : L) : dyn} \qquad \frac{\mathcal{K}, \mathcal{T} \vdash M : dyn \quad \mathcal{K} \vdash L : tyRep(\tau)}{\mathcal{K}, \mathcal{T} \vdash (M \ \mathtt{as} \ L) : \tau}$$

Fig. 2. The type system of the target calculus

To define an effective (tag-passing) operational semantics, we define the set of closed type tags (ranged over by J), the set of run-time values (ranged over by V), and run-time environments (ranged over by E).

$$J ::= \mathtt{BaseTy}^b \mid \mathtt{FunTy}(J, J) \mid \mathtt{DataTy}(T, J) \mid \mathtt{DynTy}$$
$$V ::= c^b \mid C \ V \mid Cls(E, x, M) \mid TCls(E, t, M) \mid Dyn(V, J) \mid RuntimeTypeError \mid Wrong$$
$$E ::= \{\overline{x : V}, \overline{t : J}\}$$

RuntimeTypeError represents the exception raised when the type tag check of $(M \ \mathtt{as} \ L)$ fails; it has any type. *Wrong* represents failure due to type inconsistency, which has no type.

A big-step operational semantics is given by specifying rules of the forms $E \models L \Downarrow J$ and $E \models M \Downarrow V$ indicating the fact that L evaluates to J under E and M evaluates to V under E, respectively. The set of evaluation rules is given in Fig. 3. This set of rules should be taken with the following implicit rules: if evaluation does not satisfy the specified condition represented by value patterns then the term will yield *Wrong*, and if evaluation of any component yields *Wrong* (*RuntimeTypeError*) then the entire term will yield *Wrong* (*RuntimeTypeError*).

A pair (S, E) of a substitution S and run-time environment E is a model of $\mathcal{K}$ if $(\emptyset, S)$ respects $\mathcal{K}$ and for each $t \in dom(\mathcal{K})$ such that $\mathcal{K}(t) = R$, $\emptyset \vdash E(t) : tyRep(S(t))$. Also we say that (S, E) is a model of $(\mathcal{K}, \mathcal{T})$ if it is a model of $\mathcal{K}$ and for each $x \in dom(\mathcal{T})$, $\models E(x) : S(\mathcal{T}(x))$.

To show the type soundness of the target calculus, we define value typing as a binary relation $\models V : \sigma$ as follows.

$$E\{t : J\} \models t \Downarrow J \qquad E \models \mathtt{BaseTy}^b \Downarrow \mathtt{BaseTy}^b \qquad E \models \mathtt{DynTy} \Downarrow \mathtt{DynTy}$$

$$\frac{E \models L_1 \Downarrow J_1 \quad E \models L_2 \Downarrow J_2}{E \models \mathtt{FunTy}(L_1, L_2) \Downarrow \mathtt{FunTy}(J_1, J_2)} \qquad \frac{E \models L \Downarrow J}{E \models \mathtt{DataTy}(T, L) \Downarrow \mathtt{DataTy}(T, J)}$$

$$E\{x : V\} \models x \Downarrow V \qquad E \models c^b \Downarrow c^b$$

$$E \models \lambda x.M \Downarrow Cls(E, x, M) \qquad E \models \lambda t.M \Downarrow TCls(E, t, M)$$

$$\frac{E \models M_1 \Downarrow Cls(E_0, x, M_0) \quad E \models M_2 \Downarrow V' \quad E_0\{x : V'\} \models M_0 \Downarrow V}{E \models M_1 \ M_2 \Downarrow V}$$

$$\frac{E \models M \Downarrow TCls(E_0, t, M_0) \quad E \models L \Downarrow J \quad E_0\{t : J\} \models M_0 \Downarrow V}{E \models M \ L \Downarrow V}$$

$$\frac{E \models M \Downarrow V}{E \models C \ M \Downarrow C \ V} \qquad \frac{E \models M \Downarrow C_i \ V' \quad E\{x_i : V'\} \models M_i \Downarrow V}{E \models \mathtt{case} \ M \ \mathtt{of} \ \overline{C_i \ x_i \ \texttt{=>} \ M_i} \Downarrow V}$$

$$\frac{E \models M_1 \Downarrow V' \quad E\{x : V'\} \models M_2 \Downarrow V}{E \models \mathtt{let} \ x \ \texttt{=} \ M_1 \ \mathtt{in} \ M_2 \Downarrow V} \qquad \frac{E \models M \Downarrow V \quad E \models L \Downarrow J}{E \models \mathtt{dynamic}(M : L) \Downarrow Dyn(V, J)}$$

$$\frac{E \models M \Downarrow Dyn(V, J) \quad E \models L \Downarrow J}{E \models (M \ \mathtt{as} \ L) \Downarrow V} \qquad \frac{E \models M \Downarrow Dyn(V, J_1) \quad E \models L \Downarrow J_2 \quad J_1 \neq J_2}{E \models (M \ \mathtt{as} \ L) \Downarrow Runtime\,TypeError}$$

Fig. 3. An operational semantics of the target calculus

- $\models c^b : b$ for any c^b.
- $\models C \ V : \tau$ if $\models V : \tau_1$ and $\vdash C : \tau_1 \to \tau$ for some τ_1.
- $\models Cls(E, x, M) : \tau_1 \to \tau_2$ if there exists some S, $\mathcal{K}$, $\mathcal{T}$, τ_1' and τ_2' such that (S, E) is a model of $(\mathcal{K}, \mathcal{T})$, $\mathcal{K}, \mathcal{T}\{x : \tau_1'\} \vdash M : \tau_2'$, $\tau_1 = S(\tau_1')$, and $\tau_2 = S(\tau_2')$.
- $\models V : \forall t : U.\sigma$ if $\models V : \sigma[\tau/t]$ for all τ such that $\emptyset \vdash \tau$.
- $\models TCls(E, t, M) : \forall t : R.\sigma$ if there exists some S, $\mathcal{K}$, $\mathcal{T}$, and σ' such that (S, E) is a model of $(\mathcal{K}, \mathcal{T})$, $\mathcal{K}\{t : R\}, \mathcal{T} \vdash M : \sigma$, and $S(\sigma') = \sigma$.
- $\models Dyn(V, J) : dyn$ if $\models V : \tau$ and $\emptyset \vdash J : tyRep(\tau)$ for some ground monotype τ.

The following soundness theorem is shown.

Theorem 1. *If* $\mathcal{K}, \mathcal{T} \vdash M : \sigma$, (S, E) *is a model of* $(\mathcal{K}, \mathcal{T})$, *and* $E \models M \Downarrow V$, *then* $\models V : S(\sigma)$.

3.2 Type-Directed Compilation

We define a compilation algorithm as a translation of typing derivations of the source calculus to those of the target calculus, following the idea of record compilation, which inserts an extra lambda abstraction and lambda application only when needed using kind information of type variables. We write $\mathcal{K}, \mathcal{T} \vdash e \Rightarrow M : \sigma$ to indicate that the algorithm translates the derivation

$$\mathcal{K}, \mathcal{T} \vdash c^b \Rightarrow c^b : b \qquad \mathcal{K}, \mathcal{T} \vdash x \Rightarrow x : \sigma \qquad \frac{\mathcal{K}, \mathcal{T}\{x : \tau_1\} \vdash e \Rightarrow M : \tau_2}{\mathcal{K}, \mathcal{T} \vdash \lambda x.e \Rightarrow \lambda x.M : \tau_1 \to \tau_2}$$

$$\frac{\mathcal{K}, \mathcal{T} \vdash e_1 \Rightarrow M_1 : \tau_1 \to \tau_2 \quad \mathcal{K}, \mathcal{T} \vdash e_1 \Rightarrow M_2 : \tau_1}{\mathcal{K}, \mathcal{T} \vdash e_1 \ e_2 \Rightarrow M_1 \ M_2 : \tau_2} \qquad \frac{\mathcal{K}, \mathcal{T} \vdash e \Rightarrow M : \tau'}{\mathcal{K}, \mathcal{T} \vdash C \ e \Rightarrow C \ M : \tau}$$

$$\frac{\mathcal{K}, \mathcal{T} \vdash e \Rightarrow M : \tau' \quad \overline{\vdash C_i : \tau_i \to \tau'} \quad \overline{\mathcal{K}, \mathcal{T}\{x : \tau_i\} \vdash e_i \Rightarrow M_i : \tau}}{\mathcal{K}, \mathcal{T} \vdash \text{case } e \text{ of } \overline{C_i \ x_i} \Rightarrow e_i \Rightarrow \text{case } M \text{ of } \overline{C_i \ x_i} \Rightarrow M_i : \tau}$$

$$\frac{\mathcal{K}, \mathcal{T} \vdash e \Rightarrow M : \forall t : R.\sigma \quad \mathcal{K} \vdash L : tyRep(\tau)}{\mathcal{K}, \mathcal{T} \vdash e \Rightarrow M \ L : \sigma[\tau/t]} \qquad \frac{\mathcal{K}, \mathcal{T} \vdash e \Rightarrow M : \forall t : U.\sigma}{\mathcal{K}, \mathcal{T} \vdash e \Rightarrow M : \sigma[\tau/t]}$$

$$\frac{\mathcal{K}\{t : R\}, \mathcal{T} \vdash e \Rightarrow M : \sigma}{\mathcal{K}, \mathcal{T} \vdash e \Rightarrow \lambda t.M : \forall t : R.\sigma} \qquad \frac{\mathcal{K}\{t : U\}, \mathcal{T} \vdash e \Rightarrow M : \sigma}{\mathcal{K}, \mathcal{T} \vdash e \Rightarrow M : \forall t : U.\sigma}$$

$$\frac{\mathcal{K}, \mathcal{T} \vdash e_1 \Rightarrow M_1 : \sigma \quad \mathcal{K}, \mathcal{T}\{x : \sigma\} \vdash e_2 \Rightarrow M_2 : \tau}{\mathcal{K}, \mathcal{T} \vdash \text{let } x = e_1 \text{ in } e_2 \Rightarrow \text{let } x = M_1 \text{ in } M_2 : \tau}$$

$$\frac{\mathcal{K}, \mathcal{T} \vdash e \Rightarrow M : \tau \quad \mathcal{K} \vdash L : tyRep(\tau)}{\mathcal{K}, \mathcal{T} \vdash \text{dynamic}(e) \Rightarrow \text{dynamic}(M : L) : dyn}$$

$$\frac{\mathcal{K}, \mathcal{T} \vdash e \Rightarrow M : dyn \quad \mathcal{K} \vdash L : tyRep(\tau)}{\mathcal{K}, \mathcal{T} \vdash (e \text{ as } \tau) \Rightarrow (M \text{ as } L) : \tau}$$

Fig. 4. The compilation algorithm

$\mathcal{K}, \mathcal{T} \vdash e : \sigma$ in the source calculus to the derivation $\mathcal{K}, \mathcal{T} \vdash M : \sigma$ in the target calculus. Figure 4 shows this compilation relation.

For this algorithm, the following typing preservation theorem is shown.

Theorem 2. *If $\mathcal{K}, \mathcal{T} \vdash e : \sigma$ is a derivation in the source calculus and $\mathcal{K}, \mathcal{T} \vdash e \Rightarrow M : \sigma$ then $\mathcal{K}, \mathcal{T} \vdash M : \sigma$ is a derivation in the target calculus.*

4   Pattern Matching

This section extends the type theoretical framework with pattern matching. To present the extension, it is sufficient to consider the following patterns (ranged over by P) and language extensions in the source and target calculus:

$$P ::= x \mid C \ P \mid (P, P) \mid (P : \tau)$$
$$e ::= \cdots \mid \text{case } e \text{ of } \overline{P} \Rightarrow e \mid \text{dynamiccase } e \text{ of } \overline{P} \Rightarrow e$$
$$M ::= \cdots \mid \text{case } M \text{ of } \overline{P : \tau} \Rightarrow M$$

(P_1, P_2) is a pair pattern, which is useful in analyzing various properties; for this, we implicitly assume that the source and target calculi are extended with pairs. case expressions in the source and target calculus are standard. The construct dynamiccase e of $\overline{P_i} \Rightarrow e_i$ is a generalization of "typecase" construct with arbitrary patterns. In this construct, P_i may be of different types.

We write $\mathcal{K} \vdash P : (\tau, \mathcal{T})$ if P has a type τ and yields a variable assignment $\mathcal{T}$ under a kind assignment $\mathcal{K}$. We omit this standard definition.

The type system of the extended source calculus is obtained by adding the following two rules:

$$\frac{\mathcal{K}, \mathcal{T} \vdash e : \tau' \quad \overline{\mathcal{K} \vdash P_i : (\tau', \mathcal{T}_i)} \quad \overline{\mathcal{K}, \mathcal{T}\mathcal{T}_i \vdash e_i : \tau}}{\mathcal{K}, \mathcal{T} \vdash \mathsf{case}\ e\ \mathsf{of}\ \overline{P_i\ \texttt{=>}\ e_i} : \tau}$$

$$\frac{\mathcal{K}, \mathcal{T} \vdash e : dyn \quad \overline{\mathcal{K} \vdash P_i : (\tau_i, \mathcal{T}_i)} \quad \overline{\mathcal{K}, \mathcal{T}\mathcal{T}_i \vdash e_i : \tau}}{\mathcal{K}, \mathcal{T} \vdash \mathsf{dynamiccase}\ e\ \mathsf{of}\ \overline{P_i\ \texttt{=>}\ e_i} : \tau}$$

Similarly, the typed extended target calculus is obtained by adding the following rule:

$$\frac{\mathcal{K}, \mathcal{T} \vdash M : \tau' \quad \overline{\mathcal{K} \vdash P_i : (\tau', \mathcal{T}_i)} \quad \overline{\mathcal{K}, \mathcal{T}\mathcal{T}_i \vdash M_i : \tau}}{\mathcal{K}, \mathcal{T} \vdash \mathsf{case}\ M\ \mathsf{of}\ \overline{P_i : \tau'\ \texttt{=>}\ M_i} : \tau}$$

The compilation of case expressions is a simple inductive compilation of subterms. The $\mathsf{dynamiccase}$ expression is treated as a syntactic shorthand of the combination of case expressions and $(e\ \mathsf{as}\ \tau)$ expressions. Here, we follow a technique shown in [15] for translating case dispatch on partial dynamic types and give the following translation. Suppose

$$\mathcal{K}, \mathcal{T} \vdash \mathsf{dynamiccase}\ e\ \mathsf{of}\ \overline{P_i\ \texttt{=>}\ e_i} : \tau$$

is the given typing. Let $\mathcal{K}, \mathcal{T} \vdash P_i : (\tau_i, \mathcal{T}_i)$ be the derivation of P_i in the typing. We partition the rules $\overline{P_i\ \texttt{=>}\ e_i}$ into the equivalence classes $\overline{R_j : P_{i_j} : \tau_i\ \texttt{=>}\ e_{i_j}}$ induced by the syntactic equality of τ_i such that $\bigcup_{1 \le j \le n} R_j = \overline{P_i\ \texttt{=>}\ e_i}$ and in each partition R_j the order of P_{i_j} preserves the original occurrence ordering of P_i. Let $\mathcal{K} \vdash P_{i_j} : (\tau_j, \mathcal{T}_{i_j})$. The $\mathsf{dynamiccase}$ construct is then compiled to C_1 inductively defined as follows:

$$C_j = (\mathsf{case}\ (e\ \mathsf{as}\ \tau_j)\ \mathsf{of}\ \overline{R_j})\ \mathsf{handle}\ \mathtt{RuntimeTypeError}\ \texttt{=>}\ C_{j+1}$$
$$C_n = \mathtt{raise}\ \mathtt{RuntimeTypeError}$$

This implementation of $\mathsf{dynamiccase}$ is naive and inefficient due to the sequential case-statement evaluation with runtime exception. We believe it possible to compile-out the entire pattern matching without using runtime exception using pattern matching compilation methods.

5 Introduction of Existential Type Variables

One feature that cannot be represented in ML type discipline is locally-bound type variables in pattern matching. This feature is useful in writing polymorphic function with _dynamiccase statement, such as the following:

```
fun dlen dyn = dynamiccase dyn of
            {'a} (L:'a list, len:'a list -> int) => len L
```

where {'a} is a type variable declaration local to the rule. Supporting this feature requires *existential types*. This section develops an ML-style existential type and extends the type-directed compilation with it.

Existential types in the style of [12] can be defined in an ML-style implicit calculus as follows:

$$\frac{\mathcal{K}, \mathcal{T} \vdash e \ : \ \tau[\tau'/\alpha]}{\mathcal{K}, \mathcal{T} \vdash \mathsf{pack} \ \tau', e \ \mathsf{to} \ \exists \alpha.\tau \ : \ \exists \alpha.\tau}$$

$$\frac{\mathcal{K}, \mathcal{T} \vdash e_1 \ : \ \exists \alpha.\tau_1 \quad \mathcal{K}, \mathcal{T}\{x : \tau_1\} \vdash e_2 \ : \ \tau_2 \quad \alpha \notin FTV(\mathcal{T} \cup \tau_2)}{\mathcal{K}, \mathcal{T} \vdash \mathsf{open} \ e_1 \ \mathsf{as} \ \alpha, x \ \mathsf{in} \ e_2 \ : \ \tau_2}$$

Note that the condition on α is equivalent to the generalization of type variables α of $\tau_1 \to \tau_2$, which represents the duality of existential and universal types in an ML-style type discipline. Because the universal quantification mechanism is built-in ML, we can use this property to simulate existential types as follows:

$$\frac{\mathcal{K}, \mathcal{T} \vdash e_1 \ : \ \exists \alpha.\tau_1 \quad \mathcal{K}, \mathcal{T} \vdash \lambda x.e_2 \ : \ \forall \alpha.\tau_1 \to \tau_2 \quad \alpha \notin FTV(\tau_2)}{\mathcal{K}, \mathcal{T} \vdash \mathsf{open} \ e_1 \ \mathsf{as} \ \alpha, x \ \mathsf{in} \ e_2 \ : \ \tau_2}$$

This construct can be introduced in ML with minimal extension by combining it with the case expression as follows:

$$\frac{\mathcal{K}, \mathcal{T} \vdash e_1 \ : \ \exists \alpha.\tau_1 \quad \mathcal{K}, \mathcal{T} \vdash \lambda x.e_2 \ : \ \forall \alpha.\tau_1 \to \tau_2 \quad \alpha \notin FTV(\tau_2)}{\mathcal{K}, \mathcal{T} \vdash \mathsf{case} \ e_1 \ \mathsf{of} \ \{\alpha\} \ (x : \tau_1 \ \texttt{=>} \ e_2) \ : \ \tau_2}$$

Because Standard ML has various built-in mechanisms for type abstraction, the need of general first-class existential types may not be so high. At this moment, we also do not know its impact on the type inference mechanism. Therefore, instead of allowing this form freely in source programs, we restrict the introduction of existential types to (e as τ) by adding

$$\frac{\mathcal{K}, \mathcal{T} \vdash e \ : \ dyn}{\mathcal{K}, \mathcal{T} \vdash (e \ \mathsf{as} \ \exists \alpha.\tau) \ : \ \exists \alpha.\tau}$$

and restrict the above new **case** construct with existential type variables to the result of the following syntactic elaboration for the **dynamiccase** construct

dynamiccase e_1 of $\{\alpha\}$ (x:τ => e_2) $\Longrightarrow$ case (e_1 as $\exists \alpha.\tau$) of $\{\alpha\}$ (x:τ => e_2).

Based on this general strategy, we extend the type-theoretical framework developed so far with existential dynamic elimination.

5.1   The Source Calculus with Pattern Matching and Existential Types

In this subsection, we add existential types on top of the source calculus with pattern matching. Existential types are monotypes, but their occurrences are restricted to $(e \text{ as } \exists \alpha.\tau)$. For this purpose, we introduce another layer of mono-type π. The following gives new constructs of the source calculus:

$$e ::= \cdots \mid \text{case } e \text{ of } \overline{\{\alpha\} \; (P_i \Rightarrow e_i)} \mid (e \text{ as } \exists \alpha.\tau)$$

$$\tau ::= \alpha \mid \cdots \qquad \pi ::= \tau \mid \exists \alpha.\tau \qquad \sigma ::= \pi \mid \forall t : k.\sigma$$

Existential type variables are only used in existential quantification, which is eliminated by replacing them with universal quantification. To represent this nature in the kinded context, we treat existential type variables (α) distinct from ordinary type variables (t).

The well-formedness of existential types is given below:

$$\frac{\mathcal{K}\{t : R\} \vdash \tau[t/\alpha] \; : \; R}{\mathcal{K} \vdash \exists \alpha.\tau \; : \; R}$$

There are two points to be noted this well-formedness existential type derivation. By our convention on $\mathcal{K}\{t : R\}$, the type variable t does not occur in any context kinded by $\mathcal{K}$. Furthermore, existential type variables must be replaced with ordinary type variables with R kind and therefore existential types have always R kind. These properties become important in extending our type-directed compilation algorithm.

The typing rules for the new constructs are given below:

$$\frac{\mathcal{K}, \mathcal{T} \vdash e : \exists \alpha.\tau' \quad \overline{\mathcal{K}\{t : R\} \vdash P_i[t/\alpha] \; : \; (\tau'[t/\alpha], \mathcal{T}_i)} \quad \overline{\mathcal{K}\{t : R\}, \mathcal{T}\mathcal{T}_i \vdash e_i[t/\alpha] \; : \; \tau}}{\mathcal{K}, \mathcal{T} \vdash \text{case } e \text{ of } \overline{\{\alpha\} \; (P_i \Rightarrow e_i)} \; : \; \tau}$$

$$\frac{\mathcal{K}, \mathcal{T} \vdash e : dyn \quad \mathcal{K} \vdash \exists \alpha.\tau \; : \; R}{\mathcal{K}, \mathcal{T} \vdash (e \text{ as } \exists \alpha.\tau) \; : \; \exists \alpha.\tau}$$

The rule of case comes with the constraints $\alpha \notin FTV(\tau)$.

The target calculus and compilation can also be extended with existential types, whose technical details are omitted due to space limitation.

6   Implementation and Applications

This section presents implementation and applications. For this purpose we have to refer our development of type reification and representation, summarized below:

- The compiler reifies $tyRep(\tau)$ as the user-level datatype reifiedTy.
- The compiler reifies the compiler-generated dynamic value $Dyn(V, J)$ to a user-level datatype reifiedTerm that represents both the value V and its type tag L.

The implementation is carried out by extending the SML# compiler, which is already equipped with a type directed compilation phase for record polymorphism and others. The major part of the extension includes refinement of the type directed compilation with existential types, type-tag reification, and construction of `reifiedTy` and `reifiedTerm`.

(e as τ) and `dynamiccase` are written as `_dynamic` e as τ and `_dynamiccase`. Type `dyn` is refined to *partial dynamic type* τ `dyn` developed in [15]. τ `dyn` denotes dynamic values whose actual type is a subtype of τ. Type `dyn` is represented as `void dyn`, where `void` is a primitive type of SML# denoting the root supertype. Since the manipulation of partial dynamic types in [15] is restricted to ground monotypes, this refinement does not require any additional mechanism in the type-directed compilation presented in this paper.

The implementation provides the following functions in `Dynamic` structure.

```
val dynamic : ['a#reify. 'a -> void dyn]
val view : ['a#reify. 'a dyn -> 'a]
val dynamicToTerm : void dyn -> reifiedTerm
val termToDynamic : reifiedTerm -> void dyn
```

where `['a#reify.····]` means $\forall'a : R.····$. In addition to those dynamic primitives, the implementation introduces a user-level primitive construct `_reifyTy(`τ`)` for user programs to access type tag of any type annotation τ in user programs. The rest of this section demonstrates dynamic typing through examples.

6.1   Pretty Printing/Serialization and Deserialization

The implementation provides

```
val pp : ['a#reify. 'a -> unit]
```

as a first-class polymorphic function which pretty-prints any value, as seen in the following example interactive session:

```
# datatype foo = N | C of int * foo;
datatype foo = N | C of int * foo
# fun f (n, A) = (pp A; if n = 0 then A else f (n - 1, C (n, A)));
val f = fn : int * foo -> foo
# f (2, N);
N
C (2, N)
C (1, C (2, N))
val it = C (1, C (2, N)) : foo
```

where # is the input prompt printed by the SML# interactive system.

Deserialization can also be implemented by the composition of parsing to `reifiedTerm`, the primitive function `termToDynamic`, and `_dynamic` exp as τ construct. The implementation provides the following JSON serializer/ deserializer:

```
val fromJson : string -> void dyn
val toJson : 'a dyn -> string
```

By combing `fromJson` with `_dynamic` *exp* `as 'a dyn` construct, one can write the following function which deserializes JSON string to various JSON-compatible type according to a given sample ML term (when the given JSON data represents a value of that type, otherwise yields `RuntimeTypeError` exception).

```
# fun ('a#reify) importJson {json:string, sample:'a} =
    view (_dynamic (fromJson json) as 'a dyn)
val importJson = fn : ['a#reify. {json: string, sample: 'a} -> 'a]
# importJson {json="[{\"x\":1,\"y\":2,\"speed\":1.1},
                      {\"x\":3,\"y\":4,\"color\":\"red\"}]",
              sample = [{x=0,y=0}]} ;
val it = [{x = 1, y = 2}, {x = 3, y = 4}] : {x: int, y: int} list
```

In the `importJson` function, `sample` is used to obtain the type information of the desired result value. We find this programming idiom quite useful in accessing external JSON data; one can obtain an ML value of any JSON compatible type from a JSON string by simply specifying a relevant portion of JSON data as a sample ML value.

6.2   Database Programming

A practical application of dynamic typing is communicating with relational databases. Because the modern database is implemented as a network server that receives an SQL query as a string and returns its serialized result, communication with a database can be programmed similarly as a couple of serialization and deserialization functions using reified types and terms.

A relation (or table) can be represented as a list of records in ML. We associate the name of a table with its contents by a one-field record. For example, the following is the type of `sourceTable` table consisting of `fileId` and `fileName` columns:

```
{sourceTable : {fileId : int, fileName: string} list}
```

The `'a table` type, where `'a` must be a table type, is defined as follows:

```
datatype 'a table = TABLE of {keys : string list}
```

The `keys` field is the list of column names that constitute the primary key of the table. For bulk initialization of a database, we have implemented the following two functions:

```
val createTables : ['a#reify. conn -> 'a table -> unit]
val insert : ['a#reify. conn -> 'a -> unit]
```

where `createTable` creates a new table indicated by `'a table`, and `insert`
inserts an ML value of list of records to the table specified by `'a`. These functions
obtains $tyRep('a)$ as a term of `reifiedTy` using `_reifyTy('a)` and compare it
with the system catalog of the connected database to check that the command,
and hence `'a`, respects the database schema. They then convert the argument
to a term of type `reifiedTerm`, applies a non-standard serializer to the term
to obtain the SQL command string, and execute it on the database server. For
example, the skeleton of the `insert` function is the following:

```
fun 'a#reify insert conn (rel:'a) =
  let val serverTy = getServerTy conn
      val tableTy = _reifyTy('a)
      val _ = checkTable (serverTy, tableTy)
      val relTerm = dynamicToTerm (dynamic rel)
      val query = mkInertQuery relTerm
      val _ = execQuery (conn, query)
  in () end
```

`getServerTy` accesses the database system table, obtains the scheme information in JSON format, and converts it to `reifiedTy`. `checkTable` checks that
`serverTy` contains the `tableTy` field. `mkInsertQuery` is a `insert`-command-
specific serializer, which converts, for example,

```
[{fileId = 1, fileName = "a"}, {fileId = 2, fileName = "b"}]
```

to the following string:

```
INSERT INTO "sourceTable" ("fileId", "fileName")
VALUES (1, 'a.sml'), (2, 'b.sml')
```

6.3 Meta-programming

Dynamic typing allows us to program a type-safe meta-programming similarly
to one using GADTs. We demonstrate this feature by writing a simple evaluator.
    We define the type of terms of type `'a` as follows:

```
datatype 'a term = T of void dyn
```

For constructors of object-level terms, we introduce the following tag types:

```
datatype 'a value = VAL of 'a
datatype ('a,'b) lam = LAM of 'a term -> 'b term
datatype ('a,'b) app = APP of ('a -> 'b) term * 'a term
datatype ('a,'b) pair = PAIR of 'a term * 'b term
```

All of the above data constructors are hidden from users; instead, the following
functions are provided to construct object-level terms:

```
fun 'a#reify Val (x : 'a)  : 'a term =
  T (dynamic (VAL x))
fun ('a#reify,'b#reify) Lam (x:'a term -> 'b term)  : ('a -> 'b) term =
  T (dynamic (LAM x))
```

```
fun ('a#reify,'b#reify) App (x:('a -> 'b) term, y:'a term) :'b term =
  T (dynamic (APP (x, y)))
fun ('a#reify,'b#reify) Pair (x:'a term, y:'b term)  :('a * 'b) term =
  T (dynamic (PAIR (x, y)))
```

The `eval` function, which evaluates an object-level term of type `'a term` to a meta-level value of type `'a`, is implemented by using the `_dynamiccase` expression with existential type variables as follows:

```
fun evalD x =
  let fun 'a#reify eval (T x : 'a term) = _dynamic evalD x as 'a
  in _dynamiccase x of
        {'a} VAL (x:'a) => dynamic x
      | {'a,'b} LAM (f : 'a term -> 'b term) =>
        dynamic (fn x => eval (f (Val x)))
      | {'a,'b} APP (f : ('a -> 'b) term, x : 'a term) =>
        dynamic ((eval f) (eval x))
      | {'a,'b} PAIR (x : 'a term, y : 'b term) =>
        dynamic (eval x, eval y)
  end
fun 'a#reify eval (T x : 'a term) = _dynamic evalD x as 'a
```

The following shows a simple interactive session.

```
# val t = App (App (Lam (fn (x:real term) =>
                      Lam (fn (y:int term) => Pair (x, y))),
          Val 1.0), Val 1);
val t = T _ : (real * int) term
# eval t;
val it = (1.0, 1) : real * int
```

From this simple toy example, we see that dynamic typing can represent a form of type-safe meta-programming similarly to those using GADT and others. We should note that above program is written in a standard polymorphic type system of ML extended with dynamic typing, and it does not use any elaborate typing mechanism such as GADT or higher-rank polymorphism; it does not even use polymorphic recursion. This fact suggests that dynamic typing is an independent and fundamental primitive mechanism.

7 Conclusions

We have presented an implementation method of dynamic typing in ML and have implemented the method in SML#, a full-scale native code compiler of an extension of Standard ML. The method achieves an orthogonal extension of ML polymorphism with dynamic typing. Because $\text{dynamic}(e : \tau)$ and $(e \text{ as } \tau)$ are fully polymorphic in any monotype τ including free type variables, dynamic typing freely mixes with all the ML features including polymorphic type inference and pattern matching with user-defined datatypes. We have also extended the type-directed compilation method with existential types to support existentially-bound type variable guards in `dynamiccase` construct. With this extension, our method supports most of the standard features of dynamic typing discussed in literature. We have also demonstrated the usefulness of our method through examples.

In the type-theoretical development of our method, we have observed that the essential ingredients to realize dynamic typing are the type-directed compilation and existential types. Variant of these mechanism can be found in type systems that support non-parametric programming such as GADT, gradual typing, and generic programming. An interesting future investigation is to analyze the relationship between dynamic typing and those other non-parametric typing mechanisms. Comparison of our target calculus and the second-order calculus presented by [22] could shed some light on this research direction.

Acknowledgments. The authors thank an anonymous reviewer for his/her detailed comments. This work was partially supported by JSPS KAKENHI Grant Number JP18K11233. The second author's work was also partially supported by JSPS KAKENHI Grant Number JP19K11893.

References

1. Abadi, M., Cardelli, L., Pierce, B., Rémy, D.: Dynamic typing in polymorphic languages. J. Funct. Program. **5**(1), 111–130 (1995)
2. Abadi, M., Cardelli, L., Pierce, B., Plotkin, G.: Dynamic typing in a statically typed language. ACM Trans. Program. Lang. Syst. **13**(2), 237–268 (1991)
3. Atkinson, M., Buneman, O.: Types and persistence in database programming languages. ACM Comput. Surv. **19**(2), 105–170 (1987)
4. Chakravarty, M.M.T., Keller, G., Jones, S.P., Marlow, S.: Associated types with class. In: Proceedings ACM POPL, pp. 1–13 (2005)
5. Damas, L., Milner, R.: Principal type-schemes for functional programs. In: DeMillo, R.A. (ed.) In: Proceedings ACM POPL Symposium (1982)
6. Elsman, M.: Polymorphic equality - no tags required. In: Proceedings of the 2nd International Workshop on Types in Compilation. Kyoto, March 1998
7. Hall, C.V., Hammond, K., Peyton Jones, S.L., Wadler, P.L.: Type classes in haskell. ACM Trans. Program. Lang. Syst. **18**(2), 109–138 (1996)
8. Harper, R., Morrisett, G.: Compiling polymorphism using intensional type analysis. In: Proceedings ACM POPL Symposium, pp. 130–141 (1995)
9. Hengline, F.: Dynamic typing: syntax and proof theory. Science of Computer Programming (1992)
10. Leroy, X., Doligez, D., Frisch, A., Garrigue, J., Rémy, D., Vouillon, J.: The OCaml system release 4.10 documentation and user's manual (2020). https://caml.inria.fr/pub/docs/manual-ocaml/
11. Leroy, X., Mauny, M.: Dynamics in ML. In: Hughes, J. (ed.) FPCA 1991. LNCS, vol. 523, pp. 406–426. Springer, Heidelberg (1991). https://doi.org/10.1007/3540543961_20
12. Mitchell, J.C., Plotkin, G.D.: Abstract types have existential type. ACM Trans. Program. Lang. Syst. **10**(3), 470–502 (1988)
13. Ohori, A.: A simple semantics for ML polymorphism. In: Proceedings of ACM/IFIP Conference on Functional Programming Languages and Computer Architecture, pp. 281–292 (1989)

14. Ohori, A.: A polymorphic record calculus and its compilation. ACM Trans. Prog. Lang. and Syst. **17**(6), 844–895 (1995) (An extended version of Ohori, A: A compilation method for ML-style polymorphic record calculi. ACM POPL Symposium, 154–165, 1992.)
15. Ohori, A., Ueno, K., Sasaki, T., Kikuchi, D.: A calculus with partially dynamic records for typeful manipulation of JSON objects. In: Proceedings ECOOP Conference (2016)
16. Peyton Jones, S., Vytiniotis, D., Weirich, S., Washburn, G.: Simple unification-based type inference for GADTs. SIGPLAN Not. **41**(9), 50–61 (2006)
17. Peyton Jones, S., Weirich, S., Eisenberg, R.A., Vytiniotis, D.: A reflection on types. In: Lindley, S., McBride, C., Trinder, P., Sannella, D. (eds.) A List of Successes That Can Change the World. LNCS, vol. 9600, pp. 292–317. Springer, Cham (2016). https://doi.org/10.1007/978-3-319-30936-1_16
18. Pil, M.: Dynamic types and type dependent functions. In: Hammond, K., Davie, T., Clack, C. (eds.) IFL 1998. LNCS, vol. 1595, pp. 169–185. Springer, Heidelberg (1999). https://doi.org/10.1007/3-540-48515-5_11
19. Schrijvers, T., Peyton Jones, S., Chakravarty, M., Sulzmann, M.: Type checking with open type functions. In: Proceedings ACM ICFP Conference, pp. 51–62 (2008)
20. Siek, J.G., Taha, W.: Gradual typing for functional languages. In: Proceedings of the 2006 Scheme and Functional Programming Workshop, pp. 81–92 (2006)
21. SML# Project. https://smlsharp.github.io/en/
22. Sulzmann, M., Chakravarty, M.M.T., Jones, S.P., Donnelly, K.: System F with type equality coercions. In: Proceedings ACM SIGPLAN International Workshop on Types in Languages Design and Implementation, pp. 53–66 (2007)
23. Tolmach, A.: Tag-free garbage collection using explicit type parameters. In: Proceedings ACM Conference on LISP and Functional Programming, pp. 1–11 (1994)
24. Xi, H., Chen, C., Chen, G.: Guarded recursive datatype constructors. In: Proceedings ACM POPL Symposium, pp. 224–235 (2003)

Language Design

The Choice Construct in the Soufflé Language

Xiaowen Hu(ID), Joshua Karp(ID), David Zhao(ID), Abdul Zreika(ID), Xi Wu(ID),
and Bernhard Scholz(✉)(ID)

The University of Sydney, Sydney, Australia
{xihu5895,jkar4969,dzha3983,azre6702}@uni.sydney.edu.au
{xi.wu,bernhard.scholz}@sydney.edu.au

Abstract. Datalog has become a popular implementation language for solving large-scale, real world problems, including bug finders, network analysis tools, and disassemblers. These applications express complex behaviour with hundreds of relations and rules that often require a non-deterministic choice for tuples in relations to express worklist algorithms.

This work is an experience report that describes the implementation of a *choice* construct in the Datalog engine Soufflé. With the choice construct we can express worklist algorithms such as spanning trees in a few lines of code. We highlight the differences between rule-based choice as described in prior work, and relation-based choice introduced by this work. We show that a choice construct enables certain worklist algorithms to be computed up to 10k× faster than having no choice construct.

Keywords: Static analysis · Datalog · Non-deterministic

1 Introduction

Datalog and other logic specification languages [4,22,25,28] have become popular in recent years for implementing bug finders, static program analysis frameworks [3,25], network analysis tools [24,39], security analysis tools [31] and business applications [4]. For these applications, logic programming is used as a domain specific language to allow programmers to express complex program behavior succinctly, while enabling rapid-prototyping for scientific and industrial applications in a declarative fashion. For example, logic programming has gained traction in the area of program analysis due to its flexibility in building custom program analyzers [25], points-to analyses for Java programs [7], and security analysis for smart contracts [12,13].

Although modern Datalog implementations such as Soufflé [34] have constructs (e.g., functors) that make Datalog Turing-equivalent, certain classes of algorithms are hard to implement. For example, worklist algorithms [33] that are commonly found in compilers and productivity tools [2], are challenging since they require a non-deterministic choice from a set. Without the notion of choice,

H. Oh (Ed.): APLAS 2021, LNCS 13008, pp. 163–181, 2021.
https://doi.org/10.1007/978-3-030-89051-3_10

programmers must manually introduce an (arbitrary) ordering on a set and select the elements inductively to simulate this choice. The ordering and the inductive selection in Datalog requires dozens of rules and can be highly inefficient.

In database literature [8,14–16,27], there have been Datalog extensions for non-deterministic choice. In the work of Krishnamurthy, Naqvi, Greco and Zaniolo, the non-determinism is enforced operationally by introducing functional dependency constraints on relations. A functional dependency constraint enforces that a particular subset of values in each tuple (the key) can only occur once in the relation. For example, an ternary relation (x, y, z) with the functional dependency constraint $(x, y) \rightarrow z$ ensures that the two tuples $(1, 2, 3)$ and $(1, 2, 4)$ cannot simultaneously exist in the relation, since they both contain the same values $(1, 2)$ for the key (x, y). In this system, any tuple in the relation causes all subsequent tuples that violate the functional dependency constraint to be rejected from being inserted into the relation.

In this work, we report on the experience of implementing a choice construct in Soufflé [25,34] and show (1) the simplicity of its semantics, (2) its ease of implementation, and (3) its efficiency in contrast to having no choice construct in the language. Prior work on choice has introduced functional dependencies as local, rule-based constraints, where the permissible tuples of a relation are only constrained on a rule-by-rule basis [16]. That work must be seen in the context of database research in the 90s that typically have a small number of rules. Soufflé programs have different characteristics, consisting of hundreds of rules and relations [7], where the relations are held in memory. For such applications, a rule-based choice becomes tedious and error prone because the functional dependency constraint may need to be repeated per rule. Hence, we introduce a new variant of choice called *relation-based choice*. A relation-based choice makes the underlying auxiliary relations of a ruled-based choice [10] explicit to the programmer. This approach is more amenable for logic programming with many relations/rules to ease the burden for the programmer.

The contributions of our paper are summarized as follows:

- We introduce a relation-based choice construct for the Soufflé (a Datalog engine) that enforces a global functional dependency upon a relation (not a rule). With a choice construct, algorithms such as worklists can be expressed effectively and efficiently.
- We show that the semantics of relation-based choice is easily implementable in an engine like Soufflé with its intermediate representation, called the Relational Algebra Machine (RAM).
- We explain the differences between the semantics of rule-based choice in prior work [10] and relation-based choice in Soufflé. We demonstrate that relation-based choice is easier to understand by users of large-scale Datalog programs.

2   Motivating Example

Compilers and productivity tools require worklist algorithms [33], especially for control and data-flow analysis [2]. As part of more elaborate analyses, an example

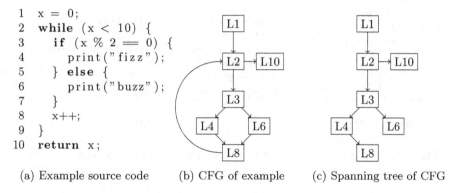

```
1    x = 0;
2    while (x < 10) {
3        if (x % 2 == 0) {
4            print("fizz");
5        } else {
6            print("buzz");
7        }
8        x++;
9    }
10   return x;
```

(a) Example source code   (b) CFG of example   (c) Spanning tree of CFG

Fig. 1. Running Example, showcasing a snippet of source code with the corresponding control flow graph and spanning tree

for a worklist algorithm is the construction of a spanning tree of a control-flow graph. This kind of application can be found for efficient placement of profiling code in programs [5], dataflow analysis [20,35], and loop reductions [19].

Control flow graphs (CFGs) express the traversal of control in a program whose nodes are basic blocks (linear code) and edges of the graph indicate potential traversal between two basic blocks. Figure 1a shows an input program whose control flow is depicted in Fig. 1b. The nodes in the control-flow graphs refer to the statements in the corresponding lines of Fig. 1a. The spanning tree of the CFG is illustrated in Fig. 1c, containing all the nodes of the CFG, but with only a subset of edges. Each node has at most one incoming edge and all nodes are connected, thus forming a spanning tree.

A standard worklist algorithm to compute a spanning tree is shown in Fig. 2a. A worklist contains all the nodes that ought to be visited in the next few iterations. The set **nodes** is used to store all visited nodes so far. The set **st** is used to store the edges of the spanning tree. The worklist is initialized with the root node, an artificial node with no incoming edge and a single out-going edge to the first basic block of the program. New nodes of the spanning tree are discovered and added to the worklist in each iteration, until no more valid nodes exist and the worklist becomes empty. Inside the loop, the worklist algorithm chooses an arbitrary node from the worklist. For this node, all adjacent nodes that haven't been visited yet will be added to the worklist and the spanning tree edges are constructed for the newly discovered nodes. With the worklist algorithm we can discover all reachable nodes and build the spanning tree in the discovery process.

While existing Datalog systems can be effectively used for many modern program analysis workloads [7,25], worklist-style algorithms are often challenging. Since standard modern Datalog engines are deterministic, they must explore *all* paths in a graph to compute a spanning tree, before making an arbitrary choice using a complex induction procedure. *Datalog* [1] represents programs as Horn clauses of the form L_0 :- L_1, ..., L_n. Each L_i has the form $R_i(x_1, ..., x_m)$; we say L_i is a *predicate* with relation R_i of arity m, and each attribute x_i is

worklist ← {root}
while worklist ≠ ∅ **do**
   v ← a choice from worklist
   nodes ← nodes ∪ {v}
   for u in adj(v) \ nodes **do**
      st ← st ∪ {(v, u)}
      worklist ← worklist ∪ {u}

```
.decl edge(v:symbol, u:symbol)
.input edge
.decl st(v:symbol, u:symbol) choice-domain u
.output st
st("root","L1").
st(v,u) :- st(_, v), edge(v,u).
```

   (a) Worklist Algorithm   (b) Soufflé with Choice

Fig. 2. Spanning tree: Worklist algorithm vs Soufflé with Relation-based choice

ether a constant or a variable. When the right hand side (the *body*) is empty, the Horn clause is interpreted as a fact; facts are unconditionally true. Otherwise, the Horn clause is interpreted as a rule, which means the head of the clause is true when all the literals in the body are evaluated to true: $L :- L_1, \ldots, L_n$. In particular, stratified negation [1], which is a standard semantics in Datalog to handle negation, does not permit a straightforward implementation of the worklist-style algorithms.

For example the spanning tree algorithm could be implemented with a rule such as st(v,u) :- st(_,v), edge(v,u), !st(_,u). However, this is illegal in standard Datalog engines because it contains a negation that is not stratified [1], i.e., the recursive relation st depends on the negation of st itself. The *choice* construct for rules overcomes the problem of choosing elements [27], which also improves the overall expressive power of Datalog programs [15]. In this work, we introduce a variation of rule-based choice which we call a relation-based choice. Consider the spanning tree example expressed in the Soufflé language as illustrated in Fig. 2. The Datalog program imposes a functional dependency constraint for relation st with the keyword **choice-domain** on attribute u. The functional dependency constraint ensures that for a given value of attribute u there exists at most one tuple. For example, if the relation st already contains the tuple (L5, L9), a subsequent insertion of a tuple such as (L7, L9) whose u's attribute value is L9 will be suppressed. With that functional dependency, the relation st becomes a function whose domain is the attribute domain of v and its co-domain is the attribute domain of u. For sake of brevity, we omit the co-domain declaration in Soufflé so that all the excluded attributes of the domain specification implicitly become the attributes of the co-domain.

Without a choice construct, the notion of non-deterministic choice must be simulated via induction. This process is quite complex due to stratified negation. Stratification ensures that a simple expression of a complement set (i.e., to eliminate nodes that have already been visited) is impossible, since doing so would involve a non-stratified negation. Instead, an algorithm written in stratified Datalog must construct an explicit complement relation, and use induction to select the next valid edge. Thus, while a spanning tree algorithm is expressible in modern Datalog engines (see Appendix of [23] for a Soufflé implementation), the native solution is very expensive in terms of runtime, memory usage, and code complexity.

To describe the native implementation in more detail, a rooted spanning tree is built incrementally from a chosen start node. The program repeatedly adds individual valid edges into the graph until no edges can be added. Since several edges may be valid at any given point, and we wish to explore only one arbitrary path, we must adorn the input edges with a total order so that ties among incoming edges can be broken. As the ordering is arbitrary, it is enough to assign a unique identifier to each edge in the graph. In Soufflé, unique numbers can be generated using the global counter, $, a unary functor which generates numbers sequentially when used, starting from the number zero (line 21). After creating an order among edges, an induction chooses the next valid edge from the worklist. A single valid edge must be chosen in each step, with elements with a lower ID being prioritized to break ties. We introduce a helper relation chosenEdgeInductive (line 127) with attributes step, edge_id and is_chosen for constructing the induction. The step number identifies the current state of construction, incrementing with each new edge added into the spanning tree. For each step, we seed the induction with a dummy base case. The recursive rule then sequentially checks every edge, incrementing the edge ID being checked while they remain invalid. As soon as a valid edge is found, it is selected, and the recursive case terminates. A tuple in the relation contains a TRUE in the final column if and only if the edge with the given edge ID was chosen at that step. We cannot simply negate validEdge to check if an edge is invalid in the recursive rule for chosenEdgeInductive, since the validity of an edge relies on the choices made in previous steps, which in turn depends on this inductive rule again. Therefore, the assumptions of stratified negation would be broken. Instead, invalidEdge must be constructed positively alongside validEdge.

The resulting program requires deeply recursive rules using inductive arguments, the notion of total orders, and the positive construction of complement sets. Hence, the simulation of choice in logic is tedious and error-prone resulting in programs with sub-optimal performance. In contrast, the choice construct enables a much simpler and far more efficient expression of a spanning tree algorithm. In contrast to the 21 Datalog rules required for the native Soufflé implementation, the running example in Fig. 1c demonstrates an implementation with 1 rule and a choice constraint for the relation st.

3   Semantics of Choice

In the previous section, we established that a choice construct in a language like Soufflé is fundamental for implementing worklist style algorithms. However, there are two options for implementing choice in a Datalog engine. The choice construct can be either (1) rule-based or (2) relation-based. In this section, we first explain the semantics of relation-based choice, which we choose to implement in Soufflé. We then explain the slight differences between the semantics of relation-based choice and rule-based choice. After that, we provide an example demonstrating why we believe relation-based choice makes more sense in modern Datalog language. Finally, we show that the expressive power of two different choice constructs are really the same and how to simulate rule-based choice semantics with relation-based choice construct.

Relation-Based Choice. Relation-based choice extends the expressiveness of logic languages (e.g., Datalog) by introducing non-determinism into the logic framework at the relation level. In particular, choice constraints are declared for a relation, allowing programs to arbitrarily make a single choice out of a set of possible candidates. For example, a relation declared with choice constraints in the Souffle Language has the form:

$$\texttt{.decl } A(X_1,\ldots,X_n) \texttt{ choice-domain } D_1,\ldots,D_k$$

Here, A is the relation name, and the sequence $X_1,\ldots,X_n$ forms the attributes of the relation. The choice constraints, `choice-domain` $D_1,\ldots,D_k$ imposes a set of relation-level constraints on the relation, where each domain D_i is a subset of attributes of the relation $D_1,\ldots,D_m \subseteq \{X_1,\ldots,X_n\}$. For example, a relation A declared with `.decl A(x:number, y:number, z:number) choice-domain x, (x,z)`. has to respect two functional dependencies: $x \to (y,z)$ and $(x,z) \to y$. Semantically, each choice constraint D_i encodes a relation-level invariant which ensures that there is at most a single tuple in the relation for any particular value for the attributes in the choice domain. This constraint is similar to the notion of primary or candidate keys in a relational database [32].

We extend the standard fixpoint semantics of Datalog [1]. The choice construct must have the ability to arbitrarily *choose* tuples in a relation such that the resulting set of tuples satisfies the choice constraint. Consider a relation A with attributes $X_1,\ldots,X_n$. Let $D \subseteq \{X_1,\ldots,X_n\}$ be a choice domain, let M_A be the Cartesian product of the attribute domains of A, let $\mathcal{A} \subseteq M_A$ be a set of tuples for A, and let $\mathcal{A}\big|_D$ be the set of instantiated values when tuples in $\mathcal{A}$ are restricted to D. A *choice function* $c_D : 2^{M_A} \to 2^{M_A}$ on a set of tuples, $\mathcal{A}$, for the relation A can be defined as

$$c_D(\mathcal{A}) := \left\{ \mathsf{SingleChoice}\left(\{t \in \mathcal{A} \mid t\big|_D \in \mathcal{A}\big|_D\}\right)\right\}$$

where $t\big|_D$ is the set of instantiated values for attributes in D for the tuple t. For each instantiation of attributes X_i in D, c_D chooses exactly one tuple matching that instantiation (via an extra function $\mathsf{SingleChoice}$ that arbitrarily chooses one element in the set). In other words, the choice function enforces uniqueness of values in the choice domain by arbitrarily choosing one tuple matching each instantiation. If M is the Cartesian product of the domain of relations in Datalog program P, then the choice function can be extended as $c : 2^M \to 2^M$, which applies c_D to each relation with choice constraints. The result of applying the choice function c to a Datalog instance is an instance that satisfies the uniqueness condition of the choice constraints, by arbitrarily choosing one tuple for each instantiated set of values for each choice domain.

The other important semantics for choice constraints is to exclude tuples that already define values for the choice domain. The exclusion semantics applies for recursive rules, where an earlier iteration may define some values for the choice domain, while a later iteration computes the same values. In this situation, the tuples in the later iteration should be rejected, since those values in the choice domain are already chosen. Given another set of tuples $\mathcal{A}'$, the instantiations in D that are already defined in $\mathcal{A}$ can be excluded by the exclusion function:

$$e_D^{\mathcal{A}}(\mathcal{A}') := \mathcal{A}' \setminus \{t \in \mathcal{A}' \mid t|_D \in \mathcal{A}|_D\}$$

The exclusion function can also be extended to an instance I, where $e^I(I')$ applies exclusion for the whole instance, excluding tuples in I' where values for the choice domain are already defined in tuples in I.

We extend the standard semantics of Datalog with choice constraints such that the result of applying the consequence operator always satisfies these constraints (using bottom-up evaluation). For this, we define a *choice consequence operator*, Γ_P^c, which applies the exclusion and choice operations, to I as follows:

$$\Gamma_P^c(I) = I \cup c(e^I(\{t \mid t :\!- t_1, \ldots, t_k \text{ is a rule instantiation with each } t_i \in I\}))$$

It can be seen that $\Gamma_P^c(I)$ is monotone. Therefore, we can show that there exists a minimum fixpoint of $\Gamma_P^c(I)$ by using *Tarski's Fixpoint Theorem* [37]. The resulting fixpoint is denoted the *choice constraint model* of Datalog program P given instance I.

We extend the semi-naive evaluation (i.e., Algorithm SEMI-NAIVE introduced in Appendix of [23]) with the choice consequence operator. The choice operator applies the choice and exclusion function and is similar to the consequence operator of semi-naive evaluation, defined as:

$$\Gamma_P^c(\Delta, I) = I \cup c \left(e^I \left(\left\{ t \,\middle|\, \begin{array}{l} t :\!- t_1, \ldots, t_k \text{ with each } t_i \in I \\ \text{and at least one } t_j \in \Delta \end{array} \right\} \right) \right)$$

The Algorithm SEMI-NAIVE in Appendix of [23] can then be modified by replacing the ordinary consequence operator Γ_P with the newly introduced choice consequence operator Γ_P^c. With this simple change, the efficient fixpoint evaluation of a choice program can be achieved.

Rule-Based Choice. Unlike relation-based choice, rule-based choice from prior work enforces the functional dependency on the rule level. That is, only the tuples generated by the rules with the choice constructs have to respect the functional dependencies. Let's consider the rule-based choice version of the rooted spanning tree as an example.

```
st("root","L1").
st(v, u) :- st(_, v), edge(v,u), choice((u), (v)).
```

The keyword `choice((X), (Y))` specifies the functional dependency $X \rightarrow Y$ on the rule-level. Unlike the relation-based implementation, only the second rule in the above program has to respect the functional dependency, while the resulting relation `st` can still have a non-injecting relation between X and Y.

In fact, the above program does not work as intended. Although the choice construct on second rule enforces that every end node u has a unique predecessor, there is nothing preventing the second rule from generating another edge to the starting node L1. This does not break the functional dependency because constraint is only enforced on rule-level and the tuple st("root", "L1") was specified in another clause in line one. To correct this, we need to rewrite the second rule as

```
st(v, u) :- st(_, v), edge(v,u), choice((u), (v)), u != "L1".
```

This program demonstrates a classic example where rule-based choice semantics can sometime become error-prone and hard to handle in large scale Datalog programs where each relation has dozens of rules.

Expressive Power. Although the user experience may differ, rule-based choice and relation-based choice have the same expressive power. We present an example of rewriting the rooted spanning tree example using rule-based choice semantics, but using relation-based choice construct. Consider the semantics of the rule-based choice implementation given under the stable model:

```
st("root","L1").
st(v, u) :- st(_, v), edge(v,u), chosen(u, v), u != "L1".
chosen(u, v) :- st(_, v), edge(v, u), !diffChoice(u, v).
diffChoice(u, v) :- chosen(u, v'), v != v'.
```

The above program cannot be computed under stratified semi-naive evaluation because of the cyclic negation between chosen and diffChoice. However, it is given by Giannotti et al. [9,10] under the stable model to formally describe the semantics of the rule-based choice implementation. The intuitive meaning of the program is to use an auxiliary table (diffChoice) to record the generated tuples and prevent the rule from generating tuples that violate the dependency. The implementation given by Giannotti et al. follows this intuition, and uses an auxiliary table internally. To mimic the effect of this with relation-based choice, we use a separate relation st' with a relation-based choice constraint to act as the auxiliary table.

```
.decl st'(v:symbol, u:symbol) choice-domain(u)
.decl st(v:symbol, u:symbol)
st("root","L1").
st'(v, u) :- st(_, v), edge(v,u), u != "L1".
st(v, u) :- st'(v, u).
```

In Sect. 4 we show that because of how relation-based choice is implemented, this emulation does not suffer from any extra overhead and has the exact same cost as the one proposed in the literature where an auxiliary table is used.

4 Implementation in Soufflé

In the following, we describe the implementation of relation-based choice in the state-of-the-art Datalog engine Soufflé [25]. A general overview of the Soufflé infrastructure is shown in Fig. 3. Soufflé parses the input Datalog program into an Abstract Syntax Tree (AST) representation. After parsing, Souffle applies a series of high-level optimizations on the AST representation. The AST contains information including all declared relations, rules and facts of the source program. After applying the AST optimisations, the AST representation is lowered into an intermediate representation called the Relational Algebra Machine (RAM). A RAM program consists of a set of relational operations along with imperative constructs. Mid-level optimizations are then applied to the RAM code, which finally is synthesized into an equivalent C++ program (or is interpreted).

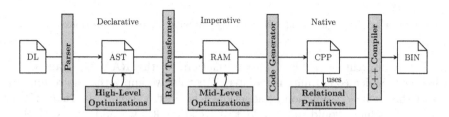

Fig. 3. Execution model of Soufflé.

A relation can be declared with zero or more choice constraints, each of which can contain a single attribute or a list of attributes. We extend the Soufflé parser to read a list of choice domains, written in the same form as shown in Sect. 3. We extend the current representation of relations in Souffle's with an extra attribute, storing each choice-domain as a list of indices representing the corresponding attributes' positions in the relation. For example, a relation declaration `.decl A(x, y) choice-domain x` will have a single choice-domain value $\{0\}$ denoting that the first attribute in A is in the choice-domain. A semantic check ensures that each choice-domain is valid (i.e., the attributes appear in the source relation), and a high-level optimization is used to reduce any redundant constraints.

At the final stage and before execution, we insert extra RAM operations to ensure the semantic for each insertion happens on a relation with choice-domain. We have various RAM elements implementing the semantics:

1. `TupleElement(t,i)` (or simply `t[i]`): It takes a runtime tuple $t = (t_1, \ldots, t_n)$ and an index i as arguments, and returns the value of the ith element of t.
2. `Insert(t,R)`: It inserts a runtime tuple $t = (t_1, \ldots, t_n)$ into a relation R.
3. `ExistenceCheck(P,R)`: It checks if the given pattern $P = (p_0, \ldots, p_n)$ exists in the relation R. p_i can be either a runtime expression (e.g., `TupleElement`), a constant or a special value $\perp$ which matches with any value.

Input: AST representation of the source program.
Output: RAM representation with insertion guarded by existence check to guarantee the choice domain.
$RAM \leftarrow$ translate the AST into RAM without concerning choice
for each insertion Insert(t, R) in RAM **do**
   if R has choice-domain **then**
      $G \leftarrow$ a new GuardedInsert(t, R, E=∅)
      for each choice-domain C **do**
         add ExistenceCheck(P, R) into E, $p_i = t[i]$ if $i \in C$ else $p_i = \bot$
         if R has prefix NEW **then**
            $R' \leftarrow$ the corresponding original relation of R.
            add ExistenceCheck(P, R') into E.
         end if
      replace the existing insertion with G in RAM.
   end if
   return RAM

Fig. 4. Augmenting a RAM program with Guarded Insertions

While inserting a tuple t into a relation R, the RAM program checks whether a choice constraints is violated. For this, we apply the choice function c and the exclusion function e^I mentioned in Sect. 3. Before an Insert(t,R) operation (which would add tuple t to relation R), we add an extra check ExistenceCheck(P,R) with pattern $P = (p_0, \ldots, p_n)$. The value of p_i is defined as:

$$p_i = \begin{cases} \text{TupleElement(t, i)} & \text{if the } i^{th} \text{ attribute is in } D \\ \bot & \text{otherwise} \end{cases}$$

where D is the choice-domain $D = \{d_0, \ldots, d_k\}$ on R. If the existence check finds a matching tuple, then the insert operation is rejected. Thus, prior to the insertion tuples are filtered so that only tuples that do not violate the functional dependency constraint of the choice domain are inserted.

For a non-recursive rule, the relation R in the ExistenceCheck would be the original relation that the tuple is inserted into. However, for a recursive rule, the relation R would denote a *new* auxiliary relation rather than the original one (for semi-naïve evaluation), which requires the exclusion function. To achieve this in RAM, a similar existence check is applied to each version of the relation, i.e., if R has the form R', then we also create an ExistenceCheck(P,R'), which ensures that any new tuples inserted into the relation will not replicate values for the choice-domains already defined in an earlier iteration, thus executing the semantics of the exclusion function.

To encapsulate the semantics of the filtering insertions, we introduce a new RAM operation, GuardedInsert(t, R, E), i.e., a regular Insert operation with an extra field E representing a list of ExistenceCheck operations. The semantics of GuardedInsert specifies that the insertion only proceeds if all existence checks in E have been done. An algorithm is given in Fig. 4, demonstrating

```
INSERT ("root", "a") INTO new_st
READ INPUT INTO delta_st.
LOOP
  IF ((NOT (delta_st = ∅)) AND (NOT (graph = ∅)))
    FOR a IN delta_st
      FOR b IN graph ON INDEX b[0] = a[1]
        IF (NOT (⊥,b[1]) ∈ new_st) AND (NOT (⊥,b[1]) ∈ st)
          INSERT (a[1], b[1]) INTO new_st
    BREAK IF (new_st = ∅)
    MERGE new_st INTO st
    SWAP (delta_st, new_st)
    CLEAR new_st
END LOOP
```

Fig. 5. Resulting RAM program from spanning tree with relation-based choice

the process of translating a Soufflé program with choice constraints. In this algorithm each existing `Insert` operation is translated into a corresponding `GuardedInsert` operation, which encodes the semantics of the choice and exclusion functions.

With the new RAM transformation, the spanning tree program (Fig. 2b) is translated into the RAM program as shown in Fig. 5. The parts highlighted in blue are the extra existence checks introduced by the new translator. Because relation-based choice only requires extra existence checks, it is easy to see the emulation we describe in Sect. 3 has the same cost as the rule-based choice implementation proposed in prior work.

Soufflé is equipped with highly-efficient data structures such as the specialized B-tree [26]. During the translation from RAM to C++, Soufflé analyzes the RAM representation to automatically compute indices for each primitive search [36]. This automatic index selection allows Soufflé to generate static C++ code that is tailored to data structures specialized for each index. As a result, the existence checks can be done efficiently with minimal overhead.

5 Experiments

This section explores the performance benefit of choice construct in Soufflé compared to native Soufflé without choice, as well as exploring any performance difference between relation-based choice and rule-based choice. Our experimental results illustrate that both choice constructs improve the environment of native Soufflé with similar performance statistics. Furthermore, we also demonstrate the applicability of choice and how it extends the expressive power of logic language. These experiments aim to answer three main research questions:

1. Does choice substantially improve runtime and memory performance over equivalent non-choice Datalog programs?

174 X. Hu et al.

2. Does choice allow for easier expressivity for Datalog programs requiring non-determinism?
3. Is there any performance difference between relation-based and rule-based choice?

Our experiments demonstrate a rooted spanning tree implementation applied on real-world input, along with 5 other algorithms that utilize choice constructs. For each algorithm, three versions are implemented:

1. **Relation-based Choice:** a Soufflé program that uses relation-based choice constraint (as implemented in Sect. 4)
2. **Rule-based Choice:** a Soufflé program that uses relation-based choice construct to emulate the rule-based choice semantics as described in Sect. 3.
3. **Native:** a Soufflé program that uses aggregates and auxiliary relations to emulate the effects of choice without using an explicit choice constraint

The experiments were conducted on a machine with an AMD Ryzen 2990WX 32-Core CPU and 126 GB of memory. All programs were run in sequential mode. Both runtime and memory usage were measured using the GNU `time` utility, observing both user time and maximum resident set size respectively.

5.1 Rooted Spanning Tree

We extract Control Flow Graphs (CFGs) from the real-world benchmark suite SpecCPU2000 [21]. These CFGs consist of large graphs with small connected components, thus the spanning forest consists of one spanning tree for each connected component. Computing the spanning tree of a program's CFG is very important for program analysis tools to identify loops, possible optimization opportunities and security flaws, etc. Since each input file contains several connected components, we modify the rooted spanning tree example in Fig. 2b by computing a spanning forest with relation-based choice construct:

```
.decl edge(module:symbol, x:symbol, y:symbol)
.input edge
.decl startNode(module:symbol, x:symbol)
.input startNode
.decl st(module:symbol, x:symbol, y:symbol) choice-domain (module, y)
.output st

st(M,X,Y) :- startNode(M,X), edge(M,X,Y).
st(M,X,Y) :- st(M,_,X), edge(M,X,Y).
```

The attribute `module` identifies the name of the function where each connected component is generated from. By providing a single root node `startNode` for each component (line 4), we compute the spanning forest for the whole graph. The choice domain of relation `st` is specified as (`module`, `y`), so that each module (connected component) contains a single spanning tree. Finally, the rule on line 9 states that a spanning tree edge from X to Y in the connected component M exists if the spanning tree reaches node X and there is an edge from X to Y.

Table 1. Performance result from Spec CPU2000, timeout set to be 30 min.

Program	Benchmark information		Runtime (seconds)		Memory usage (MBs)	
	# of components	Average size (edges)	Native	Speedup factor	Choice	Native
gzip	84	28	2.75	275.00	5.00	10.95
swim	6	26	0.02	2.00	4.72	5.20
applu	16	56	1.42	142.00	4.84	8.69
gcc	1896	50	timeout	>10k	8.00	573.72
art	26	35	1.57	157.00	4.93	9.23
equake	26	16	0.22	22.00	4.87	6.11
ammp	175	32	26.19	2619.00	5.14	28.01
sixtrack	213	49	312.8	>10k	5.30	94.32
gap	830	38	298.2	>10k	5.84	116.64
bzip2	72	34	7.8	780.00	5.07	16.64
apsi	96	30	6.41	641.00	4.84	13.70
wupwise	20	32	1.7	170.00	5.02	9.94
mgrid	10	26	0.06	6.00	4.79	5.45
vpr	261	22	18.4	1840.00	5.18	21.84
mesa	1064	29	1258.55	>10k	5.98	237.61
mcf	26	25	0.26	26.00	4.82	6.36
crafty	108	88	1037.3	>10k	5.10	176.52
parser	293	25	54.79	5479.00	4.93	34.68
perlbmk	234	44	174.4	>10k	5.09	61.21
vortex	918	29	426.92	>10k	5.66	112.27
twolf	180	62	419.25	>10k	5.12	96.55

The translated rooted spanning tree program in native Soufflé uses an inductive approach as in Sect. 2 and is modified in a similar way to calculate the spanning forest. Its implementation follows concepts from typical worklist algorithms, incrementally generating the set of edges corresponding to a spanning tree of the input graph. The inductive process ensures that each edge appears only once in the output, and the output edges correspond to a tree, which contains no cycles.

During this experiment, we find no measurable runtime or memory difference between the relation-based and rule-based choice implementations. Both of them are able to finish all the benchmarks within 0.1 s and consume a similar amount of memory. Compared with relation-based choice, rule-based choice implementation requires an extra relation to keep track of the inserted tuples, and an extra insertion to dump the result from the auxiliary relation into the final result. However, in real-world use cases, because of the functional dependency constraint, the auxiliary relation tends to have a relatively small size, which makes the extra overhead small in comparison to the overall runtime and memory consumption. Specifically, in this experiment, the auxiliary relation in the rule-based choice version contains only the edges of the result spanning tree, which is much smaller than the overall graph size. Thus, we calculated a speedup factor based on two choice implementations to demonstrate the performance

Table 2. Summary of experiment results.

Program	Input	Relation-based choice			Rule-based choice			Native		
		R#	T(s)	M(MB)	R#	T(s)	M(MB)	R#	T(s)	M(MB)
Eligible advisors	3000	1	0.01	5.5	2	0.01	5.7	4	0.11	13.7
Total order	2000	2	0.23	5.2	3	0.23	5.2	3	75.88	43.9
Bipartite matching	3000	1	2.73	93.2	2	2.73	93.2	15	timeout	771
More dogs than cats	18 000	3	4.42	7	4	4.42	7	1	0.01	6.7
Highest mark in grade	10 000	1	0.02	6	2	0.02	6.3	4	0.02	6.3

difference between the choice constructs and native Soufflé implementation in
Table 1.

The results show a significant improvement for the choice-based program
compared to the native Soufflé program, performing at least 2× faster and up to
more than 10k× faster on larger benchmarks such as gcc and mesa. In terms
of memory consumption, the choice version consumes considerably less memory
than the native Soufflé version, and achieves a consistent memory usage across
all benchmarks. In comparison, the native Soufflé version uses significantly more
memory as input size increases. This is because the choice constraint only computes and stores edges that are included in the spanning tree, which are generally
fairly small compared to the constant overheads of executing a Soufflé program.
On the other hand, the native version needs to store many intermediate computations and relies on a complex recursive scheme to obtain the same results.

Another consideration is the code complexity of both the choice constructs
and native Soufflé implementation. For this spanning tree problem, the native
Soufflé implementation requires 21 rules with complex recursive structure. On
the other hand, relation-based choice version requires a minimum amount of
code, with only 2 rules and a choice construct on the st relation. Finally, for
rule-based choice, two extra auxiliary rules and one extra constraint are used as
described in Sect. 3.

5.2   Other Applications

Along with the spanning tree example, we present five other algorithms, most
of them are classic examples of non-deterministic algorithms in Datalog [9]:

- **Eligible advisors**: Choosing an advisor for each student.
- **Total order**: Assigning an arbitrary total order over an unordered list.
- **Bipartite matching**: Computing a matching over a bipartite graph.
- **More dogs than cats**: Taking two sets of elements and deciding if one set
  contains more elements than the other one.
- **Highest mark in grade**: Finding the highest mark in a subset of marks
  subject to a condition, e.g., the highest mark among students in each grade.

Table 2 shows the results for the choice versions compared to the native
Souffé implementations. No runtime or memory difference is discovered between
relation-based and rule-based choice. The reason is exactly the same as for the

rooted spanning tree experiment, the overhead of rule-based choice implementation is extremely small because of the functional dependency constraint force upon on the extra auxiliary relation. Thus, in the followings, we discuss only relation-based choice and native implementations, unless otherwise specified.

For the majority of these benchmarks, choice constraints lead to significantly better performance than the native Soufflé version. This improvement can be attributed to native Soufflé versions usually requiring the full computation of a relation, followed by selecting a unique subset satisfying the equivalent functional dependencies as a post-processing step. On the other hand, choice constraints allow for the functional dependencies to be checked on-the-fly, thus not needing the full unconstrained relation, benefiting both memory and runtime.

The *eligible advisors* example most clearly demonstrates the improvement in performance with the choice construct. Here, the relation-based choice can simply compute the student/advisor relationship with a single rule with a choice constraint on the `advisor` relation. However, the native Soufflé implementation must compute the full unconstrained `advisor` relation, with a unique numbering scheme to enforce a total ordering. Then, as a post-processing step, the algorithm selects a subset satisfying the choice constraint by using the total ordering (for example, by choosing the minimum value for the unique number).

Similar patterns can also be observed in the *total order* and *bipartite matching* examples. These benchmarks demonstrate situations where choice constraints allow for both an easier and more effective specification of the problem.

On the other hand, the benchmark *highest mark* shows a negligible performance difference. In both implementations, an aggregation is used to summarize the highest mark of each grade and is the main performance bottleneck of the whole algorithm. The performance benefit of the choice constraint that is used to restrict the result of the aggregation becomes insignificant. However, the difference in number of rules (4 v.s. 1) still demonstrate the expressiveness of the choice constraint.

The only benchmark where the native Soufflé implementation outperformes the choice version is *more dogs than cats*. In this example, the choice version consider building an injective function between the two set of elements, and then check if the domain covers all the codomain, if so, the size of the domain set is greater than or equal to the codomain set. On the other hand, the native implementation takes a more straightforward approach, using a simple count aggregate to compute the sizes of the relations.

Importantly, for all examples, the choice version uses equal or less memory compared to the native Soufflé counterpart. This improvement is a result of the auxiliary relations each native Soufflé program utilizes to perform their computations. The difference is most evident in the *total order* example, where the native Soufflé implementation suffers an approximate 850% increase in memory usage as a result of its auxiliary relations.

Going beyond performance results, every example is implemented more elegantly using choice constraints. For most of the benchmarks, the choice version contains less than half the number of rules of the native Soufflé version, and in three of the five benchmarks, the choice version contains only a single rule. While not a perfect measurement of elegance, the small number of rules indicates that the choice-based implementations are generally more succinct and easier to understand than the native Soufflé versions. As shown, native Soufflé implementations of programs requiring arbitrary choice, as in worklist algorithms, typically involve the construction of several intertwined recursive relations with their complements, in addition to inductive rules, aggregate functions, and imposed total orderings. Such substantial overhead often obscures the meaning of the program. With the choice construct, such behavior is modeled with a simple constraint declaration. Moreover, the clearer semantics of the choice versions allows for a simpler extension and modification of the underlying program. For example, modifying the spanning tree example in Sect. 5.1 to constrain over only the attribute y rather than the pair (`module,` `y`) would involve changing only the given choice constraint. In a native Soufflé implementation, changing these functional dependencies could involve substantial structural changes to the auxiliary relations to ensure correctness.

In the context of Soufflé, these experiments demonstrate a significant impact of choice constraints, both in terms of performance overhead as well as the ease in expressing these algorithms. Thus, the introduction of choice constraints can be seen as extending the effective expressive power of the language, since certain problems that were infeasible using aggregates and auxiliary relations can now be solved using choice constraints.

6 Related Work

In relational databases, the notion of functional dependencies [6,38] is an important concept that allows a database designer to encode certain uniqueness properties as an invariant on a relation. These invariants are enforced when the relation is modified, with the database system rejecting any data that violates the uniqueness constraint. In logic programming, a deterministic computation is expressed as a set of logic rules. To extend the capabilities of this framework, previous work has introduced the choice construct [27,30] as a means of supporting non-determinism in Datalog, by enforcing uniqueness constraints similar to functional dependencies. There is some prior work on choice for Prolog [29]. Over the years, the applicability of choice has extended into the expression of greedy algorithms [16–18], as well as improving the overall expressive power of Datalog queries [11,14,15]. It has been cited to be particularly powerful when defining aggregate functions for relations, especially when used in conjunction with other predicates [8].

Choice constructs in prior work provide an intuitive foundation for enforcing non-determinism using a rule-based choice constraint, which is applied to a singular rule in the program, so that the underlying functional dependency is exclusively enforced on the local level of the specific rule that the constraint is declared on. In order to enforce these rule-based dependencies, auxiliary relations (e.g., the *chosen* relations in [16]) are required to provide an intermediate platform for computation for each rule with a constraint. The semantics of rule-based choice can be tedious and error prone when applying on Soufflé's programs that consist of hundreds of rules and relations.

7   Conclusion

Extending the expressive power of logic languages is a pertinent research area, especially with these languages becoming increasingly used in real-world problems. While languages such as Datalog have found success in a number of areas, worklist-style algorithms require notions of non-determinism which is currently challenging in modern Datalog engines. In this work, we report on implementing a choice construct in the Soufflé Language. We experiment with two flavors of the choice construct: rule-based choice (that has been reported in prior work) and relation-based choice, which we introduce in this work.

We experiment with a number of classic algorithms using the two choice constructs and show that using a choice construct significantly improves the performance, along with greater elegance in expressing non-determinism in Datalog. Our experiments indicate that there is a negligible performance difference between the two flavors of choice constructs. However, we show with an example that the semantics of rule-based choice can be tedious and error prone in Datalog programs with a large number of rules and relations.

References

1. Abiteboul, S., Hull, R., Vianu, V.: Foundations of Databases: The Logical Level, 1st edn. Addison-Wesley Longman Publishing Co., Inc., Boston (1995)
2. Aho, A.V., Lam, M.S., Sethi, R., Ullman, J.D.: Compilers: Principles, Techniques, and Tools, 2nd edn. Addison-Wesley Longman Publishing Co., Inc., Boston (2006)
3. Allen, N., Scholz, B., Krishnan, P.: Staged points-to analysis for large code bases. In: Franke, B. (ed.) CC 2015. LNCS, vol. 9031, pp. 131–150. Springer, Heidelberg (2015). https://doi.org/10.1007/978-3-662-46663-6_7
4. Aref, M., et al.: Design and Implementation of the LogicBlox System. In: SIGMOD 2015, pp. 1371–1382. ACM (2015)
5. Ball, T., Larus, J.R.: Efficient path profiling. In: Proceedings 29th Annual ACM/IEEE International Symposium on Microarchitecture, pp. 46–57. MICRO 29 (1996)
6. Beeri, C., Fagin, R., Howard, J.H.: A complete axiomatization for functional and multivalued dependencies in database relations. In: Proceedings of the 1977 ACM SIGMOD International Conference on Management of Data, pp. 47–61 (1977)
7. Bravenboer, M., Smaragdakis, Y.: Strictly declarative specification of sophisticated points-to analyses. In: Proceedings 24th ACM SIGPLAN Conference on Object Oriented Programming Systems Languages and Applications, pp. 243–262 (2009)
8. Ceri, S., Gottlob, G., Tanca, L.: Overview of research prototypes for integrating relational databases and logic programming. In: Logic Programming and Databases. SURVEYS, pp. 246–266. Springer, Heidelberg (1990). https://doi.org/10.1007/978-3-642-83952-8_12

9. Giannotti, F., Greco, S., Saccá, D., Zaniolo, C.: Programming with non-determinism in deductive databases. Ann. Math. Artif. Intell. **19**, 97–125 (2004)
10. Giannotti, F., Pedreschi, D., Saccá, D., Zaniolo, C.: Non-determinism in deductive databases. In: Delobel, C., Kifer, M., Masunaga, Y. (eds.) DOOD 1991. LNCS, vol. 566, pp. 129–146. Springer, Heidelberg (1991). https://doi.org/10.1007/3-540-55015-1_7
11. Giannotti, F., Pedreschi, D., Zaniolo, C.: Semantics and expressive power of nondeterministic constructs in deductive databases. J. Comput. Syst. Sci. **62**(1), 15–42 (2001)
12. Grech, N., Brent, L., Scholz, B., Smaragdakis, Y.: Gigahorse: thorough, declarative decompilation of smart contracts. In: ICSE 2019, pp. 1176–1186. ACM (2019)
13. Grech, N., Kong, M., Jurisevic, A., Brent, L., Scholz, B., Smaragdakis, Y.: Madmax: surviving out-of-gas conditions in ethereum smart contracts. In: SPLASH 2018 OOPSLA (2018)
14. Greco, S., Molinaro, C.: Datalog and logic databases. In: Synthesis Lectures on Data Management, vol. 10, pp. 47–57 (2016)
15. Greco, S., Saccá, D., Zaniolo, C.: DATALOG queries with stratified negation and choice: from P to D^P. In: ICDT (1995)
16. Greco, S., Zaniolo, C.: Greedy algorithms in datalog with choice and negation. In: IJCSLP (1998)
17. Greco, S., Zaniolo, C.: Greedy algorithms in datalog. Theory Pract. Log. Program. **1**(4), 381–407 (2001)
18. Greco, S., Zaniolo, C., Ganguly, S.: Greedy by choice. In: Proceedings 11th ACM SIGACT-SIGMOD-SIGART Symposium on Principles of Database Systems, 2–4 June 1992, San Diego, California, USA, pp. 105–113. ACM Press (1992)
19. Hecht, M.S., Ullman, J.D.: Characterizations of reducible flow graphs. J. ACM (JACM) **21**(3), 367–375 (1974)
20. Hecht, M.S., Ullman, J.D.: A simple algorithm for global data flow analysis problems. SIAM J. Comput. **4**(4), 519–532 (1975)
21. Henning, J.L.: SPEC CPU2000: measuring CPU performance in the new millennium. Computer **33**(7), 28–35 (2000)
22. Hoder, K., Bjørner, N., de Moura, L.: μZ – An efficient engine for fixed points with constraints. In: Gopalakrishnan, G., Qadeer, S. (eds.) CAV 2011. LNCS, vol. 6806, pp. 457–462. Springer, Heidelberg (2011). https://doi.org/10.1007/978-3-642-22110-1_36
23. Hu, X., Karp, J., Zhao, D., Zreika, A., Wu, X., Scholz, B.: The choice construct in the souffle language (2021)
24. Huang, S.S., Green, T.J., Loo, B.T.: Datalog and Emerging Applications: An Interactive Tutorial. In: SIGMOD 2011, pp. 1213–1216. ACM (2011)
25. Jordan, H., Scholz, B., Subotić, P.: SOUFFLÉ: on synthesis of program analyzers. In: Chaudhuri, S., Farzan, A. (eds.) CAV 2016. LNCS, vol. 9780, pp. 422–430. Springer, Cham (2016). https://doi.org/10.1007/978-3-319-41540-6_23
26. Jordan, H., Subotić, P., Zhao, D., Scholz, B.: A specialized B-Tree for concurrent datalog evaluation. In: PPoPP 2019, pp. 327–339. ACM (2019)
27. Krishnamurthy, R., Naqvi, S.: Non-deterministic choice in datalog. In: Proceedings International Conference on Data and Knowledge Bases, pp. 416–424. Morgan Kaufmann (1988)
28. Madsen, M., Yee, M.H., Lhoták, O.: From datalog to flix: a declarative language for fixed points on lattices. In: PLDI 2016, pp. 194–208. ACM (2016)
29. Mendelzon, A.O.: Functional dependencies in logic programs. In: VLDB - Volume 11, pp. 324–330. VLDB Endowment (1985)

30. Naqvi, S.A., Tsur, S.: A Logical Language for Data and Knowledge Bases. Computer Science Press, Cambridge (1989)
31. Ou, X., Govindavajhala, S., Appel, A.W.: MulVAL: a logic-based network security analyzer. In: Proceedings USENIX Security Symposium - Volume 14, p. 8. SSYM 2005. USENIX Association (2005)
32. Paredaens, J., De Bra, P., Gyssens, M., Van Gucht, D.: Constraints. In: The Structure of the Relational Database Model. EATCS, vol. 17, pp. 61–112. Springer, Heidelberg (1989). https://doi.org/10.1007/978-3-642-69956-6_3
33. Rayside, D., Kontogiannis, K.: A generic worklist algorithm for graph reachability problems in program analysis. In: Proceedings of the Sixth European Conference on Software Maintenance and Reengineering, pp. 67–76 (2002)
34. Scholz, B., Jordan, H., Subotić, P., Westmann, T.: On fast large-scale program analysis in datalog. In: CC 2016, pp. 196–206. ACM (2016)
35. Sharir, M.: A strong-connectivity algorithm and its applications in data flow analysis. Computers & Mathematics with Applications **7**(1), 67–72 (1981)
36. Subotic, P., Jordan, H., Chang, L., Fekete, A.D., Scholz, B.: Automatic Index Selection for Large-Scale Datalog Computation. PVLDB **12**(2), 141–153 (2018)
37. Tarski, A.: A lattice-theoretical fixpoint theorem and its applications. Pacific J. Math. **5**(2), 285–309 (1955). https://projecteuclid.org:443/euclid.pjm/1103044538
38. Wiederhold, G.: Database Design, vol. 1077. McGraw-Hill New York, New York (1983)
39. Zhou, W., Sherr, M., Tao, T., Li, X., Loo, B.T., Mao, Y.: Efficient querying and maintenance of network provenance at internet-scale. In: SIGMOD, pp. 615–626 (2010)

Latent Effects for Reusable Language Components

Birthe van den Berg[1]($\boxtimes$)(iD), Tom Schrijvers[1](iD), Casper Bach Poulsen[2](iD),
and Nicolas Wu[3](iD)

[1] KU Leuven, Leuven, Belgium
{birthe.vandenberg,tom.schrijvers}@kuleuven.be
[2] Delft University of Technology, Delft, The Netherlands
c.b.poulsen@tudelft.nl
[3] Imperial College London, London, UK
n.wu@imperial.ac.uk

Abstract. The development of programming languages can be quite complicated and costly. Hence, much effort has been devoted to the modular definition of language features that can be reused in various combinations to define new languages and experiment with their semantics. A notable outcome of these efforts is the algebra-based "datatypes à la carte" (DTC) approach. When combined with algebraic effects, DTC can model a wide range of common language features. Unfortunately, the current state of the art does not cover modular definitions of advanced control-flow mechanisms that defer execution to an appropriate point, such as call-by-name and call-by-need evaluation, as well as (multi-)staging.

This paper defines *latent effects*, a generic class of such control-flow mechanisms. We demonstrate how function abstractions, lazy computations and a MetaML-like staging can all be expressed in a *modular* fashion using latent effects, and how they can be combined in various ways to obtain complex semantics. We provide a full Haskell implementation of our effects and handlers with a range of examples.

Keywords: Effect handlers · Effects · Monads · Modularity · Staging

1 Introduction

Modern programming languages, be they general purpose or domain-specific, can be built in a flexible manner by composing simple, off-the-shelf language components. It is attractive to build languages in this way as it is useful to study language components in isolation. Furthermore, it reduces the cost of developing new and improved programming languages. Indeed, reducing the effort of building languages to the effort of composing off-the-shelf language components for features such as function abstraction, exceptions or mutable state, is likely to enable language designers with limited resources or expertise—e.g., domain

© Springer Nature Switzerland AG 2021
H. Oh (Ed.): APLAS 2021, LNCS 13008, pp. 182–201, 2021.
https://doi.org/10.1007/978-3-030-89051-3_11

experts—to build their own languages. Providing a modular definition for these advanced language features enables a more widespread use of them, especially in the development of domain-specific languages (DSLs).

To build programming languages from reusable components, we need a framework for defining those components. Two promising techniques for such a framework are *Data Types à la Carte* [23] (DTC) and *Algebraic Effects & Handlers* [18] (AE&H). Using these, language interpreters can be implemented in two steps:

$$Syntax \xrightarrow{denote} Effects \xrightarrow{handle} Result$$

The first step defines a *denote* function that maps the syntax of an object language onto effectful (*monadic* [13]) operations. By implementing *denote* using DTC, we can seamlessly compose *denote* functions from isolated cases for different *Syntax* constructors.

In the second step, *handle* defines the semantics of effectful operations and their effect interactions. Using AE&H allows cases of *denote* to be defined in an effect polymorphic way; i.e., a case maps to a monad that has *at least* the relevant operations, and possibly more. Furthermore, we can define *handle* functions for different effects in isolation, and seamlessly compose them by nesting handlers. Thus, DTC+AE&H provides a powerful framework for composing programming languages from isolated components.

However, not all language fragments have an obvious modular definition in terms of AE&H. Traditional algebraic effects and scoped effects [29] are baking in assumptions about control-flow and data-flow. These assumptions get in the way of expressing a modular semantics for some language features. In particular, control-flow mechanisms that defer execution, such as lambda abstractions with effectful bodies, lazy evaluation strategies, or (multi-)staging, are neither *algebraic* [17] nor scoped. This implies that the only way to implement these mechanisms is by means of sophisticated encodings that are often relatively low-level and non-modular. As such, these control-flow mechanisms present a severe challenge for allowing non-experts to build programming languages by composing off-the-shelf components.

This paper presents a novel form of effects and handlers that addresses this challenge: *latent effects and handlers*. Latent effect handlers defer the running of side effects, such that they are "latent" until handlers for all effects have been applied. This notion of effects can be used to directly define handlers for language components that defer execution, such as lambda abstractions with effectful bodies, lazy evaluation, and (multi-)staging.

After introducing the background (Sect. 2), our main contributions are:

- We introduce *latent effect trees*, implemented using Haskell (Sect. 3).
- We show how to encode lambda abstraction and application in terms of latent effects. We illustrate how this allows us to define lambda abstraction with effectful bodies as a composable language component (Sect. 3).
- We illustrate how to compose languages from reusable components using latent effects by showing how to encode lazy evaluation (call-by-need and call-by-name), and MetaML-like multi-staging (Sect. 4).

- We provide an effect library[1] with syntax and semantics in Haskell for various simple and advanced language features. These features can be used as isolated components to construct languages.

Finally, we discuss related work (Sect. 5) and conclude (Sect. 6). For an extended version of this work, including a library of effects and an elobarion of our two case studies, we refer to van den Berg et al. [2].

2   Background and Motivation

This section summarizes the state of the art in modular language definition by means of DTC and AE&H, discusses the challenges and problems associated with treating lambdas in this setting, and sketches how our new latent effects enable the integration of modular forms of advanced control-flow effects.

2.1   Modular Syntax and Semantics with Data Types à la Carte

Data types à la Carte [23] (DTC) solves the core problem of assembling language definitions from isolated components. It solves this for both syntax and semantics to be composed in a modular way. For an accessible introduction to DTC, we refer to [23]; we summarize the key points here.

Firstly, the abstract syntax of a language is modularized into the syntax of each isolated feature. This is achieved by defining a recursive type *Syntax S* of ASTs in terms of the shape S of its nodes. This shape S can be composed out of shapes $S_1, \dots, S_n$ of the individual features: $S = S_1 + \dots + S_n$.

Secondly, the semantic function *denote* $:: Syntax\ S \to M$ that maps ASTs *Syntax S* to their meaning M is modularized into the separate syntactic maps of the individual features. This is done by parameterizing the recursive semantic map of the AST with the semantic mapping of the individual nodes, *denote* = *fold denote$_S$* where *denote$_S$* $:: S\ M \to M$ is composed out of the semantic maps:

$$denote_{S_1} :: S_1\ M \to M \qquad denote_S = denote_{S_1} + \dots + denote_{S_n}$$
$$denote_{S_n} :: S_n\ M \to M$$

This modular approach affords great flexibility to quickly assemble a range of different languages and to explore language design: features can be added or removed, and their semantic maps can be changed. We use the DTC approach extensively when defining a library of effects in Sect. 4.3.

Unfortunately, this approach comes with a serious limitation: to be able to combine the semantic maps of different features, they must agree on the semantic domain M. This often prohibits the unanticipated combinations of features, even due to small differences in their semantic domain, such as one feature requiring access to an environment or store that the other feature does not expect.

---

[1] https://github.com/birthevdb/Latent-Effect-and-Handlers.git.

Moggi [13] observed that many of the differences in semantic domains of common language features, usually called (side-)effects, can be captured in the category-theoretical pattern of *monads*. Although not all monads compose, the state of the art in modular monads, *algebraic effects and handlers* (AE&H) [18], is well-aligned with the DTC approach of modular language features.

In fact, AE&H tackles the problem of modularly defining a monad in much the same way DTC tackles the problem of modularly defining a language. Indeed, the API of the monad (its "syntax") is modularized into separate effects; the category-theoretical concept of a free monad plays the role of an abstract syntax of API calls. A modular meaning is assigned to the free monad by means of semantic maps for the separate effects. The key difference with DTC is that the different effects do not all have to be mapped to the same semantics. Instead, by means of "modular carriers" their semantics can be layered [20].

Whereas AE&H is used to define (simpler) language features, we use latent effects and handlers, which we introduce in Sect. 3, to modularly define more complex language features.

2.2   Advanced, Non-modular Control-Flow Effects

The AE&H literature shows how to express a range of different control-flow effects such as exceptions, non-determinism and even call-with-current-continuation. However, as traditional effects and handlers rely on assumptions about data-flow and control-flow, more advanced and complicated control-flow effects are missing, such as call-by-name and call-by-need evaluation or multi-staging. These features typically defer execution and are *non-algebraic*.

An operation is *algebraic* when it meets the following requirements:

1. It can be expressed as $op :: D \to \forall a.M\ a \to ... \to M\ a$ where D represents the non-computational parameters that the operation has, M is a monad with algebraic operations, and each $M\ a$ typed parameter represents a possible continuation of the operation.
2. It satisfies the *algebraicity property*, which states that, no matter which possible continuation m_i we take, the continuation *immediately* transfers control to the current continuation k.

$$(op\ d\ m_1\ ...\ m_n) \ggg k \equiv op\ d\ (m_1 \ggg k)\ ...\ (m_n \ggg k)$$

Although many operations are algebraic, there are many common control-flow operations that are not. For instance, $catch :: \forall a.M\ a \to M\ a \to M\ a$ is an operation that executes the computation in the first argument, and if that computation raises an exception, proceeds by executing the second argument. The *catch* operation is not algebraic; i.e.,

$$(catch\ m_1\ m_2) \ggg k \not\equiv catch\ (m_1 \ggg k)\ (m_2 \ggg k)$$

since exceptions raised during evaluation of k should *not* be handled by m_2.

The lack of support for control-flow effects such as exception handling, motivated the development of *scoped effects* [29]. An operation is *scoped* when it can be expressed as having the following type:

$$op :: D \to \forall a.M\ a \to ... \to M\ a \to \forall b.(a \to M\ b) \to ... \to (a \to M\ b) \to M\ b$$

The universal quantification over a restricts data flow: for a given operation $op\ d\ m_1...m_n\ k_1...k_m$, it is *only* the possible continuations $k_1...k_m$ that can inspect values yielded by computations m_i. The allowable destinations of data produced by the computation are restricted to those determined by the operation. The *catch* operation is compatible with this restriction: it can be implemented as a scoped operation $catch' :: \forall a.M\ a \to M\ a \to \forall b.(a \to M\ b) \to M\ b$.

However, this pattern does not apply to more advanced control-flow effects for which the data produced by a computation can be used outside of the operation. For example, lambda abstractions delay the execution of computations in the body of a function until the function is applied (or not, depending on dynamic control- and data flow). To support such deferred execution, the return type V in the body of a lambda abstraction $abstr :: String \to M\ V \to M\ V$ is *not* universally quantified. Thus, $abstr$ is not a scoped operation. It is also not algebraic, as the equation $abstr\ x\ m \ggg k \equiv abstr\ x\ (m \ggg k)$ would cause k to be (wrongly) deferred, and could cause free variables in k to be captured. Other control-flow effects, such as call-by-need and call-by-name evaluation and multi-staging annotations for (dynamically) staging and unstaging code, defer execution in a similar way, and are similarly neither scoped nor algebraic.

It is theoretically possible to define the control-flow effects discussed above, by making the control flow of all operations *explicit*; e.g., by writing interpreters in continuation-passing style (CPS). However, the relatively low-level nature of CPS and its non-modular style, make this approach fall short of our goal of composing languages from simple, off-the-shelf components.

2.3   Our Approach: Latent Effects

We provide modular support for advanced control-flow effects such as function abstraction, with its different evaluation semantics, and staging. Our solution generalizes the approach of DTC and AE&H outlined above. In fact, it does not require any changes to the DTC approach for modular abstract syntax trees and modular semantic mapping. It only impacts the second part of the pipeline, replacing AE&H with a more general notion of *latent effects and handlers* (LE&H).

LE&H is based on a different, more sophisticated structure than AE&H's free monad. This structure supports non-atomic operations (e.g., function abstraction, thunking, quoting) that contain or delimit computations whose execution may be deferred. Also, the layered handling is different. The idea is still the same, to replace bit by bit the structure of the tree by its meaning. Yet, while AE&H grows the meaning around the shrinking tree, LE&H grows little "pockets of meaning" around the individual nodes remaining in the tree, and not just around the root. The latter supports deferred effects because later handlers can still re-arrange the semantic pockets created by earlier handlers.

LE&H are the first to modularly express advanced control-flow effects, such as staging and lambda abstractions, and provide different handlers, e.g., for call-by-name and call-by-need evaluation. Moreover, they combine with existing algebraic effects to express varying semantics for a large range of languages.

3   Latent Effects

This section presents *latent effects*. Latent effects generalize algebraic effects to include control-flow mechanisms that defer computation. As our running example we use lambda abstraction, which—as discussed in Sect. 2.2—is neither an algebraic nor a scoped operation. We show that it can be defined as a latent effect. We start from a non-modular version that we refine in two steps. First we add support for modular signatures, and then support for modular handlers.

3.1   Non-modular Definition of Lambda Abstraction

First we provide a non-modular definition of the lambda abstraction effect.

Monadic Syntax Tree. The type $LC\ v\ a$ is a non-modular monadic syntax tree that supports three primitive operations for a de Bruijn indexed λ-calculus.

```
data LC v a where
    Return :: a → LC v a
    Var    :: Int → (v → LC v a) → LC v a
    App    :: v → v → (v → LC v a) → LC v a
    Abs    :: LC v v → (v → LC v a) → LC v a
```

Here, the v of $LC\ v\ a$ is a value type parameter, and a represents the return type of the computation. Thus $Return\ x$ is a trivial computation that returns x. $Var\ i\ k$ retrieves the value of type v associated with the ith variable and passes it to the continuation k. The application $App\ v_1\ v_2\ k$ applies the value v_1 to the value v_2 and passes the result to the continuation. Finally, $Abs\ e\ k$ builds a closure value out of the function body e and passes it to the continuation.

For example, we can represent the lambda expression $(\lambda x \rightarrow x)\ 1$ as the LC expression $Abs\ (Var\ 0\ Return)\ (\lambda v \rightarrow App\ v\ 1\ Return)$. This computation constructs an abstraction and passes it to the continuation as a (closure) value v. The continuation applies v to 1 and passes the result to $Return$. The closure retrieves the value of variable with index 0 (i.e., x) and passes it to $Return$.

Handler. The idea of a handler is to map the syntax tree onto its meaning. We illustrate this on the $LC\ v\ a$ type, where we use the type $v = Closure$ for values.

data *Closure₁* **where**   **type** *FunPtr₁* $=$ *Int*
    Clos₁ :: *FunPtr₁* $\rightarrow$ *Env₁* $\rightarrow$ *Closure₁*   **type** *Env₁* $=$ [*Closure₁*]
type *Store₁* $=$ [*LC Closure₁ Closure₁*]

A closure contains a function pointer and an environment. The function pointer is an index into a list of deferred computations (i.e., function bodies) that we call the *(resumption) store*. The environment is a list that maps the closure's parameters (which are indexes) onto their values.

Now we are ready to define the handler *handleAbs* as a function that, given an initial environment and store, maps an *LC Closure a* computation onto its meaning, which is a tuple of the result value of type *a* and the final store.

$$
\begin{aligned}
&handleAbs :: Env_1 \rightarrow Store_1 \rightarrow LC\ Closure_1\ Closure_1 \rightarrow (Store_1, Closure_1)\\
&handleAbs\ \_\quad r\ (Return\ x)\quad = (r, x)\\
&handleAbs\ env\ r\ (Var\ n\quad k) = handleAbs\ env\ r\ (k\ (env\ !!\ n))\\
&handleAbs\ env\ r\ (App\ v_1\ v_2\ k) = handleAbs\ env\ r'\ (k\ v)\\
&\textbf{where}\ (Clos_1\ fp\ env') = v_1\\
&\qquad\quad (r', v)\qquad\quad = handleAbs\ (v_2 : env')\ r\ (r\ !!\ fp)\\
&handleAbs\ env\ r\ (Abs\ e\quad k) = handleAbs\ env\ r'\ (k\ v)\\
&\textbf{where}\ v = Clos_1\ (length\ r)\ env\\
&\qquad\quad r' = r \mathbin{+\!\!+} [e]
\end{aligned}
$$

First, the leaf case of the handler returns the value in that leaf, supplemented with the resumption store. Next, the variable case looks up the variable in the environment and passes it to the continuation. Then, the application case unpacks the closure, retrieves the corresponding function body from the resumption store and applies it to the extended environment and store. The resulting value is passed to the continuation. Finally, the abstraction case adds the function body to the resumption store, creates a closure that indexes this new entry, and calls the continuation on this closure value.

3.2   Modular Latent Effect Signatures and Trees, Naively

We now modularize the definition of *LC* by separating the recursive structure of the monadic syntax from the node shapes of the *Var*, *App* and *Abs* operations.

Latent Effect Signature. We call the node shapes the latent effect signature. In this case, it is called *Abstracting v* with *v* the type of values.

data *Abstracting v* :: $* \rightarrow (* \rightarrow *) \rightarrow *$**where**
    Var' :: *Int* $\rightarrow$ *Abstracting v v NoSub*
    App' :: $v \rightarrow v \rightarrow$ *Abstracting v v NoSub*
    Abs' ::   *Abstracting v v (OneSub v)*

Besides its first parameter v, the type *Abstracting* v p c is indexed by two further parameters: The parameter p is the return type of the primitive operations; this is the type of value they pass to their continuation. As all three primitive operations return a value of type v, we have that $p = v$. The parameter $c :: * \to *$ captures the number and result type of the subcomputations. As *Var'* and *App'* have no subcomputations, they use the type $c = NoSub$ to indicate that. However, *Abs'* has a subcomputation and it indicates this with $c = OneSub$ v. This subcomputation is the body of the function abstraction, whose return type is v. Hence, *OneSub* v has one constructor *One :: OneSub* v v.

data *NoSub* :: $* \to *$**where**   **data** *OneSub* v :: $* \to *$**where**
                                                      One :: *OneSub* v v

Latent Effect Tree, Version 1. The type *Tree*$_1$ σ a extends a latent effect signature σ into a recursive syntactic structure that is a monad in a.

data *Tree*$_1$ $(\sigma :: * \to (* \to *) \to *)$ a **where**
    Leaf$_1$ :: $a \to$ *Tree*$_1$ σ a
    Node$_1$ :: σ p $c \to (\forall x.c$ $x \to$ *Tree*$_1$ σ $x) \to (p \to$ *Tree*$_1$ σ $a) \to$ *Tree*$_1$ σ a

The *Leaf*$_1$ constructor is trivial; *Leaf*$_1$ x returns a pure computation with result x. The internal nodes are of the form *Node op sub k* where the fields have the following meaning. The first, *op*, identifies what primitive operation the node represents. Next, *sub* is a function that, in case of a non-atomic primitive, selects the subcomputations of the node. Finally, k is the continuation of further operations to perform after the current one.

Some notable characteristics are as follows:

- Every operation has a result type p that is made available to its continuation, and a number of subcomputations c. To model these two, the signature of an operation $op :: \sigma$ p c is parameterized by p and c.
- The function *sub* has type $\forall x.c$ $x \to$ *Tree*$_1$ σ x. The input of type c x determines what subcomputation to select; the parameter x indicates the result type of that subcomputation.
- Likewise, continuations take as input the operation's output value (p).
- The *Tree*$_1$ data type is monadic, with a similar notion of return and bind as the *free monad* [23]:

    instance *Monad* (*Tree*$_1$ σ) **where**
        return = *Leaf*$_1$
        (*Leaf*$_1$ x) $\ggg f = f$ x
        (*Node*$_1$ *op sub k*) $\ggg f =$ *Node*$_1$ *op sub* $(\lambda x \to k$ $x \ggg f)$

A monadic binding $t \ggg f$ thus "concatenates" the tree in f to the leaf positions in the continuation (only) of t.

$var :: (Abstracting\ v < \sigma) \Rightarrow Int \rightarrow Tree_1\ \sigma\ v$
$var\ n = Node_1\ (injSig\ (Var'\ n))\ (\lambda x \rightarrow \textbf{case}\ x\ \textbf{of}\ )\ Leaf_1$
$app :: (Abstracting\ v < \sigma) \Rightarrow v \rightarrow v \rightarrow Tree_1\ \sigma\ v$
$app\ v_1\ v_2 = Node_1\ (injSig\ (App'\ v_1\ v_2))\ (\lambda x \rightarrow \textbf{case}\ x\ \textbf{of}\ )\ Leaf_1$
$abs :: (Abstracting\ v < \sigma) \Rightarrow Tree_1\ \sigma\ v \rightarrow Tree_1\ \sigma\ v$
$abs\ t = Node_1\ (injSig\ Abs')\ (\lambda One \rightarrow t)\ Leaf_1$

Fig. 1. The modular constructor functions of the *Abstracting* effect. These functions all fix the continuation to $Leaf_1$, which can easily be replaced by an arbitrary continuation k using the $\gg\!=$ operator of $Tree_1$'s monad instance.

We can emulate the non-modular type $LC\ v\ a$ with $LC'\ v\ a$.

type $LC'\ v\ a = Tree_1\ (Abstracting\ v)\ a$

The corresponding representation for LC's *Return* constructor is $Leaf_1$. The *Var* constructor is represented with a $Node_1$.

$var_1 \quad :: Int \rightarrow (v \rightarrow LC'\ v\ a) \rightarrow LC'\ v\ a$
$var_1\ i\ k = Node_1\ (Var'\ i)\ (\lambda x \rightarrow \textbf{case}\ x\ \textbf{of}\ )\ k$

This is a $Var'\ i$ node. As there are no subcomputations, there are no branches in the pattern match in the selection function on the value x of the empty type *NoSub*. Lastly, the continuation k receives the value produced by the operation.

The encodings of the two other operations are similar. One notable aspect of abs_1 is that it does have one subcomputation. Hence, the selection function matches on the *One* constructor and returns t:

$app_1 :: v \rightarrow v \rightarrow (v \rightarrow LC'\ v\ a) \rightarrow LC'\ v\ a$
$app_1\ v_1\ v_2\ k = Node_1\ (App'\ v_1\ v_2)\ (\lambda x \rightarrow \textbf{case}\ x\ \textbf{of}\ )\ k$
$abs_1 :: LC'\ v\ v \rightarrow (v \rightarrow LC'\ v\ a) \rightarrow LC'\ v\ a$
$abs_1\ t\ k = Node_1\ Abs'\ (\lambda One \rightarrow t)\ k$

Modular Tree Constructors. We can create modular constructors for latent effect operations, similarly to how DTC admits modular syntax constructors [23]. To this end, we use a co-product operator $+$ that combines latent effect signatures, and a subtyping relation $\sigma_1 < \sigma_2$ with an associated injection function, $injSig :: \sigma_1\ p\ c \rightarrow \sigma_2\ p\ c$. Using these, we can implement the modular constructor functions in Fig. 1, that allow combining *Abstracting* with other latent and algebraic effects. The subtyping requirements in the type signatures are automatically inferrable by type class instance resolution in Haskell. The implementation details of $+$ and $<$ are given in DTC [23] or Appendix A of van den Berg et al. [2].

We can now use these modular constructors to implement denotation function cases. We can also write programs using the constructors directly. For example, the following program with a lambda abstraction with an effectful body:

$$prog :: \forall v. Num\ v \Rightarrow Tree_1\ (Mutating\ v + Abstracting\ v + Ending)\ v$$
$$prog = \mathbf{do}$$
$$\quad put\ (1 :: v)$$
$$\quad f \leftarrow abs\ (\mathbf{do}\ m \leftarrow var\ 0; (n :: v) \leftarrow get; return\ (m + n))$$
$$\quad put\ (2 :: v)$$
$$\quad app\ f\ (3 :: v)$$

The body of the function abstraction increments the function argument value (de Bruijn index 0) by the n yielded by the get operation. The signature of the program tree is the co-product of three signatures: (1) $Mutating\ V$ for mutable state; (2) function abstractions $Abstracting\ V$; and (3) the empty signature $Ending$, which provides no operations and serves as the base case. The $Mutating\ V$ effect recasts the traditional algebraic state effect as a latent effect, and has two operations, get and put. Observe that $prog$ is essentially an AST, with multiple possible interpretations. If $Mutating\ V$ is dynamic (runtime) state, then $prog$ evaluates to $3 + 2 = 5$. However, if it is for macro bindings that are expanded *statically*, then the get in the body of the abstraction is evaluated under the state at the "definition site" of the lambda, and $prog$ evaluates to $3 + 1 = 4$. Next, we show how handlers can map the $prog$ syntax tree to different semantics.

3.3 Trees with Support for Modular Handlers

In the case of a modularly composed signature $\sigma = \sigma_1 + ... + \sigma_n + Ending$, the idea is to compose the handler function from individual handlers for the different components of the signature $h = hEnd \circ h_n \circ ... \circ h_1$. The type of each handler would be $h_i :: \forall \sigma. Tree_1\ (\sigma_i + \sigma)\ a \rightarrow Tree_1\ \sigma\ (L_i\ a)$. Hence, it is polymorphic in the remaining part of the signature and preserves those nodes in the resulting tree. It only replaces the nodes of σ_i with their meaning, which is given in the form of a functor L_i that decorates the result type a.

Unfortunately, our $Tree_1$ type and, in particular, the type of its $Node_1$ constructor, needs some further refinement to fully support this idea. Indeed, if the signature is $\sigma_i + \sigma$, and we apply h_i to all the recursive occurrences of $Tree\ (\sigma_i + \sigma)$ in a σ-node $Node_1\ (Inr'\ op)\ sub\ k$, we get:

Before applying h_i	After applying h_i
$Inr'\ op :: (\sigma_i + \sigma)\ p\ c$	$op \qquad :: \sigma\ p\ c$
$sub \qquad :: \forall x.c\ x \rightarrow Tree_1\ (\sigma_i + \sigma)\ x$	$h_i \circ sub :: \forall x.c\ x \rightarrow Tree_1\ \sigma\ (\boxed{L_i\ x})$
$k \qquad :: p \rightarrow Tree_1\ (\sigma_i + \sigma)\ a$	$h_i \circ k \quad :: p \rightarrow Tree_1\ \sigma\ (L_i\ a)$

The resulting fields do not together form a node of type $Tree_1\ \sigma\ (L_i\ a)$ because the highlighted result type of the subcomputations is $(L_i\ x)$ rather than x which the $Node_1$ constructor requires sub to have as return type.

The problem is that the $Tree_1$ type is oblivious to the *effect functor* that the return type of subcomputations in the tree are decorated by. To solve this problem, we can expose the effect functor decoration in the tree type itself; e.g.,

```
data Tree₂ (σ :: * → (* → *) → *) ( l :: * → * ) a where
  Leaf₂ :: a → Tree₂ σ l a
  Node₂ :: σ p c → (∀x.c x → Tree₂ σ l ( l x))
                 → ( l p → Tree₂ σ l a) → Tree₂ σ l a
```

But the *Tree₂* type requires effect handlers to be applied to subcomputations *immediately*. Motivated by modeling constructs that defer computation, we generalize the type further by parameterizing subcomputations by the effect functor state, and making each node "remember" the effect state (the *latent effects*):

```
data Tree (σ :: * → (* → *) → *) (l :: * → *) a where
  Leaf :: a → Tree σ l a
  Node :: σ p c → l () → (∀x.c x → l () → Tree σ l (l x))
               → (l p → Tree σ l a) → Tree σ l a
```

In Sect. 3.4 we discuss how *Tree* supports deferring computation. *Tree* is a monad with a return and bind defined similarly to the ones for *Tree₁* in Sect. 3.2. We can also define modular tree constructors using similar techniques as in Sect. 3.2. For instance, using *Tree* instead of *Tree₁*, the type of *prog* from Sect. 3.2 becomes:

$$prog :: Tree~(Mutating~V + Abstracting~V + Ending)~Id~V$$

Here, the *Id* functor models the absence of latent effects in the tree. The type *V* represents a concrete value type.

Example. Figure 2 shows how the type of the *prog* tree evolves when applying successive handlers for the three parts of the signature:

$$(hEnd \circ hAbs~[]~[] \circ hMut~0)~prog$$

First, we run the modular handler for mutable state *Mutating s*, which has type:

$$hMut :: Functor~l \Rightarrow s \to Tree~(Mutating~s + \sigma)~l~a \to Tree~\sigma~(StateL~s~l)~(s, a)$$

Given an initial state of type s, this handler transforms a tree into another tree. The signature of the tree evolves from *Mutating s + σ* to *σ* because the handler interprets the mutable state, but not the other effects. Also, the latent effect functor evolves from l (the latent effects already present) to *StateL s l*, which augments l with the value of the intermediate state.

newtype $StateL~s~l~a = StateL~\{~unStateL :: (s, l~a)\}$

The result type evolves from a to (s, a), which augments it with the final state.

Second, the handler for *Abstracting V* behaves similarly to *hMut*, removing itself from the signature and growing the latent effect functor. Finally, *hEnd* handles the *Ending* base case. It takes a tree with an empty signature, which thus necessarily only contains a leaf, and extracts the final result out of it.

hEnd :: Tree Ending l a → a
hEnd (Leaf x) = x

The remainder of this section illustrates how modular handlers are implemented.

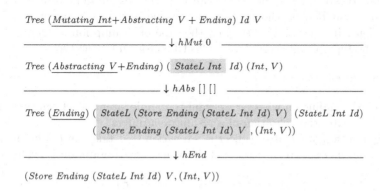

Tree (Mutating Int+Abstracting V + Ending) Id V

————————————————— ↓ *hMut* 0 —————————————————

Tree (Abstracting V+Ending) (StateL Int Id) (Int, V)

————————————————— ↓ *hAbs* [] [] —————————————————

Tree (Ending) (StateL (Store Ending (StateL Int Id) V) (StateL Int Id)
(Store Ending (StateL Int Id) V , (Int, V))

————————————————— ↓ *hEnd* —————————————————

(Store Ending (StateL Int Id) V , (Int, V))

Fig. 2. The type of *prog* after successive handling steps.

3.4 Example: Two Modular Handlers for Function Abstractions

We implement two different modular handlers for the operations in *Abstracting*, which illustrate (1) how latent effects let us write handlers for function abstraction, and (2) the kind of fine-grained control the handlers provide. The first handler we consider evaluates the body of a function abstraction using the latent effects of its *call site*. Hence, the evaluation of side-effectful operations is postponed until the function is applied. The second handler evaluates the body of the function abstraction using the latent effects of its *definition site*. This immediately enacts the latent effects introduced by previously-applied handlers.

Modular Closure Values. A concern that arises when we step away from the earlier non-modular handler for *Abstracting* is *reuse*. Notably, in a modular setting we want to allow reuse of both handlers with different notions of values. For that reason, they are parameterized in the type of values v. This type may comprise various shapes of values; all the function abstraction handlers require is that closures are one possible shape of value.

To express this requirement, we introduce another type class $v_1 <: v_2$ for subtyping, this time at kind $*$, which witnesses (1) that any v_1 can be "upcast" to the type v_2; and (2) that a v_2 can be "downcast" to type

v_1. The latter may fail, but the former does not. The minimal requirement for lambda abstractions is that the value type includes closure values.

class $v_1 <: v_2$ **where**   **data** *Closure v* **where**
   $inj_v :: v_1 \rightarrow v_2$ *Clos* :: *FunPtr* → *Env v* → *Closure v*
   $proj_v :: v_2 \rightarrow Maybe\ v_1$ **type** *Env v* = $[v]$

In the modular setting, the types *Closure v* and *Env v*, of respectively closures and value environments, are parameterized in the type of values used.

Modular Resumption Store. Recall that the resumption store keeps track of the function bodies whose execution has been deferred; i.e., it is a list of resumptions. In the modular setting, the type of resumptions is parametric in the specific type of signature, latent effect functor and value type.

type *Store* $\sigma\ l\ v = [R\ \sigma\ l\ v]$

Moreover, depending on whether we want to handle latent effects on the call site or definition site, the definition of a resumption differs.

A resumption of a call-site effect is a function that takes an l () input, which is the latent effect context of the call site where the resumption is evaluated.

type $R_{CS}\ \sigma\ l\ v = l\ () \rightarrow Tree\ (Abstracting\ v + \sigma)\ l\ (l\ v)$

The resumptions of a definition-site effect store are trees instead of functions that produce trees. Indeed, they have no dependency on the latent effects of the call site. Instead, they have been fully determined by the definition site.

type $R_{DS}\ \sigma\ l\ v = Tree\ (Abstracting\ v + \sigma)\ l\ (l\ v)$

Although the resumption store makes the handlers verbose, it is a more modular solution than storing *Trees* in values.

Modular Handlers. Figure 3 shows the modular handler $hAbs_{CS}$ that uses the call-site latent effects when executing a function body[2].

Compared to the non-modular definition, there are several differences. Firstly, the handler only interprets part of the work and thus returns the remaining tree instead. Hence, the *Leaf* case now returns a new leaf, and the other cases use monadic **do**-notation to build a new tree. Secondly, because the signature is a composition and the resulting value type is too, the pattern matching on operations involves the *Inl'* and *Inr'* tags of the + co-product. The pattern matching and construction of values involves inj_v and $proj_v$ calls for the same reason. Thirdly, the latent effects now matter and need to be properly threaded in all the operation cases. Finally, there is an additional operation case, to handle

---

[2] The function (<\$) is short for *fmap ∘ const*.

unknown operations from the remaining part of the signature by "forwarding" them, i.e., copying them to the resulting tree for later handling.

As discussed, in a modular setting a second handler is possible: one that uses the latent effects of the definition site for function bodies rather than their call site. This definition-site handler, $hAbs_{DS}$, looks much like its sibling. The key difference is the type of resumptions, which affects the code in two places (highlighted in gray). Firstly, the abstraction case applies the subtree function to the latent effect of the definition site instead of deferring the application ($st\ One\ l$ instead of $st\ One$). Dually, the application case does not have to apply the resumption to the call-site latent effect ($r\ !!\ p$ instead of $(r\ !!\ p)\ l$).

$hAbs_{CS} :: (Closure\ v <: v, Functor\ l)$
$\quad \Rightarrow Env\ v \rightarrow Store\ \sigma\ l\ v \rightarrow Tree\ (Abstracting\ v + \sigma)\ l\ a$
$\quad \rightarrow Tree\ \sigma\ (StateL\ (Store\ \sigma\ l\ v)\ l)\ (Store\ \sigma\ l\ v, a)$
$hAbs_{CS}\ \_\ \ r\ (Leaf\ x) \qquad = Leaf\ (r, x)$
$hAbs_{CS}\ nv\ r\ (Node\ (Inl'\ Abs')\ l\ st\ k) = \mathbf{do\ let}\ v\ =\ inj_v\ (Clos\ (length\ r)\ nv)$
$\qquad\qquad\qquad\qquad\qquad\qquad\qquad \mathbf{let}\ r' = r \mathbin{+\!\!+} [\ st\ One\ ]$
$\qquad\qquad\qquad\qquad\qquad\qquad\qquad hAbs_{CS}\ nv\ r'\ (k\ (v \mathbin{<\$} l))$
$hAbs_{CS}\ nv\ r\ (Node\ (Inl'\ (App'\ v_1\ v_2))\ l\ \_\ k) = \mathbf{case}\ proj_v\ v_1\ \mathbf{of}$
$\quad Just\ (Clos\ fp\ nv') \rightarrow \mathbf{do}\ (r', v) \leftarrow hAbs_{CS}\ (v_2 : nv')\ r\ (\ (r\ !!\ fp)\ l\ )$
$\qquad\qquad\qquad\qquad\qquad hAbs_{CS}\ nv\ r'\ (k\ v)$
$\quad Nothing \qquad\qquad\quad \rightarrow error\ \texttt{"application error"}$
$hAbs_{CS}\ nv\ r\ (Node\ (Inl'\ (Var'\ n))\ l\ \_\ k)\ \ = hAbs_{CS}\ nv\ r\ (k\ ((nv\ !!\ n) \mathbin{<\$} l))$
$hAbs_{CS}\ nv\ r\ (Node\ (Inr'\ op) \qquad l\ st\ k)\ \ = Node\ op\ (StateL\ (r, l))$
$\quad (\lambda c\ (StateL\ (r', l\ )) \rightarrow StateL \mathbin{<\$>} hAbs_{CS}\ nv\ r'\ (st\ c\ l))$
$\quad (\lambda\ \ (StateL\ (r', lv)) \rightarrow hAbs_{CS}\ nv\ r'\ (k\ lv))$

Fig. 3. Modular call-site abstraction handler. The gray highlights indicate the places where it differs from a definition-site handler.

Example. With the abstraction handlers in place, let us revisit the *prog* example. We run the handlers with default initial values, i.e., 0 for the state, the empty variable environment and the empty resumption store. When using the call-site abstraction handler after the state handler, the function body uses the value of the state that was written right before its invocation.

$\quad > example_{CS} = inspect\ \$\ hEnd\ \$\ hAbs_{CS}\ [\,]\ [\,]\ \$\ hMut\ 0\ prog$
$\quad 5$

If we use the definition-site handler instead, the function body uses the state value that was written right before the abstraction was created.

$\quad > example_{DS} = inspect\ \$\ hEnd\ \$\ hAbs_{DS}\ [\,]\ [\,]\ \$\ hMut\ 0\ prog$
$\quad 4$

4   Case Studies

This section reports on two advanced control-flow features implemented using this library: *call-by-need lambdas* (Sect. 4.1) and *multi-staging* (Sect. 4.2); and on a case study implementation of a library with a range of modular effects (Sect. 4.3). For the source code of these case studies, we refer to the implementation available at https://github.com/birthevdb/Latent-Effect-and-Handlers.git.

4.1   Call-by-Need Evaluation

We have implemented two different evaluation strategies, call-by-need (lazy) and call-by-value (CBV), for lambdas by using different latent effect handlers. Our approach is inspired by Levy's call-by-push-value [10], which can express both strategies. We summarize here; Appendix B of van den Berg et al. [2] has all the details.

Call-by-need evaluation lazily delays the evaluation of argument expressions of function applications, and uses *memoization* to ensure that evaluation only happens once for delayed expressions. We build a lazy semantics for function abstractions out of three primitive effects:

1. The *Reading* effect corresponds to the well-known *reader monad* from the Haskell monad transformer library [11].
2. The *Suspending* effect delays the evaluation of function bodies, without memoizing the result of the evaluation of the delayed subtrees.
3. The *Thunking* effect delays the evaluation of argument expressions of function applications, memoizing the result of forcing a thunked computation.

The definition of these effects and their handlers can be found in the effect library of Appendix A of van den Berg et al. [2]. Using these effects, we define three operations for lazy evaluation (abs_{lazy}, var_{lazy}, and app_{lazy}). Lambda abstraction suspends the body of a lambda, and pairs a pointer to the suspension with the environment that the thunk should be evaluated under. The var_{lazy} and app_{lazy} functions memoize and recall argument values (possibly by forcing the evaluation of a thunked computation), and evaluate the body of a lambda. Application evaluates the first argument to a function value, and memoizes the second argument, which is placed in the current environment. Then, the function body is executed.

The following example program evaluates to 0 when using lazy evaluation:

$$prog_{lazy} :: Tree \ (\ Mutating \ V + Reading \ [\,V\,] + Suspending \ V$$
$$+ \ Thunking \ V + Ending) \ Id \ V$$
$$prog_{lazy} = app_{lazy} \ (abs_{lazy} \ get) \ (\textbf{do} \ put \ 42; get)$$

Function application delays the evaluation of *put* in the argument, and is never executed because the function body does not reference its parameter. We can run the program with call-by-need by applying its handlers:

```
run <print "bar";
    1 + ~(print "foo"; <2>)>
```

$letbind\ (seq\ (print\ "foo")\ (quote\ (num\ 2)))$
$(unquote\ (quote\ (seq\ (print\ "bar")$
$(add\ (num\ 1)\ (splice\ (var\ 0)))))))$

Fig. 4. A MetaML program (left) and its latent effects implementation (right).

> $inspect\ \$\ hEnd\ \$\ hThunk\ [\,]\ \$\ hSuspend\ [\,]\ \$\ hRead\ [\,]\ \$\ hMut\ 0\ prog_{lazy}$
0

The inspect function extracts the final value out of the result that is decorated with the latent effect functor (in this case nested $StateL$'s).

We can also recover a CBV semantics from app_{lazy}, abs_{lazy}, and app_{lazy} by implementing an alternative handler for the *Thunking* effect. This handler eagerly evaluates subtrees and stores their value in a store.

> $inspect\ \$\ hEnd\ \$\ hEager\ [\,]\ \$\ hSuspend\ [\,]\ \$\ hRead\ [\,]\ \$\ hMut\ 0\ prog_{lazy}$
42

This case study demonstrates that modular call-by-need can be implemented by decomposing it into modular, primitive latent effects and handlers. It also shows how *overloading* the handler of the *Thunking* effect provides a means of changing the semantics of a program without touching the program itself.

4.2   Staging

Another advanced control-flow feature that we have implemented with latent effects is multi-staging. By applying effect handlers *before* the handler for the staging effect, we can control which effects should be staged, and which not. The implementation of these staging constructs can be found in Appendix C of van den Berg et al. [2].

Our inspiration are the three constructs of MetaML [25]: (1) *bracket* expressions (<_>) delay execution to a later stage; (2) *escape* expressions (~_) splice a staged expression into another; and (3) *run* expressions (**run** _) run an expression that has been dynamically generated by bracket and escape expressions.

A key feature of MetaML is that staged code is *statically typed* and *lexically scoped*. The staging constructs that we implement differ in two ways: our staging constructs are untyped, and we provide *two* constructs for splicing code (*push* and *splice*) instead of the single *escape* expression found in MetaML.

We use *push* for writing programs with escape expressions under binders in staged code. The dynamic semantics of *push* creates an environment with "holes" that represent unknown bindings, and *splice* automatically fills in these holes with bindings from the dynamic context of the *splice* expression.

The four staging constructs we implement are thus: (1) *quote*, corresponding to brackets in MetaML; (2) *unquote*, corresponding to **run** _ in MetaML; and

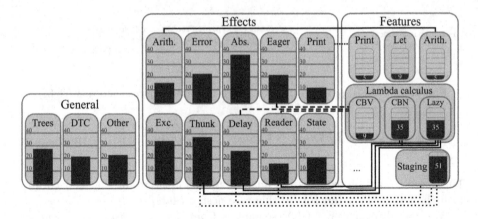

Fig. 5. Effect library with Lines of Code (LoC) per effect.

(3+4) *splice* and *push* for code splicing. The programs in Fig. 4 illustrate the difference in how splicing works. The MetaML program on the left prints the string "foobar" and returns the value 3. The program on the right desugars into latent effects. With the appropriate handlers, it gives the same output.

Yet, by switching the order of handlers for the *print* effect and staging, we obtain a different semantics that eagerly handles *print* operations inside *quoted* code. This makes the program on the right print "barfoo" instead.

4.3 Library Summary

We have given two examples where latent effects can be modularly composed to form language features. Figure 5 gives an overview of our effect library[3] and how the primitive effects are combined into language features.

The left part shows the general framework code for implementing latent effects, consisting of *Trees*, the DTC approach and helper definitions (e.g. *Id*, *Void*); the figure also indicates the associated lines of code (LoC). The middle part shows ten different effects and their LoC. Each effect comes with an effect signature, a handler, and smart constructors for their operations. For the detailed implementation of these effects, we refer to the effect library (Appendix A of van den Berg et al. [2]). The right part contains several language features that can be implemented using these effects, with their associated LoC. Each feature comes with its object language syntax and a mapping onto the effects. Each language requires an additional two LoC, to indicate the effects and handlers used and their order. A different order of effects and handlers may give different semantics.

Figure 5 only includes a few language features covered in the paper. However, as we provide ten effects and handlers, they can be modularly composed in different order, using different combinations. In theory, when algebras are fixed,

---

[3] https://github.com/birthevdb/Latent-Effect-and-Handlers.git

we can define $(10! + 9! + \ldots + 2! + 1!) = 4,037,913$ semantics, although some compositions may result in the same behaviour. Even more variations are possible, varying the algebra that maps the object language syntax to the effects.

5 Related Work

Modular Semantics and Effects. Modularity has received much attention both at the level of language definitions and of the effects used by those languages. A landmark is the formulation of the expression problem [26], the challenge to modularly extend languages with new features and new interpretation functions. As different language features use different effects, this also requires the modular composition of those effects. Monad transformers [11] are the most prominent approach, including alternative implementations such as Filinksi's layered monads [3] and Jaskelioff's Monatron [7].

Algebraic Effects. Algebraic effects [16] have been proposed as a more structured approach to monads that can also be composed [6]. The subsequent introduction of handlers [18] to deal with exceptions has enabled practical language and library implementations, e.g., [8,9,12]. Schrijvers et al. [20] identified when algebraic effect handlers are modular and related this to a subclass of monad transformers, using the notion of modules [15]. Wu et al. [29] have identified a class of what they call *scoped* effects, which cannot be expressed as algebraic operations. To remedy the situation, they have proposed a practical generalization of algebraic effects. Piróg et al. [14] have put this ad-hoc approach for scoped effects on formal footing in terms of a free monad on a level-indexed category.

Latent Effects. There are many works on specific types of latent effects. For instance, staging is a widely studied area [19,22,24]. Some works have also combined algebraic effects with staging mechanisms [21,27,30]. Yet, we are, to the best of our knowledge, the first to consider staging using effect handlers.

The call-by-push-value calculus of Levy [10] provides primitives for expressing both call-by-name and call-by-value. These have been an inspiration for our modular thunking handler. A more generic work is that of Atkey and Johann [1] on interleaving data and effects to model the incremental production of the data, and on interpreting these with f-and-m algebras.

Various forms of delimited control have been used in the literature to realize sophisticated control mechanisms, such as the simulation of call-by-need by Garcia et al. [5]. Moreover, several works [4] show the interdefinability of conventional algebraic effects and delimited control. A further investigation into the relative expressiveness of latent effects would be interesting.

In future work we would like to demonstrate the performance of latent effects, using the techniques of fusion by Wu and Schrijvers [28].

6 Conclusion

This paper has introduced the notion of latent effects. These extend algebraic effects with the ability to modularly model advanced control-flow mechanisms that can postpone the execution of certain computations and require fine-grained control over the effects inside them. Lambda abstraction, lazy evaluation, and staging were shown to be three prominent instances.

Acknowledgments. This work has been supported by EPSRC grant number EP/S028129/1 on 'Scoped Contextual Operations and Effects', by the NWO VENI project on 'Composable and Safe-by-Construction Programming Language Definitions' (VI.Veni.192.259), by FWO project G095917N, and by KU Leuven project C14/20/079.

References

1. Atkey, R., Johann, P.: Interleaving data and effects. J. Funct. Program. **25** (2015)
2. van den Berg, B., Schrijvers, T., Bach-Poulsen, C., Wu, N.: Latent effects for reusable language components: extended version (2021)
3. Filinski, A.: Representing layered monads. In: 26th Symposium on Principles of Programming Languages, POPL 1999, pp. 175–188 (1999)
4. Forster, Y., Kammar, O., Lindley, S., Pretnar, M.: On the expressive power of user-defined effects: effect handlers, monadic reflection, delimited control. J. Funct. Program. **29**, e15 (2019)
5. Garcia, R., Lumsdaine, A., Sabry, A.: Lazy evaluation and delimited control. Log. Methods Comput. Sci. **6**(3) (2010)
6. Hyland, M., Plotkin, G., Power, J.: Combining effects: sum and tensor. Theoret. Comput. Sci. **357**(1–3), 70–99 (2006)
7. Jaskelioff, M.: Monatron: an extensible monad transformer library. In: Scholz, S.-B., Chitil, O. (eds.) IFL 2008. LNCS, vol. 5836, pp. 233–248. Springer, Heidelberg (2011). https://doi.org/10.1007/978-3-642-24452-0_13
8. Kiselyov, O., Ishii, H.: Freer monads, more extensible effects. In: 8th Symposium on Haskell, pp. 94–105. ACM (2015)
9. Leijen, D.: Type directed compilation of row-typed algebraic effects. In: 44th Symposium on Principles of Programming Languages, pp. 486–499. ACM (2017)
10. Levy, P.B.: Call-by-push-value: decomposing call-by-value and call-by-name. High. Order Symb. Comput. **19**(4), 377–414 (2006)
11. Liang, S., Hudak, P., Jones, M.: Monad transformers and modular interpreters. In: Symposium on Principles of Programming Languages, pp. 333–343. ACM (1995)
12. Lindley, S., McBride, C., McLaughlin, C.: Do be do be do. In: 44th Symposium on Principles of Programming Languages. ACM (2017)
13. Moggi, E.: An abstract view of programming languages. Technical report ECS-LFCS-90-113, Edinburgh University, Department of Computer Science, June 1989
14. Piróg, M., Schrijvers, T., Wu, N., Jaskelioff, M.: Syntax and semantics for operations with scopes. In: Logic in Computer Science, pp. 809–818. ACM (2018)
15. Piróg, M., Wu, N., Gibbons, J.: Modules over monads and their algebras. In: 6th Conference on Algebra and Coalgebra in Computer Science. LIPIcs, vol. 35, pp. 290–303. Schloss Dagstuhl - Leibniz-Zentrum für Informatik (2015)

16. Plotkin, G., Power, J.: Notions of computation determine monads. In: Nielsen, M., Engberg, U. (eds.) FoSSaCS 2002. LNCS, vol. 2303, pp. 342–356. Springer, Heidelberg (2002). https://doi.org/10.1007/3-540-45931-6_24
17. Plotkin, G.D., Power, J.: Algebraic operations and generic effects. Appl. Categ. Struct. 11(1), 69–94 (2003)
18. Plotkin, G., Pretnar, M.: Handlers of algebraic effects. In: Castagna, G. (ed.) ESOP 2009. LNCS, vol. 5502, pp. 80–94. Springer, Heidelberg (2009). https://doi.org/10.1007/978-3-642-00590-9_7
19. Rompf, T., Odersky, M.: Lightweight modular staging: a pragmatic approach to runtime code generation and compiled DSLs. In: Generative Programming and Component Engineering, pp. 127–136. ACM (2010)
20. Schrijvers, T., Piróg, M., Wu, N., Jaskelioff, M.: Monad transformers and modular algebraic effects: what binds them together. In: 12th International Symposium on Haskell, pp. 98–113. ACM (2019)
21. Schuster, P., Brachthäuser, J.I., Ostermann, K.: Compiling effect handlers in capability-passing style. Proc. ACM Program. Lang. 4(ICFP), 93:1–93:28 (2020)
22. Sheard, T., Jones, S.L.P.: Template meta-programming for Haskell. ACM SIG-PLAN Not. 37(12), 60–75 (2002)
23. Swierstra, W.: Data types à la carte. J. Funct. Program. 18(4), 423–436 (2008)
24. Taha, W., Sheard, T.: Multi-stage programming with explicit annotations. In: PEPM, pp. 203–217 (1997)
25. Taha, W., Sheard, T.: MetaML and multi-stage programming with explicit annotations. Theor. Comput. Sci. 248(1), 211–242 (2000). PEPM 1997
26. Wadler, P.: The expression problem. Mailing list (1998)
27. Wei, G., Bračevac, O., Tan, S., Rompf, T.: Compiling symbolic execution with staging and algebraic effects. Proc. ACM Program. Lang. 4(OOPSLA) (2020)
28. Wu, N., Schrijvers, T.: Fusion for free. In: Hinze, R., Voigtländer, J. (eds.) MPC 2015. LNCS, vol. 9129, pp. 302–322. Springer, Cham (2015). https://doi.org/10.1007/978-3-319-19797-5_15
29. Wu, N., Schrijvers, T., Hinze, R.: Effect handlers in scope. In: Symposium on Haskell, pp. 1–12. ACM (2014)
30. Yallop, J.: Staged generic programming. Proc. ACM Program. Lang. 1(ICFP), 29:1–29:29 (2017)

Adaptable Traces for Program Explanations

Divya Bajaj[⊠], Martin Erwig, Danila Fedorin, and Kai Gay

Oregon State University, Corvallis, OR 97331, USA
{bajajd,erwig,fedorind,gayk}@oregonstate.edu

Abstract. Program traces are a sound basis for explaining the dynamic behavior of programs. Alas, program traces can grow big very quickly, even for small programs, which diminishes their value as explanations.

In this paper we demonstrate how the systematic simplification of traces can yield succinct program explanations. Specifically, we introduce operations for transforming traces that facilitate the abstraction of details. The operations are the basis of a query language for the definition of trace filters that can adapt and simplify traces in a variety of ways.

The generation of traces is governed by a variant of Call-By-Value semantics which specifically supports parsimony in trace representations. We show that our semantics is a conservative extension of Call-By-Value that can produce smaller traces and that the evaluation traces preserve the explanatory content of proof trees at a much smaller footprint.

Keywords: Semantics · Language design · Domain-specific languages

1 Introduction

Explaining program behavior has many uses, including program maintenance, debugging, and teaching. In particular, when the correctness of a program is in doubt, an explanation can help to regain the user's trust and confidence. Users often employ debuggers to understand program behavior [14], even though debugging is costly [15] and focuses more on identifying and removing bugs. Moreover, debuggers typically already assume an understanding of the program by the programmer [11]. Research on customizable debugging provides additional evidence for the limitations of generic debugging approaches [7,9].

Perera, et al. [12] use partial program traces to explain program executions. Through *backward program slicing* only those parts of a trace are retained that contribute to a selected part of the output; all irrelevant parts of the trace are replaced by holes. However, the resulting traces can still be large, even for simple programs, because much of the information that is produced through slicing techniques, while technically relevant, might not contribute to the explanation.

Partial traces can be very effective, but they may omit the wrong information. In general, no one trace works equally well as an explanation for every user, since

H. Oh (Ed.): APLAS 2021, LNCS 13008, pp. 202–221, 2021.
https://doi.org/10.1007/978-3-030-89051-3_12

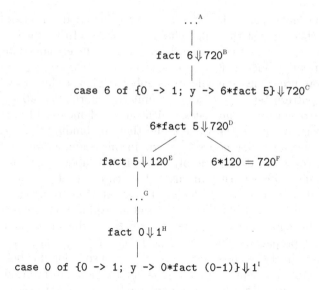

Fig. 1. Trace view for `fact` 6. (The LaTeX code for trace views was generated by our prototype implementation, with some manual adjustment of horizontal positioning.)

different users typically have different questions about the behavior of a program. The approach we present in this paper gives users the ability to manipulate program traces through a query language and thus gives them control over which parts of a trace to hide and which parts to keep. To illustrate this aspect, we demonstrate how to create a trace for the factorial function that could be used, for example, as a teaching aid. Consider the following definition.

```
fact = \x -> case x of {0 -> 1; y -> x * fact (x-1)}
```

Suppose that we want to explain the computation of `fact` 6. A proof tree generated by a typical big-step Call-By-Value operational semantics consists of 80 nodes and 22 levels, which is a lot of information. However, to understand how this computation works, one doesn't need to see all instances of the recursive function call. Specifically, one might expect a trace to execute all parts of a definition once, but generally not more than that. One might also want to filter out some of the more clerical arithmetic computations (for example, for decrementing a counter) and the lookup of variable bindings. We call such a filtered trace a *trace view*. In Fig. 1 we show a trace view with only 7 non-hidden judgments on 8 levels that meets these expectations. The trace view is obtained from a complete trace in six steps: (1) hiding top-level declarations, (2) hiding and propagating variable lookups, (3) hiding and propagating evaluations of subtractions, (4) hiding reflexive judgements, (5) hiding intermediate recursive calls, and (6) hiding pattern matching evaluations.

These steps are achieved by filter operations which hide nodes and subtrees, occasionally propagating information from hidden nodes to the rest of the trace.

204   D. Bajaj et al.

The nodes to which a particular filter is to be applied are determined by patterns that are matched against the judgments in the nodes of the trace.

First, `let` expressions that define the program to be explained are contained in nodes that carry judgements of the form `let` $x{=}e'$ `in` $e \Downarrow v$. A pattern for such a judgment can use values or a wildcard symbol $\diamond$. Thus, to hide the definition of `f` we use the pattern `let f` $= \diamond$ `in` $\diamond \Downarrow \diamond$ Similarly, information about bindings is presented by so-called *binding nodes*, which carry judgments of the form $n{:}\, x{=}v$, saying that variable x has the value v and that the binding was introduced by node n. To hide all binding nodes, as we do in this example, we use the pattern $\diamond{:}\diamond = \diamond$. However, we do not simply hide binding nodes, but also propagate the bound values to where they are used. For reasons that will become clear in Sect. 4, we call this operation *factoring*. The effect of factoring can be seen, for example, in node C where the value 6 is used instead of the variable x.

While we have hidden the binding node for `fact` (which is a premise for node B), we *haven't* propagated its value (the function definition), as can be seen again in node C in the expression 6*`fact` 5. Responsible for this behavior is our version of operational semantics, *Call-By-Named-Value*, introduced in Sect. 2, which stores names with values. As explained in Sect. 3, the presentation of traces exploits the names of function values to produce smaller and more readable traces. This effect is extremely useful for tracing the execution of higher-order functions where substituting function values for variables that are referenced (potentially multiple times) can render traces effectively unreadable.

A filter for hiding and propagating some of the arithmetic is also expressed through factoring with a pattern. In our example we use the pattern $\diamond{-}1 \Downarrow \diamond$ to hide only decrements by 1, since we want to retain some of the multiplication expressions, which are important for explaining the functioning of `fact`. Also, some of the judgements, for example, $5 \Downarrow 5$, do not add explanatory value to the trace. A filter to hide all such judgements uses a pattern $\diamond_a \Downarrow \diamond_a$, that contains indexed wildcards. Indexed wildcards force equivalence on values in different places.

Hiding recursive `fact` calls is more complicated, since we don't want to hide all applications of `fact`. We can keep the first two calls and the last call as well as the first and last expansion of the function body by modifying the set of matched nodes through a function `limitRec`. The function `limitRec` is defined with combinators described in Sect. 5. Note that we shouldn't define `limitRec` to simply remove the first and last of the matched nodes (assuming we can rely on the matched nodes to appear in a particular order), because this wouldn't work well, for example, in the expression `fact` 5+`fact` 6. The definition provided in Sect. 5 is more robust and works well with cases like these.

We also hide all pattern matching judgements of the form $v|p \rightsquigarrow \rho$ (that match a value v against a pattern p and produce a binding ρ), again using a pattern with only wildcards: $\diamond | \diamond \rightsquigarrow \diamond$. As with the recursive function calls, we only hide nodes and don't propagate any information. Finally, we also hide the definition of `fact` to focus on the evaluation steps.

hide (funDef fact)	funDef f ≡ let f = ◇ in ◇ ⇓ ◇
factor binding	binding ≡ ◇:◇ = ◇
factor dec	dec ≡ ◇-1 ⇓ ◇
hide reflexive	reflexive ≡ ◇$_a$ ⇓ ◇$_a$
hide middleFact	middleFact ≡ limitRec fact
hide patMatch	patMatch ≡ ◇| ◇ ⤳ ◇

Fig. 2. Filters used to produce the trace view for fact 6.

To summarize, the trace view in Fig. 1 can be produced from the complete trace by applying the filters shown in Fig. 2, which can be done step-by-step in the user interface of our prototype or by running a script.

Some of these filters are quite generic and can be reused in other examples. In fact, we reuse them all in the next example to illustrate more features of our approach. Consider the trace in Fig. 3 that explains the following program.

```
let twice = \f -> \x -> f (f x) in
let fact = \x -> case x of {0 -> 1; y -> x * fact (x-1)}
  in twice fact 2
```

The trace view is generated by the following filter script, which uses two more patterns (fun and fact2) whose meaning should be obvious. The two patterns illustrate how general patterns can be combined into very specific ones. Here, the first factoring step excludes the binding for f, and the sequencing combinator then is used to apply the hiding operation to recursive nodes only after the application of fact 2. (The sequencing combinator s_1 then s_2 performs the node selection s_2 to each subtrace whose root matches the result of selection s_1 and then merges the results of the s_2 selections.)

hide (funDef ◇)	funDef f ≡ let f = ◇ in ◇ ⇓ ◇
factor binding except fun	fun ≡ ◇:f = ◇
hide fact2 then middleFact	fact2 ≡ fact 2 ⇓ ◇
...	

Note that fact 2 needs to be computed twice in the above program. Thus, a trace that is based on a proof tree would have two occurrences of the subtrace for fact 2 ⇓ 2. However, explaining the same computation more than once does not provide any additional benefit. On the contrary, the extra space requirement is detrimental to an effective explanation. To address this problem, we represent traces as DAGs. Here node G is a shared premise of nodes D and F. To avoid potential clutter caused by DAG edges, we decided to represent multiple edges to the same premise by showing nodes as a reference.

We can also observe another benefit of our Call-By-Named-Value semantics in this trace. Standard Call-By-Value would have evaluated the expression in node C to \x->f (f x) where f is bound to the definition of fact. The judgement

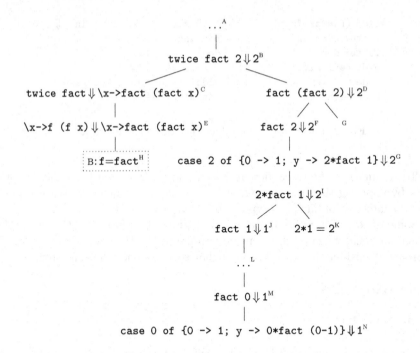

Fig. 3. Trace view for `twice fact 2`

in node D would then be `f (f 2)` $\Downarrow 2$ which is semantically correct, but can be confusing, since the introduction of the alias `f` for `fact` causes an indirection that has to be tracked by the user. Also, when `f` is applied, the reference to `f` would be replaced by its value, the definition of `fact`, leading to a more complex trace.

Finally, we can observe how bindings are represented in traces using the aforementioned binding nodes instead of as part of environments. Node H shows that `f` is bound to the function `fact` (again showing the name instead of the definition) and that the binding was generated by node B. The concept of binding nodes allows us to omit environments in evaluation judgments, and our Call-By-Named-Value semantics save us from the need to use closures as function values. The main contributions of this paper are the following.

- A new *Call-By-Named-Value* semantics that facilitates the creation of parsimonious traces by employing names for values (Sect. 2). We show that Call-By-Named-Value is a conservative extension of Call-By-Value that can generate smaller traces.
- A DAG structure for *traces* that substitutes binding nodes for environments (Sect. 3) and uses operations for trace simplifications (Sect. 4). We show that the evaluation traces preserve the explanatory content of proof trees at a much smaller footprint.
- A notion of *trace view* that encapsulates the contraction of subtraces into single nodes, plus corresponding operations for producing trace views through

$$u, v \in \mathit{Val} \quad ::= \quad c\, \nu \, \ldots \, \nu \quad | \quad \backslash x\text{->}e \quad | \quad \texttt{fix}(\backslash x\text{->}e, f)$$
$$p \in \mathit{Pat} \quad ::= \quad c\, p \ldots p \quad | \quad x$$
$$\nu \in \mathit{NVal} \quad ::= \quad v^{x \, \cdots \, x}$$
$$e \in \mathit{Expr} \quad ::= \quad x \quad | \quad e\, e \quad | \quad \texttt{case } e \texttt{ of } \{p\text{->}e; \ldots; p\text{->}e\} \quad | \quad \texttt{let } x\texttt{=}e \texttt{ in } e \quad | \quad e \; op \; e \quad | \quad \nu$$

Fig. 4. Expressions, patterns, and (named) values

the hiding and factoring of judgments, which preserve the explanatory content of traces. We show that the trace operations produce residual explanations that can be expected from the corresponding trace simplifications.

- A *trace query language* that supports the modular definition of reusable, expressive filters for trace simplifications (Sect. 5). The trace query language turns basic trace transformations into comprehensive strategies for simplifying traces.

After discussing related work in Sect. 6, we present conclusions in Sect. 7 where we also comment on future work and briefly report results from an evaluation of the space savings that can be achieved by trace views.

2 Call-By-Named-Value Semantics

Our object language is the untyped lambda calculus, extended by numbers and algebraic data types (see Fig. 4). We use c to represent integers and constructor names and x, y, and f for variables. A *pattern* is a constructor applied to a (potentially empty) list of patterns or a variable. A *value* is a constructor applied to a (potentially empty) list of (named) values, a function or a fixpoint construction. A *named value* (ν) is a plain value which has a (possibly empty) sequence of names attached to it, written as $v^{x_1 \cdots x_k}$. The names have no semantic significance but will be used to make traces shorter and more readable. A *binding* is a pair of a name and a named value $x{=}\nu$, and an environment ρ is a sequence of bindings. Environments are extended on, and searched from, the right end.

The semantics of our language are defined in Fig. 5 through rules for the judgment $\rho : e \Downarrow v^{\bar{x}}$. Notably, our definition uses named values in addition to plain values. Otherwise, the rules are a variation of Call-By-Value, and we call the semantics therefore *Call-By-Named-Value* (*CBNV*).

Names are attached to values when they are retrieved from the environment (in rule VAR). By repeatedly binding a value to different variables, the value can accumulate a list of attached names (or "aliases"). Named values lose their attached names in basic computations as described in rule BINOP. Another departure from ordinary Call-By-Value is that we use plain lambda expressions instead of closures to represent function values. The purpose, again, is to achieve simpler traces. In rules ABS and FIX we substitute all free variables in abstraction bodies (except x and f) by their bound values in ρ. This is done using the environment as a function $\rho_{\bar{x}}(e)$, defined as follows.

$$\text{Con} \quad \frac{}{\rho:c \Downarrow c} \qquad \text{Var} \quad \frac{x=v^{\bar{y}} \in \rho}{\rho:x \Downarrow v^{\bar{y}x}} \qquad \text{BinOp} \quad \frac{\rho:e_1 \Downarrow v_1^{\bar{x}} \quad \rho:e_2 \Downarrow v_2^{\bar{y}} \quad v_1 \, op \, v_2 = v}{\rho:e_1 \, op \, e_2 \Downarrow v}$$

$$\text{AppF} \quad \frac{\rho:e_1 \Downarrow (\backslash x\text{->}e')^{\bar{f}} \quad \rho:e_2 \Downarrow u^{\bar{y}} \quad \rho, x=u^{\bar{y}}:e' \Downarrow v^{\bar{x}}}{\rho:e_1 \, e_2 \Downarrow v^{\bar{x}}} \qquad \text{AppC} \quad \frac{\rho:e_1 \Downarrow c \, \bar{v}^{\bar{y}} \quad \rho:e_2 \Downarrow v^{\bar{x}}}{\rho:e_1 \, e_2 \Downarrow c \, \bar{v}^{\bar{y}} \, v^{\bar{x}}}$$

$$\text{AppFix} \quad \frac{\rho:e_1 \Downarrow \mathtt{fix}(\backslash x\text{->}e, f)^{\bar{g}} \quad \rho:e_2 \Downarrow u^{\bar{y}} \quad \rho, x=u^{\bar{y}}:[\mathtt{fix}(\backslash x\text{->}e, f)^{\bar{g}}/f]e \Downarrow v^{\bar{x}}}{\rho:e_1 \, e_2 \Downarrow v^{\bar{x}}}$$

$$\text{Case} \quad \frac{\rho:e \Downarrow u^{\bar{y}} \quad u^{\bar{y}}|p_i \rightsquigarrow \rho' \quad \rho, \rho':e_i \Downarrow v_i^{\bar{x}} \quad \nexists j.1 \le j < i \wedge u^{\bar{y}}|p_j \rightsquigarrow \rho_j}{\rho:\mathtt{case} \, e \, \mathtt{of} \, \{p_1\text{->}e_1; \dots; p_k\text{->}e_k\} \Downarrow v_i^{\bar{x}}}$$

$$\text{Abs} \quad \frac{}{\rho:\backslash x\text{->}e \Downarrow \backslash x\text{->}\rho_{\bar{x}}(e)} \qquad \text{Fix} \quad \frac{}{\rho:\mathtt{fix}(\backslash x\text{->}e, f) \Downarrow \mathtt{fix}(\backslash x\text{->}\rho_{x,f}(e), f)} \qquad \text{PVar} \quad \frac{}{v^{\bar{y}}|x \rightsquigarrow x=v^{\bar{y}}}$$

$$\text{PCon} \quad \frac{v_1^{\bar{x}_1}|p_1 \rightsquigarrow \rho_1 \quad \dots \quad v_n^{\bar{x}_n}|p_n \rightsquigarrow \rho_n}{c \, v_1^{\bar{x}_1} \dots v_n^{\bar{x}_n}|c \, p_1 \dots p_n \rightsquigarrow \rho_1, \dots, \rho_n} \qquad \text{Let} \quad \frac{\rho:e' \Downarrow u^{\bar{y}} \quad \rho, x=u^{\bar{y}}:e \Downarrow v^{\bar{x}}}{\rho:\mathtt{let} \, x=e' \, \mathtt{in} \, e \Downarrow v^{\bar{x}}}$$

Fig. 5. Big-step Call-By-Named-Value semantics

$$\rho_{\bar{x}}(e) = [\nu_1/x_1, \dots, \nu_k/x_k]e$$
$$\textbf{where } \rho|_{dom(\rho)-\bar{x}} = \{\nu_1=x_1, \dots, \nu_k=x_k\}$$

Since the only difference between CBNV and CBV semantics are the names attached to values, both evaluate expressions to the same results, except for possible attached names and the resolving of closures in CBNV. A closure $(\backslash x\text{->}e, \rho)$ can be viewed as being equivalent to its resolved form $\backslash x\text{->}\rho_{\bar{x}}(e)$.[1] Writing $v \approx v'$ for the extension of this relation to all values, we can express the relationship between CBV and CBNV as follows. (We ignore free variables in $\rho_{\bar{x}}(e)$, since such expressions are considered meaningless in both semantics.)

Theorem 1. $\rho:e \Downarrow^{CBNV} v^{\bar{x}} \wedge FV(v) = \varnothing \iff \rho:e \Downarrow^{CBV} v' \wedge v \approx v'$

3 From Proof Trees to Traces

We introduce a DAG model of traces for judgments $j = \rho:e \Downarrow \nu$ that eliminates duplicates, replaces variable lookups by *binding nodes*, replaces function values by their names in places they are not applied, and eliminates environments.

Let $P_j = (N, L, R, E)$ be the proof tree for j where N is a set of nodes, $L : N \to \mathcal{J}_\nu$ maps each node to the judgment it is labeled with, R maps each node to the name of the rule that was used to create it as a conclusion, and

---

[1] Or $\mathtt{fix}(\backslash x\text{->}\rho_{x,f}(e), f)$, if the closure is recursive.

$$j \in \mathcal{J}_\nu \ ::= \ \rho : e \Downarrow \nu \ \mid \ \nu | p \rightsquigarrow b \ \mid \ v \, op \, v = v \ \mid \ x = \nu \in \rho$$
$$j \in \mathcal{J}_w \ ::= \ e \Downarrow w \ \mid \ w | p \rightsquigarrow b \ \mid \ v \, op \, v = v \ \mid \ \overline{n \cdot n} \triangleright x = w \ \mid \ \cdots$$
$$w \in W \ ::= \ x \ \mid \ v$$

Fig. 6. Judgments stored in proof trees ($\mathcal{J}_\nu$) and traces ($\mathcal{J}_w$).

$(n, m) \in E$ iff m is a child of n in P_j. The root of P_j is labeled with j. The type of judgments $\mathcal{J}_\nu$ used in proof trees is defined in Fig. 6. In addition to evaluation judgments, $\mathcal{J}_\nu$ includes pattern matching judgments, equations for binary operations, and variable lookups.

The type of judgments $\mathcal{J}_w$ used in traces is slightly different: First, evaluation judgments don't have an environment, and expressions don't evaluate to named values but to names *or* values (W). Second, variable lookups are replaced by binding nodes, and we have placeholder nodes ($\cdots$), explained in Sect. 4.1. Finally, all judgments only use plain values v (or names or values w) instead of named values ν. The names associated with values are exploited in the translation process to replace some of the values in $e \Downarrow w$ and $w | p \rightsquigarrow \rho$.

In the first step, we generate a DAG from the proof tree. To this end, we need an equivalence predicate on the judgments $\mathcal{J}_\nu$ used in labels. Two values v and v' are equivalent (written as $v \equiv v'$) if they are identical. The same is true for variables, patterns, and expressions. Two named values are equivalent if their plain values are, that is, $v^{\bar{y}} \equiv v^{\bar{x}}$ (ignoring names increases the opportunities for sharing). The following rules define the equivalence of environments and judgments.

$$\frac{\nu_1 \equiv \nu_1' \quad \cdots \quad \nu_k \equiv \nu_k'}{\{x_1 = \nu_1, \ldots, x_k = \nu_k\} \equiv \{x_1 = \nu_1', \ldots, x_k = \nu_k'\}} \qquad \frac{\rho(e) \equiv \rho'(e') \quad \nu \equiv \nu'}{\rho : e \Downarrow \nu \equiv \rho' : e' \Downarrow \nu'}$$

$$\frac{\nu \equiv \nu' \quad \rho \equiv \rho'}{\nu | p \rightsquigarrow \rho \equiv \nu' | p \rightsquigarrow \rho'} \qquad v_1 \, op \, v_2 = v \equiv v_1 \, op \, v_2 = v \qquad \frac{\nu \equiv \nu'}{x = \nu \in \rho \equiv x = \nu' \in \rho'}$$

The equivalence of labels induces a corresponding equivalence for nodes: $n \equiv m \Leftrightarrow L(n) \equiv L(m)$. To increase the potential for sharing, we could extend equivalence to account for α-equivalence. However, this would require to use "named variables" (similar to named values), since the transformation of traces may change the binding parent of shared computations. Such a "bound variable shift" is similar to the effect of "origin shift", explained later (cf. Fig. 7). Since α-equivalence would complicate our model further, we leave it for future work.

To generate the DAG, we choose a minimal subset of N that doesn't lose any judgments, that is, we pick a smallest set $N_\equiv \subseteq N$ so that $\forall j \in rng(L).\exists n \in N_\equiv . L(n) \equiv j$. Next we redirect edges to/from nodes in $N_\equiv$.

$$E_\equiv = \{(n, m) \mid (n', m') \in E \wedge \{n, m\} \subseteq N_\equiv \wedge n \equiv n' \wedge m \equiv m'\}$$

Finally, we transform labels $\rho : e \Downarrow \nu \in rng(L)$ to $\rho |_{FV(e)} : e \Downarrow \nu$ to restrict ρ to the most recent bindings of free variables in e. We write $L_\equiv^1$ for the resulting labeling

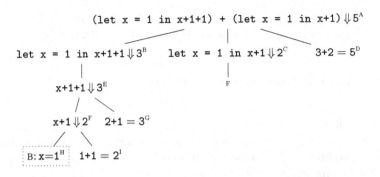

Fig. 7. Trace for (let x = 1 in x+1+1) + (let x = 1 in x+1).

function. Then $G_j = (N_\equiv, L^1_\equiv, R, E_\equiv)$ is the proof DAG for j derived from P_j. We use superscripts to disambiguate the different versions of the labeling function that result from each step.

In the second step, we tag variable bindings in environments with the nodes of the judgments that created them, as well as with the nodes of the bindings' scopes. Since some nodes are shared, it may happen that an environment contains a binding that has more than one origin and scope. Consider the trace in Fig. 7. The judgment x+1⇓2 in node F that results from the evaluation of both let expressions is shared. One of its premises is the binding node H, which has its origin in nodes B and C. We usually only show the origin of the binding for the context of the node, in this case B, but when we transitively hide all the nodes in the subtrace with root E, we still have to show node F as a premise for node C. But now the origin of the binding x=1 is node C, which should be indicated in the binding node (see Sect. 4.1).

To tag variable bindings, we must determine which nodes produce bindings that are used by other nodes. To this end, we define a relation $O \subseteq N_\equiv \times N_\equiv \times Var \times N_\equiv$, where $(n, m, x, n_j) \in O$ means "the variable x is used in the label of node n_j, and has origin n and scope m." We first define an auxiliary relation $O' \subseteq N_\equiv \times N_\equiv \times Var$ that captures which nodes are considered origins and scopes. We consider two cases: (A) For a node n with $R(n) \in \{\text{APPF}, \text{LET}, \text{APPFIX}\}$ that has a child m with label $\rho, x{=}u^{\bar{y}} : e' \Downarrow v^{\bar{x}}$, we have $(n, m, x) \in O'$. (B) For a node with $R(n) = \text{CASE}$, that has a child m_1 with $R(m_1) = \text{PVAR}$ or $R(m_1) = \text{PCON}$ (and thus having a label in the form $v | p \rightsquigarrow \rho'$) and a child m_2 with a label in the form $\rho, \rho' : e_i \Downarrow v_i^{\bar{x}}$, we have $(m_1, m_2, x) \in O'$ iff x is bound in b.

Intuitively, O' relates variables and their possible origins and scopes. However, O' is too general, since it does not include information regarding *which* occurrences of x have particular origins and scopes. We thus define a more precise O'' relation as follows.

$$O'' = \{(n, m, x, n_j) \mid (n, m, x) \in O' \land n_j \in \sigma^*_T(m)\}$$

In the above expression, $\sigma^*(m)$ is the set of nodes reachable from node m. The new relation adds nodes n_j that contain x as a free variable in their label.

Unlike O', only occurrences of x in descendants of the scope m are included. Finally, to get O from O'', we have to account for variable shadowing.

$$O = \{(n, m, x, n_j) \in O'' \mid \forall n', m' \in N_\equiv.(n', m', x, n_j) \in O'' \Rightarrow m' \notin \sigma_T^*(m)\}$$

Intuitively, only the closest origins and scopes are included in O. We finally transform each label's environment to include the origin and scope information. To this end we define scope/origin pairs for a variable x and node n_j as follows.

$$\omega(x, n_j) = \{n \cdot m \mid (n, m, x, n_j) \in O\}$$

With this definition we then extend every binding $x{=}v$ in an environment ρ by the origin/scope information, yielding $\omega(x, n_j) \triangleright x{=}v$. We thus evolve $L_\equiv^1$ as follows.

$$L_\equiv^2(n_j) = \{\omega(x, n_j) \triangleright x{=}v \mid x{=}v \in \rho\} : e \Downarrow \nu$$

The scope node of a binding is the top-most node in which that binding is available. For some operations on traces, it's necessary to know the set of *all* nodes in which a binding is available, which is given by the following function.

$$S_x(m) = \sigma_T^*(m) - \bigcup\{\sigma_T^*(m') \mid (n', m', x, n_j') \in O \land m' \in \sigma_T^*(m)\}$$

$S(m)$ includes all descendants of m, except those that are descendants of another scope node m' further down the tree, to account for shadowing.

At this point, the environments contain information that will help us tailor our traces later on. In particular, for a judgement of the form $\rho : e \Downarrow \nu$, the scopes of the variables bound in ρ can be used to determine nodes where e can be safely replaced with v. We capture this information in a function $\eta(n)$, which is defined to work on evaluation judgments in the current mapping $L_\equiv^2$.

$$\eta(n) = \begin{cases} \bigcap_{\bar{o} \triangleright x = \nu \in \rho} \bigcup_{n' \cdot m \in \bar{o}} S_x(m) & \text{if } L_\equiv^2(n) = \rho : e \Downarrow v \\ \varnothing & \text{otherwise} \end{cases}$$

This definition ensures that an expression will be replaced by its value only in labels of nodes where all free variables are defined and have the same value. If no variables are bound in ρ, then the scope of a node is the entire trace, or $N_\equiv$.

In the third step, we replace applications of the VAR rule by binding nodes: For each node $k \in N_\equiv$ with $R(k) = $ VAR and $L_\equiv^2(k) = \rho : x \Downarrow v^{\bar{y}x}$ where $\bar{o} \triangleright x{=}v^{\bar{y}} \in \rho$, we change $L_\equiv^2$ to $L_\equiv^3(k) = \bar{o} \triangleright x{=}v$ and remove the node m with $(k, m) \in E_\equiv$ as well as the edge (k, m).

In the final step, we replace named values by names or values. Specifically, we replace named functions by their names and remove names from other values, that is, we replace all $(\backslash x\text{->}e)^{z\bar{y}}$ by z (the first name assigned to the function) and $c^{\bar{x}}$ by c. As a special case, if the first name z is equal to the variable being bound, we instead use the second name (the first element of $\bar{y}$) if it is available. This is a very simple strategy, but CBNV offers opportunities to explore more refined replacement rules based on properties of the trace and guided by annotation from the user. We also eliminate the environments from all evaluation judgments, since the origins of variable bindings are captured by their node tags. This yields $L^4_{\underline{\equiv}}$.

After the transformation steps, we can drop the rule labels R, since they are no longer needed. We call the resulting DAG $T_j = (N_{\underline{\equiv}}, L^4_{\underline{\equiv}}, E_{\underline{\equiv}}, \eta)$ a *trace* for the judgment j. In the following we simply use N instead of $N_{\underline{\equiv}}$ (same for E and L) and consider the "$\underline{\equiv}$" subscript as implicitly present.

In the rest of the paper we use the following notation for accessing specific parts of traces. In the definition of $T[n]$, the notation $L[n]$, $E[n]$, and $\eta[n]$ is used to denote restrictions of the sets to element to only include nodes in $\sigma^*_T(n)$.

$$
\begin{array}{rl}
\hat{T} & \textit{root node of trace } T \\
\sigma_T(n) = \{m \mid (n,m) \in E\} & \textit{direct premises of node } n \\
\sigma^*_T(n) = \{m \mid (n,m) \in E^*\} & \textit{direct & indirect premises of node } n \\
T[n] = (\sigma^*_T(n), L[n], E[n], \eta[n])\} & \textit{subtrace of } T \textit{ with root } n
\end{array}
$$

Traces represent comprehensive explanations of program executions that are subject to systematic transformations using two specific trace operations, to be introduced next.

4   Trace Views as Explanations

As described in [5], proof trees can be viewed as explanations. Specifically, the judgment in each node is explained by the judgments in its children. In the context of operational semantics, a rule defines what counts as a valid explanation of a judgment, that is, in a rule $P_1, \ldots, P_n \implies C$ the premises $P_1, \ldots, P_n$ explain the conclusion C in the sense that the correct answer to the question "Why is C true?" is: "Because P_1, P_2, etc." A proof tree is comprehensive as an explanation of the judgment at its root, since it contains explanations for all judgments in internal nodes that might themselves be in need of an explanation.

By strictly following the rules of the semantics in building a proof tree we also ensure that the proof tree provides a *correct explanation*. This seems to be obvious, but it is important to point out that an explanation could, in principle be incorrect, and since we will use transformations of explanations in the following, we need to guard against the construction of incorrect ones. There are several ways in which an explanation can be incorrect. First, an explanation could contain an incorrect judgment. For example, $3 \Downarrow 4$ cannot be derived by the rules and thus makes any explanation it is used in incorrect. Second, an explanation could contain a correct judgment that doesn't match the rule used for building the explanation. For example, the correct explanation for $3{+}4 \Downarrow 7$ contains the three premises $3 \Downarrow 3$, $4 \Downarrow 4$, and $3{+}4 = 7$. If the first premise were replaced by $2 \Downarrow 2$ or the third premise were replaced by $2{+}5 = 7$, the resulting explanation would contain only correct judgments, but it would still be an incorrect explanation. Finally, an explanation could contain extra judgments that, while true, don't contribute anything to the explanation. An example would be to add a fourth premise $7 \Downarrow 7$ to the explanation of $3{+}4 \Downarrow 7$.

While the construction of traces described in Sect. 3 does change the structure of judgments and turns the tree into a DAG, it doesn't change the factual statements of the judgments, and it doesn't omit any facts either.

Proposition 1. *The trace T_j derived from a proof tree P_j for a judgment j is a correct and comprehensive explanation for j.*

In the following we write $T \therefore j$ when T is a correct explanation for j, that is, the correctness part of Proposition 1 can be simply rephrased as $T_j \therefore j$.

While we always want to have correct explanations, we do not necessarily need comprehensive explanations. Specifically, we don't need an explanation for a judgement that is well understood. A non-comprehensive explanation might be often even preferable to a comprehensive one, since it is smaller and can thus be understood more easily.

4.1 Hiding Judgments and Subtraces

We can consider two main cases for simplifying traces by omitting parts: removal of leaves or complete subtrees (or sub-DAGs), and removal of (one or more) internal nodes. The latter requires redirecting its incoming and outgoing edges, which may cause incorrect explanations. Consider, for example, the explanation for $\rho:$ succ (succ 1) $\Downarrow 3$, which according to the APPF rule has three premises, (A) $\rho:$ succ $\Downarrow$ \x->x+1, (B) $\rho:$ succ $1\Downarrow 2$, and (C) $\rho, \mathtt{x} = 2:\mathtt{x+1}\Downarrow 3$. If we remove (B) and replace it with its three premises (another (A), (D) $\rho:1\Downarrow 1$, and (E) $\rho, \mathtt{x} = 1:\mathtt{x+1}\Downarrow 2$), the resulting explanation now has five premises, A, A, D, E, and C. Now the premises D and E do not match the premise B required by the APPF rule, and thus, the resulting trace is an incorrect explanation.

Therefore, nodes aren't removed from a trace, but rather only hidden. More precisely, they are marked as hidden, and (maximal) groups of connected hidden nodes are shown in the trace as an ellipsis ($\cdots$) when they have non-hidden premises. Given a total order $<$ on N, we can identify any connected hidden subgraph with its smallest node. With $\sim$ being the reflexive, transitive, and symmetric closure of edges from E that are between two nodes in H, we can define a function R that performs this identification as follows.

$$R(n) = \{\min([n]_\sim) \mid n \in N\}$$

Hidden sinks are subgraphs of hidden nodes with no outgoing edges, that is, $S_H = \{n \in R(N) \mid \nexists(l,m) \in E : R(l) = n \wedge R(m) \neq n\}$. The *trace view* of T induced by H is the graph $T_H = (N_H, L_H, E_H, \eta)$ where:

$$N_H = R(N) - S_H$$
$$E_H = \{(R(m), R(n)) \mid (m,n) \in E \wedge R(m), R(n) \in N_H \wedge R(m) \neq R(n)\}$$
$$L_H(n) = \begin{cases} \cdots & \text{if } n \in H \\ L(n) & \text{otherwise} \end{cases}$$

We use τ to range over trace views.

The two basic operations for hiding and unhiding a single node are:

$$T_H - n := T_{H \cup \{n\}} \qquad\qquad T_H + n := T_{H - \{n\}}$$

Due to their type, both operations are left associative.

A trace view is a correct explanation if all hidden nodes can be substituted by (subgraphs of) judgments so that the resulting trace is a comprehensive and correct explanation. Of course, this can be easily achieved by unhiding all the hidden nodes, that is, trace views are by construction correct explanations.

Lemma 1. $\tau \therefore j \implies \tau - n \therefore j$ and $\tau \therefore j \implies \tau + n \therefore j$

To make the interaction work with trace views intuitive, it is important that node hiding and unhiding is commutative.

Lemma 2. $\tau - n - m = \tau - m - n$ and $\tau + n + m = \tau + m + n$

Commutativity of node (un)hiding supports the incremental construction of explanations, since hiding operations can be applied and undone in arbitrary order. Hiding and unhiding are idempotent, but they are not inverses of each other, because even though unhiding a hidden node will make the node visible, hiding a node after unhiding it will still hide it in the resulting trace view.

$$\tau - n - n = \tau - n \qquad\qquad \tau - n + n = \tau$$
$$\tau + n + n = \tau + n \qquad\qquad \tau + n - n = \tau - n$$

If we could only hide individual nodes one by one, the construction of explanations would be too arduous. Since it's only natural to want to transitively hide all premises of an understood judgment, we define a corresponding operation. However, we cannot simply hide all nodes $m \in \sigma_T^*(n)$, since we shouldn't hide nodes that are still used as premises in other (non-hidden) parts of the trace view. We should hide only those descendants of n that are only reachable through n. We can gather this set of *weak descendants* through the following definition.

$$\sigma_T^\circ(n) = \{n\} \cup \{m \in \sigma_T^*(n) \mid deg_{T[n]}^-(m) = deg_T^-(m)\}$$

With the help of that function we can define the following operation for hiding a node and all of its weak descendants. Similarly, we can also define transitive functions for hiding and unhiding nodes.

$$T_H \ominus n := T_{H \cup \sigma_T^\circ(n)} \qquad\qquad T_H \oplus n := T_{H \cup \sigma_T^\circ(n)}$$

The transitive (un)hiding operations enjoy the same algebraic properties as the single-node versions of the operations.

$$\tau \ominus n \ominus n = \tau \ominus n \qquad\qquad \tau \ominus n \oplus n = \tau$$
$$\tau \oplus n \oplus n = \tau \oplus n \qquad\qquad \tau \oplus n \ominus n = \tau \ominus n$$

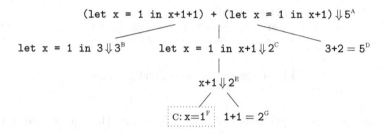

Fig. 8. Factoring judgment x+1+1 $\Downarrow$ 3 in node E (cf. Fig. 7).

4.2 Applying Judgments and Factoring Traces

In some cases traces can be simplified beyond hiding. For example, understanding the judgment `length []` $\Downarrow$ 0, we may in addition to hiding it actively employ it to replace subexpressions `length []` elsewhere by 0. We call the use of a judgment $L(n) = e \Downarrow v$ as a rewrite rule *applying a judgment*; it is used within n's scope, that is, for the set of nodes in the trace where e is certain to be evaluated to the same result v. The function η, included in each trace, contains this scope for every node. We use η with one adjustment: We consider the scope of a lambda abstraction to be only the node in which it is evaluated, and thus avoid substituting lambda abstractions.

In the following definition we write $!m$ for the condition $m \in \eta(n) \wedge L(m) = e' \Downarrow w'$, which identifies nodes that are subject to the simplification substitution.

$$(N, L, E, \eta)_H \bullet n := (N, L', E, \eta)_H \text{ where}$$
$$L'(m) = \begin{cases} [v/e]e' \Downarrow w' & \text{if } !m \wedge L(n) = e \Downarrow w \\ [w/x]e' \Downarrow w' & \text{if } !m \wedge L(n) = \bar{o} \triangleright x{=}w \\ L(m) & \text{otherwise} \end{cases}$$

For example, to apply the judgment x+1 $\Downarrow$ 2 in node F in the trace from Fig. 7, we have to substitute 2 for x+1 in the scope for x+1, which is given by the scope for variable x. Since node F is shared, the binding node for x (that is, H) has two scope nodes associated with it, namely B and C.

Applying a judgment leads to a redundant judgment of the form $w \Downarrow w$. We generally want to hide such judgments, since they don't contribute to the explanation. Therefore, we define an additional operation *factor* that applies a judgment and transitively hides it at the same time.

$$\tau \div n := (\tau \bullet n) \ominus n$$

We call the application of a factor operation *trace factorization* and also refer to the result as *factored trace*. As an example, consider the factoring of the judgment x+1+1 $\Downarrow$ 3 in node E in Fig. 7: Node E and its premise G are removed from the trace. Because F, H, and I are shared as a premise of the judgment in C, they will not be removed. The factored trace is shown in Fig. 8. Nodes F, H,

$$q ::= \text{hide } s \mid \text{hideAll } s \mid \text{apply } s \mid \text{factor } s \mid q \, \& \, q$$
$$s ::= \iota \mid s \text{ and } s \mid s \text{ or } s \mid s \text{ except } s \mid s \text{ then } s \mid \text{fix } s \mid \text{try } s \mid \text{root}$$
$$\iota ::= e^\circ \Downarrow v^\circ \mid v^\circ | e^\circ \rightsquigarrow b^\circ \mid v^\circ \, op \, v^\circ = v^\circ \mid x^\circ \triangleright x^\circ = v^\circ \mid \circ_a$$

Fig. 9. Queries, selectors, and patterns

and I from Fig. 7 now appear as E, F, and G. Note that these nodes are no longer children of B. The binding in F (which was previously H) is created in C, which means that the binding node's origin has to be changed from B to C.

Unlike the hiding of nodes, which changes merely the presentation of a trace, the applying and factoring of judgments can change traces substantially through the simplification of expressions.

In particular, when the root of an explanation is affected by $e' \Downarrow v'$, such an altered trace does not explain the original judgment in the root anymore, that is, $j = e \Downarrow v$ turns into $j' = [v'/e']e \Downarrow v$, and we have $\tau \div n \therefore j'$ but *not* $\tau \div n \therefore j$.

But that is, we argue, exactly what one should expect from an explanation: A residual explanation for $e \Downarrow v$ that omits everything related to explaining $e' \Downarrow v'$ is an explanation for $[v'/e']e \Downarrow v$, and that is the trace that one gets.

To formulate the formal relationship for factored traces, we write $\lceil j \rceil$ to denote the trace for a judgment j and $\frac{j}{j'}$ for $\lceil j \rceil \div n$ with $L(n) = j'$. In general, we have the following relationship for factored traces.

Theorem 2

$$FV(e') = \varnothing \implies \frac{e \Downarrow v}{e' \Downarrow v'} = \frac{[v'/e']e \Downarrow v}{v' \Downarrow v'}$$

We can explain the idea also in terms of factoring and hiding.

Lemma 3. $L(n) = e' \Downarrow v' \wedge FV(e') = \varnothing \implies \lceil e \Downarrow v \rceil \div n = \lceil [v'/e']e \Downarrow v \rceil \ominus n$

5   Trace Query Language

The query language consists of two parts: operations and selectors. The operations are as described in the previous sections. Selectors are used to find nodes where operations should be applied. The grammars for these two components of the language are given in Fig. 9; it also contains a grammar for patterns, which is similar to $\mathcal{J}_w$ from Fig. 6, without the ellipsis and extended by a wildcard symbol (we use e° to stand for e or $\circ$, v° to stand for v or $\circ$, etc.). Different occurrences of an non-indexed wildcard $\circ$ can be bound independently of one another. To force the occurrence of the same bound value in different places, the wildcard can be indexed, as for example in $\circ_a \Downarrow \circ_a$, which matches expressions that evaluate to themselves.

When a selector s is applied to a trace, it yields a set of nodes matching the selector, ordered according to a breadth-first traversal of the trace.

If the selector is a pattern ι, it yields the set of all nodes with matching labels (written as $l \prec \iota$). The matching relation is fairly straightforward: Each pattern ι matches the corresponding judgment, while the wildcard $\diamond$ matches anything.

A selector may also be a combination of other selectors. For instance, s_1 or s_2 finds nodes that are selected by either s_1 or s_2. Similarly, s_1 and s_2 finds nodes selected by both s_1 and s_2, and s_1 except s_2 will yield all nodes matched by s_1 that are not matched by s_2.

More sophisticated queries can be built with the selectors root, s_1 then s_2, try s, and fix s: root returns the root node of the trace, sequencing s_1 then s_2 applies s_2 to subtraces $T[n]$ of T for every node n selected by s_1 and merges the final results, and fix computes fixed points.

We can use then to find evaluations of the factorial function that occur as children of other evaluations of the function (indicating recursion).

$$(\texttt{fact} \diamond \Downarrow \diamond) \texttt{ then } ((\texttt{fact} \diamond \Downarrow \diamond) \texttt{ except root})$$

Here except root ensures that only the children of the function application are selected, and not the parent application itself. Here are a few more frequently used general-purpose selectors (where all $= \diamond$ is just a convenient alias):

> none $=$ root except root
> first $s = s$ except (s then (s except root))
>
> descendants $=$ all except root
> children $=$ first descendants

The selector first s will find all nodes selected by s that are not children of other nodes also selected by s. The selectors descendants and children find the transitive and immediate children of the trace's root node, respectively.

The combinator then in itself cannot be used to define more complicated traversals of a trace. Instead, the fix selector can be used to perform an arbitrary number of sequencing operations. It works by repeatedly sequencing s with itself until the result of the sequencing stops changing. To help avoid fixed points where no nodes are selected, the try s combinator can be used, which returns the root of the graph if s does not select any nodes. This way, we are able to terminate the sequencing right before hitting an empty result, rather than after. We can use fix to find all nodes that are used outside of a call to the factorial function.

$$\texttt{fix ((children or root) except (fact} \diamond \Downarrow \diamond))$$

The new combinator enables us to define a few more general purpose selectors.

> last $s = $ fix (try (s except root))
> uniqueChildren $s = (s$ then all) except (fix ((children or root) except s))

The last s selector will find all nodes selected by s that do not have other nodes selected by s as descendants, while uniqueChildren s will find descendants of nodes selected by s that are not referenced anywhere else in the trace.

The semantics for the selector language are given in Fig. 10. We can now use the arsenal of selectors to construct specialized queries to help with creating

$$\begin{aligned}
[\![\iota]\!](L,N,E) &= \{n \mid L(n) \prec \iota\} & [\![s \text{ then } s']\!]T &= \bigcup_{n \in [\![s]\!]T}[\![s']\!](T[n])\\
[\![s_1 \text{ and } s_2]\!]T &= [\![s_1]\!]T \cap [\![s_2]\!]T & & \\
[\![s_1 \text{ or } s_2]\!]T &= [\![s_1]\!]T \cup [\![s_2]\!]T & [\![\text{fix } s]\!]T &= \begin{cases} [\![s]\!]T & \text{if } [\![s \text{ then } s]\!]T = [\![s]\!]T \\ [\![s \text{ then } (\text{fix } s)]\!]T & \text{otherwise} \end{cases}\\
[\![s_1 \text{ except } s_2]\!]T &= [\![s_1]\!]T - [\![s_2]\!]T & & \\
[\![\text{root}]\!]T &= \{\hat{T}\} & [\![\text{try } s]\!]T &= \begin{cases} [\![\text{root}]\!]T & \text{if } [\![s]\!]T = \varnothing \\ [\![s]\!]T & \text{otherwise} \end{cases}
\end{aligned}$$

Fig. 10. Selector semantics

explanations. For instance, we may want to hide all evaluations of a recursive function except for the first and last one. This can be achieved with the `limitRec` f selector, defined as follows, where f is the name of the recursive function.

```
nonFirst s = (s except first s) then descendants
afterLast s = last s then all
limitRec f = notFirst (f ◇ ⇓◇) except afterLast (f ◇ ⇓◇)
```

We can now define the semantics of queries as a transformation of trace views through the operations introduced in Sect. 4. (Note that for any ordered set of nodes $M = \{n_1, \ldots, n_k\}$, we use for all $\odot \in \{-, \ominus, +, \oplus, \bullet, \div\}$ the notation $T \odot M$ as an abbreviation for $T \odot n_1 \odot \ldots \odot n_k$).

$$[\![\text{hide } s]\!]T = T - [\![s]\!]T \qquad\qquad [\![\text{apply } s]\!]T = T \bullet [\![s]\!]T$$
$$[\![\text{hideAll } s]\!]T = T \ominus [\![s]\!]T \qquad\qquad [\![\text{factor } s]\!]T = T \div [\![s]\!]T$$
$$[\![q_1 \text{ \& } q_2]\!]T = [\![q_2]\!]([\![q_1]\!]T)$$

Note that the `uniqueChildren` combinator was not created arbitrarily; in fact, its behavior closely aligns with that of the $\sigma_T^\circ(n)$ function (defined in Sect. 4.1). We capture this in the following lemmas (where Lemma 5 is a direct consequence of Lemma 4).

Lemma 4. $[\![\text{uniqueChildren } s]\!]T = \bigcup_{n \in [\![s]\!]T} \sigma_T^\circ(n)$

Lemma 5. $[\![\text{hideAll } s]\!]T = T - [\![\text{uniqueChildren } s]\!]T$

6   Related Work

Our *Call-By-Named-Value* semantics is similar to the work of Acar et al. [1], in which the semantics of a language are extended to support provenance. They use a fixed algorithm for *disclosure slicing* to reduce the size of traces, whereas our approach allows tailoring of traces through a query language.

Problems with the visualization of large proof trees has been addressed Dunchev et al. [3] through hiding structural rules (similar to our VAR rule) and unused contexts (similar to our hidden environments). Their *Prooftool* allows users to focus on sub-proofs, similar to our hiding and factoring operations.

They also discuss the use of proof DAGs but decided against them because of the difficulty of finding graph layouts that avoid crossing edges.

Proof trees are universal structures to trace arbitrary programs. A different kind of structure called *value decomposition* was introduced in [4] for explaining the execution of dynamic programming algorithms. This approach is based on a semiring model of dynamic programming, and while it can produce succinct explanations, it is limited to only a small set of programs.

The work on explaining (imperative) functional programs [12,13] employs program slicing as a technique to generate dynamic explanations for the part of output selected by the user. Program slicing filters out parts from traces that do not lead to the selected partial output. The approach assumes that a user would like to understand certain part of the output, which isn't always the case. Also, the generated traces can still be quite large. Our approach is somewhat orthogonal and could in principle be combined with program slicing techniques.

The idea of *algorithmic debugging* is to incrementally tailor a proof tree for a computation by repeatedly asking users about the expected results of subexpression evaluations [10]. Like most other debugging approaches, the goal is not to provide any explanation of why the output was generated in the first place.

The *Java Whyline* [8] is a debugger for Java program that allows programmers to ask questions about the output, which the debugger tries to answer by computing a backward trace of the computations that caused the output. Haskell's debugger Hood [6] generates a trace of intermediate values of computation. A programmer needs to annotate the interesting parts in the source code. When the code is recompiled and rerun, the debugger results in a trace of intermediate values along with the actual output. This is similar to our approach in that the user has some control over the form and size of the produced trace.

The selector component of our query language was inspired by the *rewrite strategies* approach presented by Visser et al. [16], which are used to define algorithms that apply optimizations to programs. Much like our query language, these strategies provide a toolbox of combinators that allow the user of the system to construct more complicated traversal and transformation algorithms. The selectors defined in this paper are more limited: they lack the ability to transform the trace, and they are not capable of maintaining a context of encountered expressions, or making decisions based on that context.

7   Conclusions and Future Work

We have presented a new approach for explaining program behavior that is based on a new Call-By-Named-Value semantics, a DAG-based representation for traces, and a query language for expressing trace manipulations. A major innovation of our traces is the economical presentation of information and an effective method for hiding large parts of uninteresting regions from a trace.

Our initial experiments with this new approach are encouraging: For a benchmark set of 21 functional programs used in an introductory CS course, we could achieve reductions between 79% and 98% (in 90% of the cases the traces have been reduced by 85% or more). For this we needed 12 standard filters (7 of these were always applied and 5 only in specific instances). (Details about this evaluation, can be found in Bajaj et al. [2].)

In future work, we can make explanation traces even more succinct through dead-code elimination, especially within expressions. For example, the `True` branch in a judgment `case False of {...; False -> 0}` $\Downarrow$ `0` can be omitted. This strategy is applicable even if part of the code is not dead but "dormant" and thus explanatorily irrelevant in the current part of the trace. Moreover, we can further exploit the Call-By-Named-Value semantics by having users tag important names, and we can also exploit the fact that named values can have an arbitrary number of names. Instead of always displaying one specific name, the decision can be made dynamically, for example, when a value acquires a more meaningful name in the evaluation of a program (such as when list elements acquire the name `pivot` during the execution of quicksort).

Acknowledgements. This work is partially supported by the National Science Foundation under the grants CCF-1717300, DRL-1923628, and CCF-2114642.

References

1. Acar, U.A., Ahmed, A., Cheney, J., Perera, R.: A core calculus for provenance. In: Degano, P., Guttman, J.D. (eds.) POST 2012. LNCS, vol. 7215, pp. 410–429. Springer, Heidelberg (2012). https://doi.org/10.1007/978-3-642-28641-4_22
2. Bajaj, D., Erwig, M., Fedorin, D., Gay, K.: A visual notation for succinct program traces. In: IEEE International Symposium on Visual Languages and Human-Centric Computing (2021, to appear)
3. Dunchev, C., et al.: PROOFTOOL: a GUI for the GAPT framework. Electron. Proc. Theor. Comput. Sci. **118**, 1–14 (2013)
4. Erwig, M., Kumar, P.: Explainable dynamic programming. J. Funct. Program. **31**, e10 (2021)
5. Ferrand, G., Lesaint, W., Tessier, A.: Explanations and proof trees. Comput. Inform. **25**, 105–125 (2006)
6. Gill, A.: Debugging Haskell by observing intermediate data structures. Electron. Notes Theor. Comput. Sci. **41**(1), 1 (2001)
7. Khoo, Y.P., Foster, J.S., Hicks, M.: Expositor: scriptable time-travel debugging with first-class traces. In: International Conference on Software Engineering, pp. 352–361 (2013)
8. Ko, A.J., Myers, B.A.: Finding causes of program output with the Java Whyline. In: SIGCHI Conference on Human Factors in Computing Systems, pp. 1569–1578 (2009)
9. Marceau, G., Cooper, G.H., Spiro, J.P., Krishnamurthi, S., Reiss, S.P.: The design and implementation of a dataflow language for scriptable debugging. Autom. Softw. Eng. **14**(1), 59–86 (2007). https://doi.org/10.1007/s10515-006-0003-z
10. Nilsson, H., Fritzson, P.: Algorithmic debugging for lazy functional languages. J. Funct. Program. **4**(3), 337–369 (1994)
11. Parnin, C., Orso, A.: Are automated debugging techniques actually helping programmers? In: International Symposium on Software Testing and Analysis, pp. 199–209 (2011)

12. Perera, R., Acar, U.A., Cheney, J., Levy, P.B.: Functional programs that explain their work. In: ACM International Conference on Functional Programming, pp. 365–376 (2012)
13. Ricciotti, W., Stolarek, J., Perera, R., Cheney, J.: Imperative functional programs that explain their work. Proc. ACM Program. Lang. 1(ICFP), 1–28 (2017)
14. Roehm, T., Tiarks, R., Koschke, R., Maalej, W.: How do professional developers comprehend software? In: International Conference on Software Engineering, pp. 255–265 (2012)
15. Vessey, I.: Expertise in debugging computer programs: an analysis of the content of verbal protocols. IEEE Trans. Syst. Man Cybern. 16(5), 621–637 (1986)
16. Visser, E., Benaissa, Z., Tolmach, A.: Building program optimizers with rewriting strategies. In: ACM International Conference on Functional Programming, pp. 13–26 (1998)

A Typed Programmatic Interface to Contracts on the Blockchain

Thi Thu Ha Doan◉ and Peter Thiemann$^{(\boxtimes)}$◉

University of Freiburg, Freiburg, Germany
{doanha,thiemann}@informatik.uni-freiburg.de

Abstract. Smart contract applications on the blockchain can only reach their full potential if they integrate seamlessly with traditional software systems via a programmatic interface. This interface should provide for originating and invoking contracts as well as observing the state of the blockchain. We propose a typed API for this purpose and establish some properties of the combined system. Specifically, we provide an execution model that enables us to prove type-safe interaction between programs and the blockchain. We establish further properties of the model that give rise to requirements on the API. A prototype of the interface is implemented in OCaml for the Tezos blockchain.

Keywords: Smart contracts · Embedded domain specific languages · Types

1 Introduction

First generation blockchains were primarily geared towards supporting cryptocurrencies. Bitcoin is the most prominent system of this kind [14]. Although Bitcoin already features a rudimentary programming language called Script, second generation blockchains like Ethereum [5] feature Turing-complete programming facilities, called *smart contracts*. They provide robust trustworthy distributed computing facilities even though the programs run on a peer-to-peer network with untrusted participants. Each peer in the network runs the same program and uses cryptographic methods to check the results among the other peers and to create a persistent ledger of all transactions, the blockchain, thus ensuring the integrity of the results. Third generation blockchains, like Tezos [8], are adaptable to new requirements without breaking participating peers (no "soft forks" required and "hard forks" can be avoided).

The strength of programs on the blockchain is also their weakness. They are fully deterministic in that they can only depend on data that is ultimately stored on the chain including the parameters of a contract invocation. Moreover, the code, the data, as well as all transactions are public. These properties make it hard to react to external stimuli like time triggers or events like a price exceeding a threshold unless these stimuli get translated to contract invocations.

© Springer Nature Switzerland AG 2021
H. Oh (Ed.): APLAS 2021, LNCS 13008, pp. 222–240, 2021.
https://doi.org/10.1007/978-3-030-89051-3_13

Arguably, smart contracts are more useful if they can be integrated with traditional software systems and thus triggered from outside the blockchain. Oracles [6,13] provide an approach for contracts to obtain outside information. A contract registers a request and a callback with an oracle. The oracle invokes the callback as soon as an answer is available.

There are other usecases for connecting a contract with traditional software. One example is automating procedures like managing an auction, bidding in an auction, optimizing fees, or initiating delivery of goods to a customer. While some of these procedures are amenable to implementation as contracts, we might want to save the fee of running them on the blockchain. In particular, for actions that happen strictly within a single domain of trust, it is not worth running them on the blockchain. For example, automated bidding runs on behalf of a single peer.

Building such automation requires a programmatic interface to implement the interactions. Current blockchains mostly provide RPC interfaces, such as the Ethereum JSON-RPC API [7] and the Tezos RPC API [8], but they require cumbersome manipulation of string data in JSON format and do not provide static guarantees (except that the response to a well-formed JSON input is also a well-formed JSON output). To improve on this situation we present a typed API for invoking contracts from OCaml programs. Our typed API supports the implementation of application programs and oracles that safely interact with smart contracts on the blockchain. Moreover, our approach provides a type-safe facility to communicate with contracts where data is automatically marshalled between OCaml and the blockchain. This interface is a step towards a seamless integration of contracts into traditional programs.

Contributions

- A typed API for originating and invoking contracts as well as querying the state of the blockchain.
- An operational semantics for functional programs running alongside smart contracts in a blockchain.
- Established various properties of the combined system with proofs in upcoming techreport.
- An implementation of a low-level OCaml-API to the Tezos blockchain, which corresponds to the operational semantics[1].

There is an extended version of the paper with further proofs[2].

2 Motivation

Suppose you want to implement a bidding strategy for an auction that is deployed on the blockchain as a smart contract. Your bidding strategy may start at a certain amount and increase the bid until a limit is reached. Of course,

---

[1] Available at https://github.com/tezos-project/Tezos-Ocaml-API.
[2] Available at https://arxiv.org/abs/2108.11867.

```
parameter (or (unit %close)
               (unit %bid));  # bid in transfer
storage (pair bool           # bidding allowed
        (pair address        # contract owner
         address             # highest bidder's address
        ));
```

Listing 1.1. Header of the auction contract

```
# let auction = Cl.make_contract_hash auction_hash
#     ~parameter:(Ct.Or (Ct.Unit, Ct.Unit))
#     ~storage:(Ct.Pair (Ct.Bool, Ct.Pair (Ct.Addr, Ct.Addr))));;
val auction :
  ((unit, unit) Either.t,
   bool * (Cl.Addr.t * Cl.Addr.t)) Cl.contract
```

Listing 1.2. Getting the auction handle

you only want to increase your bid if someone else placed a higher bid. So you want to write a program to implement this strategy.

This task cannot be implemented as a smart contract without cooperation of the auction contract because it reacts on external triggers. Bidding requires watching the current highest bid of the contract and react if another bidder places a higher bid. The auction contract could anticipate the need for such observations by allowing bidders to register callbacks that are invoked when a higher bid arrives. However, we cannot assume such cooperation of the auction contract nor would we be willing to pay the fee for running that callback.

For concreteness, Listing 1.1 shows the header of an auction contract in Michelson [12]. The parameter clause specifies the contract's parameter type. It is a sum type (indicated by **or**) and each alternative constitutes an entrypoint, named %close and %bid . The caller selects the entrypoint by injecting the argument into the left or right summand. Both entrypoints take a unit parameter. The %bid entrypoint considers the transferred tokens as the bid. The storage clause declares the state of the contract, which is a nested pair type indicating whether bidding is allowed (bool), the address of the contract owner (to prohibit unauthorized calls to %close), and the bidder's address. The highest bid corresponds to the token balance of the contract.

We only outline the implementation of the entrypoints. The %close entrypoint first checks its sender's address against the owner's address in the store. Then it transfers the funds to the owner, closes the contract by clearing the bidding flag, and leaves it to the owner to deliver the goods[3]. The %bid entrypoint immediately returns each bid that is not higher than the existing highest bid. Otherwise, it keeps the funds transferred, returns the previous highest bid to its owner, and stores the current bidder as the new highest bidder.

We present a program that implements strategic bidding by interacting with the blockchain. The bidding strategy cannot be implemented as a smart contract.

---

[3] For simplicity we elide safeguarding by a third-party oracle.

```
let rec poll limit step =
  let (bidding, (_, highest_bidder)) = Cl.get_storage auction;
  let high_bid = Cl.get_balance auction;
  if bidding && high_bid < limit then
  (if highest_bidder <> my_address then     (* entrypoint %bid *)
    try
      Cl.call_contract auction
        (right (min (high_bid + step, limit)))
    with
    | Cl.FAILWITH message -> poll limit step;
  Time.sleep(5 * 60);
  poll limit step)
```

Listing 1.3. Bidding strategy

In Listing 1.2, we use the library function Cl.make_contract_from_hash to obtain a typed handle for the contract[4]. The function takes the hash of the contract along with representations of the types of the parameter and the storage (from module Ct). It checks the validity of the hash and the types with the blockchain and returns a typed handle, which is indexed with OCaml types corresponding to parameter and storage type.

The implementation of the bidding strategy in Listing 1.3 first checks the state of the contract to find the current highest bid. As long as bidding is allowed and the current bid is below our limit, we update our bid by a given amount step, and then keep watching the state of the contract by polling it every five minutes.

The functions get_storage and get_balance obtains the storage and current balance, respectively, of a contract from the blockchain. They never fail. Function call_contract takes a typed handle and a parameter of suitable type. It indicates failure by raising an exception. If failure is caused by the FAILWITH instruction in the contract, then the corresponding Cl.FAILWITH exception is raised, which carries a string corresponding to the argument of the instruction. In our particular example, the auction may fail with signaling the message "closed" or "bid too low". Our code ignores this message for simplicity.

This code is idealized in several respects. Originating or running a contract requires proposing a fee to the blockchain, which may or may not be accepted. Starting a contract may also time out for a variety of reasons. So just invoking a contract with a fixed fee does not guarantee the contract's execution. Even if the invocation is locally accepted, it still takes a couple of cycles before we can be sure the invocation is globally accepted and incorporated in the blockchain. Hence, after starting the invocation, we have to observe the fate of this invocation. If it does not get incorporated, then we need to analyze the reason and react accordingly. For example, if the invocation was rejected because of an insufficient fee, we might want to restart with an increased fee. Or we might decide to wait until the invocation goes through without increasing the fee.

---

[4] Cl is the module containing the contract library.

Hence, we would implement a scheme similar to the bidding strategy: start with a low fee and increase (or wait) until the contract is accepted or a fee cap is reached. On the other hand, an observer function like get_state always succeeds.

The low-level interface that we propose in this paper requires the programmer to be explicit about fees, waiting, and polling the state of contract invocations.

In summary, a useful smart-contract-API has facilities to

- query the current state of the blockchain (e.g., fees in the current block),
- query storage and balance of a contract (to obtain the current highest bid),
- originate contracts, invoke contracts, and initiate transfers. Hence, the API has to run on behalf of some account (by holding its private key).

These facilities are supported by the (untyped) RPC interface of the Tezos blockchain, which is the basis of our implementation.

3   Execution Model

The context of our work is the Tezos blockchain [2,8]. Tezos is a self-amending blockchain that improves several aspects compared to established blockchains. Tezos proposes an original consensus algorithm, Liquid Proof of Stake, that applies not only to the state of its ledger, like Bitcoin [14] or Ethereum [5], but also to upgrades of the protocol and the software.

Tezos supports two types of accounts: implicit accounts, which are associated with a pair of private/public keys, and smart contracts, which are programmable accounts created by an origination operation. The address of a smart contract is a unique public hash that depends on the creation operation. No key pair is associated with a smart contract. An implicit account is maintained on the blockchain with its public key and balance. A smart contract account is stored with its script, storage, and balance. A contract script maps a pair of a parameter and a storage, which have fixed and monomorphic types, to a pair of a list of internal operations and an updated storage. An account can perform three kinds of transactions: (1) transfer tokens to an implicit account, (2) invoke a smart contract, or (3) originate a new smart contract. A contract origination specifies the script of the contract and the initial contents of the contract storage, while a contract invocation must provide input data. Each transaction contains a fee to be paid either by payment to a baker or by destruction (burning). A transaction is injected into the blockchain network via a node, which then validates the transaction before submitting it to the network. A transaction may be rejected by the node for a number of reasons. After validation, the transaction is injected into a *mempool*, which contains all pending transactions before they can be included in a block. A pending transaction may simply disappear from the mempool, for example, a transaction times out when 60 blocks have passed and it can no longer be included in a block. When a transaction is included in the blockchain, the affected accounts are updated according to the transaction result.

The execution model consists of functional (OCaml) programs that interact with an abstraction of the Tezos blockchain [8]. As the blockchain is realized by a peer-to-peer network of independent nodes, interaction happens through *local nodes* that receive requests to originate and invoke contracts from programs that run on a particular node. We model the blockchain itself as a separate, abstract global entity that represents the current consensual state of the system. Our model does not express low-level details, but relies on nondeterminism to describe the possible behaviors of the system. In particular, we do **not** formalize the execution of the smart contracts themselves, we rather consider them as black boxes and probe their observable behavior. Tezos's smart contract language Michelson and its properties have been formalized elsewhere [4].

We write ∅ for the empty set and **e** :: **s** to decompose a set nondeterministically into an element **e** and a set **s**. We generally use lowercase boldface for metavariables ranging over values of a certain syntactic category, e.g., **puk** for public keys, and the capitalized name for the corresponding type as well as for the set of these values (as in Puk).

3.1 Local Node

A local node runs on behalf of authorities, which are called *accounts* in Tezos. An account is represented by a key pair ⟨**pak**, **puk**⟩, where **pak** is a private key and **puk** the corresponding public key in a public key encryption scheme.

The local node offers operations to transfer tokens from one account to another, to invoke a contract, and to originate a contract on the blockchain.

op ::= transfer **nt** from **puk** to **addr** arg **p** fee **fee**

    | originate contract transferring **nt** from **puk** running **code** init **s** fee **fee**

In the transfer, which also serves as contract invocation, **nt** is the amount of tokens transferred, **puk** is the public key of the sender, **addr** is either a public key for an implicit account (in case of a simple transfer) or a public hash for a smart contract (for an invocation), **p** is the argument passed to the smart contract, which is empty for a simple transfer, and **fee** is the amount of tokens for the transaction fee. In originate, **code** is the script of a smart contract and **s** is the initial value of the contract's storage. Each operation returns an *operation hash* **oph**, on which we can query the status of the operation.

The local node offers several ways to query the current state of the blockchain. Some *query operators* are defined by the following grammar:

qop ::= balance | status | storage | contract | ...

We obtain the balance associated with an implicit account or a contract by its public key or public hash, respectively; the status of a submitted operation by its operation hash; the stored value of a contract by its public hash; and the public hash of a contract by the operation hash of its originating transaction.

The domain-specific types come with different guarantees. Values of type Puh and Puk as well as Addr are not necessarily valid, as there might be no contract associated with a hash/no account associated with a public key. In contrast, a

$$\textbf{c} ::= \textbf{i} \mid \text{fix} \mid \textbf{oph} \mid \textbf{puh} \mid \textbf{puk} \mid \textbf{code} \mid \textbf{nt} \mid () \mid \text{False} \mid \text{True}$$

$$\textbf{st} ::= \text{pending} \mid \text{included}(\textbf{i}) \mid \text{timeout}$$

$$\textbf{err} ::= \text{xPrg} \mid \text{xBal} \mid \text{xCount} \mid \text{xFee} \mid \text{xPub} \mid \text{xPuh} \mid \text{xArg} \mid \text{xInit}$$

$$\textbf{e} ::= \textbf{c} \mid \textbf{st} \mid \textbf{err} \mid \textbf{x} \mid \lambda \textbf{x}.\textbf{e} \mid \textbf{ee} \mid \textbf{e} + \textbf{e} \mid \textbf{e} = \textbf{e} \mid \textbf{e} \text{ and } \textbf{e} \mid \textbf{e} \text{ or } \textbf{e} \mid \text{not } \textbf{e}$$
$$\mid (\textbf{e}, \textbf{e}) \mid \text{nil} \mid \text{cons } \textbf{e} \ \textbf{e} \mid \text{left } \textbf{e} \mid \text{right } \textbf{e} \mid \text{some } \textbf{e} \mid \text{none} \mid \text{match } \textbf{e} \text{ with } \textbf{pat} \rightarrow \textbf{e} \dots$$
$$\mid \text{raise } \textbf{e} \mid \text{try } \textbf{e} \text{ except } \textbf{e} \mid (\textbf{e} : T \Rightarrow U)$$
$$\mid \textbf{qop } \textbf{e} \mid \text{transfer } \textbf{e} \text{ from } \textbf{e} \text{ to } \textbf{e} \text{ arg } \textbf{e} \text{ fee } \textbf{e}$$
$$\mid \text{originate contract transferring } \textbf{e} \text{ from } \textbf{e} \text{ running } \textbf{e} \text{ init } \textbf{e} \text{ fee } \textbf{e}$$

$$\textbf{pat} ::= \textbf{x} \mid (\textbf{pat}, \textbf{pat}) \mid \text{nil} \mid \text{cons } \textbf{pat } \textbf{pat} \mid \text{left } \textbf{pat} \mid \text{right } \textbf{pat} \mid \text{some } \textbf{pat} \mid \text{none}$$
$$\mid \text{False} \mid \text{True} \mid \textbf{st} \mid \textbf{err}$$

$$T, U ::= \text{Puh} \mid \text{Puk} \mid \text{Addr} \mid \text{Cont } T \ U \mid \text{Code } T \ U \mid \text{Oph } T \ U \mid \text{Status} \mid \text{Exc} \mid \text{Tz}$$
$$\mid \top \mid \text{Int} \mid \text{Unit} \mid \text{Bool} \mid \text{Str} \mid T \rightarrow U \mid \text{Pair } T \ U \mid \text{List } T \mid \text{Or } T \ U \mid \text{Option } T$$

Fig. 1. Syntax of expressions, e, and types, T

value of type Cont T is a public hash that is verified to be associated with a contract with parameter type T. Operation hashes **oph** are only returned from blockchain operations. As the surface language neither contains literals of type Oph nor are there casts into that type, all values of Oph are valid.

Definition 1. *The* state of a node *is a pair* $N = [\bar{e}, A]$, *where* $\bar{e}$ *is a set of programs and* $A \subseteq Pak \times Puk$ *is a set of implicit accounts.*

Queries and operations are started by closed expressions of type unit that run on the local node. Each program can send transactions on behalf of any account on the local node. Figure 1 defines the syntax of lambda calculus with sum, product, list, and option types, exceptions and fixpoint. Pattern matching is the only means to decompose values, cf. **pat**. The execution model envisions off-chain programs interacting with smart contracts on the blockchain. The programs are defined using expression scripts. The off-chain scripts run on behalf of a single entity.

Domain-specific primitive types and constants **c** support blockchain interaction, as well as several exceptional values collected in **err**. There is syntax to initiate transfers and to originate contracts as well as for the queries. Finally, there is a type cast $(\textbf{e} : T \Rightarrow U)$, which we describe after discussing types. An implementation provides all of these types and operations via a library API.

Types (also in Fig. 1) comprise some base types as well as functions, pairs, lists, sums, and option types. These types are chosen to match with built-in types of Michelson. There are domain specific types of public hashes Puh and public keys Puk subsumed by a type of addresses Addr. Cont $T \ U$ is the type of a contract with parameter type T and storage type U. Code $T \ U$ indicates a Michelson program with parameter type T and storage type U. Tezos tokens have type Tz. The type Oph $T \ U$ signifies operation hashes returned by blockchain operations.

$$\mathbf{E} ::= [\,] \mid \mathbf{sc}[\overline{\mathbf{v}}\ \mathbf{E}\ \overline{\mathbf{e}}] \mid \text{raise } \mathbf{E} \mid \text{try } \mathbf{E} \text{ except e} \mid \text{match } \mathbf{E} \text{ with } \mathbf{pat} \to \mathbf{e} \dots$$
$$\mathbf{v} ::= \mathbf{c} \mid \mathbf{st} \mid \mathbf{err} \mid \lambda x.e \mid (\mathbf{v}, \mathbf{v}) \mid \text{nil} \mid \text{cons } \mathbf{v}\ \mathbf{v} \mid \text{left } \mathbf{v} \mid \text{right } \mathbf{v} \mid \text{some } \mathbf{v} \mid \text{none}$$

Fig. 2. Evaluation contexts and values

The parameters of the hash carry the types when originating a contract. Otherwise, they are set to the irrelevant type ⊤. We take the liberty of omitting irrelevant type parameters, that is, we write Oph for Oph ⊤ ⊤. Querying the status of an operation returns a value of type Status. Exceptions have type Exc.

Figure 2 defines evaluation contexts **EC** and values **v**. Here **sc** ranges over the remaining syntactic constructors, which are treated uniformly: evaluation proceeds from left to right. Values are standard for call-by-value lambda calculus.

Type casts are only applicable to certain pairs of types governed by a relation $<:$, which could also serve as a subtyping relation. It is given by the axioms Puh $<:$ Addr, Puk $<:$ Addr, and Cont $T\ U <:$ Puh. A cast from T to U is only allowed if $T <: U$ (upcast) or $U <: T$ (downcast). Upcasts always succeed, but downcasts may fail at run time. In particular, public hashes and public keys can both stand for addresses. Moreover, a smart contract with parameter type T is represented by its public hash at run time. The corresponding downcast must check whether the public hash is valid and has the expected parameter and storage type.

Figure 3 presents selected typing rules for expressions. We rely on an external typing judgment $\vdash_C$ **code** $: T$ for the contract language, which we leave unspecified, and $\vdash_V$ **s** $: T$ for serialized values as stored on the blockchain. The latter judgment states **s** is a string parseable as a value of type T.

3.2 Global Structures

Our execution model abstracts from the particulars of the blockchain implementation, like the peer-to-peer structure or the distributed consensus protocol. Hence, we represent the blockchain by a few global entities: managers, contractors, and a pool of operations.

A *manager* keeps track of a single implicit account. Managers are represented by a partial map $\mathbf{M} : \text{Puk} \hookrightarrow \text{Bal} \times \text{Cnt}$. If $\mathbf{M}(\mathbf{puk}) = \langle \mathbf{bal}, \mathbf{cnt} \rangle$ is defined, then **puk** is the public key of an account, **bal** is its balance and **cnt** is its counter whose form is a value-flag pair $(n, b) \in \mathbf{N} \times \text{Bool}$, where n is the value of the counter and b is its flag. The counter is used internally to serialize transactions.

A *contractor* manages a single smart contract. Contractors are represented by a partial map $\mathbf{C} : \text{Puh} \hookrightarrow \text{Code} \times \mathbf{t} \times \text{Bal} \times \text{Storage}$. If $\mathbf{C}(\mathbf{puh}) = \langle \mathbf{code}, \mathbf{t}, \mathbf{bal}, \mathbf{storage} \rangle$ is defined, then **puh** is the public hash of a contract, **code** is its code, **t** is the time when it was accepted, **bal** is its current balance, and **storage** is its current storage. The hash **puh** is self-verifying as it is calculated from the fixed components **code** and **t**. All time stamps will be different in our model.

$$\Gamma \vdash \mathbf{i} : \mathrm{Int} \qquad \Gamma \vdash \mathbf{oph} : \mathrm{Oph}\; T\; U \qquad \Gamma \vdash \mathbf{puh} : \mathrm{Puh} \qquad \Gamma \vdash \mathbf{puk} : \mathrm{Puk}$$

$$\frac{\vdash_C \mathbf{code} : \mathrm{Pair}\; T_p\; T_s}{\Gamma \vdash \mathbf{code} : \mathrm{Code}\; T_p\; T_s} \qquad \Gamma \vdash \mathbf{nt} : \mathrm{Tz} \qquad \Gamma \vdash () : \mathrm{Unit} \qquad \Gamma \vdash \mathrm{False} : \mathrm{Bool}$$

$$\Gamma \vdash \mathrm{True} : \mathrm{Bool} \qquad \Gamma \vdash \mathrm{pending} : \mathrm{Status} \qquad \Gamma \vdash \mathrm{timeout} : \mathrm{Status}$$

$$\frac{\Gamma \vdash \mathbf{e} : \mathrm{Int}}{\Gamma \vdash \mathrm{included}(\mathbf{e}) : \mathrm{Status}} \qquad \Gamma \vdash \mathbf{err} : \mathrm{Exc} \qquad \Gamma \vdash \mathbf{x} : \Gamma(\mathbf{x}) \qquad \frac{\Gamma, \mathbf{x} : T' \vdash \mathbf{e} : T}{\Gamma \vdash \lambda \mathbf{x}.\mathbf{e} : T' \to T}$$

$$\frac{\Gamma \vdash \mathbf{e} : T' \to T \quad \Gamma \vdash \mathbf{e}' : T'}{\Gamma \vdash \mathbf{e}\,\mathbf{e}' : T} \qquad \frac{\Gamma \vdash \mathbf{e} : T \quad \Gamma \vdash \mathbf{e}' : T'}{\Gamma \vdash (\mathbf{e}, \mathbf{e}') : \mathrm{Pair}\; T\; T'} \qquad \frac{\Gamma \vdash \mathbf{e} : \mathrm{Exc}}{\Gamma \vdash \mathrm{raise}\; \mathbf{e} : T}$$

$$\frac{\Gamma \vdash \mathbf{e} : T \quad \Gamma \vdash \mathbf{e}' : \mathrm{Exc} \to T}{\Gamma \vdash \mathrm{try}\; \mathbf{e}\; \mathrm{except}\; \mathbf{e}' : T} \qquad \frac{\Gamma \vdash \mathbf{e} : T \quad T <: U \vee U <: T}{\Gamma \vdash (\mathbf{e} : T \Rightarrow U) : U}$$

Fig. 3. Typing rules for expressions (excerpt)

$$\frac{\Gamma \vdash \mathbf{e}_1 : \mathrm{Tz} \quad \Gamma \vdash \mathbf{e}_2 : \mathrm{Puk} \quad \Gamma \vdash \mathbf{e}_3 : \mathrm{Puk} \quad \Gamma \vdash \mathbf{e}_4 : \mathrm{Unit} \quad \Gamma \vdash \mathbf{e}_5 : \mathrm{Tz}}{\Gamma \vdash \mathrm{transfer}\; \mathbf{e}_1\; \mathrm{from}\; \mathbf{e}_2\; \mathrm{to}\; \mathbf{e}_3\; \mathrm{arg}\; \mathbf{e}_4\; \mathrm{fee}\; \mathbf{e}_5 : \mathrm{Oph}\; \top\; \top}$$

$$\frac{\Gamma \vdash \mathbf{e}_1 : \mathrm{Tz} \quad \Gamma \vdash \mathbf{e}_2 : \mathrm{Puk} \quad \Gamma \vdash \mathbf{e}_3 : \mathrm{Cont}\; T_p\; T_s \quad \Gamma \vdash \mathbf{e}_4 : T_p \quad \Gamma \vdash \mathbf{e}_5 : \mathrm{Tz}}{\Gamma \vdash \mathrm{transfer}\; \mathbf{e}_1\; \mathrm{from}\; \mathbf{e}_2\; \mathrm{to}\; \mathbf{e}_3\; \mathrm{arg}\; \mathbf{e}_4\; \mathrm{fee}\; \mathbf{e}_5 : \mathrm{Oph}\; \top\; \top}$$

$$\frac{\Gamma \vdash \mathbf{e}_1 : \mathrm{Tz} \quad \Gamma \vdash \mathbf{e}_2 : \mathrm{Puk} \quad \Gamma \vdash \mathbf{e}_3 : \mathrm{Code}\; T_p\; T_s \quad \Gamma \vdash \mathbf{e}_4 : T_s \quad \Gamma \vdash \mathbf{e}_5 : \mathrm{Tz}}{\Gamma \vdash \mathrm{originate}\; \mathrm{contract}\; \mathrm{transferring}\; \mathbf{e}_1\; \mathrm{from}\; \mathbf{e}_2\; \mathrm{running}\; \mathbf{e}_3\; \mathrm{init}\; \mathbf{e}_4\; \mathrm{fee}\; \mathbf{e}_5 : \mathrm{Oph}\; T_p\; T_s}$$

$$\frac{\Gamma \vdash \mathbf{e} : \mathrm{Addr}}{\Gamma \vdash \mathrm{balance}\; \mathbf{e} : \mathrm{Tz}} \qquad \frac{\Gamma \vdash \mathbf{e} : \mathrm{Oph}\; T\; U}{\Gamma \vdash \mathrm{status}\; \mathbf{e} : \mathrm{Status}} \qquad \frac{\Gamma \vdash \mathbf{e} : \mathrm{Cont}\; T_p\; T_s}{\Gamma \vdash \mathrm{storage}\; \mathbf{e} : T_s}$$

$$\frac{\Gamma \vdash \mathbf{e} : \mathrm{Oph}\; T\; U \quad T \neq \top \quad U \neq \top}{\Gamma \vdash \mathrm{contract}\; \mathbf{e} : \mathrm{Cont}\; T\; U}$$

Fig. 4. Typing rules for blockchain operations and queries

When an operation is started on a node, it enters a *pool* as a pending operation. A pending operation is either dismissed after some time or promoted to an included operation, which has become a permanent part of the blockchain. The pool is a partial map $\mathbf{P} = \mathrm{Oph} \hookrightarrow \mathrm{Op} \times \mathrm{Time} \times \mathrm{Status}$ where

$$\mathrm{Status} = \mathrm{pending} + \mathrm{included}\; \mathrm{Time} + \mathrm{timeout}$$

such that if $\mathbf{P}(\mathbf{oph}) = \langle \mathbf{op}, \mathbf{t}, \mathbf{st} \rangle$ is defined, then $\mathbf{oph}$ is the public hash of the operation, $\mathbf{op}$ is the operation, $\mathbf{t}$ is the time when the operation was injected, and $\mathbf{st}$ is either pending, included $\mathbf{t}'$, or timeout. A pool $\mathbf{P}$ is *well-formed* if, for all $\mathbf{oph}, \mathbf{P}(\mathbf{oph}) = \langle \mathbf{op}, \mathbf{t}, \mathrm{included}\; \mathbf{t}' \rangle$ implies $\mathbf{t}' \geq \mathbf{t}$ and $\mathbf{oph} = \mathrm{genOpHash}(\mathbf{op}, \mathbf{t})$.

A *pending operation* is represented by $\mathbf{oph} \mapsto \langle \mathbf{op}, \mathbf{t}, \text{pending} \rangle$. Once the operation is accepted, it changes its status to included: $\mathbf{oph} \mapsto \langle \mathbf{op}, \mathbf{t}, \text{included } \mathbf{t}' \rangle$, where $\mathbf{t}' \geq \mathbf{t}$ is when the operation was included in the blockchain. The operation may also be dropped at any time, which is represented by $\mathbf{oph} \mapsto \langle \mathbf{op}, \mathbf{t}, \text{timeout} \rangle$. There are several causes for dropping, primarily timeout or overflow of the pending pool which is limited in size in the implementation.

In summary, the *state of a blockchain* is a tuple $\mathbf{B} = [\mathbf{P}, \mathbf{M}, \mathbf{C}, \mathbf{t}]$ where $\mathbf{P}$ is a pool of operations, $\mathbf{M}$ is a map of managers, $\mathbf{C}$ is a map of contractors, and $\mathbf{t}$ is the current time.

We often use the dot notation to project a component from a tuple. For instance, we write $\mathbf{B}.\mathbf{M}$ to access the managers component.

A *blockchain configuration* has the form $\mathbf{B}[\mathbf{N}_1, \ldots, \mathbf{N}_n]$, for some $n > 0$, where $\mathbf{B}$ is a blockchain and the $\mathbf{N}_i$ are local nodes, for $1 \leq i \leq n$. In a *well-formed configuration*, the accounts on the local nodes are all different and each local account has a manager in $\mathbf{B}$:

1. for all $1 \leq i < j \leq n$, $\mathbf{N}_i.\mathbf{A} \cap \mathbf{N}_j.\mathbf{A} = \emptyset$;
2. for all $1 \leq i \leq n$, $\forall a \in \mathbf{N}_i.\mathbf{A} \implies a.\mathbf{puk} \in dom(\mathbf{B}.\mathbf{M})$.

4   Operational Semantics

The operational semantics is defined by several kinds of transitions:

1. $\longrightarrow_E$ single-step evaluation of an expression in a local node,
2. $\longrightarrow_N$ internal transitions of a node,
3. $\longrightarrow_B$ transitions of the blockchain state,
4. $\longrightarrow$ blockchain system transitions.

Evaluation of expressions is standard for call-by-value lambda calculus defined using evaluation contexts $\underline{\mathbf{E}}[]$. Figure 5 shows some of the reduction rules. The internal transitions of a node are just evaluation of expressions.

$$\text{NODE-EVAL}$$
$$\frac{\mathbf{e} \longrightarrow_E \mathbf{e}'}{[\underline{\mathbf{E}}[\mathbf{e}] :: \overline{\mathbf{e}}, \mathbf{A}] \longrightarrow_N [\underline{\mathbf{E}}[\mathbf{e}'] :: \overline{\mathbf{e}}, \mathbf{A}]}$$

$$\underline{\mathbf{E}}[(\lambda x.\mathbf{e})\mathbf{v}] \longrightarrow_E \underline{\mathbf{E}}[\mathbf{e}[\mathbf{v}/x]] \qquad \underline{\mathbf{E}}[\text{try } \mathbf{v} \text{ except } \mathbf{e}] \longrightarrow_E \underline{\mathbf{E}}[\mathbf{v}]$$

$$\frac{T <: U}{\underline{\mathbf{E}}[(\mathbf{v} : T \Rightarrow U)] \longrightarrow_E \underline{\mathbf{E}}[\mathbf{v}]} \qquad \frac{\text{try} \notin \underline{\mathbf{F}}[]}{\underline{\mathbf{E}}[\text{try } \underline{\mathbf{F}}[\text{raise } \mathbf{v}] \text{ except } \mathbf{e}] \longrightarrow_E \underline{\mathbf{E}}[\mathbf{e} \; \mathbf{v}]}$$

Fig. 5. Select expression reduction rules (pattern matching omitted)

Node-Inject

$$\frac{\begin{array}{ccc} \langle \mathbf{pak}, \mathbf{puk} \rangle \in \mathbf{A} & \text{chkBal}(\mathbf{M}, \mathbf{puk}, \mathbf{nt}, \mathbf{fee}) & \text{chkArg}(\mathbf{C}, \mathbf{puh}, \mathbf{p}) \\ \text{chkCount}(\mathbf{M}, \mathbf{puk}) & \text{chkPuh}(\mathbf{C}, \mathbf{puh}) & \text{chkFee}(\mathbf{C}, \mathbf{puh}, \mathbf{p}, \mathbf{fee}) \\ \mathbf{oph} = \text{genOpHash}(\mathbf{op}, \mathbf{t}) & \mathbf{op} = \text{transfer } \mathbf{nt} \text{ from } \mathbf{puk} \text{ to } \mathbf{puh} \text{ arg } \mathbf{p} \text{ fee } \mathbf{fee} \end{array}}{[\underline{\mathbf{E}}[\mathbf{op}] :: \overline{\mathbf{e}}, \mathbf{A}] \| [\mathbf{P}, \mathbf{M}, \mathbf{C}, \mathbf{t}] \longrightarrow [\underline{\mathbf{E}}[\mathbf{oph}] :: \overline{\mathbf{e}}, \mathbf{A}] \| [\mathbf{oph} \mapsto \langle \mathbf{op}, \mathbf{t}, \text{pending} \rangle :: \mathbf{P}, \\ \text{updCount}(\mathbf{M}, \mathbf{puk}, \text{True}), \mathbf{C}, \mathbf{t}]}$$

Node-Reject

$$\frac{\neg \text{ chkBal}(\mathbf{B}.\mathbf{M}, \mathbf{op}.\mathbf{puk}, \mathbf{op}.\mathbf{nt}, \mathbf{op}.\mathbf{fee})}{[\underline{\mathbf{E}}[\mathbf{op}] :: \overline{\mathbf{e}}, \mathbf{A}] \| \mathbf{B} \longrightarrow [\underline{\mathbf{E}}[\text{raise xBal}] :: \overline{\mathbf{e}}, \mathbf{A}] \| \mathbf{B}}$$

Block-Accept

$$\frac{\mathbf{op} = \text{transfer } \mathbf{nt} \text{ from } \mathbf{puk} \text{ to } \mathbf{puh} \text{ arg } \mathbf{p} \text{ fee } \mathbf{fee} \qquad \mathbf{t} - \hat{\mathbf{t}} \leq 60}{[\mathbf{oph} \mapsto \langle \mathbf{op}, \hat{\mathbf{t}}, \text{pending} \rangle :: \mathbf{P}, \mathbf{M}, \mathbf{C}, \mathbf{t}] \longrightarrow_B [\mathbf{oph} \to \langle \mathbf{op}, \hat{\mathbf{t}}, \text{included } \mathbf{t} \rangle :: \mathbf{P}, \\ \text{updSucc}(\mathbf{M}, \mathbf{puk}, \mathbf{nt}, \mathbf{fee}), \text{updConstr}(\mathbf{C}, \mathbf{puh}, \mathbf{nt}, \mathbf{p}), \mathbf{t} + 1]}$$

Block-Timeout

$$\frac{\mathbf{t} - \hat{\mathbf{t}} > 60}{[\mathbf{oph} \mapsto \langle \mathbf{op}, \hat{\mathbf{t}}, \text{pending} \rangle :: \mathbf{P}, \mathbf{M}, \mathbf{C}, \mathbf{t}] \longrightarrow_B [\mathbf{oph} \mapsto \langle \mathbf{op}, \hat{\mathbf{t}}, \text{timeout} \rangle :: \mathbf{P}, \\ \text{updCount}(\mathbf{M}, \mathbf{op}.\mathbf{puk}, \text{False}), \mathbf{C}, \mathbf{t}]}$$

Fig. 6. Lifecycle transitions of a transaction

The remaining transitions affect a local node in the context of the blockchain. To this end, any local node may be selected.

Config-System
$$\frac{\mathbf{N} \| \mathbf{B} \longrightarrow \mathbf{N}' \| \mathbf{B}'}{\mathbf{B}[\mathbf{N} :: \overline{\mathbf{N}}] \longrightarrow \mathbf{B}'[\mathbf{N}' :: \overline{\mathbf{N}}]}$$

Config-Node
$$\frac{\mathbf{N} \longrightarrow_N \mathbf{N}'}{\mathbf{B}[\mathbf{N} :: \overline{\mathbf{N}}] \longrightarrow \mathbf{B}[\mathbf{N}' :: \overline{\mathbf{N}}]}$$

Config-Block
$$\frac{\mathbf{B} \longrightarrow_B \mathbf{B}'}{\mathbf{B}[\overline{\mathbf{N}}] \longrightarrow \mathbf{B}'[\overline{\mathbf{N}}]}$$

Figure 6 shows the transitions to start and finalize a contract invocation. Node-Inject affects a local node and the blockchain. It nondeterminstically selects a program that wants to do a transfer operation. It checks whether the sender of the transfer is a valid local account, whether the balance is sufficient to pay the fee and the transferred amount, whether there is an active transition for this sender (chkCount), whether the public hash is associated with a smart contract on the blockchain, whether the type of the input parameter matchs with the smart contract's parameter type (chkArg), and whether the fee is sufficient. If these conditions are fulfilled, the transition forges an operation hash

CONTRACT-YES

$$\frac{\vdash_C \mathbf{code} : \text{Pair } T \ U \qquad \mathbf{B.C(puh)} = \langle \mathbf{code}, \tilde{\mathbf{t}}, \mathbf{nt'}, \mathbf{s'} \rangle}{[\mathbf{E}[(\mathbf{puh} : \text{Puh} \Rightarrow \text{Cont } T)] :: \bar{\mathbf{e}}, \mathbf{A}] \| \mathbf{B} \longrightarrow [\mathbf{E}[\mathbf{puh}] :: \bar{\mathbf{e}}, \mathbf{A}] \| \mathbf{B}}$$

CONTRACT-NO

$$\frac{\mathbf{B.C(puh)} = \langle \mathbf{code}, \tilde{\mathbf{t}}, \mathbf{nt'}, \mathbf{s'} \rangle \Rightarrow \vdash_C \mathbf{code} : \text{Pair } T' \ U \wedge T \neq T'}{[\mathbf{E}[(\mathbf{puh} : \text{Puh} \Rightarrow \text{Cont } T)] :: \bar{\mathbf{e}}, \mathbf{A}] \| \mathbf{B} \longrightarrow [\mathbf{E}[\text{raise xPrg}] :: \bar{\mathbf{e}}, \mathbf{A}] \| \mathbf{B}}$$

Fig. 7. Cast reductions (excerpt)

and returns it to the local node. The pending operation enters the pool and the sender's counter is set to indicate an ongoing transition.

We give just one example NODE-REJECT of the numerous transitions that cover the cases where one of the premises of NODE-INJECT is not fulfilled. Each of them raises an exception that describes which condition was violated.

Acceptance or rejection of a pending operation happens on the blockchain independent of any local node. In our model, these transitions are nondeterministic so that acceptance can happen any time in the next 60 cycles BLOCK-ACCEPT. Afterwards, a pending operation can only time out BLOCK-TIMEOUT. If the transaction is accepted, then the sender's counter is reset, the balances of sender is adjusted (updSucc), the smart contract's storage and balance are updated (updConstr), and the time stamp increases.

Whereas NODE-INJECT and BLOCK-ACCEPT are particular to the transfer operation, the timeout transition applies to all operations. It just changes the state of the operation and resets the sender's counter, thus rolling back the transaction.

4.1 Cast Reductions

Figure 7 contains the most interesting example of cast reductions, from a public hash to a typed contract. These reductions force the local node to obtain information from the blockchain. The cast succeeds on **puh** ('CONTRACT-YES'), if there is a contractor for **puh** such that the stored code has the parameter type expected by the cast. The cast fails ('CONTRACT-NO'), if **puh** is invalid or if the types do not match.

4.2 Smart Contracts

The invocation of smart contracts is similar to a transfer, so we elide the details. Figure 8 contains the transition BLOCK-ORIGINATE to originate a smart contract. The basic scheme is similar to the transfer. The preconditions for the operation are checked, but there are extra preconditions for origination: the program must be well-formed and typed, the initial storage value must match its type. The operation ends up in the pool in pending status.

BLOCK-ORIGINATE

$$\langle \mathbf{pak}, \mathbf{puk} \rangle \in \mathbf{A}$$

$$\text{chkBal}(\mathbf{M}, \mathbf{puk}, \mathbf{nt}, \mathbf{fee}) \qquad \text{chkCount}(\mathbf{M}, \mathbf{puk}) \qquad \text{chkPrg}(\mathbf{code})$$

$$\text{chkFee}(\mathbf{code}, \mathbf{s}, \mathbf{nt}, \mathbf{fee}) \qquad \text{chkInit}(\mathbf{code}, \mathbf{s}) \qquad \mathbf{oph} = \text{genOpHash}(\mathbf{op}, \mathbf{t})$$

$$\mathbf{op} = \text{originate contract transferring } \mathbf{nt} \text{ from } \mathbf{puk} \text{ running } \mathbf{code} \text{ init } \mathbf{s} \text{ fee } \mathbf{fee}$$

$$[\underline{\mathbf{E}}[\mathbf{op}] :: \overline{\mathbf{e}}, \mathbf{A}] \| [\mathbf{P}, \mathbf{M}, \mathbf{C}, \mathbf{t}] \longrightarrow [\underline{\mathbf{E}}[\mathbf{oph}] :: \overline{\mathbf{e}}, \mathbf{A}] \| [\mathbf{oph} \mapsto \langle \mathbf{op}, \mathbf{t}, \text{pending} \rangle :: \mathbf{P},$$
$$\text{updCount}(\mathbf{M}, \mathbf{puk}, \text{True}), \mathbf{C}, \mathbf{t}]$$

BLOCK-ORIGINATE-ACCEPT

$$\mathbf{op} = \text{originate contract transferring } \mathbf{nt} \text{ from } \mathbf{puk} \text{ running } \mathbf{code} \text{ init } \mathbf{s} \text{ fee } \mathbf{fee}$$

$$\mathbf{puh} = \text{genHash}(\mathbf{code}, \mathbf{t}) \qquad \mathbf{t} - \hat{\mathbf{t}} \leq 60$$

$$[\mathbf{oph} \mapsto \langle \mathbf{op}, \hat{\mathbf{t}}, \text{pending} \rangle :: \mathbf{P}, \mathbf{M}, \mathbf{C}, \mathbf{t}] \longrightarrow_B [\mathbf{oph} \mapsto \langle \mathbf{op}, \hat{\mathbf{t}}, \text{included } \mathbf{t} \rangle :: \mathbf{P},$$
$$\text{updSucc}(\mathbf{M}, \mathbf{puk}, \mathbf{nt}, \mathbf{fee}), \mathbf{puh} \mapsto \langle \mathbf{code}, \mathbf{t}, \mathbf{nt}, \mathbf{s} \rangle :: \mathbf{C}, \mathbf{t} + 1]$$

BLOCK-ACCEPT-QUERY

$$\mathbf{op} = \text{originate contract transferring } \mathbf{nt} \text{ from } \mathbf{puk} \text{ running } \mathbf{code} \text{ init } \mathbf{s} \text{ fee } \mathbf{fee}$$

$$\mathbf{P}(\mathbf{oph}) = \langle \mathbf{op}, \hat{\mathbf{t}}, \text{included } \tilde{\mathbf{t}} \rangle \qquad \mathbf{puh} = \text{genHash}(\mathbf{code}, \tilde{\mathbf{t}})$$

$$[\underline{\mathbf{E}}[\text{contract } \mathbf{oph}] :: \overline{\mathbf{e}}, \mathbf{A}] \| [\mathbf{P}, \mathbf{M}, \mathbf{C}, \mathbf{t}] \longrightarrow [\underline{\mathbf{E}}[\mathbf{puh}] :: \overline{\mathbf{e}}, \mathbf{A}] \| [\mathbf{P}, \mathbf{M}, \mathbf{C}, \mathbf{t}]$$

Fig. 8. Smart contract origination

QUERY-BALANCE-IMPLICIT

$$\mathbf{B}.\mathbf{M}(\mathbf{puk}) = \langle \mathbf{bal}, \mathbf{cnt} \rangle$$

$$[\underline{\mathbf{E}}[\text{balance } \mathbf{puk}] :: \overline{\mathbf{e}}, \mathbf{A}] \| \mathbf{B} \longrightarrow [\underline{\mathbf{E}}[\mathbf{bal}] :: \overline{\mathbf{e}}, \mathbf{A}] \| \mathbf{B}$$

QUERY-BALANCE-FAIL

$$\mathbf{puk} \notin dom(\mathbf{B}.\mathbf{M})$$

$$[\underline{\mathbf{E}}[\text{balance } \mathbf{puk}] :: \overline{\mathbf{e}}, \mathbf{A}] \| \mathbf{B} \longrightarrow [\underline{\mathbf{E}}[\text{raise xPub}] :: \overline{\mathbf{e}}, \mathbf{A}] \| \mathbf{B}$$

Fig. 9. Example queries

Acceptance of origination is slightly different as for transfers as shown in BLOCK-ACCEPT. We calculate the public hash **puh** of the contract from the code and the current time stamp and create a new contractor at that address.

We obtain the handle of the contract through a query, once the contract is accepted on the blockchain in BLOCK-ACCEPT-QUERY. The query's argument is the operation hash, which is used to obtain the code and the time stamp of its acceptance. From this information, we can re-calculate the public hash.

4.3 Queries

We conclude with two example transitions for a simple query in Fig. 9. To obtain the balance of an implicit account **puk**, we obtain the account info from the manager and extract the balance (QUERY-BALANCE-IMPLICIT). If the account is unknown, then we raise an exception (QUERY-BALANCE-FAIL). Other queries are implemented analogously.

5   Properties

Having defined our execution model, we proceed to prove properties of the combined systems that ensure type-safe interaction between programs and the blockchain.

5.1   Properties of Blockchain State Transitions

One interesting property we wish to prove is that the execution of a program that starts with valid references to accounts, operations, and contracts is not corrupted by a transition.

Proposition 1. *The following properties are preserved by a step on a well-formed configuration* $[\bar{e}, A] \| B$:

- *for all* $\boldsymbol{oph}$ *in* $\bar{e}$, $\boldsymbol{oph} \in dom(\boldsymbol{B.P})$,
- *for all* $\boldsymbol{puk}$ *in* $\bar{e}$, $\boldsymbol{puk} \in dom(\boldsymbol{B.M})$,
- *for all* $\boldsymbol{puh}$ *in* $\bar{e}$, $\boldsymbol{puh} \in dom(\boldsymbol{B.C})$.

Proposition 2. *If* $[P, M, C, t] \longrightarrow_B [P', M', C', t']$, *then*

1. $t \leq t'$
2. $dom(\boldsymbol{P}) \subseteq dom(\boldsymbol{P'})$
3. *invariant for the pool: if* $\boldsymbol{P(oph)} = \langle \boldsymbol{op}, \hat{\boldsymbol{t}}, \boldsymbol{st} \rangle$, *then* $\boldsymbol{oph} = \mathrm{genOpHash}(\boldsymbol{op}, \hat{\boldsymbol{t}})$.
4. *for all* $\boldsymbol{oph} \in dom(P)$, *if* $\boldsymbol{P(oph)} = \langle \boldsymbol{op}, \hat{\boldsymbol{t}}, \boldsymbol{st} \rangle$, *then either*
    - $\boldsymbol{P'(oph)} = \boldsymbol{P(oph)}$; *or*
    - $\boldsymbol{st} = pending$ *and* $\boldsymbol{P'(oph)} = \langle \boldsymbol{op}, \hat{\boldsymbol{t}}, timeout \rangle$; *or*
    - $\boldsymbol{st} = pending$, $\boldsymbol{t} - \hat{\boldsymbol{t}} \leq 60$, $\boldsymbol{P'(oph)} = \langle \boldsymbol{op}, \hat{\boldsymbol{t}}, included\ \boldsymbol{t} \rangle$, *and* $\boldsymbol{t'} = \boldsymbol{t} + 1$.
5. *for all* $\boldsymbol{oph} \in dom(P)$ *and* $\boldsymbol{P(oph)} = \langle \boldsymbol{op}, \hat{\boldsymbol{t}}, \boldsymbol{st} \rangle$,
    - *if* $\boldsymbol{st} = pending$ *and* $\boldsymbol{M(op.puk)} = \langle \boldsymbol{bal}, \boldsymbol{cnt} \rangle$ *then* $\boldsymbol{cnt.b} = True$ *and* $\boldsymbol{bal} \geq \boldsymbol{op.nt} + \boldsymbol{op.fee}$;
    - *if* $\boldsymbol{st} = included\ \hat{\boldsymbol{t}}$, *then* $\hat{\boldsymbol{t}} < \boldsymbol{t'}$.
6. $dom(\boldsymbol{M}) \subseteq dom(\boldsymbol{M'})$
7. *for all* $\boldsymbol{puk} \in dom(\boldsymbol{M})$
    if $\boldsymbol{M(puk)} = \langle \boldsymbol{bal}, \boldsymbol{cnt} \rangle$, *then* $\boldsymbol{M'(puk)} = \langle \boldsymbol{bal'}, \boldsymbol{cnt'} \rangle$ *and*
    - *if* $\boldsymbol{cnt.b} = True$ *and* $\boldsymbol{cnt'.b} = False$, *then* $\boldsymbol{cnt.n'} \in \{\boldsymbol{cnt.n}, \boldsymbol{cnt.n} + 1\}$,
    - *otherwise* $\boldsymbol{cnt.n} = \boldsymbol{cnt'.n}$
    - *If* $\boldsymbol{cnt.n} = \boldsymbol{cnt'.n}$, *then* $\boldsymbol{bal} = \boldsymbol{bal'}$.
8. $dom(\boldsymbol{C}) \subseteq dom(\boldsymbol{C'})$
    - *for all* $\boldsymbol{puh} \in dom(\boldsymbol{C})$, $\boldsymbol{C(puh)}.code = \boldsymbol{C'(puh)}.code$
9. *invariant for contractors: for all* $\boldsymbol{puh} \in dom(\boldsymbol{C})$,
    $\boldsymbol{C(puh)} = \langle \boldsymbol{code}, \tilde{\boldsymbol{t}}, \boldsymbol{bal}, \boldsymbol{storage} \rangle$ *implies that* $\boldsymbol{puh} = \mathrm{genHash}(\boldsymbol{code}, \tilde{\boldsymbol{t}})$.

Establishing items 4 and 7 relies on the preimage resistance of the various hash functions used to calculate operation hashes and public hashes: we always feed a fresh timestamp into the hash functions for operations and code. Items 2–5 describe an invariant and the lifecycle of operations. Items 6 and 7 describe the lifecycle of a transfer and items 8 and 9 describe invariants for contractors. The invariants establish the self-verifying property common of blockchain entities.

The proofs of these properties refer to all transitions with the detailed specifications of the related functions, such as chkCount and updSucc. Due to page limitations, not all transitions and their associated functions are presented in this paper, so the full proofs will be provided in an upcoming technical report. In this paper, we only provide the proofs for Proposition 2 at items 4 and 7.

Proof (4). After feeding into a node, the status of the operation is pending according to the transition NODE-INJECT. This operation could either be accepted by the blockchain on the condition that the elapsed time is less than 60 ($t - \hat{t} \leq 60$), and then its status is included t (the transition BLOCK-ACCEPT) or it is timed out with the timeout status (BLOCK-TIMEOUT). When an operation is accepted or timed out, its status is never changed. Therefore, if $\mathbf{P(oph)} = \langle \mathbf{op}, \hat{t}, \mathbf{st} \rangle$, then there are three cases:

(1) if the operation's status remains the same as $\mathbf{st}$ (still in pending, included or timeout), then we have $\mathbf{P'(oph)} = \langle \mathbf{op}, \hat{t}, \mathbf{st} \rangle$. This means $\mathbf{P'(oph)} = \mathbf{P(oph)}$;
(2) if the operation's status is pending ($\mathbf{st}$ = pending), and then the operation is timed out, then we have $\mathbf{P'(oph)} = \langle \mathbf{op}, \hat{t}, \text{timeout} \rangle$ according to the transition BLOCK-TIMEOUT;
(3) if the operation's status is pending, the time condition is satisfied, and then the operation is accepted, then we have $\mathbf{P'(oph)} = \langle \mathbf{op}, \hat{t}, \text{included } t \rangle$ and $t' = t + 1$ because the timestamp is incremented by one according to the transition BLOCK-ACCEPT.

From (1), (2) and (3), the item 4 of Proposition 2 is proved.

Proof (7). To prove this point, let us consider the two related functions. The function updCount($\mathbf{M}, \mathbf{puk}, \mathbf{b}$) updates the flag of the counter of the account associated with the public key $\mathbf{puk}$. Its specification is as follows:

$$\text{updCount}(\mathbf{puk} \mapsto \langle \mathbf{bal}, (\mathbf{n}, \hat{\mathbf{b}}) \rangle, \mathbf{b}) = \mathbf{puk} \mapsto \langle \mathbf{bal}, (\mathbf{n}, \mathbf{b}) \rangle$$

The function updSucc($\mathbf{M}, \mathbf{puk}, \mathbf{nt}, \mathbf{fee}$) updates the balance and the counter of the account associated with the public key $\mathbf{puk}$. Its specification is as follows:

$$\text{updSucc}(\mathbf{puk} \mapsto \langle \mathbf{bal}, (\mathbf{n}, \text{True}) \rangle, \mathbf{nt}, \mathbf{fee}) = \mathbf{puk} \mapsto \langle \mathbf{bal} - \mathbf{nt} - \mathbf{fee}, (\mathbf{n} + 1, \text{False}) \rangle$$

if $\mathbf{M(puk)} = \langle \mathbf{bal}, \mathbf{cnt} \rangle$, then $\mathbf{M'(puk)} = \langle \mathbf{bal'}, \mathbf{cnt'} \rangle$ and we have:

(1) $\mathbf{cnt}.b$ = True means that the operation is injected and its status is pending at the time t according to the transition NODE-INJECT. After that, there are only two cases where the counter's flag is reset to False. If the operation is accepted, the counter's flag is reset ($\mathbf{cnt'}.b$ = False) according to the transition BLOCK-ACCEPT and the counter's value is incremented by 1 according to the specification of the function updSucc ($\mathbf{cnt}.n' = \mathbf{cnt}.n + 1$). In another

case, if the operation is timed out, the counter's flag is also reset to False, but the value of the counter remains the same ($\mathbf{cnt}.n' = \mathbf{cnt}$) according to the transition BLOCK-TIMEOUT. That is, if $\mathbf{cnt}.b =$ True and $\mathbf{cnt}'.b =$ False, then $\mathbf{cnt}.n' \in \{\mathbf{cnt}.n, \mathbf{cnt}.n + 1\}$;

(2) otherwise, if the operation is still pending, the counter's value remains the same. This means $\mathbf{cnt}.n = \mathbf{cnt}'.n$;

(3) and then $\mathbf{cnt}.n = \mathbf{cnt}'.n$ means that the operation is either still pending or it has timed out. Therefore, the balance of the account remains the same because the balance is only changed when the operation is accepted. This means $\mathbf{bal} = \mathbf{bal}'$.

From (1), (2) and (3), the item 7 of Proposition 2 is proved.

5.2   Typing Related Properties

To describe the typing of contracts we maintain an environment $\Delta ::= \cdot \mid \mathbf{puh} :$ T, Δ that associates a public hash with a type. We define typing for blockchains, local nodes, and configurations.

$$\frac{dom(\Delta) = dom(\mathbf{B.C}) \qquad (\forall \mathbf{puh} \in dom(\Delta)) \qquad \Delta(\mathbf{puh}) = \text{Pair } T_p \ T_s}{\vdash_C \mathbf{B.C}(\mathbf{puh}).\text{code} : \text{Pair } T_p \ T_s \qquad \vdash_V \mathbf{B.C}(\mathbf{puh}).\text{storage} : T_s}{\Delta \vdash \mathbf{B}}$$

The type for a hash is a pair type, which coincides with the type of the code stored at that hash. The storage at that hash has the type expected by the code.

$$\frac{\cdot \vdash \mathbf{e}_i : \text{Unit}}{\vdash [\overline{\mathbf{e}}, \mathbf{A}] \text{ ok}} \qquad\qquad \frac{\Delta \vdash \mathbf{B} \qquad \vdash \mathbf{N}_i \text{ ok}}{\Delta \vdash \mathbf{B}[\overline{\mathbf{N}}]}$$

Lemma 1 (Preservation). *If $\mathbf{B}[\overline{\mathbf{N}}] \longrightarrow \mathbf{B}'[\overline{\mathbf{N}'}]$ and $\Delta \vdash \mathbf{B}[\overline{\mathbf{N}}]$, then there is some $\Delta' \supseteq \Delta$ such that $\Delta' \vdash \mathbf{B}'[\overline{\mathbf{N}'}]$.*

This lemma includes the standard preservation for the lambda calculus part.

Lemma 2 (Progress). *If $\Delta \vdash \mathbf{B}[\overline{\mathbf{N}}]$, then either all expressions in all nodes are unit values or there is a configuration $\mathbf{B}'[\overline{\mathbf{N}'}]$ such that $\mathbf{B}[\overline{\mathbf{N}}] \longrightarrow \mathbf{B}'[\overline{\mathbf{N}'}]$.*

The consistency lemma says that all committed transactions respect the typing.

Lemma 3 (Consistency). *Consider a blockchain state with $\Delta \vdash [P, M, C, t]$. For all $\mathbf{oph} \in dom(P)$, if $P(\mathbf{oph}) = \langle \mathbf{op}, \hat{t}, \mathbf{st} \rangle$*

- *if $\mathbf{op} = transfer \ \mathbf{nt} \ from \ \mathbf{puk} \ to \ \mathbf{puk}' \ arg \ () \ fee \ \mathbf{fee}$, then $\mathbf{puk}, \mathbf{puk}' \in dom(M)$;*
- *if $\mathbf{op} = transfer \ \mathbf{nt} \ from \ \mathbf{puk} \ to \ \mathbf{puh} \ arg \ \mathbf{p} \ fee \ \mathbf{fee}$, then*
  - *$\mathbf{puk} \in dom(M)$ and $\mathbf{puh} \in dom(C)$,*
  - *$\vdash_V \mathbf{p} : T_p$ where $\Delta(\mathbf{puh}) = \text{Pair } T_p \ T_s$;*

- if $op =$ originate contract transferring nt from puk running $code$ init s fee
  fee and $st =$ included t', then
  - $puk \in dom(M)$ and $puh = \text{genHash}(code, t') \in dom(C)$,
  - $\Delta(puh) = Pair\ T_p\ T_s$, $\vdash_C code : Pair\ T_p\ T_s$ and $\vdash_V s : T_s$.

Proof. Consider the proof of the second item of Lemma 3, which specifies the property on type for a smart contract invocation. A smart contract call op has the form transfer nt from puk to puh arg p fee fee. If $P(oph) = \langle op, \hat{t}, st \rangle$, then the operation op is injected into the node. According to the transition NODE-INJECT for a smart contract invocation, the public key is valid and the public hash must be associated with a smart contract on the blockchain. This means $puk \in dom(M)$ and $puh \in dom(C)$. Moreover, the chkArg function checks whether the type of the input parameter p matches the parameter type of the smart contract. If the casted type of the smart contract is $\Delta(puh) = Pair\ T_p\ T_s$, then the type of the parameter must be T_p. This means $\vdash_V p : T_p$. Therefore, this item is proved.

6   Related Work

The inability to access external data sources limits the potential of smart contracts. Oracles [3,6,13] can help overcome this limitation by providing a bridge between the outside sources and the blockchain network. A blockchain oracle is used to provide external data for smart contracts. When the external data is available, an oracle invokes a smart contract with that information. The invocation can conveniently be made through a programmatic interface. There has been extensive research on providing oracle solutions for blockchain. Adler et al. [11] propose a framework to explain blockchain oracles and various key aspects of oracles. This framework aims to provide developers with a guide for incorporating oracles into blockchain-based applications. The main problems with using a blockchain oracle are the untrusted data provided maliciously or inaccurately [1]. Ma et al. [10] propose an oracle equipped with verification and disputation mechanisms. Similarly, Lo et al. [9] provide a framework for performing reliability analysis of various blockchain oracle platforms.

Current blockchains such as Ethereum [5] and Tezos [8] often offer RPC APIs and use loosely structured data, such as a JSON-based format that is difficult for a programmatic program to handle. As a result, there is increasing work to provide better programmatic interfaces to blockchains. Web3.js [15] provides an Ethereum JavaScript API and offers Java Script users a convenient interface to interact with the Etherum blockchain. Later, Web3.py [16], derived from Web3.js, is developed to provide a Python library for interacting with Ethereum. Our typed API not only supports for programmatic programs, but also provides verifiable interaction with the Tezos smart contract platform.

7   Conclusion

We present a first step towards a typed API for smart contracts on the Tezos blockchain. Our formalization enables us to establish basic properties of the interaction between ordinary programs and smart contracts. We see ample scope for future work to provide a higher-level interface that exploits the similarities between blockchain programming and concurrent programs. The next step will be to formalize the typing-related results. The formalization could connect with the Mi-Cho-Coq formalization of Michelson contracts [4]. In the end, we would like to state and prove properties of a system that contains OCaml code (multi-threaded or distributed) connected to Michelson contracts on the Tezos blockchain via the typed API.

References

1. Al-Breiki, H., Rehman, M.H.U., Salah, K., Svetinovic, D.: Trustworthy blockchain oracles: review, comparison, and open research challenges. IEEE Access 8, 85675–85685 (2020)
2. Allombert, V., Bourgoin, M., Tesson, J.: Introduction to the Tezos blockchain. In: 2019 International Conference on High Performance Computing Simulation (HPCS), pp. 1–10 (2019). https://doi.org/10.1109/HPCS48598.2019.9188227
3. Beniiche, A.: A study of blockchain oracles (2020)
4. Bernardo, B., Cauderlier, R., Hu, Z., Pesin, B., Tesson, J.: Mi-Cho-Coq, a framework for certifying Tezos smart contracts. In: Sekerinski, E., et al. (eds.) FM 2019. LNCS, vol. 12232, pp. 368–379. Springer, Cham (2020). https://doi.org/10.1007/978-3-030-54994-7_28
5. Buterin, V.: A next-generation smart contract and decentralized application platform (2013). https://ethereum.org/en/whitepaper/
6. Caldarelli, G.: Understanding the blockchain oracle problem: a call for action. Information 11(11), 509 (2020)
7. Ethereum JSON-RPC API (2021). https://ethereum.org/en/developers/docs/apis/json-rpc/
8. Goodman, L.: Tezos-a self-amending crypto-ledger (2014). https://www.tezos.com/static/papers/white-paper.pdf
9. Lo, S.K., Xu, X., Staples, M., Yao, L.: Reliability analysis for blockchain oracles. Comput. Electr. Eng. 83, 106582 (2020)
10. Ma, L., Kaneko, K., Sharma, S., Sakurai, K.: Reliable decentralized oracle with mechanisms for verification and disputation. In: 2019 Seventh International Symposium on Computing and Networking Workshops (CANDARW), pp. 346–352 (2019)
11. Mammadzada, K., Iqbal, M., Milani, F., García-Bañuelos, L., Matulevičius, R.: Blockchain oracles: a framework for blockchain-based applications. In: Asatiani, A., et al. (eds.) BPM 2020. LNBIP, vol. 393, pp. 19–34. Springer, Cham (2020). https://doi.org/10.1007/978-3-030-58779-6_2
12. Michelson: The language of smart contracts in Tezos. https://tezos.gitlab.io/alpha/michelson.html
13. Mühlberger, R., et al.: Foundational oracle patterns: connecting blockchain to the off-chain world. In: Asatiani, A., et al. (eds.) BPM 2020. LNBIP, vol. 393, pp. 35–51. Springer, Cham (2020). https://doi.org/10.1007/978-3-030-58779-6_3

14. Nakamoto, S.: Bitcoin: A peer-to-peer electronic cash system (2008). https://www.tezos.com/static/papers/white-paper.pdf
15. Vogelsteller, F., Kotewicz, M., Wilcke, J., Oance, M.: web3.js - Ethereum JavaScript API. https://web3js.readthedocs.io/en/v1.3.4/
16. Vogelsteller, F., Kotewicz, M., Wilcke, J., Oance, M.: web3.py - a Python library for interacting with Ethereum. https://web3py.readthedocs.io/en/stable/

Verification

Simplifying Alternating Automata for Emptiness Testing

Pavol Vargovčík and Lukáš Holík[(✉)]

Brno University of Technology, Brno, Czechia
{ivargovcik,holik}@fit.vutbr.cz

Abstract. We propose preprocessing techniques that improve efficiency of testing language emptiness of alternating automata. We target mainly automata that come from practical application such as processing regular expressions, LTL formulae, or string solving. Such automata often have large alphabets and transition relations represented by succinct and complex Boolean formulae that are more or less unrestricted and may even mix symbols with states. Our main contribution are simplification methods that can be seen as originating from a limited form of determinisation. Our transformations simplify the transition formulae and decrease the number of states. We evaluate experimentally that our preprocessing is beneficial when used together with most of the existing algorithms. It generally improves running times and allows to solve examples that could not be solved before within the given timeout.

1 Introduction

Finite alternating automata with their conjunctive branching are exponentially more succinct than normal non-deterministic automata [10,25]. They can be especially practical in applications where automata are combined with Boolean and similar operations, as demonstrated in works on string solving, e.g. [2,35], LTL model checking, e.g. [15,17,34], testing properties of regular expressions and their combinations [11,12], and also deciding logics as WS1S [16,33] (with their "language/automata terms" or "formula derivatives" that may be seen as generalisation of AFA), and have a great potential in a number of other applications such as regular model checking (e.g. [3,6,37]) or deciding linear arithmetic with automata (e.g. [4,36]).

The price for the succinctness of AFA is the PSPACE-completeness of the language emptiness test. Using AFA instead of non-deterministic finite automata (NFA) thus does not decrease the worst case complexity, but it allows for postponing the payment of the computational cost from construction of the automata to their language emptiness test (indeed, a naïve AFA emptiness test would use a worst case exponential conversion to an NFA). The fact that only the emptiness of the AFA language is of interest, not the explicit NFA, can be used to

This work has been supported by The Czech Science Foundation (GAČR), project No. 19-24397S, and the FIT BUT internal project FIT-S-20-6427.

H. Oh (Ed.): APLAS 2021, LNCS 13008, pp. 243–264, 2021.
https://doi.org/10.1007/978-3-030-89051-3_14

a great advantage. A number of algorithms for deciding the emptiness question use sophisticated heuristics to avoid constructing of the entire NFA. We can name antichain algorithms of [38], later extended with an abstraction refinement scheme [18], the congruence closure based algorithm [13], and adaptations of model checking algorithms [22,35] such as Impact [27] or IC3/PDR [7,12,21]. These algorithms improve scalability of AFA emptiness testing a great deal. Large and complex AFA however still remain a bottleneck.

In this paper, we contribute to the state of the art of solving AFA emptiness by devising a set of lightweight AFA preprocessing steps that improve performance of language inclusion testing algorithms. We concentrate on alternating automata such as those that come from applications areas of string solving, processing of regular expressions, or translation from LTL formulae. They are characterised by large alphabets (such as UNICODE with 2^{32} symbols) that need to be encoded symbolically and a complex Boolean structure of transitions. Our heuristics simplify the Boolean structure of transitions and decrease the number of states.

We propose to use preprocessing steps of several categories. The basic preprocessing uses transformations of the Boolean structure of the transition formulae such as absorption or idempotence. Although relatively simple and common sense, they are efficient and may even solve the emptiness problem by themselves. We do not claim these transformations as entirely novel, similar and more sophisticated heuristics in this spirit are used for simplification of and-inverter graphs [28]. Yet, our version has some differences (such as n-ary $\wedge$ and $\vee$-nodes that give a larger reach to some local transformations) and our particular implementation of the basic transformations seems to be working well on our experimental data and does not seem superseded by the implementation of [28] in the model checker ABC [8].

Our main contribution is a pair of heuristics that simplify the transition formulae and decrease the number of states. They assume the transition formulae in the form of a directed acyclic graph (transition formulae DAG) with nodes being sub-formulae of transition formulae (different occurrences of the same formula share the same DAG node).

The first of the new preprocessing steps may be seen as a limited, local variant of determinisation. Even though the full determinisation of AFA could be even doubly exponential in the worst case, its limited forms may be used to remove redundancies and ultimately decrease the automata size. An example of this is the Brzozovski minimisation [9] where an NFA is transformed into its minimum DFA by inverting, determinising by subset construction, and inverting and determinising again. The determinisation by subset construction can be generalised to AFA as a "configuration formula" construction where the states of the DFA are not sets of states but Boolean formulae. To prevent the construction from exploding, which the full determinisation would be prone to, we limit the determinisation to local parts of the automaton where it indeed tends to reduce the size of the automaton rather than increase it. We also call this optimisation up-shifting, since in the transition formulae DAG view of the transition function, the construction may be seen as shifting states upwards through the sub-formulae that are purely made of states (they do not talk about symbols). Figure 1 shows an example.

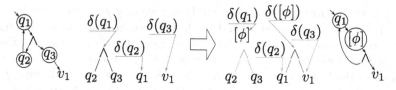

Fig. 1. State up-shifting. The left-most graph is an input AFA (its transition graph) with states q_1, q_2, q_3, initial state q_1, a symbol variable v_1, and the transition function δ assigning transition formulae to states so that $\delta(q_1) = q_2 \wedge q_3, \delta(q_2) = q_1, \delta(q_3) = v_1$. The second graph from left is the transition function δ of the input AFA as a function assigning nodes of the transition formulae DAG to states. The right part of the figure shows δ and the AFA after the up-shifting. The conjunction of states $\phi = q_2 \wedge q_3$ is up-shifted—it is replaced by a single state $[\phi]$. After the currently unreachable states q_2, q_3 are removed, the resulting automaton has a smaller number of states.

The second novel construction arises by extrapolating the intuition behind the local determinisation—instead of upwards, we can also shift states downwards through the formulae DAG. This may in theory lead to reverting the effect of the up-shifting, but when applied carefully, it gives significant additional savings in the number of states. The heuristic namely finds minimum cut through the transition formulae DAG and replaces the existing set of states by states transitioning to the nodes of the cut. The minimality of the cut guarantees that the new states will be at most as many as there were the old states. We call this heuristic down-shifting. Down-shifting may slightly resemble the concept of retiming from hardware circuit optimisation [23,29]. Nevertheless, we have verified experimentally that turning retiming on in the ABC tool does not have a significant impact on model checking of the automata problems, while down-shifting has.

We design the heuristics carefully in order for them to be implementable with a small cost relative to the overall cost of the emptiness testing. Especially the local determinisation requires a well though algorithm to achieve this. Indeed, we experimentally verify that our implementation, despite made in Haskell without thorough focus on optimisation, is fast enough for the preprocessing cost to be almost negligible. We have tested the power of the preprocessing on AFA from several applications, namely, translated from LTL formulae [13], created during deciding string constraints [22], and combinations of regular expressions [12,13]. Our experiments show that depending on the type of benchmark, the preprocessing may have significant impact on performance of emptiness checkers and allows them to solve some examples that could not be solved before by any of the checkers within a relatively generous timeout.

2   Preliminaries

A *Boolean formula* ψ over a set X is constructed as $\psi ::= 0 \mid 1 \mid x \mid \bigvee \Phi \mid \bigwedge \Phi \mid \neg\phi$ where $x \in X$, ϕ is a Boolean formula, and Φ is a set of Boolean formulae. Note that the commutativity of the operators is implicit in this definition and we will treat it as such through the paper, even though we may write e.g. $\phi \wedge \psi$ to denote $\bigwedge\{\phi, \psi\}$. The constants 0 and 1 stand for the false and true formulae, respectively. We use $\mathcal{B}(X)$ to denote the set of all Boolean formulae over X. A *positive Boolean formula* is a Boolean formula without negation and 0 and $\mathcal{B}^+(X)$ is the set of all positive Boolean formulae over X. The semantics is standard, with $f \models \phi$ denoting that the assignment $f : X \rightarrow \{0, 1\}$ *satisfies (is a solution of)* ϕ.

Alphabet. Let $V = \{v_1, v_2, \ldots\}$ be a set of *symbol-variables*. An assignment $a : V \rightarrow \{0, 1\}$ is a *symbol* and Σ is the *alphabet*, the set of all symbols. A *word* is a sequence of symbols and Σ^* is the set of all (finite) words.

Alternating Automata. We consider alternating automata in a succinct form (in which they naturally arise in some applications in string solving or processing of regular expressions). This form handles large alphabets symbolically by means of encoding symbols as bit-vectors, and the transition relation for each state is given as a Boolean formula over states and symbol-variables. The solutions of the transition formula encodes both the symbol as well as the set of states into which the state can transition. The formula allows to mix symbol variables and states almost arbitrarily, the only restriction is that states do not appear under negation.

Formally, an *alternating finite automaton (AFA)* is a quadruple $\mathcal{M} = (Q, V, \delta, \iota, F)$ where 1) Q is a finite set of *states*; 2) V is a finite set of *symbol-variables*; 3) $\delta : Q \rightarrow \mathcal{B}^+(Q \cup \mathcal{B}(V))$ is a *transition function*; 4) $\iota \in Q$ is the *initial state*; and 5) $F \subseteq Q$ is a set of *final/accepting states*. An example of an AFA is in Fig. 1.

A *configuration* of $\mathcal{M}$ is a mapping $c : Q \rightarrow \{0, 1\}$. We will often abuse the notation and treat configurations c as the sets $\{q \mid c(q) = 1\}$ of which they are characteristic functions (we write $q \in c$ to denote $c(q) = 1$ and relate configurations using $\subseteq$). A *run* of $\mathcal{M}$ over a word $a_1 \cdots a_n \in \Sigma^*$ is a sequence $c_0, a_1, c_1, a_2, \ldots, a_n, c_n$ of the letters interleaved with configurations where $\iota \in c_0$, and for all $i : 0 \leq i < n$, $\bigwedge_{q \in c_i} \delta(q) \models a_{i+1} \cup c_{i+1}$. The run is *accepting* if $c_n \subseteq F$. The *language* of $\mathcal{M}$ is the set $L(\mathcal{M})$ of all accepted words.

Special Forms of AFA. The AFA is *separated* if every transition formula $\delta(q), q \in Q$ is a disjunction of the formulae $(\alpha_1 \wedge \psi_1) \vee (\alpha_n \wedge \psi_n)$ where $\alpha_i \in \mathcal{B}(V)$ and $\psi_i \in \mathcal{B}^+(Q)$ for all i. δ is then usually given in the form of a function that returns for α_i and q the state formula $\delta(q, \alpha_i) = \psi_i$.

The standard notion of a *non-deterministic (symbolic) finite automaton (NFA)* then corresponds to a separated automaton where every $\delta(q, \alpha_i)$ is a literal $r \in Q$. The triple q, α_i, r is called a *transition* and denoted $q \xrightarrow{\alpha_i} r$. A *deterministic (symbolic) finite automaton DFA* is an NFA where for every $q \in Q$ and transitions $q \xrightarrow{\alpha} r$ and $q \xrightarrow{\alpha'} r'$ with $r \neq r'$, $\alpha \wedge \alpha'$ is not satisfiable. We get the standard, non-symbolic variants of NFA and DFA if the predicate α on their transitions is satisfied by exactly one symbol.

AFA Without Final States and Language Emptiness. For simplicity, we will present our preprocessing only for AFA with the empty set of final states (note that an AFA without final states accepts at the empty configuration). The decision problem of language emptiness of an AFA with final states can be easily reduced to the language emptiness of an AFA without final states: intuitively, the AFA without final states has the alphabet extended with a new symbol-variable $v_\$$ and under $v_\$ = 1$ it can transition to the empty configuration instead of to a configuration consisting only of final states.

Technically, we transform an AFA $M = (Q, V, \delta, \iota, F)$ to the automaton M' with the empty set of final states as follows. We introduce a new symbol-variable $v_\$$. We replace every occurrence of a non-final state $q \in Q \setminus F$ in the transition formulae by $(q \wedge \neg v_\$)$ and every occurrence of a final state $q_f \in F$ by $q_f \vee v_\$$. Then we empty the set of final states. The new automaton may then transition to an empty configuration under a symbol with $v_\$ = 1$ if the old automaton could transition to a final configuration. Otherwise it must use the old transitions with $v_\$ = 0$.

Notice that after the modification of δ and emptying of F, the automaton can accept only by a transition to an empty configuration, and so it cannot accept the empty word ϵ (accepted because $\iota \in F$). To remedy this, we start the transformation of M to M' by replacing the initial states by a fresh state ι' with the transition formula $\delta(\iota') = \iota$. The modification of δ and emptying of F is done after that.

The resulting automaton M' without final states then accepts exactly words of $L(M)$ prefixed with an arbitrary symbol, and so the language of M is empty if and only if the language of M' is.

Lemma 1. *The language obtained from $L(M')$ by projecting the variable $v_\$$ away from symbols equals $\Sigma.L(M)$.*

Shared AFA Representation. Through the paper, we will work with *shared representation* of the transition formulae. Most of the implementations we have experimented with do actually adopt such shared DAG representation. In it, the sub-formulae of the formulae in the image of δ are nodes of a directed acyclic graph G_δ, called the *transition formulae DAG* (*formulae DAG* for short), which has an edge from each $\neg \phi$ to ϕ and from each $\phi \circ \phi'$ to ϕ and to ϕ', for $\circ \in \{\wedge, \vee\}$ (that is, from a formula to its immediate sub-formulae). An example of a formulae DAG is shown in Fig. 1.

In some phases of preprocessing of the AFA, the shared representation may become only partially shared, meaning that some sub-formulae may correspond to more than one DAG node. Formally, in a *partially shared representation*, δ maps states to nodes of a DAG G which is a domain of a graph homomorphism $h : G \to G_\delta$.

Besides the formulae DAG, we will use a concept of a *transition graph*. It arises from the formulae DAG by adding the edge from q to the node $\delta(q)$ for every $q \in Q$. We also define reachability of nodes of G_δ and states based on it: a node or a state is *reachable* if it is reachable in the transition graph from the state ι.

3   Basic Simplification

The basic simplification of the transition function uses mostly standard equivalences of Boolean formulae, removes obvious redundancies in the formulae DAG to achieve the fully shared form, and merges states with identical transition formulae.

The *basic simplification algorithm* iterates three sub-procedures until fixpoint (the formulae DAG can no longer be changed by either of them). The first sub-procedure is a bottom-up sweep through the formulae DAG (starting from the leaves and processing a node after all its children were processed) during which the following Boolean transformations of the encountered nodes are performed:[1]

- *idempotence laws*, that replaces $\phi \wedge \phi$ or $\phi \vee \phi$ by ϕ,
- *identity laws*, that replace $\phi \vee 0$ and $\phi \wedge 1$ by ϕ,
- *domination laws*, that replace $\phi \vee 0$ and $\phi \wedge 1$ by 0 or 1 respectively,
- *double negation law*, that replace $\neg\neg\phi$ by ϕ,
- *absorption laws*, that replace $\phi \wedge (\phi \vee \psi)$ and $\phi \vee (\phi \wedge \psi)$ by ϕ;
- *laws of common identities*, that replace $\phi \vee (\neg\phi \wedge \psi)$ by $\phi \vee \psi$, and, dually, replace $\phi \wedge (\neg\phi \vee \psi)$ by $\phi \wedge \psi$,
- *propagation of 0 and 1*, that replaces in the formulae DAG every state $q \neq \iota$ with $\delta(q) = x, x \in \{0,1\}$ by x,[2]
- *associative flattening*, in which nested conjunctions are flattened into a single n-ary conjunction. The conjuncts that are originally referenced from multiple parents must however be kept as separate DAG nodes. Analogously for disjunctions.

The bottom-up sweep also removes duplicities. Nodes are identified by the set of their children (that are already supposed to appear uniquely in the DAG), and if a currently processed node is found to have the same children and the same top-most logical operator as another already existing node, the two are merged.

The second sub-procedure is merging duplicate states. When two states with $\delta(q) = \delta(r)$ are found, all occurrences of r are replaced by q and r is removed. We note that the combination of identity and double negation law and propagation of 0 and 1 iterated until fixpoint removes all literals 0 and 1 from the transition formulae, except the case when even $\delta(\iota)$ becomes 1 or 0 in which the language emptiness becomes trivial.

The third sub-procedure removes unreachable nodes.

4   Local Determinisation (State Up-Shifting)

The first novel heuristic we use is inspired by the classical determinisation construction. This may seem counter-intuitive, since already non-determinisation of

---

[1] Although we use n-ary operators $\wedge$ and $\vee$, for simplicity we describe the transformations with binary versions.

[2] Note that is the only step which may alter the language: the new automaton can now accept earlier, and thus accept a prefix of a word accepted by the original. The (non)emptiness of the language however stays preserved.

AFA (transformation to NFA) is exponential, which is the main reason for deciding emptiness directly on alternating automata at the first place, and determinisation may lead to yet another level of exponential blow-up. Yet, when applied in a limited manner, determinisation may simplify the transition relation and decrease the number of states (a witness of a similar effect is the Brzozowski's construction of the minimal DFA [9], where two rounds of determinisation by subset construction, backward followed by forward, transform any NFA to the minimal DFA).

The idea is to use determinisation on local parts of the automaton where it stays cheap and has a good chance of decreasing the size of the automaton. Here we mean by AFA determinisation a construction similar to that used e.g. in [26] for Boolean automata. Roughly, for a separated AFA, states of the DFA are "state formulae"—Boolean formulae over states. The initial DFA state is the atomic formula q_0, the and the successor of a state formula φ over a letter α is obtained from φ by substituting each state q in it by $\delta(q, \alpha)$. To guarantee termination, the constructed successor state formulae are taken modulo logical equivalence or are transformed to some normal form. With not separated AFA, the substitution would be replaced by a more complex operation, which would involve some kind of transformation to a separated form, or existential quantification over the symbol α and quantifier elimination.

The step with a potential to simplify the automaton is the substitution of a Boolean combination of states by a single state. An example of this is shown in Fig. 1, where the conjunction of states $q_2 \wedge q_3$ is replaced by a new state $[q_2 \wedge q_3]$. Whether or not this indeed leads to a simplification depends on whether the involved states, q_2 and q_3 in the example, appear in other configuration formula. Since in the example they do not appear elsewhere, they can be removed. We note that the name up-shifting comes from that states are moved upwards in the formulae DAG, as Fig. 1 also shows.

Next, to keep our preprocessing on the level of a lightweight and cheap heuristic, we replace the equivalence check of formulae/transformation to a normal form (used in determinisation) by a less precise but cheaper mechanism.

In the following paragraphs, we describe the local determinisation in detail. We describe the sub-procedures and then connect them in a fixed-point iteration. We assume an AFA $\mathcal{M} = (\iota, Q, \delta, \emptyset)$ on the input, with the transition function in the shared form, i.e., δ assigning nodes of the formulae DAG G_δ to states.

4.1 Up-Shifting of States

The main step of local determinisation is the *up-shifting*. Let us first define notation needed in its description. We will say that a node of the formulae DAG or the corresponding formula is *pure* if it belongs to $\mathcal{B}^+(Q)$ (its literals are only states). We also define the function Δ that generalizes δ to all formulae in $\mathcal{B}^+(Q)$. It is defined by the structural induction: for a state $q \in Q$, $\Delta(q) = \delta(q)$ and for a pure formula ϕ other than a state, $\Delta(\phi)$ is obtained from ϕ by replacing each immediate sub-formula ψ by $\Delta(\psi)$.

Given a pure node ϕ of the formulae DAG, the operation of *up-shifting towards* ϕ substitutes ϕ by a new *state* $[\phi]$ with the transition formula defined as $\delta([\phi]) = \Delta(\phi)$.

Technically, if the node $\Delta(\phi)$ is already present in the formulae DAG, then it may be directly used. If the node $\Delta(\phi)$ is not present, then it is constructed following the inductive definition of $\Delta(\phi)$: We call a recursive procedure with the input parameter ϕ that returns $\Delta(\phi)$ if it exists in the DAG, and otherwise the procedure recursively calls itself on the immediate sub-formulae of ϕ and constructs $\Delta(\phi)$ from the returned nodes.

Figure 1 shows an example where up-shifting decreases the size of an automaton.

Lemma 2. *Up-shifting preserves language (non)emptiness, and, assuming that the formulae DAG does not contain the literal 1, it also preserves the language.*[3]

Proof (idea). The proof of Lemma 2 is based on showing that the language accepted from the state $[\phi]$ created by the up-shifting is obtained inductively to the structure of ϕ from the languages of the literal states of ϕ. Recall that ϕ is pure, that is, it is a boolean combination of states, and a boolean combination of states can be expressed by a single state as outlined above. $\qquad\square$

4.2   Preventing Nested Substitution

Up-shifting will be iterated until it has an effect. The procedure that generates $\Delta(\phi)$ during up-shifting may generate new pure nodes and these may be eventually also up-shifted. Due to loops in the reachability graph, this may cause nontermination of up-shifting, as illustrated in Fig. 2. Essentially, the repetitive application of up-shifting creates logically equivalent nodes and states with an unboundedly nested structure.

A conceptually easy and natural way to prevent this would be the following: Whenever a new node ϕ is created within up-shifting, search for an existing node ϕ' with $\phi \equiv \phi'$ and, if found, use ϕ' in place of ϕ (similarly for states—we can test logical equivalence of states after pruning from them all, possible nested, square brackets). However, comparing the semantics of all existing nodes with ϕ would be expensive. We hence opt for a much cheaper and light-weight termination criterion. Even though it is, in theory, more strict, it is still sufficiently liberal according to our empirical experience.

Namely, prior to the up-shifting procedure, we perform the depth first traversal through transition graph starting at the initial state ι and we collect a set of *back edges* (edges that lead in the tree induced by the DFS from a descendant to a predecessor). Every cycle in the transition graph must contain a back edge. Since we then work with the formulae DAG, which does not include the edges from states q to their transition formulae $\delta(q)$, some of the back edges could be lost. To prevent this, we modify the set of back edges after the DFS: every back

---

[3] The assumption will be satisfied in our context since up-shifting will always be preceded by the basic preprocessing from Sect. 3 that eliminates the literals 0 and 1.

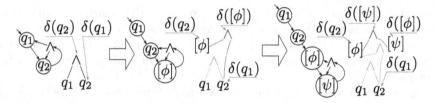

Fig. 2. Nontermination of unrestricted repeatition of up-shifting. The figure shows two repetitions of up-shifting, proceeding from left to right. The first one replaces node $\phi = q_1 \wedge q_2$ with the state $[\phi]$, the second replaces $\psi = q_2 \wedge [\phi]$ with state $[\psi] = [q_2 \wedge [\phi]] = [q_2 \wedge [q_1 \wedge q_2]]$. Notice the nested structure of the new state $[\psi]$ and also that the sub-graphs of all the three transition graphs induced by the bottom three nodes are isomorphic. Further repetition of up-shifting would lead to creation of more and more nested states and transition graphs where the same isomorphic sub-graph is reached through a longer and longer initial string of states. (the figure uses the graphical convention as in Fig. 1)

edge leading from a state q to $\delta(q)$ is removed from the set of back edges and in its place, we add all the edges leading to q. The new set of back edges still has a back edge in every cycle of the transition graph and all the back-edges now stay fully preserved also in the formulae DAG.

The rule restricting the up-shifting then applies when every path from the node of the DAG to its leaf states contains a back edge. We call such DAG node a *loop head*. Up-shifting is not applied on loop heads.

Through the run of local determinisation, the formulae DAG is modified and we need to preserve the invariant that every cycle in the transition graph has a back edge. Running the entire DFS after every change of the DAG would be expensive and we would have to resolve the problem that variability in the returned set of back edges (caused possibly by non-determinism or by that the transition graph may change in between various invocations of the DFS) could again lead to non-termination. We therefore update the set of back edges after every modification locally: When recursively constructing a DAG node $\Delta(\phi)$ from the immediate subnodes $\Delta(\psi)$, then the new edge $(\Delta(\phi), \Delta(\psi))$ becomes a back edge iff (ϕ, ψ) is a back edge.

4.3 Purification

The up-shifting can be applied only on conjunctions or disjunctions which are pure. This limit its applicability significanlty. We therefore use the following simple purification rules that separate impure sub-formulae from pure parts and allow up-shifting to be applied on them:

- *Associative extraction*: $(\chi \wedge \phi) \wedge \psi$ where ϕ and ψ are pure while χ is not gets transformed to $\chi \wedge (\phi \wedge \psi)$.
- *Distributive extraction*: $(\chi \circ \phi) \bar{\circ} (\chi \circ \psi)$ where $\{\circ, \bar{\circ}\} = \{\wedge, \vee\}$ and ϕ and ψ are pure while χ is not gets transformed to $\chi \circ (\phi \bar{\circ} \psi)$.

These rules are a compromise between the power of the transformation and its cost. They are simple, cheap, and do not increase the size of the formulae. We do not use for instance the opposite direction of the distributive law, which would indeed allow to separate more impurities, but could lead to a blow-up in the formula size.

Since the purification rules modify the edges of the DAG, we have to update the set of back edges used at cycle prevention. The rules are simple: 1) a back edge into the original formula is replaced by a back edge into the modified formula, and 2) if the path from the original formula to some of its sub-formulae χ, ϕ, ψ had a back edge, then the edges in the new formula reaching this sub-formula are also marked as back edges.

4.4   Local Determinisation Algorithm

Finally, local determinisation is implemented as bottom-up traversal through the formulae DAG that combines up-shifting, purification, and prevention of nested substitution discussed in the previous sections. It iteratively extends a set *Ground* of "ground" nodes, initialised as the DAG leaves, and serving as a pool of possible children of nodes that are candidates for up-shifting. One iteration consists of the following steps:

1. Choose a *candidate* DAG node $\phi \notin Ground$ with all children in *Ground*.
2. If the candidate ϕ is not pure, apply purification if possible (as described in Sect. 4.3) and return to step 1.
3. If ϕ is pure, then check whether it is a loop head (as discussed in Sect. 4.2).
4. If ϕ is pure and not a loop head, apply the up-shifting (as discussed in Sect. 4.1, this introduces the state $[\phi]$).
5. Add ϕ to *Ground*. Or instead, add $[\phi]$ to *Ground* if up-shifting has been applied in the step 4.

The algorithm requires testing purity of nodes (in step 2 and also within the purification procedure) and testing whether a node is a loop head (in step 3). To do that efficiently, it maintains an auxiliary set *Pure* which records visited nodes known to be pure, and an auxiliary set *LoopHead* that records visited nodes that are known to be loop heads.

An invariant of the algorithm is that the set *Pure* is the set of pure nodes contained in *Ground*. Testing purity of a node then reduces to testing whether all its children are in *Pure*. To satisfy the invariant, *Pure* is initialised as Q and nodes are added to *Pure* in step 2, when pure nodes are created within the purification procedure, and also in step 3, when the candidate is identified as pure.

The invariant of *LoopHead* is that it is the set of loop heads contained in *Ground*. Testing whether a node is a loop head then reduces to testing whether each of its children is either in *LoopHead* or is connected by a back-edge (recall that by definition, a node is a loop head if all paths in the DAG from it to a leaf contain a back edge, which is equivalent to the condition we are testing).

LoopHead is initialised as $\emptyset$ and nodes are added to it in step 4 when they are identified as loop heads.

The algorithm also keeps the formulae DAG in the shared form. Whenever a new node is generated, we search for a duplicate node in the formulae DAG and merge it with the new node if found. Since the shared form is invariant, the duplicate node can be found simply as one with the same top-most logical operator and the same children.

The bottom-up traversal terminates when there is no candidate (no node outside *Ground* with children in ground). As the last step, the basic simplification from Sect. 3 is applied again, mainly to remove all unreachable nodes and states that may arise during the bottom-up traversal, but also to use new opportunities for the Boolean and other transformations that the local determinisation may have opened.

Algorithm 1: Local Determinisation

---

1 Perform DFS on the transition graph, mark back edges in the formulae DAG G_δ;
2 *Ground* := $Q \cup V$; *Pure* := Q; *LoopHead* := $\emptyset$;
3 **while** $nodes(G_\delta) \not\subseteq Ground$ **do**
4   Choose $\phi \in nodes(G_\delta) \setminus Ground$ such that $children(\phi) \subseteq Ground$;
5   **if** $children(\phi) \subseteq Pure$ **then**
6 | *Pure* := *Pure* $\cup \{\phi\}$
7   **if** $\phi \notin Pure$ and purification from Section 4.3 is applicable **then**
8 | Replace ϕ in G_δ with its purified image; **continue**
9   **if** $children(\phi) \setminus back\text{-}edge\text{-}children(\phi) \subseteq LoopHead$ **then**
10 | *LoopHead* := *LoopHead* $\cup \{\phi\}$
11   **if** $\phi \in Pure \setminus LoopHead$ **then**   // Up-shifting
12   Construct the node $\Delta(\phi)$ if it does not already exist in G_δ;
13         $[\phi]$:= new state; $\delta([\phi])$:= $\Delta(\phi)$;
14   Replace ϕ with $[\phi]$ in G_δ (i.e. all edges that led to ϕ are redirected to $[\phi]$);
15   *Ground* := *Ground* $\cup \{[\phi]\}$; *Pure* := *Pure* $\cup \{[\phi]\}$
16   **else** *Ground* := *Ground* $\cup \{\phi\}$

Algorithm 1 sums up the above description of local determinisation. Note that the formulae DAG is modified in lines 8 and 12, implicitly updating the set of back edges (as described in the end of Sects. 4.2 and 4.3) and merging duplicates.

Lemma 3. *Local determinisation preserves the language and terminates after at most square of the number of nodes in the input formulae DAG iterations.*

Proof (Idea). Let f be a function that assigns to every node ϕ the number of states on longest path in the transition graph that starts in ϕ and does not have a back edge, where by longest we mean one that traverses the highest number of states. Note that since every cycle has a back edge, $f(\phi) \le |Q|$ for any DAG node. Consider a set X of the DAG nodes that are at the beginning of an iteration outside *Ground*. Let $f(X) = \sum_{\phi \in X} f(\phi)$. The termination argument is based on showing that $f(X)$ decreases with every iteration: Essentially, when not taking purification into account, the iteration either removes a candidate ϕ from X (by adding ϕ to *Ground* without up-shifting) or replaces it in X with a new candidate $\Delta(\phi)$ which has a smaller f value.[4] The argument with purification taken into account would be similar but more technical. The complexity bound is then derived from that the initial $f(X)$ cannot be larger than the number of DAG nodes (the maximum size of X) multiplied by the number of states (the maximum value of $f(\phi)$).   □

5   Down-Shifting of States Towards Minimal Cut

The number of automata states can also be decreased by an operation which is complementary to the up-shifting of the local determinisation. Intuitively, while the up-shifting moves states upwards through pure parts of the formulae DAG, down-shifting moves states downwards through the pure parts of the formulae DAG. Our algorithm implementing this idea is more informed than the local determinisation, which up-shifts greedily. We down-shift the states towards the *minimum state cut* through the formulae DAG to guarantee optimal savings in the number of states. Figure 3 shows an example.

Formally, a cut of the formulae DAG is a set of its nodes C such that every maximal path contains an element of C. We find a cut of a minimal size such that none of its nodes is reachable in the DAG from a *negation node*, a node of the form $\neg\phi$. The restriction on the negation nodes is present in order for

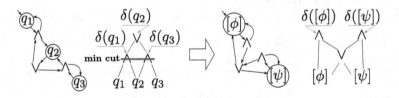

Fig. 3. Down-shifting. The input AFA is on the left, with a minimum cut $C = \{\phi = q_1 \wedge q_2, \psi = q_2 \wedge q_3\}$ in the formulae DAG, the resulting automaton is on the right. The resulting AFA has one state less. (the figure uses the graphical convention as in Fig. 1)

---

[4] We also have to account for that while creating the node $\Delta(\phi)$, the recursive procedure in Sec. 4.1 might have to create also some of its descendands. Luckily, the f values of these nodes will amount to zero: if a descendant $\Delta(\psi)$ was newly created, then ψ must have been a loop head (otherwise ψ would have been up-shifted, creating $\Delta(\psi)$), and therefore $\Delta(\psi)$ is also a loop head (since back edges are copied) and hence its f value is zero.

the transformed automaton to conform to our definition of AFA, where the states cannot appear in the transition formulae under negation.[5] Another, rather technical, restriction is that node $\delta(\iota)$ must be in the cut. This is needed for the down-shifting to preserve the original initial state ι.[6] With the minimum cut C fixed, the automaton is transformed as follows:

1. The set of states Q of $\mathcal{M}$ is replaced by the set $\{[\phi] \mid \phi \in C\}$ of new states created from the nodes in the cut, with the transitions formulae $\delta([\phi]) = \phi$ (note that since $\delta(\iota) \in C$, the state $[\delta(\iota)]$ is created and can now serve as the new initial state),
2. every node $\phi \in C$ of the formulae DAG is replaced by the new state $[\phi]$,
3. every DAG edge to a state $q \in Q$ is replaced by an edge to the node $\delta(q)$ and the nodes $q \in Q$ are removed from the DAG.[7]

Lemma 4. *Down-shifting preserves the language.*

Proof (idea). Lemma 4 follows from that down-shifting is an operation which is an inverse to up-shifting. A sequence of up-shifting steps applied on nodes that are in the third step of the description of down-shifting referred to as $\delta(q)$ would revert the automaton to the original form. Lemma 4 then follows from Lemma 2.

□

A Note on Computation of the Minimum Cut C. We note that the minimum cut C that is above all negation nodes can be computed by reduction to the standard graph problem of computing a minimum edge cut of a flow network. Namely, the transition graph G_δ is transformed into a flow network W by

1. adding a source node S that originates an edge to every node in the image of δ,
2. adding a sink node E which is the target of an edge from every symbol-variable, state, negation node of G_δ, and the node $\delta(\iota)$ (to keep the initial state),
3. assigning an infinite capacity to every existing edge,
4. replacing every node ϕ with a pair of nodes ϕ_0, ϕ_1 such that all the original incoming edges of ϕ are redirected to ϕ_0, the origin of all the outgoing edges of ϕ are changed to ϕ_1, and the two nodes are connected with a new edge from ϕ_0 to ϕ_1 of capacity 1.

The minimum edge cut (which we obtain in a standard manner, using max-flow min-cut theorem and Ford-Fulkerson's method) contains only the new edges from the step 4, from which the minimum state cut is obtained by mapping each edge (ϕ_0, ϕ_1) to ϕ. It is well known that the minimum edge cut can be computed with a complexity $O(|E| \cdot |C|)$ where E is the set of edges of G_δ.

---

[5] This restriction could be lifted for Boolean automata [26] that allow negated states.
[6] This restriction could be lifted if we allowed an initial formulae instead of just an initial state.
[7] Note that if C was not a cut, the formulae DAG would keep some states from Q. But Q has been entirely replaced in the first step, hence the result would not be a valid AFA.

6   Experimental Evaluation

In this section, we experimentally evaluate the proposed AFA simplification. We focus on evaluation of the novel simplification techniques of local determinisation and of down-shifting. We do not put emphasis on the Basic simplification, as it is mostly covered by more advanced heuristics in [28], whereas the basic simplification in Sect. 3 is simpler and mostly rather common sense. Therefore, we start from an automaton already processed by the basic simplification and focus on the impact of the two novel heuristics. We evaluate their impact on the performance on a number of existing tools and algorithms for deciding language emptiness of AFA against benchmarks from several sources, including benchmarks found in the literature, benchmarks from practical applications, and randomly generated ones. Our experiments were done on a machine with Intel(R) Core(TM) i7-8565U CPU @ 1.80 GHz and 16 GB RAM.

Benchmark Collection. The first benchmark, called *LTL*, is a benchmark inspired by [13] and based on randomly generated LTL_F formulae (linear temporal logic over finite traces [14]). Concretely, satisfiability of randomly generated LTL_F formulae are checked by their transformation to AFA and checking their language emptiness. Our random generator is controlled by several parameters: 1) the *maximum* depth of the formula syntax tree 2) the *average* depth of the formula syntax tree, and 3) for each logical connective or variables, a probability of that it will be generated next within a top-down construction of the tree. We have experimented with various settings of these parameters to obtain 13700 formulae with different characteristics (the maximum depth ranges between 5 do 17, the average depth between 4 and 14, and we have three different settings for probability distribution between the syntactic elements).

The second benchmark, *RegexLib*, is also taken from [13]. It is based on the collection of regular expressions RegexLib [1]. From [13], we took 1000 instances of the equality testing problem of the form $r_1 \wedge r_2 \wedge r_3 \wedge r_4 = r_1 \wedge r_2 \wedge r_3 \wedge r_4 \wedge r_4$ (where the r_is are regular expressions from the RegexLib for email filtering) and 423 problems of the form $r_1 \wedge r_2 \wedge r_3 = r_1 \wedge r_2 \wedge r_3 \wedge r_4$ (this is 1423 automata overall). The alternating automaton for the equality is constructed from the AFA A and B for the two equality sides, respectively, and combining them into an AFA for $(L(A) \cap L(B)') \cup (L(A)' \cap L(B))$ which has empty language if and only if the equality holds. A similar benchmark was used also in [11,12] (although we were not able to obtain the concrete examples).

Besides those three sets of formulae, we also use two artificial parametric benchmarks used in [13]. The first one, *Lift*, is a parametric LTL_F formula from [19] describing a lift operating on a parametric number of floors. The second one, *Counter*, is a parametric LTL_F formula from [32] describing a counter incremented modulo the parameter (Lift as well as Counter formulae are satisfiable in LTL but not in LTL_F).

We have also tested our preprocessing on a 406 AFA emptiness problems generated while solving satisfiability of practical string constraints by the algorithm of [2]. Our heuristics did not have a significant impact here and so we do not discuss the results in detail. This result, even though negative, underlines the fact that will be apparent also further in this section—that the source of benchmarks is a crucial factor influencing effectiveness of our preprocessing (as well as of the relative performance of AFA emptiness checkers).

The Top Level Preprocessing Algorithm. In our experiments, we use a preprocessing algorithm that uses the discussed simplification steps in the following way: 1) local determinisation (which will be further referred to only as up-shifting); 2) basic simplification; 3) down-shifting iterated until fixpoint (until it cannot decrease the number of states); and 4) basic simplification. This algorithm is called the *UpDown*. We have observed that the impact of down-shifting is less predictable—although it is often significantly helpful, it can also harm the performance of the emptiness checkers. We therefore propose to run the algorithm *UpDown* in parallel with the version which skips the steps 2 and 3, denoted *Up*, and call the parallel version *UpDown|Up*.

Emptiness Checkers. We evaluate the impact of our preprocessing on the performance of several AFA language emptiness checkers and algorithms from the literature:

- Our own implementation of the backward antichain algorithm of [38], written in C++, generalized to our form of symbolic AFA. It uses the SAT solver MiniSAT [5] to construct predecessors of configurations, denoted *Antichain*.[8]
- An algorithm that uses bisimulation up to congruence of [13], implemented by the authors in Java, denoted *Bisimulation.*
- A highly optimized implementation of the algorithm IC3 within the model checker ABC [8,20,30,31], written in C++, run on the *forward* reduction of the AFA language emptiness problem to reachability in Boolean transition systems (BTS). The forward reduction is similar to the one used in [22] (the BTS transitions between configurations in the same way as the AFA, starting in ι, terminating at the empty configuration). This is denoted *ABC.*[9]
- IC3 within ABC but this time run on the *backward/reverse* reduction of the AFA language emptiness problem to reachability in BTS, similar to the reduction used in [11,12]. Essentially, in the backward reduction we are checking whether ι is reachable from $\bigwedge_{q \in Q} \neg q$ (satisfied only by the empty configuration) by transitions specified by $\bigwedge (q' \implies \delta(q))$. This is denoted *reverse ABC.*
- The emptiness checker *JAltImpact* implementing the algorithm [24], written in Java. The algorithm is meant for so called data AFA that allow complex reasoning about integers. It uses the model checking algorithm Impact [27].

---

[8] It would be also interesting to test the algorithm of [18] which extends the antichain algorithm of [38] with a overapproximating abstraction and a refinement scheme, however, we are not aware of an implementation that could handle our form of AFA and generalizing [18] to this case would not be trivial.

[9] As suggested in [28], we run the following ABC preprocessing: *b; rw; rf; b; rw; rwz; b; rfz; rwz; b; pdr.*

To represent our AFA by the data AFA, symbol-variables v in a transition formula are substituted by the integer predicates $v = 1$.

Finally, let us emphasize that our experimentation is not intended as a comparison of the emptiness checking algorithms or tools. Although our measurements may provide some insides into this, they must be taken with a grain of salt. The tools target different kinds of inputs and are implemented in different languages with different levels of engineering and optimisation. Our intention is to demonstrate that our preprocessing has a generally positive impact on the performance of a wide spectrum of algorithms rather than to compare the emptiness checkers and their algorithms.

6.1   Experiment "Best of Checkers"

In the first experiment, we investigate the impact of our optimisations on the solving capabilities of all the emptiness checkers put together. For every benchmark, we pick the time of the best checker without preprocessing and the best time with the preprocessing $UpDown|Up$. Recall that the automata on the input are already preprocessed using basic simplification, thus the following results show just the impact of Up and $UpDown$. The results for benchmarks LTL and RegexLib are shown in Fig. 4.

The figures show that the preprocessing techniques have improved running times significantly. They also allowed the checkers to solve 34 RegexLib examples in the 15 s timeout that could not be solved before by any checker. The LTL benchmark was absolutely dominated by ABC reverse, which solved all the benchmarks within 2 s (see Fig. 5) regardless the preprocessing. We therefore exclude the results of ABC reverse from the charts showing RegexLib in Fig. 4, so that the impact of the preprocessing on the other checkers remains visible. The figures clearly show that checkers behave differently on different kinds of benchmarks, as discussed more in Sect. 6.2. The figures also show that the best times were almost always achieved with the preprocessing Up. Section 6.2 however shows that $UpDown$ actually often helps the individual checkers more.

6.2   Experiment "Individual Checkers"

Here we investigate the impact of the preprocessing on the individual checkers. The results are shown in Fig. 5 and Table 1. The figures indicate that the impact of the preprocessing as well as the overall performance varies significantly depending on the combination of a checker and benchmark.

On RegexLib, only Antichain and Bisimulation perform well, ABC struggles in both versions, and JAltImpact is not able to solve any examples, regardless the preprocessing. Preprocessing allows all checkers to solve more examples within the 15 s timeout (except JAltImpact). For antichain, Up is clearly very beneficial while $UpDown$ rather harms, but for the other checkers both $UpDown$ and Up can significantly improve performance. On LTL, all solvers perform quite well, preprocessing always reduces the number of timeouts and generally improves

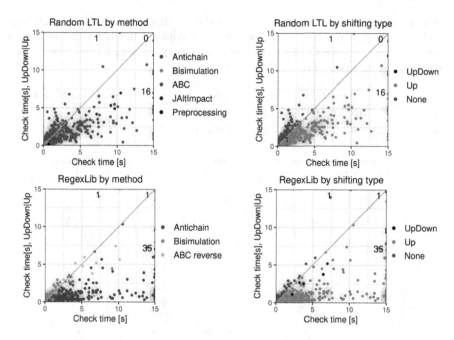

Fig. 4. The impact of preprocessing on the collective best time. The top graphs show results on LTL, the bottom on RegexLib. The results of ABC reverse are excluded from the RegexLib benchmark. The vertical axis is the time without preprocessing, the horizontal with *UpDown| Up*. The colour code on the left indicates the checker that achieved the best time (*Preprocessing* means that the case has been already decided in preprocessing, by replacing the initial state with 0 or 1), while on the right the colour indicates the preprocessing with which the best time was obtained: *UpDown*, *Up*, or *None* which means no preprocessing (recall that the input is already preprocessed using basic simplification).

running times, with the exception of ABC reverse which solves all examples within 2 s regardless preprocessing (the slightly worse time for ABC reverse with preprocessing is caused by the summation with the time of preprocessing, but the preprocessing does not harm its performance).

It is often the case that preprocessing can both improve and harm the performance significantly. We consider the mixed effect also a good news since it shows that preprocessing does have a large chance of improving the running time, gives a better chance of solving difficult examples, and offers a potential for portfolio solvers that run several algorithms in parallel. None of the two preprocessing variants, *UpDown* and *Up*, strictly supersedes the other. Although Fig. 4 and Fig. 5 favour mostly *Up* preprocessing, Fig. 6 indicates that *UpDown* preprocessing is superior to *Up* on RegexLib benchmarks using ABC model checker.

Table 1. Impact of preprocessing on the number of timeouts (15 ss). For each combination of checker and benchmark, we report a triple of numbers: the number of timeouts of the checker without preprocessing, with preprocessing by *UpDown| Up*, and the number of examples that timed out in both cases.

	Antichain	Bisim	ABC	ABC reverse	JAltImpact
LTL (13700)	303, 223, 183	530, 525, 519	56, 4, 3	0, 0, 0	133, 52, 52
RegexLib (1423)	188, 12, 12	120, 143, 112	1065, 1000, 984	107, 25, 17	1423, 1423, 1423

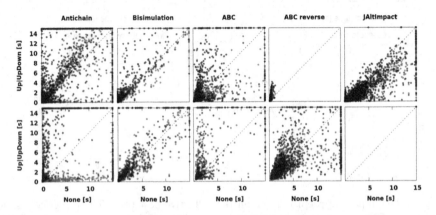

Fig. 5. Impact of preprocessing on individual checkers. The top row show results with LTL, the bottom row with RegexLib. The vertical axis is the time without preprocessing (in seconds), the horizontal with *UpDown| Up*. The colour of the dots indicates the preprocessing method which obtained the best time, blue for *UpDown* and red for *Up*.

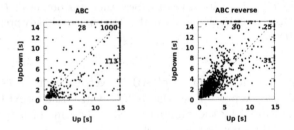

Fig. 6. RegexLib model checking time: comparison of *Up* and *UpDown*.

6.3   Parametric LTL Benchmarks

For the parametric benchmarks Lift and Counter, we measure the impact of preprocessing with increasing parameter on every combination of checker and preprocessing algorithm (none, *Up*, *UpDown*).

For Lift, only JAltImpact and ABC could handle more than 9 floors in the 15 s timeout. JAltImpact could handle about 80 floors, but ABC reverse outclassed any other method, and handled 200 floors in 0.3 s. The preprocessing slightly improved the running times of JAltImpact, by about 30%, but did not noticeably influence running times of ABC reverse or any other tool.

Much more exciting result was achieved by preprocessing on the parametric family Counter (a notoriously hard benchmark according to [13]). ABC again outperforms the other solvers by order of magnitude even in its slowest variant. Its running times with increasing parameter values are shown in Fig. 7. Without preprocessing, the best of the solvers, ABC reverse, can handle parameter values up to 290 in the 15 s timeout, however, with preprocessing by *Up*, ABC handles parameter values up to 500 in less than 2 s and ABC reverse in less than 1 s. ABC reverse performs similarly with *UpDown*.

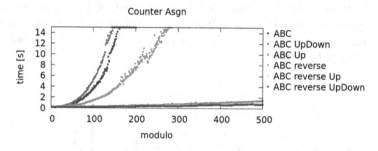

Fig. 7. The time taken by the variants of the ABC checker and of the preprocessing *Up* on AFA translated from parametric LTL_F formula Counter with increasing parameter.

A Note on the Running Time of Preprocessing. In all the experiments (Sects. 6.1, 6.2, and 6.3), the time taken by preprocessing is included in the overall time of testing emptiness. Preprocessing was taking time almost negligible compared to the time taken by the checkers on examples that took more than one second. In cases that took less than one second, the time of preprocessing was becoming comparable to that taken by the checkers. We note that the preprocessing is implemented as an unoptimised Haskell code and its running time can be probably much improved.

6.4   Basic Simplification

In this section, we briefly discuss the impact of basic simplification from Sect. 3. Although the performance of basic simplification was not our primary concern (recall that the experiments discussed above start from automata already processed by basic simplification), its impact on the performance of the checkers is quite significant and seems worth reporting on. Its impact on the best time of all checkers on the united benchmark LTL and RegexLib is shown in Fig. 8 on the left. Using basic simplification allowed the solvers to finish 118 more examples within the 15 s timeout.

As mentioned before, the techniques of Basic simplification cannot be claimed conceptually novel, and similar and even more sophisticated ones are used in

ABC [28]. Surprisingly, our particular implementation of these techniques is not superseded by ABC, and has a notable positive impact on its performance. This is shown in Fig. 8, the second and third graph from the left. Basic preprocessing allowed ABC to solve 113 more examples and reverse ABC solved 108 more examples with their help.

6.5 Impact of Preprocessing on Size of Automata

As shown in Fig. 9, for LTL benchmarks, the preprocessing often decreases the number of automata states, most often by about 25% and increases the number of DAG nodes and edges by about the same percentage. On the other hand, it changes these numbers rather slightly in the case of RegexLib benchmark. These numbers suggest that the impact on the solver performance is not only in decreasing the size of the formulae DAG or the number of states, but also in restructuring of the automaton.

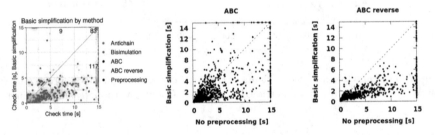

Fig. 8. Impact of the basic simplification in the united benchmarks RegexLib and LTL. Its impact on the best time of all checkers is shown on the left, the impact on the performance of ABC and reverse ABC is shown in the other two figures.

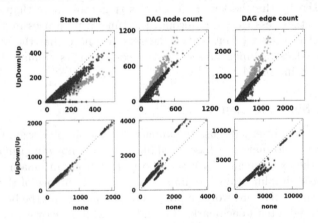

Fig. 9. Random LTL (row 1) and RegexLib (row 2) benchmarks: Impact of *Up* (red) and *UpDown* (blue) preprocessing on automaton size. (Color figure online)

References

1. RegexLib. http://www.regexlib.com/, http://www.regexlib.com/
2. Abdulla, P.A., et al.: Efficient handling of string-number conversion. In: PLDI 2020, pp. 943–957. ACM (2020)
3. Abdulla, P.A., Jonsson, B., Nilsson, M., d'Orso, J.: Regular model checking made simple and efficient. In: CONCUR 2002. LNCS, vol. 2421, pp. 116–130. Springer (2002)
4. Boigelot, B., Wolper, P.: Representing arithmetic constraints with finite automata: an overview. In: Stuckey, P.J. (ed.) ICLP 2002. LNCS, vol. 2401, pp. 1–20. Springer, Heidelberg (2002). https://doi.org/10.1007/3-540-45619-8_1
5. Boigelot, B., Wolper, P.: Representing arithmetic constraints with finite automata: an overview. In: Stuckey, P.J. (ed.) ICLP 2002. LNCS, vol. 2401, pp. 1–20. Springer, Heidelberg (2002). https://doi.org/10.1007/3-540-45619-8_1
6. Bouajjani, A., Jonsson, B., Nilsson, M., Touili, T.: Regular model checking. In: Emerson, E.A., Sistla, A.P. (eds.) CAV 2000. LNCS, vol. 1855, pp. 403–418. Springer, Heidelberg (2000). https://doi.org/10.1007/10722167_31
7. Bradley, A.R., Manna, Z.: Checking safety by inductive generalization of counterexamples to induction. In: FMCAD 2007, pp. 173–180. IEEE Computer Society (2007)
8. Brayton, R., Mishchenko, A.: ABC: an academic industrial-strength verification tool. In: Touili, T., Cook, B., Jackson, P. (eds.) CAV 2010. LNCS, vol. 6174, pp. 24–40. Springer, Heidelberg (2010). https://doi.org/10.1007/978-3-642-14295-6_5
9. Brzozowski, J.A.: Canonical regular expressions and minimal state graphs for definite events. In: Proceedings of the Symposium of Mathematical Theory of Automata, pp. 529–561 (1962)
10. Chandra, A.K., Kozen, D.C., Stockmeyer, L.J.: Alternation. J. ACM **28**(1), 114–133 (1981)
11. Cox, A.: Model checking regular expressions. In: Presented at MOSCA 2019 (2019). https://mosca19.github.io/slides/cox.pdf
12. Cox, A., Leasure, J.: Model checking regular language constraints. CoRR abs/1708.09073 (2017)
13. D'Antoni, L., Kincaid, Z., Wang, F.: A symbolic decision procedure for symbolic alternating finite automata. CoRR abs/1610.01722 (2016)
14. De Giacomo, G., Vardi, M.Y.: Linear temporal logic and linear dynamic logic on finite traces. In: IJCAI 2013, pp. 854–860. ACM (2013)
15. De Wulf, M., Doyen, L., Maquet, N., Raskin, J.-F.: Antichains: alternative algorithms for LTL satisfiability and model-checking. In: Ramakrishnan, C.R., Rehof, J. (eds.) TACAS 2008. LNCS, vol. 4963, pp. 63–77. Springer, Heidelberg (2008). https://doi.org/10.1007/978-3-540-78800-3_6
16. Fiedor, T., Holík, L., Janků, P., Lengál, O., Vojnar, T.: Lazy automata techniques for WS1S. In: Legay, A., Margaria, T. (eds.) TACAS 2017. LNCS, vol. 10205, pp. 407–425. Springer, Heidelberg (2017). https://doi.org/10.1007/978-3-662-54577-5_24
17. Finkbeiner, B., Sipma, H.: Checking finite traces using alternating automata. Formal Methods Syst. Des. **24**(2), 101–127 (2004)
18. Ganty, P., Maquet, N., Raskin, J.: Fixed point guided abstraction refinement for alternating automata. Theor. Comput. Sci. **411**(38–39), 3444–3459 (2010)
19. Harding, A.: Symbolic strategy synthesis for games with LTL winning conditions. Ph.D. thesis, University of Birmingham (2005)

20. Hassan, Z., Bradley, A.R., Somenzi, F.: Better generalization in IC3. In: FMCAD 2013, pp. 157–164. IEEE (2013)
21. Hoder, K., Bjørner, N.: Generalized property directed reachability. In: Cimatti, A., Sebastiani, R. (eds.) SAT 2012. LNCS, vol. 7317, pp. 157–171. Springer, Heidelberg (2012). https://doi.org/10.1007/978-3-642-31612-8_13
22. Holík, L., Janku, P., Lin, A.W., Rümmer, P., Vojnar, T.: String constraints with concatenation and transducers solved efficiently. In: Proceedings of the ACM Programming Language, vol. 2 (POPL) (2018)
23. Hurst, A.P., Mishchenko, A., Brayton, R.K.: Fast minimum-register retiming via binary maximum-flow. In: FMCAD 2007, pp. 181–187 (2007). https://doi.org/10.1109/FAMCAD.2007.31
24. Iosif, R., Xu, X.: Abstraction refinement for emptiness checking of alternating data automata. In: Beyer, D., Huisman, M. (eds.) TACAS 2018. LNCS, vol. 10806, pp. 93–111. Springer, Cham (2018). https://doi.org/10.1007/978-3-319-89963-3_6
25. Kupferman, O., Vardi, M.Y.: Weak alternating automata are not that weak. ACM Trans. Comput. Logic 2(3), 408–429 (2001)
26. Leiss, E.: Succinct representation of regular languages by Boolean automata. Theor. Comput. Sci. 13(3), 323–330 (1981)
27. McMillan, K.L.: Lazy abstraction with interpolants. In: Ball, T., Jones, R.B. (eds.) CAV 2006. LNCS, vol. 4144, pp. 123–136. Springer, Heidelberg (2006). https://doi.org/10.1007/11817963_14
28. Mishchenko, A., Chatterjee, S., Brayton, R.: DAG-aware AIG rewriting a fresh look at combinational logic synthesis. In: 2006 43rd ACM/IEEE Design Automation Conference (DAC 2006), pp. 532–535. ACM (2006)
29. Mishchenko, A., Chatterjee, S., Brayton, R.: Integrating logic synthesis, technology mapping, and retiming. In: Proceedings ot the IWLS 2005. Tech. rep., (2006)
30. Mishchenko, A., Een, N., Brayton, R., Baumgartner, J., Mony, H., Nalla, P.: Gla: gate-level abstraction revisited. In: DATE 2013, pp. 1399–1404. EDA Consortium (2013)
31. Robert, Y.S.H.A.M., Een, B.N.: Enhancing PDR/IC3 with localization abstraction
32. Rozier, K.Y., Vardi, M.Y.: LTL satisfiability checking. In: Bošnački, D., Edelkamp, S. (eds.) SPIN 2007. LNCS, vol. 4595, pp. 149–167. Springer, Heidelberg (2007). https://doi.org/10.1007/978-3-540-73370-6_11
33. Traytel, D.: A coalgebraic decision procedure for WS1S. In: CSL2015. LIPIcs, vol. 41, pp. 487–503. Schloss Dagstuhl - Leibniz-Zentrum fuer Informatik (2015)
34. Vardi, M.Y.: An automata-theoretic approach to linear temporal logic. In: Logics for Concurrency - Structure versus Automata, LNCS, vol. 1043, pp. 238–266. Springer, Berlin (1996).https://doi.org/10.1007/3-540-60915-6
35. Wang, H.-E., Tsai, T.-L., Lin, C.-H., Yu, F., Jiang, J.-H.R.: String analysis via automata manipulation with logic circuit representation. In: Chaudhuri, S., Farzan, A. (eds.) CAV 2016. LNCS, vol. 9779, pp. 241–260. Springer, Cham (2016). https://doi.org/10.1007/978-3-319-41528-4_13
36. Wolper, P.: On the use of automata for deciding linear arithmetic. In: Giese, M., Waaler, A. (eds.) TABLEAUX 2009. LNCS (LNAI), vol. 5607, pp. 16–16. Springer, Heidelberg (2009). https://doi.org/10.1007/978-3-642-02716-1_2
37. Wolper, P., Boigelot, B.: Verifying systems with infinite but regular state spaces. In: CAV 1998, pp. 88–97. Springer,Cham (1998)
38. De Wulf, M., Doyen, L., Henzinger, T.A., Raskin, J.-F.: Antichains: a new algorithm for checking universality of finite automata. In: Ball, T., Jones, R.B. (eds.) CAV 2006. LNCS, vol. 4144, pp. 17–30. Springer, Heidelberg (2006). https://doi.org/10.1007/11817963_5

Termination Analysis for the π-Calculus by Reduction to Sequential Program Termination

Tsubasa Shoshi[1]([✉])[ID], Takuma Ishikawa[1], Naoki Kobayashi[1][ID],
Ken Sakayori[1][ID], Ryosuke Sato[1][ID], and Takeshi Tsukada[2][ID]

[1] The University of Tokyo, Tokyo, Japan
shoshi@kb.is.s.u-tokyo.ac.jp
[2] Chiba University, Chiba, Japan

Abstract. We propose an automated method for proving termination of π-calculus processes, based on a reduction to termination of sequential programs: we translate a π-calculus process to a sequential program, so that the termination of the latter implies that of the former. We can then use an off-the-shelf termination verification tool to check termination of the sequential program. Our approach has been partially inspired by Deng and Sangiorgi's termination analysis for the π-calculus, and checks that there is no infinite chain of communications on replicated input channels, by converting such a chain of communications to a chain of recursive function calls in the target sequential program. We have implemented an automated tool based on the proposed method and confirmed its effectiveness.

1 Introduction

We propose a fully automated method for proving termination of π-calculus processes. Although there have been a lot of studies on termination analysis for the π-calculus and related calculi [11–13, 19, 25, 28, 29], most of them have been rather theoretical, and there have been surprisingly little efforts in developing fully automated termination verification methods and tools based on them. To our knowledge, Kobayashi's TyPiCal [18, 19] is the only exception that can prove termination of π-calculus processes (extended with natural numbers) fully automatically, but its termination analysis is quite limited (see Sect. 6).

Our method is based on a reduction to termination analysis for sequential programs: we translate a π-calculus process P to a sequential program S_P, so that if S_P is terminating, so is P. The reduction allows us to use powerful, mature methods and tools for termination analysis of sequential programs [7, 14, 17, 21, 23].

The idea of the translation is to convert a chain of communications on replicated input channels to a chain of recursive function calls of the target sequential program. Let us consider the following Fibonacci process:

© Springer Nature Switzerland AG 2021
H. Oh (Ed.): APLAS 2021, LNCS 13008, pp. 265–284, 2021.
https://doi.org/10.1007/978-3-030-89051-3_15

$* fib?(n, r).$**if** $n < 2$ **then** $r!(1)$
     else $(\nu s_1)(\nu s_2)(fib!(n - 1, s_1) \mid fib!(n - 2, s_2) \mid s_1?(x).s_2?(y).r!(x + y))$
$\mid fib!(m, r)$

Here, the process $*fib?(n, r)....$ is a function server that computes the n-th Fibonacci number in parallel and returns the result to r, and $fib!(m; r)$ sends a request for computing the m-th Fibonacci number; those who are not familiar with the syntax of the π-calculus may wish to consult Sect. 2 first. To prove that the process above is terminating for any integer m, it suffices to show that there is no infinite chain of communications on fib:

$$fib(m, r) \rightarrow fib(m_1, r_1) \rightarrow fib(m_2, r_2) \rightarrow \cdots .$$

We convert the process above to the following program:[1]

```
let rec fib(n) = if n<2 then () else (fib(n-1) [] fib(n-2)) in
fib(m)
```

Here, [] represents the non-deterministic choice. Note that, although the calculation of Fibonacci numbers is not preserved, for each chain of communications on fib, there is a corresponding sequence of recursive calls:

$$\texttt{fib}(m) \rightarrow \texttt{fib}(m_1) \rightarrow \texttt{fib}(m_2) \rightarrow \cdots .$$

Thus, the termination of the sequential program above implies the termination of the original process. As shown in the example above, (i) each communication on a replicated input channel is converted to a function call, (ii) each communication on a non-replicated input channel is just removed (or, in the actual translation, replaced by a call of a trivial function defined by $f(\tilde{x}) = ()$), and (iii) parallel composition is replaced by a non-deterministic choice. We formalize the translation outlined above and prove its correctness.

   The basic translation sketched above sometimes loses too much information. For example, consider the following process:

$* pred?(n, r).r!(n - 1)$
$\mid *f?(n, r).$**if** $n < 0$ **then** $r!(1)$ **else** $(\nu s)(pred!(n, s) \mid s?(x).f!(x, r))$
$\mid f!(m, r)$

The translation sketched above would yield:

```
let pred(n) = () in
let rec f(n) = if n<0 then () else (pred(n) [] f(*)) in
f(m)
```

---

[1] The actual translation given later is a little more complex.

Here, $*$ represents a non-deterministic integer: since we have removed the input $s?(x)$, we do not have information about the value of x. As a result, the sequential program above is non-terminating, although the original process is terminating. To remedy this problem, we also refine the basic translation above by using a refinement type system for the π-calculus. Using the refinement type system, we can infer that the value of x in the original process is less than n, so that we can refine the definition of f to:

```
let rec f(n) = ... else (pred(n) [] let x=* in assume(x<n);f(x))
```

The target program is now terminating, from which we can deduce that the original process is also terminating. We have implemented an automated tool based on the refined translation above.

The contributions of this paper are summarized as follows.

- The formalization of the basic translation from the π-calculus (extended with integers) to sequential programs, and a proof of its correctness.
- The formalization of a refined translation based on a refinement type system.
- An implementation of the refined translation, including automated refinement type inference based on CHC solving, and experiments to evaluate the effectiveness of our method.

The rest of this paper is structured as follows. Section 2 introduces the source and target languages of our translation. Section 3 formalizes the basic translation, and proves its correctness. Section 4 refines the basic translation by using a refinement type system. Section 5 reports an implementation and experiments. Section 6 discusses related work, and Sect. 7 concludes the paper.

2 Source and Target Languages

This section introduces the source and target languages for our reduction. The source language is the polyadic π-calculus [22] extended with integers and conditional expressions, and the target language is a first-order functional language with non-determinism.

2.1 π-Calculus

Syntax. Below we assume a countable set of variables ranged over by $x, y, z, w, \ldots$ and write $\mathbb{Z}$ for the set of integers, ranged over by i. We write $\tilde{\ }$ for (possibly empty) finite sequences; for example, $\tilde{x}$ abbreviates a sequence $x_1, \ldots, x_n$. We write $\mathrm{len}(\tilde{x})$ for the length of $\tilde{x}$ and ϵ for the empty sequence.

The sets of *processes* and *simple expressions*, ranged over by P and v respectively, are defined inductively by:

$$P \text{ (processes)} ::= \mathbf{0} \mid x!(\tilde{v}; \tilde{w}).P \mid x?(\tilde{y}; \tilde{z}).P \mid *x?(\tilde{y}; \tilde{z}).P \mid (P_1 \mid P_2) \mid (\nu x : \kappa)P$$
$$\mid \mathbf{if}\ v\ \mathbf{then}\ P_1\ \mathbf{else}\ P_2 \mid \mathbf{let}\ \tilde{x} = \tilde{*}\ \mathbf{in}\ P$$
$$v \text{ (simple expressions)} ::= x \mid i \mid op(\tilde{v})$$

The syntax of processes on the first line is fairly standard, except that the values sent along each channel consist of two parts: $\tilde{v}$ for integers, and $\tilde{w}$ for channels; this is for the sake of technical convenience in presenting the translation to sequential programs. The process $\mathbf{0}$ denotes an inaction, $x!(\tilde{v}; \tilde{w}).P$ sends a tuple $(\tilde{v}, \tilde{w})$ along the channel x and behaves like P, and the process $x?(\tilde{y}; \tilde{z}).P$ receives a tuple $(\tilde{v}, \tilde{w})$ along the channel x, and behaves like $[\tilde{v}/\tilde{y}, \tilde{w}/\tilde{z}]P$. We often just write $\tilde{v}$ for $\tilde{v}; \epsilon$ or $\epsilon; \tilde{v}$. The process $*x?(\tilde{y}; \tilde{z}).P$ represents infinitely many copies of $x?(\tilde{y}; \tilde{z}).P$ running in parallel. The process $P_1 \mid P_2$ runs P_1 and P_2 in parallel, and $(\nu x : \kappa)P$ creates a fresh channel x of type κ (where types will be introduced shortly) and behaves like P. The process **if** v **then** P_1 **else** P_2 executes P_1 if the value of v is non-zero, and P_2 otherwise. The process **let** $\tilde{x} = \tilde{*}$ **in** P instantiates the variables $\tilde{x}$ to some integer values in a non-deterministic manner, and then behaves like P. The meta-variable op ranges over integer operations such as $+$ or $\leq$.

The free and bound variables are defined as usual. The only binders are $(\nu x : \kappa)$ (which binds x), **let** $\tilde{x} = \tilde{*}$ **in** (which binds $\tilde{x}$), $x?(\tilde{y}; \tilde{z}).$ and $*x?(\tilde{y}; \tilde{z}).$ (which bind $\tilde{y}$ and $\tilde{z}$). Processes are identified up to renaming of bound variables, and we implicitly apply α-conversions as necessary.

We write $P \rightarrow Q$ for the standard one-step reduction relation on processes. The base cases of the communication are given by:

$$x?(\tilde{y}; \tilde{z}).P_1 \mid x!(\tilde{v}; \tilde{w}).P_2 \rightarrow [\tilde{i}/\tilde{y}, \tilde{w}/\tilde{z}]P_1 \mid P_2$$
$$*x?(\tilde{y}; \tilde{z}).P_1 \mid x!(\tilde{v}; \tilde{w}).P_2 \rightarrow *x?(\tilde{y}; \tilde{z}).P_1 \mid [\tilde{i}/\tilde{y}, \tilde{w}/\tilde{z}]P_1 \mid P_2$$

provided that $\tilde{v}$ evaluates to $\tilde{i}$. The full definition is given in the extended version [26]. We say that a process P is *terminating* if there is no infinite reduction sequence $P \rightarrow P_1 \rightarrow P_2 \rightarrow \cdots$.

In the rest of the paper, we consider only well-typed processes. We write ι for the type of integers. The set of channel types, ranged over by κ, is given by:

$$\kappa ::= \mathbf{ch}_\rho(\tilde{\iota}; \tilde{\kappa})$$

The type $\mathbf{ch}_\rho(\tilde{\iota}; \tilde{\kappa})$ describes channels used for transmitting a tuple $(\tilde{v}; \tilde{w})$ of integers $\tilde{v}$ and channels $\tilde{w}$ of types $\tilde{\kappa}$. Below we will just write $\tilde{\iota}$ for $\tilde{\iota}; \epsilon$ and $\tilde{\kappa}$ for $\epsilon; \tilde{\kappa}$. The subscript ρ, called a *region*, is a symbol that abstracts channels; it is used in the translation to sequential programs. For example, $\mathbf{ch}_{\rho_1}(\iota; \mathbf{ch}_{\rho_2}(\iota))$ is the type of channels that belong to the region ρ_1 and are used for transmitting a pair (i, r) where r is a channel of region ρ_2 used for transmitting integers. We use a meta-variable σ for an integer or channel type.

Type judgments for processes and simple expressions are of the form $\Gamma; \Delta \vdash P$ and $\Gamma; \Delta \vdash v : \sigma$, where Γ and Δ are sequences of bindings of the form $x : \iota$ and $x : \kappa$, respectively. The typing rules are shown in Fig. 1. Here $\Gamma; \Delta \vdash \tilde{v} : \tilde{\sigma}$ means $\Gamma; \Delta \vdash v_i : \sigma_i$ holds for each $i \in \{1, \ldots, \text{len}(\tilde{v})\}$. We omit the explanation of the typing rules as they are standard.

$$\frac{}{\Gamma; \Delta \vdash 0} \qquad \frac{\Gamma; \Delta \vdash v : \iota \qquad \Gamma; \Delta \vdash P_1 \qquad \Gamma; \Delta \vdash P_2}{\Gamma; \Delta \vdash \text{if } v \text{ then } P_1 \text{ else } P_2}$$

$$\frac{\Gamma; \Delta \vdash P_1 \qquad \Gamma; \Delta \vdash P_2}{\Gamma; \Delta \vdash P_1 \mid P_2} \qquad \frac{\Gamma; \Delta, x : \kappa \vdash P}{\Gamma; \Delta \vdash (\nu x : \kappa) P} \qquad \frac{\Gamma, \tilde{x} : \tilde{\iota}; \Delta \vdash P}{\Gamma; \Delta \vdash \text{let } \tilde{x} = \tilde{\star} \text{ in } P}$$

$$\frac{\Gamma; \Delta \vdash x : \mathbf{ch}_\rho(\tilde{\iota}; \tilde{\kappa}) \qquad \Gamma, \tilde{y} : \tilde{\iota}; \Delta, \tilde{z} : \tilde{\kappa} \vdash P}{\Gamma; \Delta \vdash x?(\tilde{y}; \tilde{z}).P}$$

$$\frac{\Gamma; \Delta \vdash x : \mathbf{ch}_\rho(\tilde{\iota}; \tilde{\kappa}) \qquad \Gamma; \Delta \vdash \tilde{v} : \tilde{\iota} \qquad \Gamma; \Delta \vdash \tilde{w} : \tilde{\kappa} \qquad \Gamma; \Delta \vdash P}{\Gamma; \Delta \vdash x!(\tilde{v}; \tilde{w}).P}$$

$$\frac{\Gamma; \Delta \vdash x : \mathbf{ch}_\rho(\tilde{\iota}; \tilde{\kappa}) \qquad \Gamma, \tilde{y} : \tilde{\iota}; \Delta, \tilde{z} : \tilde{\kappa} \vdash P}{\Gamma; \Delta \vdash *x?(\tilde{y}; \tilde{z}).P}$$

$$\frac{x : \iota \in \Gamma}{\Gamma; \Delta \vdash x : \iota} \qquad \frac{x : \kappa \in \Delta}{\Gamma; \Delta \vdash x : \kappa} \qquad \frac{}{\Gamma; \Delta \vdash i : \iota} \qquad \frac{\Gamma; \Delta \vdash \tilde{v} : \tilde{\iota}}{\Gamma; \Delta \vdash op(\tilde{v}) : \iota}$$

Fig. 1. The typing rules of the simple type system for the π-calculus

2.2 Sequential Language

We define the target language of our translation, which is a first-order functional language with non-determinism.

A *program* is a pair $(\mathcal{D}, E)$ consisting of (a set of) *function definitions* $\mathcal{D}$ and an *expression* E, defined by:

$$\mathcal{D} \text{ (function definitions)} :: = \{f_1(\tilde{x}_1) = E_1, \ldots, f_n(\tilde{x}_n) = E_n\}$$
$$E \text{ (expression)} :: = () \mid \text{let } \tilde{x} = \tilde{\star} \text{ in } E \mid f(\tilde{v}) \mid E_1 \oplus E_2$$
$$\mid \text{if } v \text{ then } E_1 \text{ else } E_2 \mid \mathbf{Assume}(v); E$$
$$v \text{ (simple expressions)} :: = x \mid i \mid op(\tilde{v})$$

In a function definition $f_i(x_1, \ldots, x_{k_i}) = E_i$, the variables $x_1, \ldots, x_{k_i}$ are bound in E_i; we identify function definitions up to renaming of bound variables, and implicitly apply α-conversions. The function names $f_1, \ldots, f_n$ need not be distinct from each other. If there are more than one definition for f, then one of the definitions will be non-deterministically used when f is called. We explain the informal meanings of the non-standard expressions. The expression $\text{let } \tilde{x} = \tilde{\star} \text{ in } E$ instantiates $\tilde{x}$ to some integers in a non-deterministic manner. The expression $E_1 \oplus E_2$ non-deterministically evaluates to E_1 or E_2. The expression $\mathbf{Assume}(v); E$ evaluates to E if v is non-zero; otherwise the whole program is aborted. The other expressions are standard and their meanings should be clear.

We write $(\mathcal{D}, E) \rightsquigarrow (\mathcal{D}, E')$ for the one-step reduction relation, whose definition is given in the extended version [26]. We say that a program is terminating if there is no infinite reduction sequence.

3 Basic Transformation

This section presents our transformation from a π-calculus process to a sequential program, so that if the transformed program is terminating then the original process is terminating.

As explained in Sect. 1, the idea is to transform an infinite chain of message passing on replicated input channels to an infinite chain of recursive function calls. Table 1 summarizes the correspondence between processes and sequential programs. As shown in the table, a replicated input process is transformed to a function definition, whereas a non-replicated input process is just ignored, and integer bound variables are non-deterministically instantiated. Note that channel arguments $\tilde{z}$ are ignored in both cases. Instead, we prepare a global function name f_ρ for each region ρ; ρ_x in the table indicates the region assigned to the channel type of x.[2]

Table 1. Correspondence between processes and sequential programs

Processes	Sequential programs
Replicated input $(*x?(\tilde{y}; \tilde{z}). \cdots)$	Function definition $f_{\rho_x}(\tilde{y}) = \cdots$
Non-replicated input $(x?(\tilde{y}; \tilde{z}). \cdots)$	Non-deterministic instantiation $(\textbf{let } \tilde{y} = \tilde{*} \textbf{ in } \cdots)$
Output $(x!(\tilde{v}; \tilde{w}). \cdots)$	Function call $(f_{\rho_x}(\tilde{v}) \oplus \cdots)$
Parallel composition $(\cdots \mid \cdots)$	Non-deterministic choice $(\cdots \oplus \cdots)$

We define the transformation relation $\Gamma; \Delta \vdash P \Rightarrow (\mathcal{D}, E)$, which means that the π-calculus process P well-typed under $\Gamma; \Delta$ is transformed to the sequential program $(\mathcal{D}, E)$. The relation is defined by the rules in Fig. 2.

We explain some key rules. In SX-NIL, **0** is translated to $(\mathcal{D}, (\,))$, where $\mathcal{D}$ is the set of trivial function definitions. In SX-IN, a (non-replicated) input is just removed, and the bound variables are instantiated to non-deterministic integers; this is because we have no information about $\tilde{y}$; this will be refined in Sect. 4. In contrast, in SX-RIN, a replicated input is converted to a function definition. Since $\mathcal{D}$ generated from P may contain $\tilde{y}$, they are bound to non-deterministic integers and merged with the new definition for f_ρ. In SX-OUT, an output is replaced by a function call. In SX-PAR, parallel composition is replaced by non-deterministic choice.

Example 1. Let us revisit the Fibonacci example used in the introduction to explain the actual translation. Using the syntax we introduced, the Fibonacci process P_{fib} can now be defined as:

---

[2] Thus, the simple type system with "regions" introduced in the previous section is used here as a simple may-alias analysis. If x and y may be bound to the same channel during reductions, the type system assigns the same region to x and y, hence x and y are mapped to the same function name f_{ρ_x} by our transformation.

$$\frac{}{\Gamma; \Delta \vdash \mathbf{0} \Rightarrow (\{f_\rho(\tilde{y}) = () \mid x : \mathbf{ch}_\rho(\tilde{\iota}; \tilde{\kappa}) \in \Delta, \mathrm{len}(\tilde{y}) = \mathrm{len}(\tilde{\iota})\}, ())} \quad \text{(SX-Nil)}$$

$$\frac{\Gamma; \Delta \vdash x : \mathbf{ch}_\rho(\tilde{\iota}; \tilde{\kappa}) \qquad \Gamma, \tilde{y} : \tilde{\iota}; \Delta, \tilde{z} : \tilde{\kappa} \vdash P \Rightarrow (\mathcal{D}, E)}{\Gamma; \Delta \vdash x?(\tilde{y}; \tilde{z}).P \Rightarrow (\mathbf{let}\ \tilde{y} = \tilde{\star}\ \mathbf{in}\ \mathcal{D}, \mathbf{let}\ \tilde{y} = \tilde{\star}\ \mathbf{in}\ E)} \quad \text{(SX-In)}$$

$$\frac{\Gamma; \Delta \vdash x : \mathbf{ch}_\rho(\tilde{\iota}; \tilde{\kappa}) \qquad \Gamma, \tilde{y} : \tilde{\iota}; \Delta, \tilde{z} : \tilde{\kappa} \vdash P \Rightarrow (\mathcal{D}, E)}{\Gamma; \Delta \vdash *x?(\tilde{y}; \tilde{z}).P \Rightarrow (\{f_\rho(\tilde{y}) = E\} \cup (\mathbf{let}\ \tilde{y} = \tilde{\star}\ \mathbf{in}\ \mathcal{D}), ())} \quad \text{(SX-RIn)}$$

$$\frac{\Gamma; \Delta \vdash x : \mathbf{ch}_\rho(\tilde{\iota}; \tilde{\kappa}) \qquad \Gamma; \Delta \vdash \tilde{v} : \tilde{\iota} \qquad \Gamma; \Delta \vdash \tilde{w} : \tilde{\kappa} \qquad \Gamma; \Delta \vdash P \Rightarrow (\mathcal{D}, E)}{\Gamma; \Delta \vdash x!(\tilde{v}; \tilde{w}).P \Rightarrow (\mathcal{D}, f_\rho(\tilde{v}) \oplus E)} \quad \text{(SX-Out)}$$

$$\frac{\Gamma; \Delta \vdash P_1 \Rightarrow (\mathcal{D}_1, E_1) \qquad \Gamma; \Delta \vdash P_2 \Rightarrow (\mathcal{D}_2, E_2)}{\Gamma; \Delta \vdash P_1 \mid P_2 \Rightarrow (\mathcal{D}_1 \cup \mathcal{D}_2, E_1 \oplus E_2)} \quad \text{(SX-Par)}$$

$$\frac{\Gamma; \Delta, x : \kappa \vdash P \Rightarrow (\mathcal{D}, E)}{\Gamma; \Delta \vdash (\nu x : \kappa)P \Rightarrow (\mathcal{D}, E)} \quad \text{(SX-Nu)}$$

$$\frac{\Gamma; \Delta \vdash v : \iota \qquad \Gamma; \Delta \vdash P_1 \Rightarrow (\mathcal{D}_1, E_1) \qquad \Gamma; \Delta \vdash P_2 \Rightarrow (\mathcal{D}_2, E_2)}{\Gamma; \Delta \vdash \mathbf{if}\ v\ \mathbf{then}\ P_1\ \mathbf{else}\ P_2 \Rightarrow (\mathcal{D}_1 \cup \mathcal{D}_2, \mathbf{if}\ v\ \mathbf{then}\ E_1\ \mathbf{else}\ E_2)} \quad \text{(SX-If)}$$

$$\frac{\Gamma, \tilde{x} : \tilde{\iota}; \Delta \vdash P \Rightarrow (\mathcal{D}, E)}{\Gamma; \Delta \vdash \mathbf{let}\ \tilde{x} = \tilde{\star}\ \mathbf{in}\ P \Rightarrow (\mathbf{let}\ \tilde{x} = \tilde{\star}\ \mathbf{in}\ \mathcal{D}, \mathbf{let}\ \tilde{x} = \tilde{\star}\ \mathbf{in}\ E)} \quad \text{(SX-LetND)}$$

$$\mathbf{let}\ \tilde{x} = \tilde{\star}\ \mathbf{in}\ \mathcal{D} := \{f(\tilde{y}) = (\mathbf{let}\ \tilde{x} = \tilde{\star}\ \mathbf{in}\ E) \mid f(\tilde{y}) = E \in \mathcal{D}\}$$

Fig. 2. The rules of simple type-based program transformation

$$(\nu fib : \mathbf{ch}_{\rho_1}(\iota; \mathbf{ch}_{\rho_2}(\iota))) * fib?(n; r).$$
$$\mathbf{if}\ n < 2\ \mathbf{then}\ r!(1)\ \mathbf{else}\ (\nu r_1 : \mathbf{ch}_{\rho_2}(\iota))(\nu r_2 : \mathbf{ch}_{\rho_2}(\iota))$$
$$(fib!(n - 1; r_1) \mid fib!(n - 2; r_2) \mid r_1?(x).r_2?(y).r!(x + y))$$
$$\mid \mathbf{let}\ m = \star\ \mathbf{in}\ (\nu r : \mathbf{ch}_{\rho_2}(\iota))fib!(m; r)$$

Note that (νfib) and $\mathbf{let}\ m = \star\ \mathbf{in}$ have been added to close the process. We can derive $\emptyset; \emptyset \vdash P_{\mathrm{fib}} \Rightarrow (\mathcal{D}, E)$, where $\mathcal{D}$ and E are given as follows:[3]

$$\mathcal{D} = \{f_{\rho_1}(z) = \mathbf{if}\ z < 2\ \mathbf{then}\ f_{\rho_2}(1)\ \mathbf{else}\ (f_{\rho_1}(z - 1) \oplus f_{\rho_1}(z - 2)$$
$$\oplus \mathbf{let}\ x = \star\ \mathbf{in}\ \mathbf{let}\ y = \star\ \mathbf{in}\ f_{\rho_2}(x + y)),$$
$$f_{\rho_2}(z) = ()\}$$
$$E = \mathbf{let}\ m = \star\ \mathbf{in}\ f_{\rho_1}(m)$$

---

[3] The program written here has been simplified for the sake of readability. For instance, we removed some redundant (), trivial function definitions, and unused non-deterministic integers. The other examples that will appear in this paper are also simplified in the same way.

Here f_{ρ_1} is the "Fibonacci function" because ρ_1 is the region assigned to the channel fib in P_{fib}. The function call $f_{\rho_2}(x+y)$ corresponds to the output $r!(x+y)$; the argument of the function call is actually a nondeterministic integer because $r?(x)$ and $r?(y)$ are translated to non-deterministic instantiations. Since the program $(\mathcal{D}, E)$ is terminating, we can verify that P_{fib} is also terminating.   □

Example 2. To help readers understand the rule SX-RIN, we consider the following process, which contains a nested input:

$$*f?(x;r). *g?(y,z).(\text{if } y \leq 0 \text{ then } r!(z) \text{ else } g!(y-1,x+z)) \mid f!(2;r).g!(3,0)$$

where $f : \mathbf{ch}_{\rho_1}(\iota; \mathbf{ch}_{\rho_2}(\iota))$ and $g : \mathbf{ch}_{\rho_3}(\iota, \iota)$. This process computes $x*y+z$ (which is 6 in this case) and returns that value using r. This program is translated to:

$$f_{\rho_1}(x) = ()   \quad f_{\rho_2}(z) = ()$$
$$f_{\rho_3}(y,z) = \text{let } x = \star \text{ in if } y \leq 0 \text{ then } f_{\rho_2}(z) \text{ else } f_{\rho_3}(y-1,x+z)$$

with the main expression $f_{\rho_1}(2) \oplus f_{\rho_3}(3,0)$. Note that the body of f_{ρ_1}, which is the function corresponding to f, is $()$. This is because when the rule SX-RIN is applied to $*g?(y,z)\ldots$, the main expression of the translated program becomes $()$. Observe that the function definition for f_{ρ_3} still contains a free variable x at this moment. Then f_{ρ_3} is closed by $\text{let } x = \star \text{ in}$ when we apply the rule SX-RIN to $*f?(x;r)\ldots$. We can check that the above program is terminating, and thus we can verify that the original process is terminating. Note that some precision is lost in the application of SX-RIN above since we cannot track the relation between the argument of f_{ρ_1} and the value of x used inside f_{ρ_3}. This loss causes a problem if, for example, the condition $y \leq 0$ in the process above is replaced with $y \leq x$. The body of f_{ρ_3} would then become $\text{let } x = \star \text{ in if } y \leq x \cdots$, hence the sequential program would be non-terminating.   □

Remark 1. A reader may wonder why a non-replicated input is removed in SX-IN, rather than translated to a function definition as done for a replicated input. It is actually possible to obtain a sound transformation even if we treat non-replicated inputs in the same manner as replicated inputs, but we expect that our approach of removing non-replicated inputs often works better. For example, consider $x?(y).x!(y) \mid x!(0)$. Our translation generates $(\{f_{\rho_x}(z) = ()\}, (\text{let } y = \star \text{ in } f_{\rho_x}(y)) \oplus f_{\rho_x}(0))$ which is terminating, whereas if we treat the input in the same way as a replicated input, we would obtain $(\{f_{\rho_x}(z) = f_{\rho_x}(z)\}, f_{\rho_x}(0))$ which is not terminating. Our approach also has some defect. For example, consider $x!(0) \mid x?(y).\text{if } y = 0 \text{ then } \mathbf{0} \text{ else } \Omega$ where Ω is a diverging process. Our translation yields $(\{f_{\rho_x}(z) = ()\}, f_{\rho_x}(0) \oplus \text{let } y = \star \text{ in if } y = 0 \text{ then } () \text{ else } \Omega')$ which is non-terminating. On the other hand, if we treat the input like a replicated input, we would obtain $(\{f_{\rho_x}(z) = \text{if } z = 0 \text{ then } () \text{ else } \Omega'\}, f_{\rho_x}(0))$ which is terminating. This issue can, however, be mitigated by the extension with refinement types in Sect. 4. Our choice of removing non-replicated inputs is also consistent with Deng and Sangiorgi's type system [13], which prevents an infinite chain of communications on replicated input channels by using types and ignores non-replicated inputs.   □

The following theorem states the soundness of our transformation.

Theorem 1 (soundness). *Suppose* $\emptyset; \emptyset \vdash P \Rightarrow (\mathcal{D}, E)$*. If* $(\mathcal{D}, E)$ *is terminating, then so is* P*.*

We briefly explain the proof strategy; see the extended version [26] for the actual proof. Basically, our idea is to show that the translated program simulates the original process. Then we can conclude that if the original process is non-terminating then so is the sequential program. However, there is a slight mismatch between the reduction of a process and that of the sequential program that we need to overcome. Recall that $*f?(x).P \mid f!(1) \mid f!(2)$ is translated to $f_{\rho_f}(1) \oplus f_{\rho_f}(2)$ with a function definition for f_{ρ_f}. In the sequential program, we need to make a "choice", e.g. if $f_{\rho_f}(1)$ is called, we cannot call $f_{\rho_f}(2)$ anymore. On the other hand, the output $f!(2)$ can be used even if $f!(1)$ has been used before. To fill this gap, we introduce a non-standard reduction relation, which does not discard branches of non-deterministic choices and show the simulation relation using that non-standard semantics. Then we show that if there is an infinite non-standard reduction sequence, then there is an infinite subsequence that corresponds to a reduction along a certain choice of non-deterministic branches. This step is essentially a corollary of the König's Lemma. This is because the infinite non-standard reduction sequence can be reformulated as an infinite tree in which branches correspond to non-deterministic choices $\oplus$ (thus the tree is finitely branching) and paths correspond to reduction sequences.

The following example indicates that the basic transformation is sometimes too conservative.

Example 3. Let us consider the following process P_{dec}:

$* \, pred?(n; r).r!(n - 1)$

$\mid *f?(n; r).\textbf{if } n < 0 \textbf{ then } r!(1) \textbf{ else } (\nu s : \textbf{ch}_{\rho_2}(\iota))(pred!(n; s) \mid s?(x).f!(x; r))$

$\mid f!(m; r)$

where $pred : \textbf{ch}_{\rho_1}(\iota; \textbf{ch}_{\rho_2}(\iota))$, $f : \textbf{ch}_{\rho_3}(\iota; \textbf{ch}_{\rho_4}(\iota))$ and $r : \textbf{ch}_{\rho_4}(\iota)$. This process, which also appeared in the introduction, keeps on decrementing the integer m until it gets negative and then returns 1 via r. We can turn this process into a closed process P'_{dec} by restricting the names $pred$, f, r and adding $\textbf{let } m = \star \textbf{ in}$ in front of the process. Note that P'_{dec} is terminating.

The process P'_{dec} is translated to:

$$f_{\rho_1}(n) = f_{\rho_2}(n - 1), \qquad f_{\rho_2}(x) = (\,), \qquad f_{\rho_4}(x) = (\,),$$
$$f_{\rho_3}(n) = \textbf{if } n < 0 \textbf{ then } f_{\rho_4}(1)$$
$$\textbf{else } (f_{\rho_1}(n) \oplus \textbf{let } x = \star \textbf{ in } f_{\rho_3}(x))$$

with the main expression $\textbf{let } m = \star \textbf{ in } f_{\rho_3}(m)$. Observe that the function f_{ρ_3} is applied to a non-deterministic integer, not $n - 1$. Thus, this program is not terminating, meaning that we fail to verify that the original process is terminating. This is due to the shortcoming of our transformation that all the integer values received by non-replicated inputs are replaced by non-deterministic integers. This problem is addressed in the next section. □

4 Improving Transformation Using Refinement Types

In this section, we refine the basic transformation in the previous section by using a refinement type system.

Recall that in Example 3, the problem was that information about values received by non-replicated inputs was completely lost. By using a refinement type system for the π-calculus, we can statically infer that $x < n$ holds between x and n in the process in Example 3. Using that information, we can transform the process in Example 3 and obtain

$$f_{\rho_3}(n) = \textbf{if } n < 0 \textbf{ then } \cdots \textbf{ else } (f_{\rho_1}(n) \oplus \textbf{let } x = \star \textbf{ in Assume}(x < n); f_{\rho_3}(x))$$

for the definition of f_{ρ_3}. This is sufficient to conclude that the resulting program is terminating.

In the rest of this section, we first introduce a refinement type system in Sect. 4.1 and explain the refined transformation in Sect. 4.2. We then discuss how to automatically infer refinement types and achieve the refined transformation in Sect. 4.3.

4.1 Refinement Type System

The set of *refinement channel types*, ranged over by κ, is given by:

$$\kappa ::= \textbf{ch}_\rho(\tilde{x}; \phi; \tilde{\kappa})$$

Here, ϕ is a formula of integer arithmetic. We sometimes write just $\textbf{ch}_\rho(\tilde{x}; \phi)$ for $\textbf{ch}_\rho(\tilde{x}; \phi; \epsilon)$. Intuitively, $\textbf{ch}_\rho(\tilde{x}; \phi; \tilde{\kappa})$ describes channels that are used for transmitting a tuple $(\tilde{x}; \tilde{y})$ such that (i) $\tilde{x}$ are integers that satisfy ϕ, and (ii) $\tilde{y}$ are channels of types $\tilde{\kappa}$. For example, the type $\textbf{ch}_{\rho_1}(x; \textbf{true}; \textbf{ch}_{\rho_2}(z; z < x))$ describes channels used for transmitting a pair (x, y), where x may be any integer, and y must be a channel of type $\textbf{ch}_{\rho_2}(z; z < x)$, i.e., a channel used for passing an integer z smaller than x. Thus, if u has type $\textbf{ch}_{\rho_1}(x; \textbf{true}; \textbf{ch}_{\rho_2}(z; z < x))$, then the process $u?(n; r).r!(n-1)$ is allowed but $u?(n; r).r!(n)$ is not.

Type judgments for processes and expressions are now of the form $\Gamma; \Phi; \Delta \vdash P$ and $\Gamma; \Phi; \Delta \vdash v : \sigma$, where Φ is a sequence of formulas. Intuitively, $\Gamma; \Phi; \Delta \vdash P$ means that P is well-typed under the environments Γ and Δ assuming that all the formulas in Φ holds.

The selected typing rules are shown in Fig. 3. The rules for the other constructs are identical to that of the simple type system; the complete list of typing rules appears in the extended version [26]. The rules shown in Fig. 3 are fairly standard rules for refinement type systems. In RT-OUT, the notation $\Phi \vDash \phi$ means that ϕ is a logical consequence of Φ; for example, $x < y, y < z \vDash x < z$ holds. In the typing rules, we implicitly require that all the type judgments are well-formed, in the sense that all the integer variables occurring in a formula is properly declared in Γ or bound by a channel type constructor; see the extended version [26] for the well-formedness condition.

$$\frac{\Gamma;\Phi;\Delta \vdash x : \mathbf{ch}_\rho(\tilde{y};\phi;\tilde{\kappa}) \qquad \Gamma,\tilde{y}:\tilde{\iota};\Phi,\phi;\Delta,\tilde{z}:\tilde{\kappa} \vdash P}{\Gamma;\Phi;\Delta \vdash x?(\tilde{y};\tilde{z}).P} \qquad \text{(RT-In)}$$

$$\frac{\Gamma;\Phi;\Delta \vdash x : \mathbf{ch}_\rho(\tilde{y};\phi;\tilde{\kappa}) \qquad \Gamma;\Phi;\Delta \vdash \tilde{v}:\tilde{\iota} \qquad \Phi \models [\tilde{v}/\tilde{y}]\phi}{\Gamma;\Phi;\Delta \vdash \tilde{w} : [\tilde{v}/\tilde{y}]\tilde{\kappa} \qquad \Gamma;\Phi;\Delta \vdash P}{\Gamma;\Phi;\Delta \vdash x!(\tilde{v};\tilde{w}).P} \qquad \text{(RT-Out)}$$

$$\frac{\Gamma;\Phi;\Delta \vdash x : \mathbf{ch}_\rho(\tilde{y};\phi;\tilde{\kappa}) \qquad \Gamma,\tilde{y}:\tilde{\iota};\Phi,\phi;\Delta,\tilde{z}:\tilde{\kappa} \vdash P}{\Gamma;\Phi;\Delta \vdash *x?(\tilde{y};\tilde{z}).P} \qquad \text{(RT-RIn)}$$

$$\frac{\Gamma;\Phi;\Delta \vdash v:\iota \qquad \Gamma;\Phi,v \neq 0;\Delta \vdash P_1 \qquad \Gamma;\Phi,v = 0;\Delta \vdash P_2}{\Gamma;\Phi;\Delta \vdash \mathbf{if}\ v\ \mathbf{then}\ P_1\ \mathbf{else}\ P_2} \qquad \text{(RT-If)}$$

$$\frac{x:\kappa \in \Delta}{\Gamma;\Phi;\Delta \vdash x:\kappa} \qquad \text{(RT-Var-Ch)}$$

Fig. 3. Selected typing rules of the refinement type system for the π-calculus

4.2 Program Transformation

Based on the refinement type system above, we refine the transformation relation to $\Gamma;\Phi;\Delta \vdash P \Rightarrow (\mathcal{D},E)$. The only change is in the following rule for non-replicated inputs.[4]

$$\frac{\Gamma;\Phi;\Delta \vdash x : \mathbf{ch}_\rho(\tilde{y};\phi;\tilde{\kappa}) \qquad \Gamma,\tilde{y}:\tilde{\iota};\Phi,\phi;\Delta,\tilde{z}:\tilde{\kappa} \vdash P \Rightarrow (\mathcal{D},E)}{\Gamma;\Phi;\Delta \vdash x?(\tilde{y};\tilde{z}).P} \qquad \text{(RX-In)}$$
$$\Rightarrow (\mathbf{let}\ \tilde{y} = \tilde{*}\ \mathbf{in}\ \mathbf{Assume}(\phi);\mathcal{D}, \mathbf{let}\ \tilde{y} = \tilde{*}\ \mathbf{in}\ \mathbf{Assume}(\phi);E)$$

Here, we insert $\mathbf{Assume}(\phi)$, based on the refinement type of x. The expression $\mathbf{let}\ \tilde{y} = \tilde{*}\ \mathbf{in}\ \mathbf{Assume}(\phi);E$ first instantiates $\tilde{y}$ to some integers in a non-deterministic manner, but proceeds to evaluate E only if the values of $\tilde{y}$ satisfy ϕ. Thus, the termination analysis for the target sequential program may assume that $\tilde{y}$ satisfies ϕ in E.

Example 4. Let us explain how the process P_{dec} introduced in Example 3 is translated by the refined translation. Recall that the following simple types were assigned to the channels:

$$pred : \mathbf{ch}_{\rho_1}(\iota;\mathbf{ch}_{\rho_2}(\iota)), \quad f : \mathbf{ch}_{\rho_3}(\iota;\mathbf{ch}_{\rho_4}(\iota)), \quad r : \mathbf{ch}_{\rho_4}(\iota), \quad s : \mathbf{ch}_{\rho_2}(\iota).$$

By the refinement type system, the above types can be refined as:

$$pred : \mathbf{ch}_{\rho_1}(n;\mathbf{true};\mathbf{ch}_{\rho_2}(x;x < n)), \quad f : \mathbf{ch}_{\rho_3}(n;\mathbf{true};\mathbf{ch}_{\rho_4}(x;\mathbf{true})),$$
$$r : \mathbf{ch}_{\rho_4}(x;\mathbf{true}), \quad s : \mathbf{ch}_{\rho_2}(x;x < n).$$

For example, one can check that the output $r!(n-1)$ on the first line of P_{dec} is well-typed because $\models [n-1/x]x < n$ holds. Note that this r is the variable bound by $pred?(n;r)$ and thus has the type $\mathbf{ch}_{\rho_2}(x;x < n)$.

---

[4] The rule for replicated inputs is also modified in a similar manner.

Therefore, by the rule RX-IN, the input $s?(x).f!(x;r)$ is now translated as follows:

$$\frac{\Gamma; \Phi; \Delta \vdash s : \mathbf{ch}_{\rho_2}(x; x < n) \quad \Gamma, x : \iota; \Phi, x < n; \Delta \vdash f!(x;r) \Rightarrow (\mathcal{D}, f_{\rho_3}(x))}{\Gamma; \Phi; \Delta \vdash s?(x).f!(x;r)}$$
$$\Rightarrow ((\mathbf{let} \ x = \star \ \mathbf{in} \ \mathbf{Assume}(x < n); \mathcal{D}), (\mathbf{let} \ x = \star \ \mathbf{in} \ \mathbf{Assume}(x < n); f_{\rho_3}(x)))$$

with suitable Γ, Φ and Δ. By translating the whole process, we obtain

$$f_{\rho_3}(n) = \mathbf{if} \ n < 0 \ \mathbf{then} \ f_{\rho_4}(1)$$
$$\mathbf{else} \ (f_{\rho_1}(n) \oplus \mathbf{let} \ x = \star \ \mathbf{in} \ \mathbf{Assume}(x < n); f_{\rho_3}(x))$$

as desired. The other function definitions are given as in the case of Example 3 (except for the fact that some redundant assertions $\mathbf{let} \ x = \star \ \mathbf{in} \ \mathbf{Assume}(x < n)$ are added).   □

The soundness of the refined translation is obtained from the following argument. We first extend the π-calculus with the **Assume** statement. Then the refined translation can be decomposed into the following two steps: (a) given a π-calculus process P, insert **Assume** statements based on refinement types and obtain a process P'; and (b) apply the translation of Sect. 3 to P' (where **Assume** is just mapped to itself) and obtain a sequential program S. The soundness of step (b) follows by an easy modification of the proof for the basic transformation (just add the case for **Assume**). So, the termination of S would imply that of P'. Now, from the soundness of the refinement type system (which follows from a standard argument on type preservation and progress), it follows that the **Assume** statements inserted in step (a) always succeed. Thus, the termination of P' would imply that of P. We can, therefore, conclude that if S is terminating, so is P.

4.3   Type Inference

This section discusses how to infer refinement types automatically to automatically achieve the transformation. As in refinement type inference for functional programs [5, 24, 27], we can reduce refinement type inference for the π-calculus to the problem of CHC (Constrained Horn Clauses) solving [4].

We explain the procedure through an example. Once again, we use the process P_{dec} introduced in Example 3. We first perform type inference for the simple type system in Sect. 2, and (as we have seen) obtain the following simple types for *pred* and f:

$$pred : \mathbf{ch}_{\rho_1}(\iota; \mathbf{ch}_{\rho_2}(\iota)), \quad f : \mathbf{ch}_{\rho_3}(\iota; \mathbf{ch}_{\rho_4}(\iota))$$

Here, we have omitted the types for other (bound) channels r, s, as they can be determined based on those of *pred* and f. Based on the simple types, we prepare the following templates for refinement types.

$$pred : \mathbf{ch}_{\rho_1}(n; P_1(n); \mathbf{ch}_{\rho_2}(x; P_2(n, x))), \quad f : \mathbf{ch}_{\rho_3}(n; P_3(n); \mathbf{ch}_{\rho_4}(x; P_4(n, x))).$$

Here, P_i ($i \in \{1, \ldots, 4\}$) is a predicate variable that represents unknown conditions.

Based on the refinement type system, we can generate the following constraints on the predicate variables.

$$\forall n.(P_1(n) \implies P_2(n, n-1)) \qquad \forall n.(P_3(n) \wedge n < 0 \implies P_4(n, 1))$$
$$\forall n.(P_3(n) \wedge n \geq 0 \implies P_1(n))$$
$$\forall n, x.(P_3(n) \wedge n \geq 0 \wedge P_2(n, x) \implies P_3(x))$$
$$\forall m.(\mathbf{true} \implies P_3(m))$$

Here, the first constraint comes from the first line of the process, and the second constraint (the third and fourth constraints, resp.) comes from the then-part (the else-part, resp.) of the second line of the process. The last constraint comes from $f!(m; r)$.

The generated constraints are in general a set of *Constrained Horn Clauses* (CHCs) [4] of the form $\forall \tilde{x}.(P_1(\tilde{v}_1) \wedge \cdots \wedge P_k(\tilde{v}_k) \wedge \phi \implies H)$, where $P_1, \ldots, P_k$ are predicate variables, ϕ is a formula of integer arithmetic (without predicate variables), and H is either of the form $P(\tilde{v})$ or ϕ'. The problem of finding a solution (i.e. an assignment of predicates to predicate variables) of a set of CHCs is undecidable in general, but there are various automated tools (called CHC solvers) for solving the problem [5,20]. Thus, by using such a CHC solver, we can solve the constraints on predicate variables, and obtain refinement types by substituting the solution for the templates of refinement types.

For the example above, the following is a solution.

$$P_1(n) \equiv \mathbf{true} \qquad P_2(n, x) \equiv x < n \qquad P_3(x) \equiv \mathbf{true} \qquad P_4(n, x) \equiv \mathbf{true}.$$

This is exactly the predicates we used in Example 4 to translate P_{dec} using the refined approach.

Adding Extra CHCs. Actually, a further twist is necessary in the step of CHC solving. As in the example above, all the CHCs generated based on the refinement typing rules are of the form $\cdots \implies P_i(\tilde{v})$ (i.e., the head of every CHC is an atomic formula on a predicate variable). Thus, there always exists a trivial solution for the CHCs, which instantiates all the predicate variables to **true**. For the example above,

$$P_1(n) \equiv \mathbf{true} \qquad P_2(n, x) \equiv \mathbf{true} \qquad P_3(n) \equiv \mathbf{true} \qquad P_4(n, x) \equiv \mathbf{true}$$

is also a solution, but using the trivial solution, our transformation yields the non-terminating program. This program is essentially the same as the one in Example 3 since **let** $x = \star$ **in** $\mathbf{Assume}(\mathbf{true}); E$ is equivalent to **let** $x = \star$ **in** E. Typical CHC solvers indeed tend to find the trivial solution.

To remedy the problem above, in addition to the CHCs generated from the typing rules, we add extra constraints that prevent infinite loops. For the example above, the definition of f_{ρ_3} (which corresponds to the channel f) in the translated program is of the form

$$f_{\rho_3}(n) = \mathbf{if}\, n < 0\, \mathbf{then}\, (\,)\, \mathbf{else}\, f_{\rho_1}(n) \oplus (\mathbf{let}\, x = \star\, \mathbf{in}\, \mathbf{Assume}(P_2(n, x)); f_{\rho_3}(x)).$$

Thus we add the clause:

$$P_2(n, x) \implies n \neq x$$

to prevent an infinite loop $f_{\rho_3}(m) \to f_{\rho_3}(m) \to \cdots$. With the added clause, a CHC solver HOICE [5] indeed returns $x < n$ as the solution for $P_2(n, x)$.

In general, we can add the extra CHCs in the following, counter-example-guided manner.

1. $\mathcal{C} :=$ the CHCs generated from the typing rules
2. $\theta :=$ *callCHCsolver*$(\mathcal{C})$
3. $S :=$ the sequential program generated based on the solution θ
4. if S is terminating then return OK; otherwise, analyze S to find an infinite reduction sequence, add an extra clause to $\mathcal{C}$ to disable the infinite sequence, and go back to 2.

More precisely, in the last step, the backend termination analysis tool generates a lasso as a certificate of non-termination. We extract a chain $f(\tilde{x}) \to \cdots \to f(\tilde{x}')$ of recursive calls from the lasso, and add an extra clause requiring $\tilde{x} \neq \tilde{x}'$ to $\mathcal{C}$. This is naive and insufficient for excluding out an infinite sequence like $f(1) \to f(2) \to f(3) \to \cdots$. We plan to refine the method by incorporating more sophisticated techniques developed for sequential programs [16].

5   Implementation and Preliminary Experiments

5.1   Implementation

We have implemented a termination analysis tool for the π-calculus based on the method described in Sects. 3 and 4. This tool was written in OCaml. We chose C language as the actual target of our translation, and used ULTIMATE AUTOMIZER [17] (version 0.2.1) as a termination analysis tool for C.

For the refinement type inference described in Sect. 4.3, we have used HOICE [5] (version 1.8.3) and Z3 [20] (version 4.8.10) as backend CHC solvers. Since a stronger solution for CHCs is preferable as discussed at the end of Sect. 4.3, if HOICE and Z3 return different solutions $\{P_1 \mapsto \phi_1, \ldots, P_n \mapsto \phi_n\}$ and $\{P_1 \mapsto \phi_1', \ldots, P_n \mapsto \phi_n'\}$, then we used the solution $\{P_1 \mapsto \phi_1 \wedge \phi_1', \ldots, P_n \mapsto \phi_n \wedge \phi_n'\}$ for inserting **Assume** commands.

To make the analysis precise, the implementation is actually based on an extension of the refinement type system in Sect. 4.1 with subtyping; see the extended version [26].

5.2   Preliminary Experiments

We prepared a collection of π-calculus processes, and ran our tool on them. Our experiment was conducted on Intel Core i7-10850H CPU with 32 GB memory. For comparison, we have also run the termination analysis mode of TYPI-CAL [18,19] on the same instances.

Table 2. Results of the experiments

Test case	Basic	Refined	TYPICAL
client-server	2.5	2.7	0.006
stateful-server-client	FAIL	FAIL	0.006
parallel-or	2.4	2.9	0.006
broadcast	3.6	3.3	0.004
btree	FAIL	FAIL	0.011
stable	FAIL	FAIL	0.003
ds-ex5-1	FAIL	FAIL	0.002
factorial	3.9	4.4	0.002
ackermann	22.4	26.0	0.003
fibonacci	4.8	4.4	0.003
even/odd	7.0	7.6	0.002
factorial-pred	FAIL	28.2	FAIL
fibonacci-pred	FAIL	28.2	FAIL
even/odd-pred	FAIL	10.1	FAIL
sum-neg	7.6	13.1	FAIL
upperbound	3.8	3.9	FAIL
nested-replicated-input1	2.3	2.4	FAIL
nested-replicated-input2	FAIL	FAIL	FAIL
nested-replicated-input3	3.7	4.0	0.010
deadlock	FAIL	2.9	FAIL

The experimental results are summarized in Table 2. The columns "Basic" and "Refined" show the results for the basic method in Sect. 3 and the refined method in Sect. 4 respectively. The numbers show the running times measured in seconds, and "FAIL" means that the verification failed due to the incompleteness of the reduction; non-terminating sequential programs were obtained in those cases. The column "TYPICAL" shows the analogous result for TYPICAL. The termination analysis of TYPICAL roughly depends on Deng and Sangiorgi's method [13]. "FAIL" in the column means that the process does not satisfy the (sufficient) conditions for termination [13]. The termination analysis of TYPICAL treats numbers as natural numbers, and is actually unsound in the presence of arbitrary integers (for example, $f!(m; r) \mid *f?(x; r).\textbf{if } x = 0 \textbf{ then } r!(1) \textbf{ else } f!(x - 1; r)$ is judged to be terminating for any m).

The test cases consist of two categories. The first one, shown above the horizontal line, has been taken from the sample programs of TYPICAL. Among them, we have excluded out those that are not related to termination analysis (note that TYPICAL can perform deadlock/lock-freedom analysis and information flow analysis besides termination analysis). The second category, shown below the horizontal line, consists of those prepared by us,[5] including the samples discussed in the paper. All the processes in the test cases are terminating.

For "stateful-server-client", "btree", "stable", and "ds-ex5-1" in the first category, and "nested-replicated-input2" in the second category, our analysis fails for essentially the same reason. The following is a simplified version of "ds-ex5-1":

$$a!() \mid b!() \mid *a?().b?().a!().$$

The process above is terminating because each run of the third process consumes a message on b. Our reduction however ignores communications on b and produces the following non-terminating program:

$$(\{f_{\rho_a}() = f_{\rho_a}(), f_{\rho_b}() = ()\}, f_{\rho_a}() \oplus f_{\rho_b}()).$$

For the second category, our refined method clearly outperforms the basic method and TYPICAL. We explain some of the test cases in the second category. The test cases "fibonacci" and "nested-replicated-input3" are from Example 1 and 2 respectively, and "even/odd" is a mutually recursive process that judges whether a given number is even or odd. The process "deadlock" is the following one:

$$*loop?().loop!() \mid r?().loop!().$$

This process is terminating, because the subprocess $r?().loop!()$ is blocked forever, without ever sending a message to $loop$. With the refinement type system, the channel r is given type: $\mathbf{ch}_\rho(\epsilon; \mathbf{false})$, and $r?().loop!()$ is translated to:

$$\mathbf{let}\ \epsilon = \epsilon\ \mathbf{in}\ \mathbf{Assume(false)}; f_{\rho_{loop}}(),$$

which is terminating by **Assume(false)**. The process "upperbound" is the following process:

$$f!(0) \mid *f?(x).\mathbf{if}\ x > 10\ \mathbf{then}\ \mathbf{0}\ \mathbf{else}\ f!(x+1).$$

It is terminating because the argument of f monotonically increases, and is bounded above by 10. TYPICAL cannot make such reasoning.

6   Related Work

As mentioned in Sect. 1, there have been a number of studies on termination of the π-calculus [11–13,19,25,28,29], but most of them have been rather theoretical, and few tools have been developed. Our technique has been partially inspired by Deng and Sangiorgi's work [13], especially by their observation that a process is terminating just if there is no infinite chain of communications on replicated input processes. Deng and Sangiorgi ensured the lack of infinite chains by using a type system. They actually proposed four system, a core system and three kinds

---

[5] Unfortunately, there are no standard benchmark set for the termination analysis for the π-calculus.

of extensions. Our approach roughly corresponds to the first extension of their system ([13], Sect. 4), which requires that, in every chain of communications, the values of messages monotonically decrease. An advantage of our approach is that we can use mature tools for sequential programs to reason about how the values of messages change. Our approach does not subsume the second and third extensions of Deng and Sangiorgi's system, which take into account synchronizations over multiple channels; it is left for future work to study whether such extensions can be incorporated in our approach.

To our knowledge, TYPICAL [18, 19] is the only automated termination analysis tool. TYPICAL's termination analysis is based on Deng and Sangiorgi's method [13], but is quite limited in reasoning about the values sent along channels; it only considers natural numbers, and the ordering on them is limited to the standard order on natural numbers. Thus, for example, TYPICAL cannot prove the termination of the process "upperbound" as described in Sect. 5.

Recently, there have been studies on type systems for estimating the (time) complexity of processes for the π-calculus [1,2] and related session calculi [8,9]. Since the existence of a finite upper-bound implies termination, those analyses can, in principle, be used also for reasoning about termination, but the resulting termination analysis would be too conservative. It would be interesting to investigate whether our approach of reduction to sequential programs can be extended to achieve complexity analysis for the π-calculus. Refinement types for variants of the π-calculus have been studied before [3,15]. Our contribution in this regard is the application to termination analysis.

Cook et al. [6] proposed a method for proving termination of multi-threaded programs. Their technique also makes use of a termination tool for sequential programs. As their language model is quite different from ours (they deal with imperative programs with shared memory and locks, rather than message-passing programs), however, their method is quite different from ours.

7   Conclusion

We have proposed a method for reducing termination verification for the π-calculus to that for sequential programs and implemented an automated termination analysis tool based on the method. Our approach allows us to reuse powerful termination analysis tools developed for sequential programs.

Future work includes (i) a further refinement of our reduction and (ii) applications of our method to other message-passing-style concurrent programming languages. As for the first point, there are a few known limitations in the current reduction. Besides the issues mentioned at the end of Example 2 and Sect. 5, there is a limitation that channels of the same region are merged to the same function, which leads to the loss of precision. For example, consider:

$$* c?(x).\textbf{if } x < 0 \textbf{ then } 0 \textbf{ else } c!(x-1)$$
$$|\ *d?(x).\textbf{if } x > 0 \textbf{ then } 0 \textbf{ else } d!(x+1)$$
$$|\ e!(c)\ |\ e!(d)\ |\ c!(0)$$

The process is terminating, but our approach fails to prove it. Since the same region is assigned to c and d (because both are sent along e), the replicated input processes are translated to non-deterministic function definitions:

$$f_\rho(x) = \textbf{if } x < 0 \textbf{ then } (\ ) \textbf{ else } f_\rho(x - 1)$$
$$f_\rho(x) = \textbf{if } x > 0 \textbf{ then } (\ ) \textbf{ else } f_\rho(x + 1),$$

which cause an infinite reduction $f_\rho(0) \to f_\rho(-1) \to f_\rho(0) \to \cdots$. One remedy to this problem would be to introduce region polymorphism and translate processes to higher-order functional programs.

Acknowledgments. We would like to thank anonymous referees for useful comments. This work was supported by JSPS KAKENHI Grant Number JP20H05703.

References

1. Baillot, P., Ghyselen, A.: Types for complexity of parallel computation in pi-calculus. In: ESOP 2021. LNCS, vol. 12648, pp. 59–86. Springer, Cham (2021). https://doi.org/10.1007/978-3-030-72019-3_3
2. Baillot, P., Ghyselen, A., Kobayashi, N.: Sized types with usages for parallel complexity of pi-calculus processes. In: Proceedings of CONCUR 2021. LIPIcs, vol. 203, pp. 34:1–34:22. Schloss Dagstuhl - Leibniz-Zentrum für Informatik (2021). https://doi.org/10.4230/LIPIcs.CONCUR.2021.34
3. Baltazar, P., Mostrous, D., Vasconcelos, V.T.: Linearly refined session types. Electron. Proc. Theoret. Comput. Sci. **101**, 38–49 (2012). https://doi.org/10.4204/eptcs.101.4
4. Bjørner, N., Gurfinkel, A., McMillan, K., Rybalchenko, A.: Horn clause solvers for program verification. In: Beklemishev, L.D., Blass, A., Dershowitz, N., Finkbeiner, B., Schulte, W. (eds.) Fields of Logic and Computation II. LNCS, vol. 9300, pp. 24–51. Springer, Cham (2015). https://doi.org/10.1007/978-3-319-23534-9_2
5. Champion, A., Chiba, T., Kobayashi, N., Sato, R.: ICE-based refinement type discovery for higher-order functional programs. J. Autom. Reason. **64**(7), 1393–1418 (2020). https://doi.org/10.1007/s10817-020-09571-y
6. Cook, B., Podelski, A., Rybalchenko, A.: Proving thread termination. In: Proceedings of PLDI 2007, pp. 320–330. ACM Press (2007). https://doi.org/10.1145/1250734.1250771
7. Cook, B., Podelski, A., Rybalchenko, A.: Proving program termination. Commun. ACM **54**(5), 88–98 (2011). https://doi.org/10.1145/1941487.1941509
8. Das, A., Hoffmann, J., Pfenning, F.: Parallel complexity analysis with temporal session types. Proc. ACM Program. Lang. **2**(ICFP), 91:1–91:30 (2018). https://doi.org/10.1145/3236786
9. Das, A., Hoffmann, J., Pfenning, F.: Work analysis with resource-aware session types. In: Proceedings of LICS 2018, pp. 305–314. ACM (2018). https://doi.org/10.1145/3209108.3209146
10. de Moura, L., Bjørner, N.: Z3: an efficient SMT solver. In: Ramakrishnan, C.R., Rehof, J. (eds.) TACAS 2008. LNCS, vol. 4963, pp. 337–340. Springer, Heidelberg (2008). https://doi.org/10.1007/978-3-540-78800-3_24

11. Demangeon, R., Hirschkoff, D., Kobayashi, N., Sangiorgi, D.: On the complexity of termination inference for processes. In: Barthe, G., Fournet, C. (eds.) TGC 2007. LNCS, vol. 4912, pp. 140–155. Springer, Heidelberg (2008). https://doi.org/10. 1007/978-3-540-78663-4_11
12. Demangeon, R., Hirschkoff, D., Sangiorgi, D.: Termination in higher-order concurrent calculi. J. Log. Algebraic Methods Program. **79**(7), 550–577 (2010). https:// doi.org/10.1016/j.jlap.2010.07.007
13. Deng, Y., Sangiorgi, D.: Ensuring termination by typability. Info. Comput. **204**(7), 1045–1082 (2006). https://doi.org/10.1016/j.ic.2006.03.002
14. Fedyukovich, G., Zhang, Y., Gupta, A.: Syntax-guided termination analysis. In: Chockler, H., Weissenbacher, G. (eds.) CAV 2018. LNCS, vol. 10981, pp. 124–143. Springer, Cham (2018). https://doi.org/10.1007/978-3-319-96145-3_7
15. Griffith, D., Gunter, E.L.: LiquidPi: inferrable dependent session types. In: Brat, G., Rungta, N., Venet, A. (eds.) NFM 2013. LNCS, vol. 7871, pp. 185–197. Springer, Heidelberg (2013). https://doi.org/10.1007/978-3-642-38088-4_13
16. Hashimoto, K., Unno, H.: Refinement type inference via horn constraint optimization. In: Blazy, S., Jensen, T. (eds.) SAS 2015. LNCS, vol. 9291, pp. 199–216. Springer, Heidelberg (2015). https://doi.org/10.1007/978-3-662-48288-9_12
17. Heizmann, M., et al.: Ultimate automizer with two-track proofs. In: Chechik, M., Raskin, J.-F. (eds.) TACAS 2016. LNCS, vol. 9636, pp. 950–953. Springer, Heidelberg (2016). https://doi.org/10.1007/978-3-662-49674-9_68
18. Kobayashi, N.: TyPiCal: a type-based static analyzer for the pi-calculus (2005). Tool available at https://www-kb.is.s.u-tokyo.ac.jp/~koba/typical/
19. Kobayashi, N., Sangiorgi, D.: A hybrid type system for lock-freedom of mobile processes. ACM Trans. Prog. Lang. Syst. **32**(5), 1–49 (2010). https://doi.org/10. 1145/1745312.1745313
20. Komuravelli, A., Gurfinkel, A., Chaki, S.: SMT-based model checking for recursive programs. Formal Methods Syst. Des. **48**(3), 175–205 (2016). https://doi.org/10. 1007/s10703-016-0249-4
21. Kuwahara, T., Terauchi, T., Unno, H., Kobayashi, N.: Automatic termination verification for higher-order functional programs. In: Shao, Z. (ed.) ESOP 2014. LNCS, vol. 8410, pp. 392–411. Springer, Heidelberg (2014). https://doi.org/10.1007/978-3-642-54833-8_21
22. Milner, R.: The polyadic π-calculus: a tutorial. In: Bauer, F.L., Brauer, W., Schwichtenberg, H. (eds.) Logic and Algebra of Specification, pp. 203–246. Springer, Heidelberg (1993). https://doi.org/10.1007/978-3-642-58041-3_6
23. Podelski, A., Rybalchenko, A.: Transition invariants. In: Proceedings of LICS 2004, pp. 32–41 (2004). https://doi.org/10.1109/LICS.2004.1319598
24. Rondon, P.M., Kawaguchi, M., Jhala, R.: Liquid types. In: PLDI 2008, pp. 159–169 (2008). https://doi.org/10.1145/1375581.1375602
25. Sangiorgi, D.: Termination of processes. Math. Struct. Comput. Sci. **16**(1), 1–39 (2006). https://doi.org/10.1017/S0960129505004810
26. Shoshi, T., Ishikawa, T., Kobayashi, N., Sakayori, K., Sato, R., Tsukada, T.: Termination analysis for the π-calculus by reduction to sequential program termination (2021). https://arxiv.org/abs/2109.00311. An extended version
27. Unno, H., Kobayashi, N.: Dependent type inference with interpolants. In: Proceedings of PPDP 2009, pp. 277–288. ACM (2009). https://doi.org/10.1145/1599410. 1599445

28. Venet, A.: Automatic determination of communication topologies in mobile systems. In: Levi, G. (ed.) SAS 1998. LNCS, vol. 1503, pp. 152–167. Springer, Heidelberg (1998). https://doi.org/10.1007/3-540-49727-7_9
29. Yoshida, N., Berger, M., Honda, K.: Strong normalisation in the pi-calculus. Info. Comput. **191**(2), 145–202 (2004). https://doi.org/10.1016/j.ic.2003.08.004

Proving LTL Properties of Bitvector Programs and Decompiled Binaries

Yuandong Cyrus Liu[1]([✉]), Chengbin Pang[1], Daniel Dietsch[2], Eric Koskinen[1], Ton-Chanh Le[1], Georgios Portokalidis[1], and Jun Xu[1]

[1] Stevens Institute of Technology, Hoboken, USA
yliu195@stevens.edu
[2] University of Freiburg, Freiburg im Breisgau, Germany

Abstract. There is increasing interest in applying verification tools to programs that have bitvector operations. SMT solvers, which serve as a foundation for these tools, have thus increased support for bitvector reasoning through bit-blasting and linear arithmetic approximations.

In this paper we show that similar linear arithmetic approximation of bitvector operations can be done at the source level through transformations. Specifically, we introduce new paths that over-approximate bitvector operations with linear conditions/constraints, increasing branching but allowing us to better exploit the well-developed integer reasoning and interpolation of verification tools. We show that, for reachability of bitvector programs, increased branching incurs negligible overhead yet, when combined with integer interpolation optimizations, enables more programs to be verified. We further show this exploitation of integer interpolation in the common case also enables competitive termination verification of bitvector programs and leads to the first effective technique for linear temporal logic (LTL) verification of bitvector programs. Finally, we provide an in-depth case study of decompiled ("lifted") binary programs, which emulate X86 execution through frequent use of bitvector operations. We present a new tool DARKSEA, the first tool capable of verifying reachability, termination and LTL of lifted binaries.

1 Introduction

There is increasing interest in using today's verification tools in domains where bitvector operations are commonplace. Toward this end, there has been a variety of efforts to enable bitvector reasoning in Satisfiability Modulo Theory (SMT) solvers, which serve as a foundation for program analysis tools. One common strategy employed by these SMT solvers is *bit-blasting*, which translates the input bitvector formula to an equi-satisfiable propositional formula and utilizes Boolean Satisfiability (SAT) solvers to discharge it. Another strategy is to approximate bitvector operations with integer linear arithmetic [14]. CVC4 now employs a new approach called *int-blasting* [53], which reasons about bitvector formulas via integer nonlinear arithmetic.

© Springer Nature Switzerland AG 2021
H. Oh (Ed.): APLAS 2021, LNCS 13008, pp. 285–304, 2021.
https://doi.org/10.1007/978-3-030-89051-3_16

Inspired by these SMT strategies, this paper explores the use of linear approximations of bitvector operations through source-level transformations, toward enabling Termination/LTL verification of bitvector programs. Our *bitwise branching* introduces new conditional, linear arithmetic paths that overapproximate many but not all bitvector behaviors. These paths cover the common cases and, in the remaining cases, other paths fall back on the exact bitvector behavior. As a result, in the common case, the reasoning burden is shifted to linear arithmetic conditions/constraints, a domain more suitable to today's automated termination/LTL techniques. We created source-translation rewriting rules for expressions as well as assignment statements and implemented them as a transformation on Boogie programs, within the Ultimate verifier [31].

We first examine the impact of bitwise branching on reachability and experimentally demonstrate that the translation imposes negligible overhead (from introducing additional paths), yet allows existing tools to verifying more bitvector programs. There are limited SV-COMP bitvector benchmarks (existing benchmarks require little or no real bitvector reasoning) so we first prepared 26 new bitvector reachability benchmarks, including examples drawn from Sean Anderson's "BitHacks" repository[1], which use bitvector operations for various purposes. Without bitwise branching, ULTIMATE's default setting (Z3 and SMT-Interpol) is only able to verify 2 of the 26 benchmarks. We show that bitwise branching allows us to verify these benchmarks with comparable performance with existing tools across a variety of back-end SMT solvers (MATHSAT, Z3, CVC4, SMTInterpol). We also show that bitwise branching is comparable in performance (both time and problems solved) with Z3.

The ability to use integer interpolation in the common case has far-reaching consequences, which we explore in the remainder of the paper. In Sect. 6 we show that, for bitwise termination benchmarks, bitwise branching improves ULTIMATE and is competitive with other tools that support termination of bitvector programs (*e.g.*, APROVE, KITTEL, CPACHECKER). Again SV-COMP does not have sufficient benchmarks for termination of bitvector programs, so we created new benchmarks by extending examples from the SV-COMP termination category [6], as well as the APROVE bitvector benchmarks [1].

More notably, our work leads to one of the first tools for verifying temporal logic (LTL) properties of bitvector programs. To our knowledge, the only existing tool is ULTIMATE, and we show that bitwise branching improves ULTIMATE's ability to verify LTL from merely 3 examples to a total of 59 new LTL benchmarks (out of a total of 67 benchmarks), adapted from ULTIMATE's LTL repository [7] and the BitHacks repository.

Case Study: Temporal Verification of Lifted Binaries. In Sect. 7 we explore how bitwise branching can be used as part of a novel strategy for verifying decompiled ("lifted") binaries. Lifted binaries have lost their source data-types and instead emulate the behavior of the architecture with extensive use of bitvector operations. We developed a new tool called DARKSEA, built on top of our ULTIMATE-based bitwise branching, as well as IDA PRO [48] and MCSEMA [25]. Although these

---

[1] https://graphics.stanford.edu/~seander/bithacks.html.

decompilation tools generate IR/C programs and today's verification tools do parse C programs, we also describe some critical translations that were needed to make the output of McSema suitable for verification (rather than re-compilation).

We experimentally validated our work and show that DarkSea is the first tool for verifying temporal properties of lifted binaries. DarkSea is able to prove or disprove LTL properties of 8 lifted binaries. The most comparable alternative is Ultimate, which cannot prove any of them without DarkSea's translations, and can only verify 6 of them without bitwise branching.

Contributions. In summary, our contributions are:

- (Section 4) Bitwise branching, introducing paths with linear approximations.
- (Section 5) An evaluation showing that it allows one to prove reachability of more bitvector programs, with negligible overhead.
- (Section 6) An evaluation showing competitive performance on termination, and the first effective technique for LTL of bitvector programs.
- (Section 7) A case study and new tool called DarkSea, the first temporal verification technique for decompiled (lifted) binaries.
- New suites of bitvector benchmarks for reachability (23), termination (31), LTL (41) and lifted binaries (8).

We conclude with related work (Sect. 8). All code, proofs and benchmarks are available online[2]. Our benchmarks have also been submitted to SV-COMP.

2 Motivating Examples

Ex. 1. Reachability	Ex. 2. Termination	Ex. 3. LTL $\varphi = \Box(\Diamond(n < 0))$
| ```
int r, s, x;
while (x>0){
  s = x >> 31;
  x--;
  r = x + (s&(1-s));
  if (r<0) error();
}
``` | ```
a = *;
assume(a>0);
while (x>0){
  a--;
  x = x & a;
}
``` | ```
while(1) {
  n = *; x = *; y = x-1;
  while (x>0 && n>0) {
    n++;
    y = x | n;
    x = x - y;
  }
  n = -1;
}}
``` |
| and_reach1.c | and-01.c | or_loop3.c |

We will refer to the above bitvector programs throughout the paper. To prove error unreachable in the **Ex. 1**, a verifier must be able to reason about the bitvector >> and & operations. Specifically, it must be able to conclude that expression s&(1-s) is always positive (so r cannot be negative) which also depends on the earlier x>>31 expression. We will use this example to explain our work in Sect. 4, and compare performance of Ultimate using state-of-the-art SMT solvers, with and without bitwise branching.

We will see that the key benefits of bitwise branching arise when concerned with termination and LTL. **Ex. 2** involves a simple loop, in which a is decremented, but the loop condition is on variable x, whose value is a bitvector expression over a. Today's tools for *termination* of bitvector programs struggle with

---
[2] github.com/cyruliu/darksea.
```

this example: APROVE, CPACHECKER and ULTIMATE report unknown and KITTEL and 2LS timeout after 900 s (details in the Appendix of the extended version [40]). Critical to verifying termination of this program are (1) proving the invariant $x > 0 \wedge a > 0$ on Line 3 within the body of the loop and (2) synthesizing a rank function. To prove the invariant $\mathcal{I}$, tools must show that it holds after a step of the loop's transition relation $T = x{>}0 \wedge a'{=}a{-}1 \wedge x'{=}x\&a'$, which requires reasoning about the bitwise-& operation because if we simply treat the & as an uninterpreted function, $\mathcal{I} \wedge T \wedge x'{>}0 \not\Longrightarrow \mathcal{I}'$.

The bitwise branching strategy we describe in this paper helps the verifier infer these invariants (and later synthesize rank functions) by transforming the bitvector assignment to x into linear constraint x<=a, but only under the condition that x>=0 and a>=0. That is, bitwise branching translates the loop in **Ex. 2** as depicted in the gray boxes to the right. This changes the transition relation of the loop body from T (the original program) to T':

```
a = *; assume(a > 0);
while (x > 0) {
  { x > 0 ∧ a > 0 }
  a--;

  if (x >= 0 && a >= 0)

  then { x = *; assume(x <= a); }

  else { x = x & a; }
}
```

$$T' = x{>}0 \wedge a'{=}a{-}1 \wedge ((x{\geq}0 \wedge a'{\geq}0 \wedge x'{\leq}a') \vee (\neg(x{\geq}0 \wedge a'{\geq}0) \wedge x'{=}x\&a'))$$

Importantly, when $\mathcal{I}$ holds, the else branch with the & is infeasible, and thus we can treat the & as an uninterpreted function and yet still prove that $\mathcal{I} \wedge T' \wedge x'{>}0 \Longrightarrow \mathcal{I}'$. With the proof of $\mathcal{I}$ a tool can then move to the next step and synthesizes a rank function $\mathcal{R}(x, a)$ that satisfies $\mathcal{I} \wedge T' \Longrightarrow \mathcal{R}(x, a){\geq}0 \wedge \mathcal{R}(x, a){>}\mathcal{R}(x', a')$, namely, $\mathcal{R}(x, a) = a$.

Bitwise branching also enables LTL verification of bitvector programs. We examine the behavior of programs such as **Ex. 3** above, with LTL property $\Box(\Diamond(n < 0))$. The state of the art program verifier for LTL is ULTIMATE, but ULTIMATE cannot verify this program due to the bitvector operations. (ULTIMATE's internal overapproximation is too imprecise so it returns Unknown.) In Sect. 6 we show that with bitwise branching, our implementation can prove this property of this program in 8.04 s.

Case Study: Decompiled Binary Programs. In recent years many tools have been developed for decompiling (or "lifting") binaries into a source code format [9,15,25,45,51]. The resulting code, however, has long lost the original source abstractions and instead emulates the hardware. These programs are an interesting case study because their frequent use of bitvector operations places them beyond the capabilities of existing tools for LTL verification.

```
while (1) {
  y = 1; x = *;
  while (x>0) {
    x--;
    if (x <= 1)
      y = 0; } } }
```

Consider the (source) program shown to the right. This program, which does not contain any bitvector operations, is taken from the ULTIMATE repository[3]. Some existing techniques

[3] http://github.com/ultimate-pa/ultimate/blob/dev/trunk/examples/LTL/simple/ PotentialMinimizeSEVPABug.c.

and tools [7,20] can prove that the LTL property $\Box(\text{x} > 0 \;\Rightarrow\; \Diamond(\text{y} = 0))$ holds. However, after the program is compiled (with gcc) and then disassembled and lifted (with IDPro and McSEMA), the resulting code has many bitvector operations. The resulting lifted code is quite non-trivial. (The full version is given in the extended version [40]). It required substantial engineering efforts just to parse and analyze the lifted code with existing verifiers (see Sect. 7). Let us first focus on the bitvector complexities; here is a fragment of the lifted IR (in C for readability):

```
1   while(true) {
2       tmp_x = load i32, i32* bitcast (%x_type* @x to i32*)
3       ...
4       if ( ((tmp_x >> 31) == 0) & ((tmp_x == 0) ^ true) ) {
5           tmp_40 = add i32 tmp_x, -1
6           store i32 tmp_40, i32* bitcast (%x_type* @x to i32*)
7           tmp_xp = load i32, i32* bitcast (%x_type* @x to i32*)
8           tmp_42 = tmp_xp + -1; tmp_45 = tmp_42 >> 31;
9           tmp_43 = tmp_xp + -2; tmp_44 = tmp_43 >> 31;
10          if ((((((tmp_42 != 0u)&1)) & ((((tmp_44 == 0u)&1)) ^ ((((tmp_44
            ^ tmp_45) + tmp_45)) == 2u)&1)))&1)))&1))) {
11              store i32 0, i32* bitcast (%y_type* @y to i32*)
12          }
13      } else { break; }
14  }
```

Roughly, Line 4 corresponds to the x>0 comparison, and Line 10 corresponds to the x<=1 comparison. These bitvector operations, introduced to emulate the behavior of the binary, make the program challenging for existing verifiers.

We describe a new tool DARKSEA that uses bitwise branching in the context of a decompilation toolchain involving IDA PRO, McSEMA and ULTIMATE. The lifting performed by tools like McSEMA is geared toward *re*compilation rather than verification, thus foiling existing tools. In Sect. 7.2 we describe translations performed by DARKSEA to tailor lifted binaries for verification. In Sect. 7.3, our experimental results show that DARKSEA is the first tool capable of proving reachability, termination and LTL of lifted binaries.

3 Preliminaries

Our formalization is based on Boogie programs [12], denoted P. Our implementations parse input source C programs (or binaries decompiled to C) that may have bitvector operations. These programs are then translated into Boogie programs, in which bitvector operations are represented as uninterpreted functions. Figure 1 includes the standard syntax of a statement *Stmt* in a Boogie program P. For bitvector programs, we assume the following abbreviated expression *Expr* syntax, which includes bitvector operations:

$$Expr ::= BinOp \mid UnOp \mid UninterpFn \mid \ldots$$
$$BinOp ::= + \mid - \mid * \mid / \mid \% \mid \&\& \mid \mid\mid \mid \texttt{==>} \mid \texttt{<==>} \mid \ldots$$
$$UnOp ::= - \mid ! \mid \ldots$$
$$UninterpFn ::= bwAnd \mid bwOr \mid bwXor \mid bwShL \mid bwShR \mid bwCompl$$

$Stmt ::= $ **assume** $Expr$;	**assert** $Expr$;
$\mid$ **call forall** Id ($NondetExpr$);	$Id : Stmt$
$\mid$ $Lhs($, $Lhs)^* := Expr($, $Expr)^*$;	**break** Id;
$\mid$ **if** ($NondetExpr$){ $Stmt^*$ } $Else$	**goto** $Id($, $Id)^*$;
$\mid$ **while** ($NondetExpr$) $LoopInv^*$ {$Stmt^*$ }	**call** $CallLhs$ Id ();
$\mid$ **call** $CallLhs$ Id ($Expr($, $Expr)^*$);	**havoc** $Id($, $Id)^*$;
$\mid$ **call forall** Id ($Expr($, $Expr)^*$);	**return**;
$Lhs ::= Id$	$Id[Expr($, $Expr)^*]$
$NondetExpr ::= * \mid Expr$	
$Else ::= $ **else if** ($NondetExpr$){ $Stmt^*$ }$Else$	**else** { $Stmt^*$ }
$CallLhs ::= Id($, $Id)^* :=$	
$LoopInv ::= $ **free invariant** $Expr$;	

Fig. 1. Boogie statement syntax in Ultimate framework.

We assume conditional branching has been transformed to non-deterministic branching: **if** * **then** {assume(b);s_1} **else** {assume(!b);s_2}. As discussed later, ULTIMATE (used in our implementation) has two modes: "bitvector mode," in which these uninterpreted expressions are translated into SMT bitvector sorts and "integer mode," in which they remain uninterpreted.

For the semantics, we assume a state space $\Sigma : Var \rightarrow Val$, mapping variables to values. We let $[\![e]\!] : \Sigma \rightarrow Val$ and $[\![s]\!] : \Sigma \rightarrow \mathcal{P}(\Sigma)$ be the semantics of expressions and statements, respectively, and $[\![P]\!]$ denotes traces of P.

4 Bitwise-Branching

We build our *bitwise-branching* technique on the known strategy of transforming bitvector operations into integer approximations [14,53] but explore a new direction: source-level transformations to introduce new conditional paths that approximate many (but not all) behaviors of a bitvector program. These new paths through the program have linear input conditions and linear output constraints and frequently cover all of the program's behavior (with respect to the goal property), but otherwise fall back on the original bitvector behavior when none of the input conditions hold. We provide two sets of bitwise-branching rules:

1. Rewriting rules of the form $\mathcal{C} \vdash_E e_{bv} \rightsquigarrow e_{int}$ in Fig. 2a. These rules are applied to bitwise arithmetic expressions e_{bv} and specify a condition $\mathcal{C}$ for which one can use integer approximate behavior e_{int} of e_{bv}. In other words, rewriting rule $\mathcal{C} \vdash_E e_{bv} \rightsquigarrow e_{int}$ can be applied only when $\mathcal{C}$ holds and a bitwise arithmetic expression e in the program structurally matches its e_{bv} with a substitution δ. Then, e will be transformed into a conditional approximation: $\mathcal{C}\delta$? $e_{int}\delta : e_{bv}$. Note that, although modulo-2 is computationally more

$$e_1 = 0 \vdash_E e_1 \& e_2 \rightsquigarrow 0$$
$$(e_1 = 0 \vee e_1 = 1) \wedge e_2 = 1 \vdash_E e_1 \& e_2 \rightsquigarrow e_1$$
$$(e_1 = 0 \vee e_1 = 1) \wedge (e_2 = 0 \vee e_2 = 1) \vdash_E e_1 \& e_2 \rightsquigarrow e_1 \&\& e_2$$
$$e_1 \geq 0 \wedge e_2 = 1 \vdash_E e_1 \& e_2 \rightsquigarrow e_1 \% 2$$
$$e_2 = 0 \vdash_E e_1 | e_2 \rightsquigarrow e_1$$
$$(e_1 = 0 \vee e_1 = 1) \wedge e_2 = 1 \vdash_E e_1 | e_2 \rightsquigarrow 1$$
$$e_2 = 0 \vdash_E e_1 \char`\^ e_2 \rightsquigarrow e_1$$
$$e_1 = e_2 = 0 \vee e_1 = e_2 = 1 \vdash_E e_1 \char`\^ e_2 \rightsquigarrow 0$$
$$(e_1 = 1 \wedge e_2 = 0) \vee (e_1 = 0 \wedge e_2 = 1) \vdash_E e_1 \char`\^ e_2 \rightsquigarrow 1$$
$$e_1 \geq 0 \wedge e_2 = \texttt{CHAR\_BIT} * \texttt{sizeof}(e_1) - 1 \vdash_E e_1 \texttt{>>} e_2 \rightsquigarrow 0$$
$$e_1 < 0 \wedge e_2 = \texttt{CHAR\_BIT} * \texttt{sizeof}(e_1) - 1 \vdash_E e_1 \texttt{>>} e_2 \rightsquigarrow -1$$

(a) Rewriting rules for arithmetic expressions.

$$e_1 \geq 0 \wedge e_2 \geq 0 \vdash_S r \ \texttt{op}_{le} \ e_1 \& e_2 \rightsquigarrow \texttt{r<=}e_1 \ \texttt{\&\&} \ \texttt{r<=}e_2$$
$$e_1 < 0 \wedge e_2 < 0 \vdash_S r \ \texttt{op}_{le} \ e_1 \& e_2 \rightsquigarrow \texttt{r<=}e_1 \ \texttt{\&\&} \ \texttt{r<=}e_2 \ \texttt{\&\&} \ \texttt{r<0}$$
$$e_1 \geq 0 \wedge e_2 < 0 \vdash_S r \ \texttt{op}_{eq} \ e_1 \& e_2 \rightsquigarrow \texttt{0<=r} \ \texttt{\&\&} \ \texttt{r<=}e_1$$
$$(e_1 = 0 \vee e_1 = 1) \wedge (e_2 = 0 \vee e_2 = 1) \vdash_S (e_1 | e_2) \texttt{==}0 \rightsquigarrow e_1 \texttt{==}0 \ \texttt{\&\&} \ e_2 \texttt{==}0$$
$$e_1 \geq 0 \wedge \texttt{is\_const}(e_2) \vdash_S r \ \texttt{op}_{ge} \ e_1 | e_2 \rightsquigarrow \texttt{r>=}e_2$$
$$e_1 \geq 0 \wedge e_2 \geq 0 \vdash_S r \ \texttt{op}_{ge} \ e_1 | e_2 \rightsquigarrow \texttt{r>=}e_1 \ \texttt{\&\&} \ \texttt{r>=}e_2$$
$$e_1 < 0 \wedge e_2 < 0 \vdash_S r \ \texttt{op}_{eq} \ e_1 | e_2 \rightsquigarrow \texttt{r>=}e_1 \ \texttt{\&\&} \ \texttt{r>=}e_2 \ \texttt{\&\&} \ \texttt{r<0}$$
$$e_1 \geq 0 \wedge e_2 < 0 \vdash_S r \ \texttt{op}_{eq} \ e_1 | e_2 \rightsquigarrow e_2 \texttt{<=r} \ \texttt{\&\&} \ \texttt{r<0}$$
$$e_1 \geq 0 \wedge e_2 \geq 0 \vdash_S r \ \texttt{op}_{ge} \ e_1 \char`\^ e_2 \rightsquigarrow \texttt{r>=0}$$
$$e_1 < 0 \wedge e_2 < 0 \vdash_S r \ \texttt{op}_{ge} \ e_1 \char`\^ e_2 \rightsquigarrow \texttt{r>=0}$$
$$e_1 \geq 0 \wedge e_2 < 0 \vdash_S r \ \texttt{op}_{le} \ e_1 \char`\^ e_2 \rightsquigarrow \texttt{r<0}$$
$$e_1 \geq 0 \vdash_S r \ \texttt{op}_{le} \ {\sim}e_1 \rightsquigarrow \texttt{r<0}$$
$$e_1 < 0 \vdash_S r \ \texttt{op}_{ge} \ {\sim}e_1 \rightsquigarrow \texttt{r>=0}$$

(b) Weakening rules for relational expressions and assignments. $\texttt{op}_{le} \in \{\texttt{<},\texttt{<=},\texttt{==},\texttt{:=}\}$, $\texttt{op}_{ge} \in \{\texttt{>},\texttt{>=},\texttt{==},\texttt{:=}\}$, and $\texttt{op}_{eq} \in \{\texttt{==},\texttt{:=}\}$

Fig. 2. Rewriting rules. Commutative closures omitted for brevity.

expensive, it is often more amenable to integer reasoning strategies. For conciseness, we omitted variants that arise from commutative re-ordering of the rules (in both Figs. 2a and 2b).

For example, consider the bitvector arithmetic expression `s&(1-s)` in **Ex. 1** of Sect. 2. If we apply the rewriting rule $e_1 \geq 0 \wedge e_2 = 1 \vdash_E e_1 \& e_2 \rightsquigarrow e_1 \% 2$ with the substitution `s`/e_1, `1-s`/e_2 then the expression is transformed into `s>=0&&(1-s)==1 ? s%2 : (s&(1-s))`. Since `s` reflects the sign bit of the positive variable `x`, it is always 0 and the `if` condition is feasible. In general, we can further replace the remaining bitwise operation in the `else` expression with other applicable rules. There may still be executions that fall into the final catch-all case where the bitwise operation is performed. However, as we see in the subsequent sections of this paper, these case splits are nonetheless practically significant because often the final `else` is infeasible.

2. Weakening rules of the form $C \vdash_S s_{bv} \rightsquigarrow s_{int}$ are in Fig. 2b. These rules are applied to relational condition expressions (*e.g.*, from assumptions) and assignment statements s_{bv}, specifying an integer condition C and over-approximation transition constraint s_{int}. When the rule is applied to a statement (as opposed to a conditional), replacement s_{int} can be implemented as assume(s_{int}). When a weakening rule $C \vdash_S s_{bv} \rightsquigarrow s_{int}$ is applied to an assignment s with substitution δ, the transformed statement is if $C\delta$ assume($s_{int}\delta$) else s_{bv}. In addition, when s_{bv} of a weakening rule can be matched to the condition c in an assume(c) of the original program via a substitution δ, then the assume(c) statement is transformed to if $C\delta$ then assume($s_{int}\delta$) else assume(c). The assignment operator in Figs. 2a and 2b, denoted :=, is included in three group of operators (op_{le}, op_{ge}, op_{eq}).

Proofs for each rule were done with Z3. Details are in the extended version [40]. The rules in Fig. 2a and Fig. 2b were developed empirically, from the reachability/termination/LTL benchmarks in the next sections and, especially, based on patterns found in decompiled binaries (Sect. 7). We then generalized these rules to expand coverage.

Translation Algorithm. We implemented bitwise branching via a translation algorithm, on top of ULTIMATE, denoted ULTIMATEBWB. Our translation acts on the AST of the program, with one method T_E : exp -> exp to translate expressions and another method T_S : stmt -> stmt to translate assignment statements, each according to the set of available rules (algorithms of T_E and T_S are given in the extended version [40]). In brief, when we reach a node with a bitwise operator, we recursively translate the operands, match the current operator against our collection of rules, and apply all matching rules to construct nested if-then-else expressions/statements. We found that, when multiple rules matched, the order did not matter much.

Let $T_E\{e\} : e$ denote the result of applying substitutions to e, and similar for $T_S\{s\} : s$. We lift this to a translation on a Boogie program P with $T_E\{P\} : P$ and $T_S\{P\} : P$, referring to all expressions and statements in P, respectively.

Lemma 1 (Rule correctness). *For every rule* $C \vdash_E e \rightsquigarrow e'$, $\forall \sigma. C(\sigma) \Rightarrow [\![e]\!]\sigma = [\![e']\!]\sigma$. *For every* $C \vdash_S s \rightsquigarrow s'$, $\forall \sigma. C(\sigma) \Rightarrow [\![s]\!]\sigma \subseteq [\![s']\!]\sigma$.

Theorem 1 (Soundness). *For every* P, T_E, T_S, $[\![P]\!] \subseteq [\![T_S\{T_E\{P\}\}]\!]$.

Proof. See Appendix A.

Control-Flow Automata. We have formalized *bitwise branching* via ASTs for readability but it can also be represented as a transformation on a program represented as a control-flow automaton. A (deterministic) *control flow automaton* (CFA) [35] is a tuple $\mathcal{A} = \langle Q, q_0, X, s, \longrightarrow \rangle$ where Q is a finite set of control locations and q_0 is the initial control location, X is a finite sets of typed variables, s is the loop/branch-free statement language and $\longrightarrow \subseteq Q \times s \times Q$ is a finite set of labeled edges.

Continuing with **Ex. 2**, an edge of the CFA labeled with statement x = x& a is shown to the right. Next shown is the result after applying the first weakening rule in Fig. 2b. Conditional edges are introduced (*e.g.*, $x \geq 0 \wedge q \geq 0$ to q_b) along with linear constraints (*e.g.*, assume($x \leq a$)) and bitvector operations remain in the fallback case.

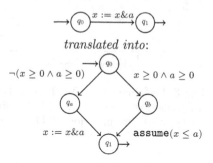

translated into:

5 Reachability of Bitvector Programs

We now evaluate the effectiveness of bitwise branching (BwB), as implemented in our ULTIMATEBwB, toward reachability verification. Existing SV-COMP benchmarks require little or no bitvector reasoning; even when bitvector operations are present, they are often irrelevant to the property and can be abstracted away. We therefore created a new suite of 28 bitvector programs, including 12 simple programs (ReachBit) and 16 programs adapted from the existing code snippets "BitHacks" [10], which use bitwise operations for various tasks.

ULTIMATE can verify bitvector programs in two modes: *integer* and *bitvector*. In the integer mode, bitvector operations are overapproximated to nondeterminism and overflow/underflow is accounted for with assume statements. In the bitvector mode, ULTIMATE utilizes a variety of back-end SMT solvers with internal bitvector reasoning strategies, such as CVC4, Z3 and MATHSAT (MS). Our implementation of bitwise branching, embodied in ULTIMATEBwB, does not use bitvector mode but instead transforms bitvector programs (through bitwise branching) and verifies them in ULTIMATE's integer mode using the same set of back-end SMT solvers.

We ran our experiments with BENCHEXEC [13] on a Linux 5.4.65 machine with an AMD Ryzen 3970X 32-core 3.7 GHz CPU and 256 GB RAM. We limited CPU time to 5 min, memory to 8 GB, and restricted each run to two cores.

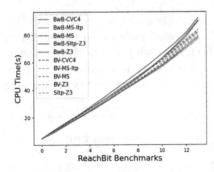
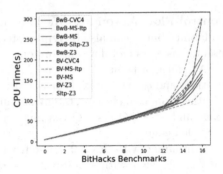

Fig. 3. Performance of ULTIMATEBwB with bitwise branching "BwB" in *integer mode* (solid lines) versus ULTIMATE (dashed lines, "BV" indicating *bitvector mode*) on bitvector programs, using various SMT solvers.

Figure 3 plots the number of ReachBit and BitHacks benchmarks solved versus the cumulative time between ULTIMATEBwB with bitwise branching (solid lines) and ULTIMATE (dashed lines). These results show that the performance of ULTIMATEBwB is comparable to ULTIMATE's bitvector mode, despite the fact that the bitwise branching transformation introduces new paths.

Because ULTIMATE's verification algorithms heavily utilize interpolation for optimizations, we also ran the experiment with interpolation enabled when possible, using MATHSAT's interpolation (MS-Itp, in both modes) and SMTINTERPOL (SItp, only in the integer mode because SMTINTERPOL does not support bitvectors). Notably, without bitwise branching, ULTIMATE with the default setting (integer mode SItp-Z3 in Fig. 3) returns *Unknown* for 10/12 "ReachBit" and 16/16 "BitHacks" benchmarks, despite the fact that it has a good trend in terms of runtime, while ULTIMATEBwB can verify all 28 programs in the same settings. Moreover, while interpolation is less effective in the bitvector mode (see BV-MS-Itp vs. BV-MS), when combined with bitwise branching in the integer mode, it improves over those solvers and has the best results (BwB-SItp-Z3). The detailed result can be found in the extended version [40].

6   Termination and LTL of Bitvector Programs

We now evaluate bitwise branching on the main target: liveness properties of bitvector programs. There are few comparable tools that support bitvector reasoning and these properties; the most comparable (and mature) tools are listed to the right, along with their limitations.

Tool	BitVec.	Term.	LTL
ULTIMATE	Limited	Yes	Yes
APROVE [29]	Yes	Yes	No
KITTEL [26]	Yes	Yes	No
CPACHECKER [50]	Limited	Yes	No
2LS [18]	Yes	Yes	No
ULTIMATEBwB	Yes	Yes	Yes

Termination. We compare bitwise branching with these termination provers in the table. We applied these tools to two benchmarks suites: **(i)** We first used 18 bitvector terminating programs selected from APROVE's bitvector benchmarks [34]. Notably, those benchmarks were designed with general bitvector arithmetic in mind so that there is only a small portion of bitvector programs in it (i.e. 18/118 or 15%). **(ii)** We therefore built a second set of 31 termination benchmarks, including 18 terminating programs (✔) and 13 non-terminating programs (✗), called TermBitBench with bitvector operations including bitwise |, &, ^, <<, >>, ~.

	(ii) TermBitBench						(i) AproveBench					
	APROVE	CPACHECKER	KITTEL	2LS	ULTIMATE	ULTIMATEBWB	APROVE	CPACHECKER	KITTEL	2LS	ULTIMATE	ULTIMATEBWB
✔	5	1	7	8	2	18	1	3	3	14	2	2
⚡✔	1	-	-	-	-	-	-	-	-	-	-	-
✗	6	10	-	8	-	13	-	-	-	-	-	-
⚡✗	2	7	-	3	-	-	-	10	-	-	2	6
?	14	13	-	-	29	-	10	3	-	1	14	8
T	3	-	19	12	-	-	7	-	10	2	-	1
M	-	-	-	-	-	-	-	-	-	1	-	1
⚡	-	-	5	-	-	-	-	2	5	-	-	-

Results. To the right is a table summarizing our results (details in [40]). For the APROVE benchmarks, our tool can correctly prove the termination or non-termination of 2 programs, which is less than the number of programs that can be proved by CPACHECKER (3), KITTEL (3), and 2LS (14). However, for TermBitBench, while ULTIMATEBWB can prove *all* 31 programs, CPACHECKER, KITTEL, and 2LS can only prove at most 16 programs. Moreover, while our tool was built on top of ULTIMATE, it outperforms ULTIMATE in proving termination and non-termination of bitwise programs. This is because ULTIMATE's algorithms for synthesizing termination [32] and non-termination proofs [39] are not applicable to SMT formulas containing bitvectors, as discussed in Sect. 2. As a consequence, ULTIMATE relies on integer-based encodings of source programs together with overapproximations of bitwise operations. The 6 false results in AproveBench are spurious counterexamples that arise due to Ultimate's overapproximation of unsigned integers. Our results here confirm that bitwise branching provides an effective means for termination of bitvector programs.

Linear Temporal Logic. We compared our tool against ULTIMATE, which is the state-of-the-art LTL prover and the only mature LTL verifier that supports bitvector programs. To our knowledge, there are no available bitwise benchmarks with LTL properties so we create new benchmarks for this purpose: (iii) New hand-crafted benchmarks called LTLBitBench of 42 C programs with LTL properties, in which bitwise operations are heavily used in assignments, loop conditions, and branching conditions. There are 22 programs in which the provided LTL properties are satisfied (✔) and 20 programs in which the LTL properties are violated (✗). (iv) Benchmarks adapted from the "BitHacks" programs, consisting of 26 programs with LTL properties (18 satisfied and 8 violated).

The table to the right summarizes the result of applying ULTIMATE and ULTIMATEBwB on these two bitvector benchmarks (see [40] for details). ULTIMATEBwB outperforms ULTIMATE: ULTIMATEBwB can successfully verify 41 of 42 programs in LTLBitBench and 18 of 26 BitHacks programs while ULTIMATE can only handle a few of them. Note that we have more out-of-memory results in BitHacks Benchmarks, perhaps due to memory consumption reasoning about the introduced paths. In conclusion, bitwise branching appears to be the first effective technique for verifying LTL properties of bitvector programs.

	(iv) Bithacks		(iii) LTLBit Bench	
	ULTIMATE	w. BwB	ULTIMATE	w. BwB
✔	3	10	-	21
✘	-	7	-	20
?	21	5	42	-
T	1	1	-	1
M	1	3	-	-

Bitwise-branching can be combined with other tools beyond ULTIMATE, making it an appealing general strategy. In this paper, we implemented bitwise branching within ULTIMATE [31] source code (during the C-to-Boogie translation) so that we could compare against unmodified Ultimate, which is already one of the more effective Termination/LTL verifiers. Furthermore, to our knowledge other tools do not allow one to flip a switch to enable their own bit-precise analysis (i.e., CBMC's Bitblasting or CPACHECKER's FixedSizeBitVectors theory) or disable that analysis, abstracting with integers.

7   Case Study: LTL of Decompiled Binaries

Decompiled binary executables are rife with bitvector operations, making them an interesting domain for a case study. Many tools [8,24,25,27,28,36,48] have been developed for decompilation. Similar to compilation, the decompilation process consists of multiple phases, beginning with disassembly. Some techniques have emerged for verifying low-level aspects of decompiled binaries such as architectural semantics [11,23,47], decompilation into logic [43–45,51], and translation validation [22] (discussed in Sect. 8).

Further along the decompilation process, other tools aim to represent a binary at a higher level of abstraction through a process called *lifting*. A lifted binary can be represented in IR or source code, but includes only some of the source-level abstractions of the original program. Instead, a lifted "program" emulates the machine itself, with data structures that mimic the hardware (*e.g.*, registers, flags, stack, heap, etc.) and control that mimics the behavior of the binary.

While some of the above mentioned works involve manual or semi-automated proofs of safety properties, we have not yet seen many automated techniques for verifying reachability, termination and temporal properties of those lifted binaries. To a large extent today's automated verification techniques have relied on source abstractions (*e.g.*, invariants and rank functions over loop variables, structured control flow, procedure boundaries, etc.).

7.1   Bitvector Operations in Lifted Binaries

Lifted binaries frequently use bitvector operations *e.g.*, to reflect signed/unsigned comparison of variables whose type was lost in compilation. As we show in Sect. 7.3, lifted programs are beyond the capabilities of termination verification tools such as ULTIMATE, CPACHECKER, APROVE or KITTEL.

While the source code for the inner loop of PotentialMinimizeSEVPABug.c in **Ex. 3** is straight-forward (decrement x; assign 0 to y if x <= 1) the corresponding expressions in the lifted binaries involve multiple bitvector operations:

```
(((tmp_42 != 0u)&1) &
((((tmp_44 == 0u)&1 ^ (((((tmp_44 ^ tmp_45) + tmp_45) == 2u)&1)))&1)))&1
```

This expression simulates branch comparisons that the machine would perform on values whose type was discarded during compilation. The source code variable x is a signed integer, but compilation has stripped its type. During decompilation, to approximate, lifting procedures consider these tmp variables (and all integer variables) to be unsigned. Meanwhile, in the binary, the condition x<=0 is compiled to be a *signed* comparison. Therefore, lifting recreates a signed comparison using the unsigned tmp variables. Lifted binaries are good candidates for bitwise branching; in this example 3 rules can be applied.

7.2   DARKSEA: A Toolchain for Temporal Verification of Lifted Binaries

Bitvector operations are not the only issue: lifted binaries have several other wrinkles that preclude them from being verified with today's tools. We briefly discuss these issues and how we address them in a new toolchain called DARK-SEA, the first tool capable of verifying reachability, termination and LTL properties of lifted binaries. DARKSEA is comprised of several components:

DARKSEA takes as input a lifted binary (obtained from IDA PRO and MCSEMA) in LLVM IR format, which then can be converted to C via llvm-cbe.

Lifting tools like MCSEMA [9,25] are often designed with the goal of *recompilation* rather than verification. Consequently, the MCSEMA IR, even if converted to C, cannot be analyzed by existing tools (see Sect. 7.3) which either crash, timeout, memout, or fail during parsing. We therefore perform a series of translations discussed below to re-target the lifted binaries into a format more amenable to verification, which we then input to ULTIMATEBWB. The translations below work with LLVM-8.0 and consist of around 500 lines of C++ and 200 lines of bash. We also identified and fixed several defects in MCSEMA [3–5].

1. *Run-time environment.* For *re*-compilation, lifting yields code that switches context between the run-time environments and the simulated code, akin

to how a loader moves environment variables onto the stack. A first pass of DARKSEA analyzes lifted output to discover the original program's `main`, decouples the surrounding context-switch code, and removes it.

2. *Passing emulation state through procedures.* MCSEMA generates lifted programs in which function arguments pass emulation state that is used for re-compilation. We found this to make it difficult for verifiers to track state. We thus eliminate these arguments from every function call, creating a single global pointer to the emulation state struct and replacing all uses of the first argument in the function body with a use of our new pointer.

3. *Nested structures.* Lifted binaries simulate hardware features (*e.g.,* registers, arithmetic flags, FPU status flags) and, for cache efficiency, represent them as nested structures, *e.g.,* `state->general_registers.register13.union .uint64cell`. DARKSEA flattens these nested data structures, creating individual variables for all the innermost and separable fields, and then translates accesses to these nested structures.

4. *Property-directed slicing.* Not all the instructions are relevant to the properties we aim to verify, so we further slice the program to keep only property-dependent code, using DG [17] in termination-sensitive mode. For LTL properties, we use the atomic propositions' variables to seed our slicing criteria.

A longer discussion of these translations can be found in [40].

7.3   Experiments

We evaluated whether our translations (Sect. 7.2) and bitwise branching (Sect. 4) enabled tools to verify termination and LTL properties of decompiled binaries.

Termination of Lifted Binaries. As discussed in Sect. 6, there are several termination provers that support bitvector programs. We thus applied those termination provers to today's lifting results on both the raw output of MCSEMA and then on the output of our translation. We used a standard termination benchmark (*i.e.,* 18 small, but challenging programs in literature selected from the SV-COMP `termination-crafted` benchmark). As discussed in Sect. 7.2, lifted code is more complicated than its corresponding source (*e.g.,* >10k vs 533 LOC in total). Although today's termination provers can verify the source of these programs, they struggle to analyze the corresponding code lifted from the programs' binaries, as seen in the **Raw McSema** columns in Table 1 (details in [40]).

Table 1. Termination of lifted binaries, with and without DARKSEA translations.

	Raw McSema						DARKSEA transl.					
	AProVE	CPACHECKER	KITTEL	2LS	ULTIMATE	ULTIMATEBwB	AProVE	CPACHECKER	KITTEL	2LS	ULTIMATE	ULTIMATEBwB
✔	-	-	-	-	-	-	-	-	-	-	18	18
✚	-	18	-	-	3	-	-	-	-	-	-	-
M	-	-	-	-	-	3	-	-	-	-	-	-
T	-	-	18	-	15	15	-	18	18	-	-	-
?	18	-	-	18	-	-	18	-	-	18	-	-

We devoted genuine effort to overcome small hurdles but, fundamentally, without the DARKSEA translations, tools struggled for the following reasons:

- APROVE: Errors in conversion from LLVM IR to internal representation.
- KITTEL: Parsing (from C to KITTEL's format via LLVM bitcode with LLVM2KITTEL) succeeded, but then KITTEL silently hung until timeout.
- CPACHECKER: Crashes on all benchmarks, while parsing system headers.
- ULTIMATE: Crashes on 3 benchmarks, due to inconsistent type exceptions.

Table 1 also shows the verification results of those termination provers when applied to DARKSEA's translated output (second set of columns).

In sum, the results show that our translations benefit both CPACHECKER and ULTIMATE (which already have sophisticated parsers), reducing crashes in analyzing lifted code. As highlighted in green, DARKSEA translations enabled ULTIMATE to prove termination on all of the 18 lifted programs, as compared to ULTIMATE timing out on 15 of the programs without DARKSEA's translations.

LTL of Lifted Binaries. We finally evaluate the effectiveness of DARKSEA on LTL properties of 8 lifted binaries. In Table 2 we report the LTL property and expected verification result of each, as well as the verification time and result of ULTIMATE and DARKSEA on them. Green cells use slightly different settings for single block encoding. DARKSEA's translations eliminate unsoundness results that come from applying ULTIMATE directly to McSEMA IR.

Table 2. ULTIMATE vs. DARKSEA on lifted programs with LTL properties.

Benchmark	Property	Exp.	ULTIMATE Time	ULTIMATE Result	DARKSEA Time	DARKSEA Result
01-exsec2.s.c	$\Diamond(\Box x = 1)$	✔	4.45 s	☢	11.23 s	✔
01-exsec2.s.f.c.c	$\Diamond(\Box x \neq 1)$	✗	6.31 s	☢	10.36 s	✗
SEVPA_gccO0.s.c	$\Box(x > 0 \Rightarrow \Diamond y = 0)$	✔	6.31 s	☢	22.92 s	✔
SEVPA_gccO0.s.f.c	$\Box(x > 0 \Rightarrow \Diamond y = 2)$	✗	5.16 s	?	14.92 s	✗
acqrel.simplify.s.c	$\Box(x = 0 \Rightarrow \Diamond y = 0)$	✔	5.17 s	☢	9.00 s	✔
acqrel.simplify.s.f.c.c	$\Box(x = 0 \Rightarrow \Diamond y = 1)$	✗	6.06 s	☢	17.60 s	✗
exsec2.simplify.s.c	$\Box\Diamond x = 1$	✔	4.92 s	☢	5.60 s	✔
exsec2.simplify.s.f.c.c	$\Box\Diamond x \neq 1$	✗	4.55 s	☢	6.28 s	✗

In summary, we have shown that DARKSEA can verify reachability, termination and LTL properties of lifted binaries. To our knowledge, DARKSEA is the first to do so.

8 Related Work

Bitvector Reasoning. Many works support bitvector reasoning in SMT solvers (*e.g.*, [52]). Kroening *et al.* [38] perform predicate image over-approximation.

Niemetz *et al.* [46] propose a translation from bitvector formulas with parametric bit-width to formulas in a logic supported by SMT solvers, making SMT-based procedures available for variant-size bitvector formulas.

He and Rakamarić [30] build on spurious counterexamples from overapproximations of bitvector operations. Mattsen *et al.* [41] use a BDD-based abstract domain for indirect jump reasoning. Bryant *et al.* [16] iterative construct an abstraction of a bit vector formula.

Other works have targeted reasoning about *termination* of bitvector programs. Cook *et al.* [21] use Presburger arithmetic for representing rank functions. Chen *et al.* [19] employ lexicographic rank function synthesis for bit precision and rely on the bit-precision of an underlying SMT solver. Falke *et al.* [26] propose an approach, implemented in KITTeL, which derives linear approximations of bitvector operations using some rules similar to our bitwise-branching rules for expressions. However, Falke *et al.* create a large disjunction of cases which puts a large burden on the solver. By contrast, our bitwise-branching creates multiple verification paths, but solver queries for most of them can be avoided through integer interpolation. As we show in Sect. 6, our ULTIMATEBWB was able to solve 33/49 benchmarks, where as KITTeL solved only 10. Moreover, KITTeL does not support LTL properties and crashes on lifted binaries.

Tools for Disassembly and Decompilation. Jakstab [37] focuses on accurate control flow reconstruction in the *disassembly* process. BAP [15] performs static disassembly of stripped binaries. Angr [49] includes symbolic execution and value-set analysis used especially for control flow reconstruction. IDA Pro [48] (used in DARKSEA) demonstrated high accuracy and uses value-set-analysis. Hex-Rays Decompiler [2], Ghidra [8], and Snowman [24] further de-compile disassembled output to higher level representations such as LLVM IR or C code.

Verifying Binaries. Some works focus on the low-level aspects of the binary and aim at precise de-compilation. Roessle *et al.* [47] de-compile x86-64 into a big step semantics. Earlier, others performed "decompilation-into-logic" (DiL) [43–45], translating assembly code into logic. While DiL provides a rich environment for precise reasoning about fine-grained instruction-level details, it incurs high complexity for reasoning about more coarse-grained properties such as reachability, termination, and temporal logic. In more recent work, Verbeek *et al.* [51] use the semantics of Roessle *et al.* [47] and describe techniques to decompile into re-compilable code.

Others focus on verifying the decompilation/lifting process itself. Dasgupta *et al.* [22] describe a translation validation on x86-64 instructions that employs their semantics for x86-64 (Dasgupta *et al.* [23]). Metere *et al.* [42] use HOL4 to verify a translation from ARMv8 to BAP. Hendrix *et al.* [33] discuss their ongoing work on verifying the translation performed by their lifting tool reopt. Numerous other works (*e.g.,* Sail [11]) provide formal semantics of ISAs.

9   Conclusion

We have shown that a source-level translation to approximate bitvector operations leads to tools that are competitive to the state-of-the-art in reachability and termination of bitvector programs. We show that bitwise branching incurs negligible overhead, yet enables more programs to be verified. Notably, we showed that this approach leads to the first effective technique for verifying LTL of bitvector programs and, to our knowledge, the first technique for verifying reachability, termination and LTL of lifted binary programs.

Acknowledgments. We thank the anonymous reviewers for their helpful feedback. This work is supported by ONR Grant #N00014-17-1-2787.

A   Proof of Theorem 1

Proof. Induction on traces, showing equality on expression translation T_E via induction on expressions/statements and then inclusion on statement translations T_S. First show that T_E preserves traces equivalence. Structural induction on e, with base cases being constants, variables, etc. In the inductive case, for a bitvector operation $e_1 \otimes e_2$, assume e_1, e_2 has been (potentially) transformed to e_1', e_2' (resp.) and that Lemma 1 holds for each $i \in \{1, 2\}$: $\forall \sigma. [\![e_i]\!]\sigma = [\![e_i']\!]\sigma$. Since $\otimes$ is deterministic, $[\![e_1' \otimes e_2']\!]\sigma = [\![e_1 \otimes e_2]\!]\sigma$. Finally, applying the transformation to $\otimes$, we show that $[\![T_E\{e_1' \otimes e_2'\}]\!] = [\![e_1' \otimes e_2']\!]$ again by Lemma 1. Next, for each statement s or relational condition c step, we prove T_S preserves trace inclusion: that $[\![s]\!] \subseteq [\![T_S\{s\}]\!]$ or that $[\![c]\!] \subseteq [\![T_S\{c\}]\!]$. We do not recursively weaken conditional boolean expressions, which would require alternating strengthening/weakening. Thus, inclusion holds directly from Lemma 1.

References

1. AProVE. aprove.informatik.rwth-aachen.de/eval/Bitvectors/
2. Hex-rays decompiler. www.hex-rays.com/products/decompiler/
3. MCSEMA jump table bug. github.com/lifting-bits/mcsema/issues/558
4. MCSEMA bug, missing data cross reference due to resetting ida's analysis flag. github.com/lifting-bits/mcsema/issues/561
5. MCSEMA var. bug. github.com/lifting-bits/mcsema/issues/566
6. SV-COMP Termination Benchmarks. github.com/sosy-lab/sv-benchmarks/tree/master/c/termination-crafted
7. Ultimate's LTL benchmarks. github.com/ultimate-pa/ultimate/tree/dev/trunk/examples/LTL/
8. National Security Agency: Ghidra. www.nsa.gov/resources/everyone/ghidra/
9. Altinay, A., et al.: BinRec: dynamic binary lifting and recompilation. In: EuroSys, pp. 36:1–36:16 (2020)
10. Anderson, S.: Bit twiddling hacks. graphics.stanford.edu/ seander/bithacks.html
11. Armstrong, A., et al.: ISA semantics for ARMv8-a, RISC-v, and CHERI-MIPS. Proc. ACM Program. Lang. **3**(POPL), 1–31 (2019)

12. Barnett, M., Chang, B.-Y.E., DeLine, R., Jacobs, B., Leino, K.R.M.: Boogie: a modular reusable verifier for object-oriented programs. In: de Boer, F.S., Bonsangue, M.M., Graf, S., de Roever, W.-P. (eds.) FMCO 2005. LNCS, vol. 4111, pp. 364–387. Springer, Heidelberg (2006). https://doi.org/10.1007/11804192_17

13. Beyer, D., Löwe, S., Wendler, P.: Reliable benchmarking: requirements and solutions. Int. J. Softw. Tools Technol. Transfer **21**(1), 1–29 (2017). https://doi.org/10.1007/s10009-017-0469-y

14. Bozzano, M., et al.: Encoding RTL constructs for MathSAT: a preliminary report. Electron. Notes Theor. Comput. Sci. **144**(2), 3–14 (2006)

15. Brumley, D., Jager, I., Avgerinos, T., Schwartz, E.J.: BAP: a binary analysis platform. In: Gopalakrishnan, G., Qadeer, S. (eds.) CAV 2011. LNCS, vol. 6806, pp. 463–469. Springer, Heidelberg (2011). https://doi.org/10.1007/978-3-642-22110-1_37

16. Bryant, R.E., Kroening, D., Ouaknine, J., Seshia, S.A., Strichman, O., Brady, B.: Deciding bit-vector arithmetic with abstraction. In: Grumberg, O., Huth, M. (eds.) TACAS 2007. LNCS, vol. 4424, pp. 358–372. Springer, Heidelberg (2007). https://doi.org/10.1007/978-3-540-71209-1_28

17. Chalupa, M.: mchalupa/dg, January 2021. github.com/mchalupa/dg

18. Chen, H., David, C., Kroening, D., Schrammel, P., Wachter, B.: Synthesising interprocedural bit-precise termination proofs (T). In: ASE, pp. 53–64 (2015)

19. Chen, H.Y., David, C., Kroening, D., Schrammel, P., Wachter, B.: Bit-precise procedure-modular termination analysis. ACM Trans. Program. Lang. Syst. **40**, 1–38 (2018)

20. Cook, B., Koskinen, E.: Making prophecies with decision predicates. In: Proceedings of the 38th Annual ACM SIGPLAN-SIGACT Symposium on Principles of Programming Languages, POPL 2011, pp. 399–410 (2011)

21. Cook, B., Kroening, D., Rümmer, P., Wintersteiger, C.M.: Ranking function synthesis for bit-vector relations. In: Esparza, J., Majumdar, R. (eds.) TACAS 2010. LNCS, vol. 6015, pp. 236–250. Springer, Heidelberg (2010). https://doi.org/10.1007/978-3-642-12002-2_19

22. Dasgupta, S., Dinesh, S., Venkatesh, D., Adve, V.S., Fletcher, C.W.: Scalable validation of binary lifters. In: Proceedings of the 41st ACM SIGPLAN Conference on Programming Language Design and Implementation, pp. 655–671, June 2020

23. Dasgupta, S., Park, D., Kasampalis, T., Adve, V.S., Roşu, G.: A complete formal semantics of x86-64 user-level instruction set architecture, p. 16 (2019)

24. Derevenets, Y.: Snowman. derevenets.com/

25. Dinaburg, A., Ruef, A.: McSema: static translation of x86 instructions to LLVM. In: ReCon 2014 Conference, Montreal, Canada (2014)

26. Falke, S., Kapur, D., Sinz, C.: Termination analysis of imperative programs using bitvector arithmetic. In: Joshi, R., Müller, P., Podelski, A. (eds.) VSTTE 2012. LNCS, vol. 7152, pp. 261–277. Springer, Heidelberg (2012). https://doi.org/10.1007/978-3-642-27705-4_21

27. Galois, I.: Macaw. github.com/GaloisInc/macaw

28. Galois, I.: Reopt vcg. github.com/GaloisInc/reopt-vcg

29. Giesl, J., et al.: Analyzing program termination and complexity automatically with AProVE. J. Autom. Reason. **58**(1), 3–31 (2016). https://doi.org/10.1007/s10817-016-9388-y

30. He, S., Rakamarić, Z.: Counterexample-guided bit-precision selection. In: Chang, B.-Y.E. (ed.) APLAS 2017. LNCS, vol. 10695, pp. 534–553. Springer, Cham (2017). https://doi.org/10.1007/978-3-319-71237-6_26

31. Heizmann, M., et al.: Ultimate program analysis framework, p. 1
32. Heizmann, M., Hoenicke, J., Podelski, A.: Termination analysis by learning terminating programs. In: Biere, A., Bloem, R. (eds.) CAV 2014. LNCS, vol. 8559, pp. 797–813. Springer, Cham (2014). https://doi.org/10.1007/978-3-319-08867-9_53
33. Hendrix, J., Wei, G., Winwood, S.: Towards verified binary raising, p. 4
34. Hensel, J., Giesl, J., Frohn, F., Ströder, T.: Proving termination of programs with bitvector arithmetic by symbolic execution. In: De Nicola, R., Kühn, E. (eds.) SEFM 2016. LNCS, vol. 9763, pp. 234–252. Springer, Cham (2016). https://doi.org/10.1007/978-3-319-41591-8_16
35. Henzinger, T.A., Necula, G.C., Jhala, R., Sutre, G., Majumdar, R., Weimer, W.: Temporal-safety proofs for systems code. In: Brinksma, E., Larsen, K.G. (eds.) CAV 2002. LNCS, vol. 2404, pp. 526–538. Springer, Heidelberg (2002). https://doi.org/10.1007/3-540-45657-0_45
36. Kinder, J.: Jakstab. http://www.jakstab.org/
37. Kinder, J., Veith, H.: Precise static analysis of untrusted driver binaries. In: Formal Methods in Computer Aided Design, pp. 43–50. IEEE (2010)
38. Kroening, D., Sharygina, N.: Approximating predicate images for bit-vector logic. In: Hermanns, H., Palsberg, J. (eds.) TACAS 2006. LNCS, vol. 3920, pp. 242–256. Springer, Heidelberg (2006). https://doi.org/10.1007/11691372_16
39. Leike, J., Heizmann, M.: Geometric nontermination arguments. In: Beyer, D., Huisman, M. (eds.) TACAS 2018. LNCS, vol. 10806, pp. 266–283. Springer, Cham (2018). https://doi.org/10.1007/978-3-319-89963-3_16
40. Liu, Y.C., et al.: Proving LTL properties of bitvector programs and decompiled binaries (extended). CoRR abs/2105.05159 (2021). https://arxiv.org/abs/2105.05159
41. Mattsen, S., Wichmann, A., Schupp, S.: A non-convex abstract domain for the value analysis of binaries. In: SANER, pp. 271–280 (2015)
42. Metere, R., Lindner, A., Guanciale, R.: Sound transpilation from binary to machine-independent code, vol. 10623, pp. 197–214. arXiv:1807.10664 [cs] (2017)
43. Myreen, M.O., Gordon, M.J.C.: Hoare logic for realistically modelled machine code. In: Grumberg, O., Huth, M. (eds.) TACAS 2007. LNCS, vol. 4424, pp. 568–582. Springer, Heidelberg (2007). https://doi.org/10.1007/978-3-540-71209-1_44
44. Myreen, M.O., Gordon, M.J.C., Slind, K.: Machine-code verification for multiple architectures - an application of decompilation into logic. In: Formal Methods in Computer-Aided Design, FMCAD 2008, pp. 1–8 (2008)
45. Myreen, M.O., Gordon, M.J.C., Slind, K.: Decompilation into logic - improved. In: Formal Methods in Computer-Aided Design, FMCAD 2012, Cambridge, UK, 22–25 October 2012, pp. 78–81 (2012)
46. Niemetz, A., Preiner, M., Reynolds, A., Zohar, Y., Barrett, C., Tinelli, C.: Towards bit-width-independent proofs in SMT solvers. In: Fontaine, P. (ed.) CADE 2019. LNCS (LNAI), vol. 11716, pp. 366–384. Springer, Cham (2019). https://doi.org/10.1007/978-3-030-29436-6_22
47. Roessle, I., Verbeek, F., Ravindran, B.: Formally verified big step semantics out of x86-64 binaries. In: Proceedings of the 8th ACM SIGPLAN International Conference on Certified Programs and Proofs (2019)
48. IDA Support: Hex Rays: IDA pro. www.hex-rays.com/products/ida/
49. Shoshitaishvili, Y., et al.: SOK: (state of) the art of war: offensive techniques in binary analysis. In: 2016 IEEE Symposium on S&P (2016)
50. SoSy-Lab: CPACHECKER. cpachecker.sosy-lab.org/

51. Verbeek, F., Olivier, P., Ravindran, B.: Sound C code decompilation for a subset of x86-64 binaries. In: de Boer, F., Cerone, A. (eds.) SEFM 2020. LNCS, vol. 12310, pp. 247–264. Springer, Cham (2020). https://doi.org/10.1007/978-3-030-58768-0_14

52. Wintersteiger, C.M., Hamadi, Y., de Moura, L.: Efficiently solving quantified bit-vector formulas. Formal Methods Syst. Des. **42**, 3–23 (2013). https://doi.org/10.1007/s10703-012-0156-2

53. Zohar, Y., et al.: Bit-Precise Reasoning via Int-Blasting (2021)

Solving Not-Substring Constraint
with Flat Abstraction

Parosh Aziz Abdulla[1], Mohamed Faouzi Atig[1], Yu-Fang Chen[2(✉)],
Bui Phi Diep[2], Lukáš Holík[3], Denghang Hu[4], Wei-Lun Tsai[2], Zhillin Wu[4],
and Di-De Yen[2]

[1] Uppsala University, Uppsala, Sweden
{parosh,mohamed_faouzi.atig}@it.uu.se
[2] Academia Sinica, Taipei, Taiwan
{yfc,alan23273850,bottle}@iis.sinica.edu.tw, bui.phi-diep@it.uu.se
[3] Brno University of Technology, Brno, Czech Republic
holik@fit.vutbr.cz
[4] State Key Laboratory of Computer Science, Institute of Software, Chinese
Academy of Sciences, Beijing, China
{hudh,wuzl}@ios.ac.cn

Abstract. Not-substring is currently among the least supported types
of string constraints, and existing solvers use only relatively crude heuristics. Yet, not-substring occurs relatively often in practical examples and
is useful in encoding other types of constraints. In this paper, we propose
a systematic way to solve not-substring using based on flat abstraction.
In this framework, the domain of string variables is restricted to flat
languages and subsequently the whole constraints can be expressed as
linear arithmetic formulae. We show that non-substring constraints can
be flattened efficiently, and provide experimental evidence that the proposed solution for not-substring is competitive with the state of the art
string solvers.

Keywords: String constraints · Not-substring relation · Flat
abstraction · Formal verification

1 Introduction

Due to the fast growth of web applications, string data type plays an increasingly
important role in computer software. Many software security vulnerabilities, such
as cross-site scripting and injection attack, are caused by careless treatment of
strings in programs [1], which jeopardize the end-users' trust in digital technology. There is therefore a crucial need of rigorous engineering techniques to ensure
the correctness of string manipulating programs. Such techniques (e.g. (bounded)

This work has been supported by the Czech Ministry of Education, Youth and Sports
ERC.CZ project LL1908, the FIT BUT internal project FIT-S-20-6427, Guangdong
Science and Technology Department grant (No. 2018B010107004), the NSFC grants
(No. 61872340), and the INRIA-CAS joint research project VIP.

© Springer Nature Switzerland AG 2021
H. Oh (Ed.): APLAS 2021, LNCS 13008, pp. 305–320, 2021.
https://doi.org/10.1007/978-3-030-89051-3_17

model checking [10,15,21], symbolic execution techniques [11,19], and concolic testing [17,24]) are highly based on efficient symbolic encodings of executions into a formula, and rely on highly performing constraint solvers for computing on such encodings. The types of constraints needed depend on the types of program expressions to be analyzed. In the case of scripting languages, constraint solvers need to support different combinations of string operations.

Thus, *string constraint solvers* such as [3–5,7,8,12,18,20,25] are the engine of modern web program analysis techniques. Due to the high demand, there is a boosting amount of publications on this subject in recent years (e.g., [3,9,13,22]). Implementing a constraint solver to cover all standard string libraries in programming languages is a challenging task. One can choose to develop a specialized solving procedure for each string operation, but it requires enormous maintenance efforts. A more feasible solution is to define a minimal set of core constraints that is expressive to encode all others and develop solving procedures only for these core constraints. A common set of such constraints includes: (1) *equality constraints*, e.g., $x.y = y.z$, which says the concatenation of string variables x and y equals the concatenation of y and z, (2) *membership constraints*, e.g., $x \in L(ab^*)$, which says the value of x is the character a followed by a sequence of b's, and (3) *length constraints*, e.g., $|x| = |y| + 3$, which says the length of x is the length of y plus 3, and (4) *"not substring constraints"*, e.g., $\texttt{NotSubstr}(x,y)$, which says x is not a substring of y. Most of the early works focused on the first three types of constraints. The "not substring" constraints have not been systematically studied before[1]. In fact, many common string operations, such as, indexOf and replace, cannot be precisely expressed without using "not substring constraints". Previous study [23] suggests that those operations are among the most commonly used string operation in the applications they studied. The same observation holds while checking existing string constraint benchmarks [2].

More concretely, for two string variables x, y, the operations indexOf(x, y) should return the first occurrence of y in x. We can use the equality and length constraints to encode the position y in x as follows. We need two extra free variables p and s. Then we can use $x = p.y.s$ to express that y is a substring of x and in this case, $|p|$ is the position of y in x. However, there is no guarantee that this y is the first occurrence in x. To do so, we still need to make sure y never occurs in $p.y'$ where y' is the prefix of y with only the last character removed, i.e., $y'.z = y \wedge |z| = 1$ for some z. This can be guaranteed using the constraint NotSubStr(y, $p.y'$). In fact, this is exactly how the Z3 SMT solver encodes indexOf constraint [20].

Observe that the positive version $x \sqsubseteq y$ (i.e., x is a substring of y) can be easily encoded as $y = p.x.s$ using two extra variables. However, the negated version of $x \sqsubseteq y$ is not equivalent to $y \neq p.x.s$. For example, $(x,y,p,s) = ($"a", "ab", ϵ, $\epsilon)$ is a model for this latter formula, but x is a substring of y in this case. To capture the not-substring relation precisely, we need to establish that,

---

[1] More precisely, *"replace all"* constraints [5] and string-integer conversion constraints [3] are not covered by these common set of constraints. Nevertheless, both have been systematically discussed in recent years.

for all strings p and s, y does not equal $p.x.s$; or more formally $\forall p, s : y \neq p.x.s$. Unfortunately, it is known that equality constraint with universal quantifiers is undecidable [16]. Although state-of-the-art solvers, such as Z3, reduce the indexOf and replace constraints by the not-substring constraint, their procedures for solving the latter do not provide much guarantee regarding completeness. It is not hard to find instances with not-substring constraints that the most advanced solvers like CVC4 and Z3 fail to solve (see Fig. 1).

$$v.u = u.v \wedge u = p_1.\text{“123456”}.s_1 \wedge v = p_2.\text{“12345”}.s_2 \wedge |u| = 21 \wedge u.\text{“a”}.v \not\sqsubseteq v.\text{“a”}.y$$

Fig. 1. An example that both CVC4 and Z3 fail to solve in 3 min

In this work, we extend the framework of flat underapproximation [3–5] to handle not substring. The framework has been shown efficient and easily extensible to a rich set of string constraints. It was for instance one of the first approaches to handle string-to-int constraints [3] and it is competitive in efficiency with the best solvers. It relies on construction of so called *flattening* as an underapproximation of string constraints. Namely, it restricts domains of string variables to flat languages of the form $w_1^* w_2^* \cdots w_n^*$, where n and the length of the words $w_1, \ldots, w_n$ are parameters controlling the balance between the cost and the precision of the underapproximation. Under this restriction, string constraints are losslesly translated into quantifier-free linear integer arithmetic formula. The formula is then efficiently handled by the state-of-art SMT solvers. The flat underapproximation is then combined with an overapproximation module capable of proving unsatisfiability. In this work, we are using particularly the method of [13,14], implemented in the tool OSTRICH, to prove the unsatisfiability. The overapproximation module either solves the constraint as is, if it fits the straight-line fragment of OSTRICH, or it solves an overapproximation of the constraints that fits the fragment. Namely, not-substring constraints of the form $t_1 \not\sqsubseteq t_2$ are first overapproximated as disequalities $t_1 \neq t_2$, and if the straight-line restriction is broken after that, it is recovered by replacing certain occurrences of variables by fresh variables. String-integer conversion constraints, that are not handled by OSTRICH, are simply removed.

A main contribution of this work is a construction that allows to flatten also non-substring constraints. Our solution is efficient despite that the final arithmetic formula for not-substring is not entirely quantifier free—it contains a single universal quantifier. The SMT solver Z3 apparently solves the formulae generated by our implementation fast.

We have evaluated our implementation of the extended framework on a large set of benchmarks from the literature, and a new benchmark collected from executions of the symbolic executor Py-Conbyte[2] on three GitHub projects. Our experimental results show that our prototype, STR, is among the best tools for

---

[2] https://github.com/alan23273850/py-conbyte.

solving basic string constraints and outperforms all other tools on benchmarks with not substring constraints.

2   Preliminaries

We use $\mathbb{N}$ (resp., $\mathbb{Z}^+$) to denote the set of non-negative integers (resp., positive integers). For $m, n \in \mathbb{Z}^+$, we write $[n]$ (resp. $[m, n]$) to denote the set $\{1, \ldots, n\}$ (resp. $\{m, m+1, \ldots, n\}$). We use x, y, ... to denote the integer variables.

In this paper, we assume that Σ is a finite alphabet satisfying $\Sigma \subseteq \mathbb{N}$. The elements of Σ are called *characters*. We use $a, b, \ldots$ to denote the characters. A *string* u over Σ is a sequence $a_1 \ldots a_n$ where $a_i \in \Sigma$ for all i. We use ε to represent the empty string. For two strings u and v, u is said to be a *substring* of v if there exist strings w and w' such that $v = wuw'$. For a string $u = a_1 \ldots a_n$, $|u|$ represents the *length* of u, that is n; moreover, for $i \in [n]$, $u(i) = a_i$ represents the i-th character of u. In addition, for a string u and $a \in \Sigma$, we use $|u|_a$ to denote the number of occurrences of a in u. We use Σ^* to denote the set of strings over Σ, and $\Sigma^{\leq n}$ to denote the set of strings in Σ^* of length at most n. For convenience, we assume that ε is encoded by a fixed natural number from $\mathbb{N} \setminus \Sigma$, and let Σ_ε denote $\Sigma \cup \{\varepsilon\}$.

We use $x, y, \ldots$ to denote *string variables* ranging over Σ^* and we use X to denote the set of string variables. A *string term* is a sequence over $\Sigma_\varepsilon \cup X$.

A *linear integer arithmetic* (LIA) formula is defined by $\phi ::= t \circ 0 \mid t \equiv c \bmod c \mid \phi \wedge \phi \mid \phi \vee \phi \mid \neg\phi \mid \exists x. \phi \mid \forall x. \phi$ and $t ::= c \mid x \mid t + t \mid t - t$, where $\circ \in \{=, \neq, <, >, \leq, \geq\}$ and x, c are integer variables and constants respectively. A *quantifier-free* LIA (QFLIA) formula is an LIA formula containing no quantifiers. The set of free variables of ϕ, denoted by $\mathsf{Var}(\phi)$, is defined in a standard manner. Given an LIA formula ϕ, and an integer interpretation of $\mathsf{Var}(\phi)$, i.e. a function $I : \mathsf{Var}(\phi) \to \mathbb{Z}$, we denote by $I \models \phi$ that I satisfies ϕ (which is defined in the standard manner), and call I a *model* of ϕ. We use $[\![\phi]\!]$ to denote the set of models of ϕ.

Finally, the *Parikh image* of a word $w \in \Sigma^*$ maps each Parikh (integer) variable $\#a$, where $a \in \Sigma$, to the number of occurrences of a in w. Let $\#\Sigma = \{\#a \mid a \in \Sigma\}$. The Parikh image of w is a function $\mathbb{P}(w) : \#\Sigma \to \mathbb{N}$ such that $\mathbb{P}(w)(\#a) = |w|_a$, for each $a \in \Sigma$. The Parikh image of a language L is defined as $\mathbb{P}(L) = \{\mathbb{P}(w) \mid w \in L\}$. It is well known that the Parikh image of a regular language can be characterized by an LIA formula.

3   String Constraints

In this paper, we extend the class of atomic constraints handled in the framework of [3–5] with not-substring. We focus especially on the core constraints, conjunctions of the atomic constraints of the following forms:

- a string equality constraint $t_1 = t_2$, where t_1, t_2 are string terms,
- a not-substring constraint $t_1 \not\sqsubseteq t_2$, where t_1, t_2 are string terms,

- a QFLIA formula over the integer variables $|x|$ for string variables x,
- a regular constraint $x \in \mathcal{A}$, where x is a string variable and $\mathcal{A}$ is an FA.

We note that presented extension is compatible also with the other types of constraints handled by [3–5], especially context-free membership, transducer constraints, string-integer conversions, negated membership, and disequality. We omit these for simplicity of presentation. For a string constraint ϕ, let us use StrVar(ϕ) and LenVar(ϕ) to denote the set of string variables and the set of length (integer) variables respectively.

While the semantics of linear integer constraints and regular constraints are standard, let us explain the semantics of the string equality constraints and string not-substring constraints:

- A string equality constraint $t_1 = t_2$ has a solution iff there is a homomorphism h from $(X \cup \Sigma)^*$ to Σ^* such that $h(u) = u$ for all $u \in \Sigma^*$ and $h(t_1) = h(t_2)$. For instance, let $t_1 = abxc$, $t_2 = yc$, and $t_3 = ya$. Then $h(x) = \epsilon$ and $h(y) = ab$ is a solution of $t_1 = t_2$. However, for all homomorphisms h, $h(t_1) \neq h(t_3)$, thus $t_1 = t_3$ is not satisfiable.
- A not-substring constraint $t_1 \not\sqsubseteq t_2$ has a solution iff there is a homomorphism h from $(X \cup \Sigma)^*$ to Σ^* such that $h(u) = u$ for all $u \in \Sigma^*$ and $h(t_1)$ is *not* a substring of $h(t_2)$. For instance, let $t_1 = ax$, $t_2 = abxc$, and $t_3 = bx$. Then $h(x) = a$ is a solution of $t_1 \not\sqsubseteq t_2$. However, $t_3 \not\sqsubseteq t_2$ is not satisfiable since $t_3 = bx$ is a subterm of $t_2 = abxc$.

We would like to remark that although the aforementioned class of string constraints does not include explicitly the constraint that t_1 is a substring of t_2, they can be encoded by the string equality constraint $t_2 = xt_1y$, where x, y are the freshly introduced string variables.

4   Solving String Constraints with Flattening

In this section, we will recall the principles of the flattening approach to string solving used in the works [3–5], which we will then extend with not-substring constraints in Sect. 5.

4.1   (Parametric) Flat Languages

We will present our underapproximations in terms of *flat languages*, which are used to restrict the domain of string variables, and *parametric flat languages*, that are used to specify them.

For integers k and ℓ and a string variable x, we define the family of indexed *character variables* CharVar$_{k,\ell}(x) = \{x_j^i \mid 1 \leq i \leq k, 1 \leq j \leq \ell\}$. A *parametric flat language* (PFL) with the *period* ℓ and the *cycle count* k is the language PFL$_{k,\ell}$ of strings over the alphabet CharVar$_{k,\ell}(x)$ that conform to the regular expression

$$(x_1^1 \ldots x_\ell^1)^* \cdot \ldots \cdot (x_1^k \ldots x_\ell^k)^*$$

That is, the words of $\mathrm{PFL}_{k,\ell}$ consist of k consecutive parts, each created by iterating a *cycle*, a string $x_1^i \ldots x_\ell^i$ of ℓ unique character variables.

A word $w = x_1 \ldots x_n \in \mathrm{PFL}_{k,\ell}$ will be interpreted respective to an interpretation of the character variables $I_{\mathsf{Char}} : \mathsf{CharVar}_{k,\ell}(x) \to \Sigma_\varepsilon$ as a string $I_{\mathsf{Char}}(w) = I_{\mathsf{Char}}(x_1) \cdots I_{\mathsf{Char}}(x_n)$ over Σ.

The property of a PFL that is central in our approach is that every PFL is fully characterised by its Parikh image. Let $\mathsf{ParVar}_{k,\ell}(x) = \{\#x_i^j \mid 1 \leq i \leq \ell, 1 \leq j \leq k\}$ be the set of Parikh variables for $\mathsf{CharVar}_{k,\ell}(x)$. Their interpretation $I_{\mathsf{Par}} : \mathsf{ParVar}_{k,\ell}(x) \to \mathbb{N}$ can be unambiguously decoded as a word from the language $\mathrm{PFL}_{k,\ell}$:

Proposition 1. *There is a function* $\mathbb{P}_{k,\ell}^{-1} : (\mathsf{ParVar}_{k,\ell}(x) \to \mathbb{N}) \to \mathrm{PFL}_{k,\ell}$ *which acts as the inverse function of* $\mathbb{P}$, *namely,* $\mathbb{P}_{k,\ell}^{-1}(\mathbb{P}(w)) = w$ *for each* $w \in \mathrm{PFL}_{k,\ell}$.

Intuitively, the function $\mathbb{P}_{k,\ell}^{-1}$ computes the word $w \in \mathrm{PFL}_{k,\ell}$ by repeating each cycle several times, the number of repetitions of the i-the cycle being $\mathbb{P}(w)(\#x_1^i)$ (note that $\mathbb{P}(w)(\#x_j^i)$ is the same for all $x_j^i, j \in [\ell]$).

Hence, an interpretation of Parikh variables $I_{\mathsf{Par}} : \mathsf{ParVar}_{k,\ell}(x) \to \mathbb{N}$ together with an interpretation of character variables $I_{\mathsf{Char}} : \mathsf{CharVar}_{k,\ell}(x) \to \Sigma_\varepsilon$ encode a word over Σ, namely the word $I_{\mathsf{Char}}(\mathbb{P}_{k,\ell}^{-1}(I_{\mathsf{Par}}))$.

The set of all strings over Σ that can be encoded as such pair of interpretations $I_{\mathsf{Char}}, I_{\mathsf{Par}}$ is the *flat language* with the cycle count k and period ℓ:

$$\mathrm{FL}_{k,\ell} = \{I_{\mathsf{Char}}(\mathbb{P}_{k,\ell}^{-1}(I_{\mathsf{Par}})) \mid I_{\mathsf{Char}} : \mathsf{CharVar}_{k,\ell}(x) \to \Sigma_\epsilon, I_{\mathsf{Par}} : \mathsf{ParVar}_{k,\ell}(x) \to \mathbb{N}\}$$

We note that we implement parametric flat languages as parametric flat automata. A parametric flat automaton is a finite automaton with a restricted structure—a sequence of cycles, each representing a cycle of the parametric language, as illustrated on Fig. 2. The automata form is needed for computing flattening of regular, context free, and other constraints (presented in [3,4]). Flattening of non-substring constraints, the subject of this paper, can be however explained using the simpler language view, hence we can abstract from the technicalities of automata in the current paper.

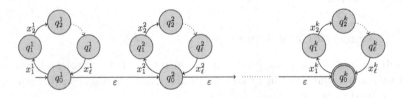

Fig. 2. The flat automaton $\mathcal{A}$ accepting the language $\mathrm{PFL}_{k,\ell}$.

4.2   Flattening of String Constraints

Let us now formalise the notion of flattening, a construction of LIA formulas that encode string constraints restricted to the domain of flat languages.

A *flat semantics* for a string constraint ϕ is obtained from the semantics of ϕ by restricting the domain of each string variable to the language $\mathrm{FL}_{k,\ell}$, for chosen k and ℓ. Let k and ℓ be fixed for the rest of this section.

An assignment I of $\mathsf{Var}(\phi)$ is called k, ℓ-*flat* if for each $x \in \mathsf{StrVar}(\phi)$, $I(x) \in \mathrm{FL}_{k,\ell}$. The flat semantics of ϕ is then defined as

$$\llbracket \phi \rrbracket_{k,\ell} = \{ I \in \llbracket \phi \rrbracket \mid I \text{ is } k, \ell\text{-flat} \}$$

Our approach to string solving is built on that the flat semantics of the string constraint can be precisely encoded by a QFLIA formula in which every string variable $x \in \mathsf{StrVar}(\phi)$ is represented by the character and Parikh variables $\mathsf{CharVar}_{k,\ell}(x)$ and $\mathsf{ParVar}_{k,\ell}(x)$, respectively, and which inherits the integer variables.

A flat solution of ϕ, $I \in \llbracket \phi \rrbracket_{k,\ell}$, is encoded as an assignment $I' = I_{\mathsf{Flat}} \cup I_{\mathsf{Int}}$. I_{Flat} is the assignment of flattening variables that encodes the values of the original string variables. In other words, I' is the union of assignments $I_{\mathsf{CharVar}_{k,\ell}(x)}$: $\mathsf{CharVar}_{k,\ell}(x) \to \Sigma_\varepsilon$ and $I_{\mathsf{ParVar}_{k,\ell}(x)}$: $\mathsf{ParVar}_{k,\ell}(x) \to \mathbb{N}$ for every $x \in \mathsf{StrVar}(\phi)$ satisfying that

$$I(x) = I_{\mathsf{CharVar}_{k,\ell}(x)}(\mathbb{P}_{k,\ell}^{-1}(I_{\mathsf{ParVar}_{k,\ell}(x)}))$$

The encoding is not unique (a string can often be k, ℓ-encoded in multiple ways), hence the encoding function returns the set of all encodings of I, denote $encode_{k,\ell}(I)$.

Decoding is the inverse of encoding, though, due to Proposition 1 it is unambiguous, as stated by this lemma:

Lemma 1. *If* $encode_{k,\ell}(I) \cap encode_{k,\ell}(J) \neq \emptyset$, *then* $I = J$.

Hence we can define the decoding as a function that returns an unique interpretation of variables (not a set, as in the case of encoding):

$$decode_{k,\ell}(I') = I \text{ iff } I' \in encode_{k,\ell}(I)$$

We can now specify the required properties of the flattening QFLIA of ϕ. It is formula $flatten_{k,\ell}(\phi)$ that encodes the flat semantics of ϕ, that is

$$\llbracket \phi \rrbracket_{k,\ell} = decode_{k,\ell}(\llbracket \exists \mathsf{AuxVar} : flatten_{k,\ell}(\phi) \rrbracket) \tag{1}$$

The existential quantification is above used to abstract away additional auxiliary variables AuxVar, variables other than $\mathsf{FlatVar}(\phi)$ and $\mathsf{LenVar}(\phi)$, which the formula $flatten_{k,\ell}(\phi)$ is sometimes constructed with.

The formula $flatten_{k,\ell}(\phi)$ is constructed inductively by following the structure of ϕ: $flatten_{k,\ell}(\phi_1 \wedge \phi_2) = flatten_{k,\ell}(\phi_1) \wedge flatten_{k,\ell}(\phi_2)$. Therefore, it is sufficient to show how to construct $flatten_{k,\ell}(\phi)$ for atomic constraints ϕ. Later on in Sect. 5, we will show how to construct $flatten_{k,\ell}(t_1 \not\sqsubseteq t_2)$. The construction of $flatten_{k,\ell}(\phi)$ for the other atomic constraints is discussed in [3].

For the inductive construction to work, flattening of the atomic constraint has to satisfy a stronger condition than Eq. 1. Namely, the obtained QFLIA formula must capture *all* encodings of the solutions of the string constraint, not only *some* of them. Otherwise for instance the inductive construction of flattening of a conjunction from flattenings of its conjuncts could be incorrect (the intersection of solution encodings could be empty while the sets of solutions themselves do intersect). Formally, the flattening of the atomic constraints must satisfy that:

$$encode_{k,\ell}(\llbracket\phi\rrbracket_{k,\ell}) = \llbracket\exists\mathsf{AuxVar} : flatten_{k,\ell}(\phi)\rrbracket \tag{2}$$

where, again, AuxVar contains auxiliary variables of $flatten_{k,\ell}(\phi)$ other than $\mathsf{FlatVar}(\phi)$ and $\mathsf{LenVar}(\phi)$). A major point of this paper is a construction of flattening of non-substring constraints satisfying Eq. 2, as presented in Sect. 5.

4.3   String Constraint Solving Algorithm

We now shortly recall the whole string solving algorithm. It uses an underapproximation module based on the flat abstraction and an overapproximation module. The two modules are run in parallel. The main loop is summarised in Algorithm 1.

The underapproximation module tries to prove satisfiability of a flat underapproximation, gradually incrementing both the period and cycle count, until the underapproximation is SAT or a limit is reached.

The overapproximation can use any algorithm capable of proving UNSAT. We do not claim any contribution in the overapproximation part, but to demonstrate that such combination indeed yields a capable tool, we combine our underapproximation technique with the method of [13,14] implemented in the tool OSTRICH. It is a complete method for the so called straight-line fragment of string constraints that supports regular and transducer constraints, replace-all, word-equations and other constraints. The straight-line restriction imposes, intuitively, that the constraint must have been obtained from a program in a single static assignment form in which every string variables is assigned at most once and is not used on the right side of an assignment before it is itself assigned. The length constraints are unrestricted (we refer the reader to [13,14] for the precise definition). The overapproximation module either solves the constraint as is, if it fits the straight-line fragment, or it solves an overapproximation of the constraints that fits the fragment. Namely, not-substring constraints of the form $t_1 \not\sqsubseteq t_2$ are first overapproximated as disequalities $t_1 \neq t_2$, and if the straight-line restriction is broken after that, it is recovered by replacing certain occurrences of variables by fresh variables. String-integer conversion constraints, that are not handled by OSTRICH, are simply removed.

5   Flattening of Not-Contains Constraints

We will now describe the construction of the flattening formula for not-substring, the formula $flatten_{(1,\ell)}(t_1 \not\sqsubseteq t_2)$, for given terms t_1, t_2.

Algorithm 1: String solving via flattening

Input: string constraint ϕ, initial period k_0 and cycle count ℓ_0, flattening limit
  $flim$
do in parallel
  | **for** i *from 0 to* $flim$ **do**
  | | **if** $flatten_{k_0+i,\ell_0+i}(\phi)$ *is SAT* **then return** *SAT*
  | **if** $Overapproximate(\phi)$ *is UNSAT* **then return** *UNSAT*
return *UNKNOWN*

5.1 Simplifying Assumptions

To simplify the presentation, we will consider flat domain restrictions with the cycle count $k = 1$ only. This is without loss of generality since using a flat domain restriction $FL_{k,\ell}$ with $k > 1$ is equivalent to replacing every substituting string variable x by the concatenation $x_1 \cdots x_k$ and using $FL_{1,\ell}$. The assumption of $k = 1$ makes the upper index 1 of the character variables x_i^1 superfluous, hence we will omit it and write only x_i.[3]

We also make the following simplifying assumptions on the input string constraint ϕ:

1. We assume that $\mathsf{StrVar}(t_1) \cap \mathsf{StrVar}(t_2) = \emptyset$. Note that any string constraint can be made to satisfy this by replacing one of the occurrences of a string variable $y \in \mathsf{StrVar}(t_1) \cap \mathsf{StrVar}(t_2)$ by its fresh primed variant y' and introducing an additional constraint $y = y'$.
2. We assume that t_1 and t_2 do *not* contain constant strings, that is, they are concatenations of string variables. Every equality or not substring constraint can be transformed into this form by replacing each occurrence of a constant a with a fresh variable x_{oc} (each occurrence with a unique fresh variable) together with the regular constraint $x_{oc} \in \{a\}$. Such modification does not influence the constraints membership in the decidable fragment used for overapproximation (whereas replacing all occurrences of a by a single fresh variable could).

5.2 Construction of the Flattening Formula

The construction of $flatten_{(1,\ell)}(t_1 \not\sqsubseteq t_2)$ is based on the following observation.

Observation 1. *For every two strings $u, v \in \Sigma^*$, $u \not\sqsubseteq v$ iff either $|u| > |v|$ or $|u| \leq |v|$ and for every shift $\in [0, |v| - |u|]$, there exists $pos \in [|u|]$, $u(pos) \neq v(shift + pos)$.*

Intuitively, either t_1 is longer than t_2, or, as illustrated on Fig. 3, for any position *shift* where we try to fit t_1 inside t_2, we can find a position *pos* in t_1 which will not match the corresponding position *shift* + *pos* in t_2.

The core of the flattening formula will be constructed as a disjunction of two formulae that express the two cases of Observation 1, $\psi_{|t_1|>|t_2|}$ and $\psi_{|t_1|\leq|t_2|}$.

---

[3] Our implementation however handles cycle counts k larger than one directly.

String Lengths and Effective Periods. To express the two cases of Observation 1, we will speak about *effective periods* of string variables and about their *lengths*, for which we introduce auxiliary constants and variables.

First, the *effective period* of a string variable z is the number ℓ_z of character variables in $\mathsf{CharVar}_{(1,\ell)}(z)$ that are assigned a non-ε value (a character from Σ) under a given assignment of character variables. Whenever a constant representing an effective period is used, we must ensure that it is indeed the effective period.

To make this test easier and the formula testing this more compact, we restrict the space of encodings of strings by requiring that the interpretations of the variables $x \in \mathsf{StrVar}(\phi)$ to ones that are *sorted*. That means that character variables x_j assigned ε appear only *at the end* of the cycle, namely *after* all character variables that are assigned letters of Σ. This is achieved by conjoining the flattening of ϕ with the formula $\psi_{\varepsilon\text{-end}}$:

$$\psi_{\varepsilon\text{-end}} = \bigwedge_{x \in \mathsf{StrVar}(\phi)} \bigwedge_{j \in [\ell-1]} (x_j = \varepsilon \rightarrow x_{j+1} = \varepsilon)$$

Note that this only restricts the encodings of the solutions of ϕ but not the set of solutions itself, since every solution has among its encodings one with aligned ε's.

In sorted interpretations, it holds that $\ell_z \in [\ell]$ if and only if z_{ℓ_z} is the last character variable assigned a non-ε character, and $\ell_z = 0$ if and only if z_1 is assigned ε. This is checked by the formula $\psi_{\text{period}}^{(z,\ell_z)}$:

$$\psi_{\text{period}}^{(z,\ell_z)} = \begin{cases} z_{\ell_z} \neq \varepsilon \wedge z_{\ell_z+1} = \varepsilon & \text{if } \ell_z \in [\ell-1] \\ z_\ell \neq \varepsilon & \text{if } \ell_z = \ell \\ z_1 = \varepsilon & \text{if } \ell_z = 0 \end{cases}$$

The length len_z of z is then determined from ℓ_z and the value of the Parikh variable $\#z_1$ as $len_z = \ell_z * \#z_1$. Indeed, $\#z_1$, the number of occurrences of z_1, is the number of iterations of the cycle $z_1 \cdots z_\ell$, and each iteration of the cycle produces a string of the length equals to the effective period ℓ_z. Additionally, we also need to ensure that $\#z_1, \ldots, \#z_\ell$ are the same, since $z_1 \cdots z_\ell$ is iterated as a whole, which is captured by $\bigwedge_{i \in [\ell-1]} \#z_i = \#z_{i+1}$. Put together, we create the formula ψ_{len}:

$$\psi_{len} = \psi_{\varepsilon\text{-end}} \wedge \bigwedge_{z \in \mathsf{StrVar}(t_1 \not\sqsubseteq t_2)} \psi_{\text{period}}^{(z,\ell_z)} \wedge len_z = \ell_z * \#z_1 \wedge \bigwedge_{i \in [\ell-1]} \#z_i = \#z_{i+1}$$

Since ℓ_z is a constant, $len_z = \ell_z * \#z_1$ is not a multiplication of two integer variables, but only an abbreviation of ℓ_z-fold addition of $\#z_1$.

Formula for Observation 1, case t_1 longer than t_2. Using the effective periods and lengths, the first case of Observation 1 with t_1 longer than t_2 can now be expressed as the formula $\psi_{|t_1|>|t_2|}$.

Suppose that $t_1 = x_1 \cdots x_m$ and $t_2 = y_1 \cdots y_n$. The case $|t_1| > |t_2|$ is specified simply by the formula

$$\psi_{|t_1|>|t_2|} = \sum_{i\in[m]} len_{x_i} > \sum_{i\in[n]} len_{y_i}$$

Formula for Observation 1, case t_1 not longer than t_2. The second case of Observation 1, with t_1 no longer than t_2, is expressed as the formula $\psi_{|t_1|\leq|t_2|}$. It is more complicated than the previous case.

Recall that it states that $|t_1| \leq |t_2|$ and for every *shift* $\in [0, |t_2| - |t_1|]$, there exists *pos* $\in [|t_1|]$, $t_1(pos) \neq t_2(shift + pos)$, as shown on Fig. 3. The formula, that allows to check this, is constructed as follows:

1. For every positions *shift* where t_1 could fit into t_2 ($|t_1| + shift \leq |t_2|$),
2. find a position *pos* in t_1 such that t_2 could fit inside t_1 at this position,
3. find a string variable $(x_{m'})_\alpha$ and a string variable $(y_{n'})_\beta$ of t_2 which appear at positions *pos* and *pos* + *shift*, respectively, and
4. verify $(x_{m'})_\alpha \neq (y_{n'})_\beta$ (hence t_1 at *pos* differs from t_2 at *pos* + *shift*).

First, t_1 shifted by *shift* must still "fit" inside t_2, that is:

$$\psi_{shift} = (0 \leq shift \leq \sum_{i\in[n]} len_{y_i} - \sum_{i\in[m]} len_{x_i})$$

Second, there are *conflict variables* $x_{m'}$ and $y_{n'}$, $m' \in [m]$ and $n' \in [n]$ such that $t_1(pos)$ corresponds to some character of $x_{m'}$ and such that $t_2(shift + pos)$ corresponds to some character of $y_{n'}$. This is formally expressed by the formulas

$$\psi_{x_{m'}} = \sum_{i\in[m'-1]} len_{x_i} < pos \leq \sum_{i\in[m']} len_{x_i}$$
$$\psi_{y_{n'}} = \sum_{i\in[n'-1]} len_{y_i} < shift + pos \leq \sum_{i\in[n']} len_{y_i}$$

Third, $t_1(pos)$ and $t_2(shift+pos)$ must correspond to the values of some character variables $(x_{m'})_\alpha$ in $(x_{m'})_1 \cdots (x_{m'})_{\ell_{x_{m'}}}$ and $(y_{n'})_\beta$ in $(y_{n'})_1 \cdots (y_{n'})_{\ell_{y_{n'}}}$. The indices α and β are specified as follows:

- The following formula checks that $(x_{m'})_\alpha$ is indeed at the position *pos* in t_1. The formula assumes an effective period of $x_{m'}$ and also verifies that assumption:

$$\psi_{x_{m'}}^{(\ell_{x_{m'}},\alpha)} = \psi_{period}^{(x_{m'},\ell_{x_{m'}})} \wedge (pos - \sum_{i\in[m'-1]} len_{x_i}) \equiv \alpha \mod \ell_{x_{m'}}$$

- Similarly, the following formula checks that $(y_{n'})_\beta$ is indeed at the position *shift* + *pos* in t_2. It assumes an effective period of $y_{n'}$ and verifies that assumption:

$$\psi_{y_{n'}}^{(\ell_{y_{n'}},\beta)} = \psi_{period}^{(y_{n'},\ell_{y_{n'}})} \wedge (shift + pos - \sum_{i\in[n'-1]} len_{y_i}) \equiv \beta \mod \ell_{y_{n'}}$$

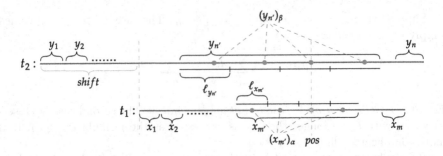

Fig. 3. An overview of the construction of $\psi_{|t_1|\geq|t_2|}$.

Fourth, having the indices α, β of character variables specified as above, $t_1(pos) \neq t_2(shift+pos)$ can be expressed as $(x_{m'})_\alpha \neq (y_{n'})_\beta$. The entire formula $\psi_{|t_1|\leq|t_2|}$ then is:

$$\psi_{|t_1|\leq|t_2|} = \sum_{i\in[m]} len_{x_i} \leq \sum_{i\in[n]} len_{y_i} \wedge \forall shift \exists pos.\ \psi_{shift} \rightarrow$$

$$\bigvee_{\substack{m'\in[m],\\n'\in[n]}} \left(\begin{array}{c} \psi_{x_{m'}} \wedge \psi_{y_{n'}} \wedge \\ \bigvee_{\ell_{x_{m'}},\ell_{y_{n'}}\in[\ell]} \bigvee_{\substack{\alpha\in[\ell_{x_{m'}}],\\\beta\in[\ell_{y_{n'}}]}} \left(\begin{array}{c} \psi_{x_{m'}}^{(\ell_{x_{m'}},\alpha)} \wedge \psi_{y_{n'}}^{(\ell_{y_{n'}},\beta)} \wedge \\ (x_{m'})_\alpha \neq (y_{n'})_\beta \end{array} \right) \end{array} \right)$$

Finally, we construct the flattening of the not substring constraint as:

$$flatten_{(1,\ell)}(t_1 \not\sqsubseteq t_2) = \psi_{len} \wedge (\psi_{|t_1|>|t_2|} \vee \psi_{|t_1|\leq|t_2|})$$

Theorem 1 states that the construction is indeed correct in the sense that it satisfies Eq. 2, only with modified, primed, variant of $encode_{(1,\ell)}$, restricted only to sorted interpretations (satisfying $\psi_{\varepsilon\text{-end}}$). This is still enough for Eq. 2 to be true for conjunctive constraints that contain non-substring atomic predicates. AuxVar are variables other than string and length variables x and $|x|$, $x \in \mathsf{Var}(t_1 \not\sqsubseteq t_2)$.

Theorem 1. $encode'_{(1,\ell)}(\llbracket t_1 \not\sqsubseteq t_2 \rrbracket_{(1,\ell)}) = \llbracket \exists \mathsf{AuxVar} : flatten_{(1,\ell)}(t_1 \not\sqsubseteq t_2) \rrbracket$

6   Implementation and Evaluation

We compare STR[4] with the other state-of-the-art string solvers, namely, CVC4 (version 1.8)[5] [8] and Z3 (version 4.8.9)[6] [20]. For these tools, the versions we

---

[4] The github link will be made available after the double blind review process.

[5] https://github.com/CVC4/CVC4/releases/tag/1.8.

[6] https://github.com/Z3Prover/z3/releases/tag/z3-4.8.9.

used are the latest release version. Observe that CVC4 and Z3 are DPLL(T)-based string solvers. We do not compare with Sloth [18] since it does not support length constraints, which occur in most of our benchmarks. Moreover, we do not compare with ABC [7] (a model counter for string constraints) and Trau+ [4–6] as well, because they do not support many string functions occurring in our benchmarks, especially those containing the "not contains" functionality.

We performed the experiments on two benchmark suites. The first benchmark suite is new and obtained by running the symbolic executor Py-Conbyte[7] on the following three GitHub projects,

- biopython[8]: freely available Python tools for computational molecular biology and bioinformatics,
- django[9]: a high-level Python Web framework that encourages rapid development and clean, pragmatic design,
- thefuck[10]: an app that corrects errors in previous console commands, inspired by a @liamosaur tweet.

The symbolic executor Py-Conbyte produces files in the SMT2 format. We only keep those SMT2 files where the function "$(str.contains\ x\ y)$" or "$(str.indexof\ x\ y\ n)$" with a non-constant first or second argument occurs.

The second benchmark suite contains sets of standard benchmarks from [3] that have been used previously in the comparison of existing string solvers.

We carry out the experiments on a PC with an Intel Core i7-10700 (2.90 GHz) processor with 8 cores and 16 threads, a 48 GB of RAM, and a 1.8 TB, 7200 rpm hard disk drive running the Ubuntu 20.04.1 LTS operating system. The timeout was set to 10s for each SMT file. In the implementation of STR, we modify the SAT handling component of Trau to the version described in this paper, and use it to handle SAT instances. Then STR run Ostrich and the modified Trau in parallel, and terminate when Ostrich reports UNSAT or Trau reports SAT. The experimental results are summarized in Table 1. Columns with heading SAT (resp. UNSAT) show the number of SAT (resp. UNSAT) test cases for which the solver returns correct answers. Column with heading FAILED indicates the number of test cases for which the solver returns UNKNOWN or cannot finished with 10 s.

From Table 1, we can see that overall STR is better than Z3 and has a similar performance to CVC4 in handling SAT instances. The handling of UNSAT instances is worse than the others, but this is mainly due to the use of OSTRICH. Observe that the over-approximation module is not the main focus of this paper since our main goal is to address the major weakness of the flattening framework of handling not-substring constraint and to provide an under-approximation technique which has at least as good, and in many cases better, performance than the state-of-the-art tools.

---

[7] https://github.com/alan23273850/py-conbyte.
[8] https://github.com/biopython/biopython.
[9] https://github.com/django/django.
[10] https://github.com/nvbn/thefuck.

Table 1. Results on new and existing benchmarks

BENCHMARK	SAT			UNSAT			FAILED		
	z3	cvc4	STR	z3	cvc4	STR	z3	cvc4	STR
biopython (77222)	5180	5707	5770	70190	70518	62435	1852	997	9017
django (52645)	8404	9297	9487	41871	42161	33471	2370	1187	9687
thefuck (19872)	1883	2313	2194	17545	17530	16018	444	29	1660
Leetcode (2666)	880	881	876	1785	1785	1658	1	0	132
PyEx (25421)	16656	20651	21420	3775	3857	3316	4990	913	685
aplas (600)	122	54	132	100	205	1	378	341	467
cvc4-str (1880)	22	18	25	1802	1841	184	56	21	1671
full-str-int (21571)	2875	4379	4433	16708	16985	12234	1988	207	4904
slog (3391)	1296	1309	1290	2082	2082	2054	13	0	47
stringfuzz (1065)	429	716	534	208	243	62	428	106	469

7   Conclusion and Future Work

We have proposed an extension of the flattening techniques for string constraints that handles constraints of the type not-substring. Our techniques generates flattening formulae that express the flat semantics of string constraints precisely. Although they do contain a single universal quantifier, they can still be handled efficiently by existing solvers. Our experimental results show that our prototype can solve not-substring constraints better than other tools (especially SAT cases) and it is competitive on the other types of constraints.

An interesting possibility for future is to solve string logic with not substring constraint precisely, not only under the flat abstraction. A possibility of flat abstraction of not substring which would be fully quantifier free is also not closed and is worth further investigation.

References

1. OWASP top ten web application security risk (2017). https://owasp.org/www-project-top-ten
2. Trauc string constraints benchmark collection (2020). https://github.com/plfm-iis/trauc_benchmarks
3. Abdulla, P.A., et al.: Efficient handling of string-number conversion. In: Donaldson, A.F., Torlak, E. (eds.) Proceedings of the 41st ACM SIGPLAN International Conference on Programming Language Design and Implementation, PLDI 2020, London, UK, 15–20 June 2020, pp. 943–957. ACM (2020). https://doi.org/10.1145/3385412.3386034

4. Abdulla, P.A., et al.: Flatten and conquer: a framework for efficient analysis of string constraints. In: Cohen, A., Vechev, M.T. (eds.) Proceedings of the 38th ACM SIGPLAN Conference on Programming Language Design and Implementation, PLDI 2017, Barcelona, Spain, 18–23 June 2017, pp. 602–617. ACM (2017)

5. Abdulla, P.A., et al.: Trau: SMT solver for string constraints. In: Bjørner, N., Gurfinkel, A. (eds.) 2018 Formal Methods in Computer Aided Design, FMCAD 2018, Austin, TX, USA, October 30–November 2 2018, pp. 1–5. IEEE (2018)

6. Abdulla, P.A., Atig, M.F., Diep, B.P., Holík, L., Janků, P.: Chain-free string constraints. In: Chen, Y.-F., Cheng, C.-H., Esparza, J. (eds.) ATVA 2019. LNCS, vol. 11781, pp. 277–293. Springer, Cham (2019). https://doi.org/10.1007/978-3-030-31784-3_16

7. Aydin, A., et al.: Parameterized model counting for string and numeric constraints. In: Leavens, G.T., Garcia, A., Pasareanu, C.S. (eds.) Proceedings of the 2018 ACM Joint Meeting on European Software Engineering Conference and Symposium on the Foundations of Software Engineering, ESEC/SIGSOFT FSE 2018, Lake Buena Vista, FL, USA, 04–09 November 2018, pp. 400–410. ACM (2018)

8. Barrett, C., et al.: CVC4. In: Gopalakrishnan, G., Qadeer, S. (eds.) CAV 2011. LNCS, vol. 6806, pp. 171–177. Springer, Heidelberg (2011). https://doi.org/10.1007/978-3-642-22110-1_14

9. Berzish, M., et al.: A length-aware regular expression SMT solver. CoRR abs/2010.07253 (2020). https://arxiv.org/abs/2010.07253

10. Biere, A., Cimatti, A., Clarke, E., Zhu, Y.: Symbolic model checking without BDDs. In: Cleaveland, W.R. (ed.) TACAS 1999. LNCS, vol. 1579, pp. 193–207. Springer, Heidelberg (1999). https://doi.org/10.1007/3-540-49059-0_14

11. Cadar, C., Sen, K.: Symbolic execution for software testing: three decades later. Commun. ACM 56(2), 82–90 (2013)

12. Chen, T., Chen, Y., Hague, M., Lin, A.W., Wu, Z.: What is decidable about string constraints with the replaceall function. PACMPL 2(POPL), 3:1–3:29 (2018)

13. Chen, T., et al.: A decision procedure for path feasibility of string manipulating programs with integer data type. In: Hung, D.V., Sokolsky, O. (eds.) ATVA 2020. LNCS, vol. 12302, pp. 325–342. Springer, Cham (2020). https://doi.org/10.1007/978-3-030-59152-6_18

14. Chen, T., Hague, M., Lin, A.W., Rümmer, P., Wu, Z.: Decision procedures for path feasibility of string-manipulating programs with complex operations. PACMPL 3(POPL), 49:1–49:30 (2019)

15. Clarke, E.M., Emerson, E.A.: Design and synthesis of synchronization skeletons using branching time temporal logic. In: Kozen, D. (ed.) Logic of Programs 1981. LNCS, vol. 131, pp. 52–71. Springer, Heidelberg (1982). https://doi.org/10.1007/BFb0025774

16. Day, J.D., Ganesh, V., He, P., Manea, F., Nowotka, D.: The satisfiability of extended word equations: the boundary between decidability and undecidability. CoRR abs/1802.00523 (2018). http://arxiv.org/abs/1802.00523

17. Godefroid, P., Klarlund, N., Sen, K.: DART: directed automated random testing. In: PLDI, pp. 213–223. ACM (2005)

18. Holík, L., Janku, P., Lin, A.W., Rümmer, P., Vojnar, T.: String constraints with concatenation and transducers solved efficiently. PACMPL 2(POPL), 4:1–4:32 (2018)

19. King, J.C.: Symbolic execution and program testing. Commun. ACM 19(7), 385–394 (1976)

20. de Moura, L., Bjørner, N.: Z3: an efficient SMT solver. In: Ramakrishnan, C.R., Rehof, J. (eds.) TACAS 2008. LNCS, vol. 4963, pp. 337–340. Springer, Heidelberg (2008). https://doi.org/10.1007/978-3-540-78800-3_24
21. Queille, J.P., Sifakis, J.: Specification and verification of concurrent systems in CESAR. In: Dezani-Ciancaglini, M., Montanari, U. (eds.) Programming 1982. LNCS, vol. 137, pp. 337–351. Springer, Heidelberg (1982). https://doi.org/10.1007/3-540-11494-7_22
22. Reynolds, A., Nötzli, A., Barrett, C.W., Tinelli, C.: Reductions for strings and regular expressions revisited. In: 2020 Formal Methods in Computer Aided Design, FMCAD 2020, Haifa, Israel, 21–24 September 2020, pp. 225–235. IEEE (2020). https://doi.org/10.34727/2020/isbn.978-3-85448-042-6_30
23. Saxena, P., Akhawe, D., Hanna, S., Mao, F., McCamant, S., Song, D.: A symbolic execution framework for Javascript. In: 31st IEEE Symposium on Security and Privacy, S&P 2010, Berleley/Oakland, California, USA, 16–19 May 2010, pp. 513–528. IEEE Computer Society (2010). https://doi.org/10.1109/SP.2010.38
24. Sen, K., Marinov, D., Agha, G.: CUTE: a concolic unit testing engine for C. In: ESEC/SIGSOFT FSE, pp. 263–272. ACM (2005)
25. Zheng, Y., Zhang, X., Ganesh, V.: Z3-str: a z3-based string solver for web application analysis. In: Meyer, B., Baresi, L., Mezini, M. (eds.) Joint Meeting of the European Software Engineering Conference and the ACM SIGSOFT Symposium on the Foundations of Software Engineering, ESEC/FSE 2013, Saint Petersburg, Russian Federation, 18–26 August 2013, pp. 114–124. ACM (2013)

Author Index

Abate, Carmine 83
Abdulla, Parosh Aziz 305
Ameen, Mahmudul Faisal Al 23
Atig, Mohamed Faouzi 305

Bajaj, Divya 202
Borgna, Agustín 121
Busi, Matteo 83

Chen, Yu-Fang 38, 305
Choi, Wonhyuk 47

Diep, Bui Phi 305
Dietsch, Daniel 285
Doan, Thi Thu Ha 222

Erwig, Martin 202

Fedorin, Danila 202

Gay, Kai 202

Holík, Lukáš 243, 305
Hu, Denghang 305
Hu, Xiaowen 163

Ishikawa, Takuma 265

Karp, Joshua 163
Kasai, Nobuhiro 62
Khoo, Siau-Cheng 3
Kimura, Daisuke 23
Kobayashi, Naoki 265
Koskinen, Eric 285

Le, Ton-Chanh 285
Liu, Yuandong Cyrus 285
Luo, Tianzuo 3

Nakazawa, Koji 23

Ohori, Atsushi 140

Pang, Chengbin 285
Perdrix, Simon 121
Portokalidis, Georgios 285
Poulsen, Casper Bach 182

Sakayori, Ken 265
Santolucito, Mark 47
Sasano, Isao 62
Sato, Ryosuke 265
Scholz, Bernhard 163
Schrijvers, Tom 182
Shoshi, Tsubasa 265
Sulzmann, Martin 102

Ta, Quang-Trung 3
Tatsuta, Makoto 23
Thiemann, Peter 222
Tsai, Wei-Lun 38, 305
Tsampas, Stelios 83
Tsukada, Takeshi 265

Ueno, Katsuhiro 140

Valiron, Benoît 121
van den Berg, Birthe 182
Vargovčík, Pavol 243
Vazirani, Michel 47

Wehr, Stefan 102
Wu, Nicolas 182
Wu, Wei-Cheng 38
Wu, Xi 163
Wu, Zhillin 305

Xu, Jun 285

Yen, Di-De 38, 305
Yu, Fang 38

Zhang, Fanlong 3
Zhao, David 163
Zhong, Yuyi 3
Zreika, Abdul 163

Printed in the United States
by Baker & Taylor Publisher Services